AN INTRODUCTION TO PROGRAMMING USING PYTHON™

GLOBAL EDITION

David I. Schneider

University of Maryland

PEARSON

Boston • Columbus • Indianapolis • New York • San Francisco • Hoboken
Amsterdam • Cape Town • Dubai • London • Madrid • Milan • Munich • Paris • Montreal • Toronto
Delhi • Mexico City • São Paulo • Sydney • Hong Kong • Seoul • Singapore • Taipei • Tokyo

Vice President and Editorial Director, ECS: *Marcia J. Horton*
Executive Editor: *Tracy Johnson*
Assistant Acquisitions Editor, Global Editions: Aditee Agarwal
Executive Marketing Manager: *Tim Galligan*
Marketing Assistant: *Jon Bryant*
Team Lead Product Management: *Scott Disanno*
Production Project Manager: *Greg Dulles and Pavithra Jayapaul*
Project Editor, Global Editions: K.K. Neelakantan
Program Manager: *Carole Snyder*
Director of Operations: *Mary Fischer*

Operations Specialist: *Maura Zaldivar-Garcia*
Senior Manufacturing Controller, Global Editions: Trudy Kimber
Cover Designer: *Lumina Datamatics*
Global HE Director of Vendor Sourcing and Procurement: *Diane Hynes*
Manager, Rights and Permissions: Rachel Youdelman
Associate Project Manager, Rights and Permissions: *William Opaluch*
Media Production Manager, Global Editions: Vikram Kumar
Full-Service Project Management: *Shylaja Gattupalli, Jouve India*

Pearson Education Limited
Edinburgh Gate
Harlow
Essex CM20 2JE
England

and Associated Companies throughout the world

Visit us on the World WideWeb at:
www.pearsonglobaleditions.com

British Library Cataloguing-in-Publication Data
A catalogue record for this book is available from the British Library

10 9 8 7 6 5 4 3 2 1

ISBN 10: 1-292-10343-4
ISBN 13: 978-1-292-10343-3

Typeset in 11/13 Goudy Old Style MT Std by Jouve India
Printed and bound by RR Donnelley Kendallville in The United States of America.

Guide to VideoNotes

www.pearsonglobaleditions.com/schneider

VideoNote

Guide to Application Topics

Business and Economics

Admission fee, 240
Analyze fuel economy, 257
Annual percentage yield (APY), 119
Annuity, 50, 132, 133, 148
Automobile depreciation, 148
Balance in a savings account, 136, 181, 182
Balance on a car loan, 131, 148, 155
Balance on a mortgage, 292
Bond yield-to-maturity, 91
Break-even analysis, 49
Calculate a sale price, 119, 354
Calculate a tip, 64, 72, 116
Calculate monthly payment for a mortgage, 321, 322
Calculate weekly pay, 117, 164, 309
Change from a purchase, 118
Check out purchases from a website, 310
Compare interest rates, 119
Compare salary options, 149, 179
Compare simple and compound interest, 148
Compound interest, 49, 50, 119, 124, 132, 133, 148, 165
Consumer price index (CPI), 131
Cost of electricity, 63
Credit card payment, 197
Crop production, 50, 149
Currency exchange rates, 258
Depreciation, 205
Determine a company's payroll, 326
Discounted price, 49, 62
Distribution of a mortgage payment, 197
Dogs of the DOW, 231
Doubling time of CPI, 131
DOW industrial average, 230, 231
Earnings, 197
Effects of a change in salary, 72, 73, 354, 355
Evaluate effects of different interest rates and compounding periods, 361
Excel, 227
FICA tax, 110, 179
Future value, 73, 165
Growth of an investment, 148
Income tax, 119
Individual retirement account, 156
Interest earned in a savings account, 181, 182
Interest-only mortgage, 322
Journal subscriptions, 221
Lifetime earnings, 148
Make change, 90
Manage a bank account, 133, 325

Monetary units of countries, 258
Monthly payment on a car loan, 91, 355
Mortgage with points, 322
Municipal bonds, 64
Net income, 72
Number of restaurants in United States, 50
Pay raise, 179, 197
Pension calculation, 180, 362
Percentage markup, 64
Percentage profit, 50
Pizza consumption, 50
PNC Christmas price index, 233
Postage costs, 193
Present value, 73
Price-to-earnings ratio, 63
Profit, 49, 109, 120
Profit margin, 64
Retirement plan, 156
Rule of 88, 156
Sales receipt, 236, 310
Savings plan, 132
Simple interest, 148
Small dogs of the DOW, 231
Stock portfolio, 91
Stock purchase, 49
Supply and demand, 149
Toll booth register, 310
Total cost, 116, 117
Total interest payments on a car loan, 155
U.S. national debt, 51
Unit price, 91
Validate credit card number, 157
Validate ISBN, 205
Withdrawal from a savings account, 118

General Interest

Academy award winners, 235, 357
American flag, 295
Anagrams, 194
Analyze a sentence, 87, 250
Bachelor degrees, 256
Boston accent, 151
Caffeine absorption, 156
Calculate number of calories, 51
Calculate semester grades, 311, 312, 314
Computer pioneers, 234
Country flags, 277
Crayon colors, 179, 221, 222
Determine day of week, 236

Mathematics

Sports and Games

CONTENTS

PREFACE

Since its introduction in the 1990s, Python has become one of the most widely used programming languages in the software industry. Also, students learning their first programming language find Python the ideal tool to understand the development of computer programs.

My objectives when writing this text were as follows:

1. *To develop focused chapters.* Rather than covering many topics superficially, I concentrate on important subjects and cover them thoroughly.

2. *To use examples and exercises with which students can relate, appreciate, and feel comfortable.* I frequently use real data. Examples do not have so many embellishments that students are distracted from the programming techniques illustrated.

3. *To produce compactly written text that students will find both readable and informative.* The main points of each topic are discussed first and then the peripheral details are presented as comments.

4. *To teach good programming practices that are in step with modern programming methodology.* Problem-solving techniques, structured programming, and object-oriented programming are thoroughly discussed.

5. *To provide insights into the major applications of computers.*

Unique and Distinguishing Features

Programming Projects. Beginning with Chapter 2, every chapter contains programming projects. The programming projects reflect the variety of ways that computers are used. The large number and range of difficulty of the programming projects provide the flexibility to adapt the course to the interests and abilities of the students. Some programming projects in later chapters can be assigned as end-of-the-semester projects.

Exercises for Most Sections. Each section that teaches programming has an exercise set. The exercises both reinforce the understanding of the key ideas of the section and challenge the student to explore applications. Most of the exercise sets require the student to trace programs, find errors, and write programs. The answers to every odd-numbered exercise in the book, with the exception of Section 6.3 (Turtle Graphics) and Chapter 8 (Graphical User Interface), are given at the end of the text. (The answers to every other odd-numbered exercise from Section 6.3 are given. The Student Solutions Manual contains the answer to every odd-numbered exercise in the book.) A possible output accompanies nearly every programming exercise and programming project.

Practice Problems. Practice Problems are carefully selected exercises located at the end of a section, just before the exercise set. Complete solutions are given following the exercise set. The practice problems often focus on points that are potentially confusing or are best appreciated after the student has thought about them. The reader should seriously attempt the practice problems and study their solutions before moving on to the exercises.

Comments. Extensions and fine points of new topics are deferred to the "Comments" portion at the end of each section so that they will not interfere with the flow of the presentation.

Key Terms and Concepts. In Chapters 2 through 8, the key terms and concepts (along with examples) are summarized at the end of the chapter.

Guide to Application Topics. This section provides an index of programs that deal with various topics including Business, Economics, Mathematics, and Sports.

VideoNotes. Twenty-four VideoNotes are available at www.pearsonhighered.com/schneider. VideoNotes are Pearson's visual tool designed for teaching key programming concepts and techniques. VideoNote icons are placed in the margin of the text book to notify the reader when a topic is discussed in a video. Also, a Guide to Video Notes summarizing the different videos throughout the text is included.

Solution Manuals. The Student Solutions Manual contains the answer to every odd-numbered exercise (not including programming projects). The Instructor Solutions Manual contains the answer to every exercise and programming project. Both solution manuals are in pdf format and can be downloaded from the Publisher's website.

Source Code and Data Files. The programs for all examples and the data files needed for the exercises can be downloaded from the Publisher's website.

How to Access Instructor and Student Resource Materials

Online Practice and Assessment with MyProgrammingLab™

MyProgrammingLab helps students fully grasp the logic, semantics, and syntax of programming. Through practice exercises and immediate, personalized feedback, MyProgrammingLab improves the programming competence of beginning students who often struggle with the basic concepts and paradigms of popular high-level programming languages.

A self-study and homework tool, a MyProgrammingLab course consists of hundreds of small practice problems organized around the structure of this textbook. For students, the system automatically detects errors in the logic and syntax of their code submissions and offers targeted hints that enable students to figure out what went wrong—and why. For instructors, a comprehensive gradebook tracks correct and incorrect answers and stores the code inputted by students for review.

For a full demonstration, to see feedback from instructors and students, or to get started using MyProgrammingLab in your course, visit www.myprogramminglab.com.

Instructor Resources

The following protected instructor resource materials are available on the Publisher's website at www.pearsonglobaleditions.com/schneider.

- Test Item File
- PowerPoint Lecture Slides

- Instructor Solutions Manual
- VideoNotes
- Programs for all examples and answers to exercises and programming projects (Data files needed for the exercises are included in the Programs folder.)

Student Resources

Access to the Premium website and VideoNotes tutorials is located at www .pearsonglobaleditions.com/schneider. Students must use the access card located in the front of the book to register and access the online material. Instructors must register on the site to access the material.

The following content is available through the Premium website:

- VideoNotes
- Student Solutions Manual
- Programs for examples (Data files needed for the exercises are included in the Programs folder.)

ACKNOWLEDGMENTS

Many talented instructors and programmers provided helpful comments and constructive suggestions during the writing of this text and I am most grateful for their contributions. The book benefited greatly from the valuable comments of the following reviewers:

Daniel Solarek, University of Toledo
David M. Reed, Capital University
Debraj De, Georgia State
Desmond Chun, Chabot College
Mark Coffey, Colorado School of Mines
Randall Alexander, College of Charleston
Vineyak Tanksale, Ball State University
Zhi Wei, New Jersey Institute of Technology

Many people are involved in the successful publication of a book. I wish to thank the dedicated team at Pearson whose support and diligence made this textbook possible, especially Carole Snyder, Program Manager for Computer Science, Kelsey Loanes, Editorial Assistant for Computer Science, and Scott Disanno, Team Lead Product Management.

I would like to thank Jacob Saina for his assistance with every stage in the writing of the book. Production Editors Pavithra Jayapaul and Greg Dulles did a fantastic job producing the book and keeping it on schedule. I am grateful to John Russo of the Wentworth Institute of Technology for producing the VideoNotes, to Dr. Kathy Liszka of the University of Akron for producing the test bank, and to Dr. Steve Armstrong of LeTourneau University for producing the PowerPoint slides that accompany the book. The competence and graciousness of Shylaja Gattupalli at Jouve India made for a pleasant production process.

I extend special thanks to my editor Tracy Johnson. Her ideas and enthusiasm helped immensely with the preparation of the book.

David I. Schneider
dis@alum.mit.edu

Pearson would like to thank and acknowledge Shaligram Prajapat, Devi Ahilya University for contributing to the Global Edition and Somitra Sanadhya, Indian Institute of Delhi, Rosanne Els, University of Kwazulu-Natal, and Shivani Pandit for reviewing the Global Edition.

1

An Introduction to Computing and Problem Solving

1.1   An Introduction to Computing and Python

An Introduction to Programming Using Python is about problem solving using computers. The programming language used is Python, but the principles apply to most modern programming languages. Many of the examples and exercises illustrate how computers are used in the real world. Here are some questions that you may have about computers and programming.

Question: *How do we communicate with the computer?*

Answer: Programming languages are used to communicate with the computer. At the lowest level, there is *machine language*, which is understood directly by the microprocessor but is difficult for humans to understand. Python is an example of a *high-level language*. It consists of instructions to which people can relate, such as *print*, *if*, and *input*. Some other well-known high-level languages are Java, C++, and Visual Basic.

Question: *How do we get computers to perform complicated tasks?*

Answer: Tasks are broken down into a sequence of instructions, called a **program**, that can be expressed in a programming language. Programs can range in size from two or three instructions to millions of instructions. The process of executing the instructions is called *running* the program.

Question: *Why did you decide to use Python as the programming language?*

Answer: Many people consider Python to be the best language to teach beginners how to program. We agree. Also, Python is being used by major software companies. Python is powerful, easy to write and read, easy to download and install, and it runs under Windows, Mac, and Linux operating systems.

Question: *How did the language Python get its name?*

Answer: It is named for the British comedy group *Monty Python*. Python's creator, Guido van Rossum, is a fan of the group.

Question: *This book uses the editor IDLE to create programs. How did IDLE get its name?*

Answer: IDLE stands for **I**ntegrated **D**eve**L**opment **E**nvironment. (Some people think the name was chosen as a tribute to Eric Idle, a founding member of the Monty Python group.) The IDLE editor has many features (such as color coding and formatting assistance) that help the programmer.

Question: *Python is referred to as an interpreted language. What is an interpreted language?*

Answer: An interpreted language uses a program called an *interpreter* that translates a high-level language one statement at a time into machine language and then runs the program. The interpreter will spot several types of errors and terminate the program when one is encountered.

Question: *What are the meanings of the terms "programmer" and "user"?*

Answer: A *programmer* (also called a *developer*) is a person who solves problems by writing programs on a computer. After analyzing the problem and developing a plan for solving it, the programmer writes and tests the program that instructs the computer how to carry out the plan. The program might be run many times, either by the programmer or by others. A *user* is any person who runs the program. While working through this text, you will function both as a programmer and as a user.

Question: *What is the meaning of the term "code"?*

Answer: The Python instructions that the programmer writes are called *code*. The processes of writing a program is often called *coding*.

Question: *Are there certain characteristics that all programs have in common?*

Answer: Most programs do three things: take in data, manipulate data, and produce results. These operations are referred to as *input*, *processing*, and *output*. The input data might be held in the program, reside on a disk, or be provided by the user in response to requests made by the computer while the program is running. The processing of the input data occurs inside the computer and can take from a fraction of a second to many hours. The output data are displayed on a monitor, printed on a printer, or recorded on a disk. As a simple example, consider a program that computes sales tax. An item of input data is the cost of the thing purchased. The processing consists of multiplying the cost by the sales tax rate. The output data is the resulting product, the amount of sales tax to be paid.

Question: *What are the meanings of the terms "hardware" and "software"?*

Answer: *Hardware* refers to the physical components of the computer, including all peripherals, the central processing unit (CPU), disk drives, and all mechanical and electrical devices. Programs are referred to as *software*.

Question: *How are problems solved with a program?*

Answer: Problems are solved by carefully reading them to determine what data are given and what outputs are requested. Then a step-by-step procedure is devised to process the given data and produce the requested output.

Question: *Many programming languages, including Python, use a zero-based numbering system. What is a zero-based numbering system?*

Answer: In a zero-based numbering system, numbering begins with *zero* instead of *one*. For example, in the word "code", "*c*" would be the zeroth letter, "*o*" would be the first letter, and so on.

Question: *Are there any prerequisites to learning Python?*

Answer: You should be familiar with how folders (also called *directories*) and files are managed on your computer. Files reside on storage devices such as hard disks, USB flash drives, CDs, and DVDs. Traditionally, the primary storage devices for personal computers were hard disks and floppy disks. Therefore, the word *disk* is frequently used to refer to any storage device.

Question: *What is an example of a program developed in this textbook?*

Answer: Figure 1.1 shows a possible output of a program from Chapter 3. When it is first run, the statement "Enter a first name:" appears. After the user types in a first name and

```
Enter a first name: James
James Madison
James Monroe
James Polk
James Buchanan
James Garfield
James Carter
```

FIGURE 1.1   **A possible output for a program in Chapter 3.**

presses the *Enter* (or *return*) key, the names of the presidents who have that first name are displayed.

Question: How does the programmer create the aforementioned program?

Answer: For this program, the programmer writes about 10 lines of code that search a text file named `USpres.txt`, and extracts the requested names.

Question: What conventions are used to show keystrokes?

Answer: The combination *key1+key2* means "hold down key1 and then press key2". The combination Ctrl+C places selected material into the Clipboard. The combination *key1/ key2* means "press and release key1, and then press key2". The combination Alt/F opens the *File* menu on a menu bar.

Question: How can the programs for the examples in this textbook be obtained?

Answer: See the preface for information on how to download the programs from the Pearson website.

Question: Where will new programs be saved?

Answer: Before writing your first program, you should create a special folder to hold your programs.

1.2   Program Development Cycle

We learned in Section 1.1 that hardware refers to the machinery in a computer system (such as the monitor, keyboard, and CPU) and software refers to a collection of instructions, called a **program**, that directs the hardware. Programs are written to solve problems or perform tasks on a computer. Programmers translate the solutions or tasks into a language the computer can understand. As we write programs, we must keep in mind that the computer will do only what we instruct it to do. Because of this, we must be very careful and thorough when writing our instructions.

■ Performing a Task on the Computer

The first step in writing instructions to carry out a task is to determine what the **output** should be—that is, exactly what the task should produce. The second step is to identify the data, or **input**, necessary to obtain the output. The last step is to determine how to **process** the input to obtain the desired output—that is, to determine what formulas or ways of doing things should be used to obtain the output.

This problem-solving approach is the same as that used to solve word problems in an algebra class. For example, consider the following algebra problem:

How fast is a car moving if it travels 50 miles in 2 hours?

The first step is to determine the type of answer requested. The answer should be a number giving the speed in miles per hour (the output). The information needed to obtain the answer is the distance and time the car has traveled (the input). The formula

$$\text{speed} = \text{distance/time}$$

is used to process the distance traveled and the time elapsed in order to determine the speed. That is,

$$\text{speed} = 50 \text{ miles/2 hours}$$
$$= 25 \text{ miles per hour}$$

A graphical representation of this problem-solving process is shown in Fig. 1.2.

FIGURE 1.2 **The problem-solving process.**

We determine what we want as output, get the needed input, and process the input to produce the desired output.

In the chapters that follow, we discuss how to write programs to carry out the preceding operations. But first we look at the general process of writing programs.

■ Program Planning

A baking recipe provides a good example of a plan. The ingredients and the amounts are determined by what is to be baked. That is, the *output* determines the *input* and the *processing*. The recipe, or plan, reduces the number of mistakes you might make if you tried to bake with no plan at all. Although it's difficult to imagine an architect building a bridge or a factory without a detailed plan, many programmers (particularly students in their first programming course) try to write programs without first making a careful plan. The more complicated the problem, the more complex the plan must be. You will spend much less time working on a program if you devise a carefully thought out step-by-step plan and test it before actually writing the program.

Many programmers plan their programs using a sequence of steps, referred to as the **Software Development Life Cycle**. The following step-by-step process will enable you to use your time efficiently and help you design error-free programs that produce the desired output.

1. *Analyze:* Define the problem.

   Be sure you understand what the program should do—that is, what the output should be. Have a clear idea of what data (or input) are given and the relationship between the input and the desired output.

2. *Design:* Plan the solution to the problem.

   Find a logical sequence of precise steps that solve the problem. Such a sequence of steps is called an **algorithm**. Every detail, including obvious steps, should appear in the algorithm. In the next section, we discuss three popular methods used to develop the logic plan: flowcharts, pseudocode, and hierarchy charts. These tools help the programmer break a problem into a sequence of small tasks the computer can perform to solve the problem. Planning also involves using representative data to test the logic of the algorithm by hand to ensure that it is correct.

3. *Code:* Translate the algorithm into a programming language.

   Coding is the technical word for writing the program. During this stage, the program is written in Python and entered into the computer. The programmer uses the algorithm devised in Step 2 along with a knowledge of Python.

4. *Test and correct:* Locate and remove any errors in the program.

   Testing is the process of finding errors in a program. (An error in a program is called a **bug** and testing and correcting is often referred to as **debugging**.) As the program is typed, Python points out certain kinds of program errors. Other kinds of errors are detected by Python when the program is executed—however, many errors due to typing mistakes, flaws in the algorithm, or incorrect use of the Python language rules, can be uncovered and corrected only by careful detective work. An example of such an error would be using addition when multiplication was the proper operation.

5. **Complete the documentation:** Organize all the material that describes the program.

   Documentation is intended to allow another person, or the programmer at a later date, to understand the program. Internal documentation (comments) consists of statements in the program that are not executed, but point out the purposes of various parts of the program. Documentation might also consist of a detailed description of what the program does and how to use it (for instance, what type of input is expected). For commercial programs, documentation includes an instruction manual and on-line help. Other types of documentation are the flowchart, pseudocode, and hierarchy chart that were used to construct the program. Although documentation is listed as the last step in the program development cycle, it should take place as the program is being coded.

1.3   Programming Tools

This section discusses some specific algorithms and describes three tools used to convert algorithms into computer programs: flowcharts, pseudocode, and hierarchy charts.

You use algorithms every day to make decisions and perform tasks. For instance, whenever you mail a letter, you must decide how much postage to put on the envelope. One rule of thumb is to use one stamp for every five sheets of paper or fraction thereof. Suppose a friend asks you to determine the number of stamps to place on an envelope. The following algorithm will accomplish the task.

1. Request the number of sheets of paper; call it Sheets.   (*input*)
2. Divide Sheets by 5.   (*processing*)
3. If necessary, round the quotient up to a whole number; call it Stamps.   (*processing*)
4. Reply with the number Stamps.   (*output*)

The preceding algorithm takes the number of sheets (Sheets) as input, processes the data, and produces the number of stamps needed (Stamps) as output. We can test the algorithm for a letter with 16 sheets of paper.

1. Request the number of sheets of paper; Sheets = 16.
2. Dividing 5 into 16 gives 3.2.
3. Rounding 3.2 up to 4 gives Stamps = 4.
4. Reply with the answer, 4 stamps.

This problem-solving example can be illustrated by Fig. 1.3.

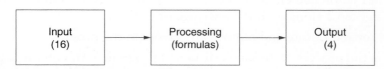

FIGURE 1.3   The problem-solving process for the stamp problem.

Of the program design tools available, three popular ones are the following:

Flowcharts: Graphically depict the logical steps to carry out a task and show how the steps relate to each other.
Pseudocode: Uses English-like phrases with some Python terms to outline the task.
Hierarchy charts: Show how the different parts of a program relate to each other.

■ Flowcharts

A flowchart consists of special geometric symbols connected by arrows. Within each symbol is a phrase presenting the activity at that step. The shape of the symbol indicates the type of operation that is to occur. For instance, the parallelogram denotes input or output. The arrows connecting the symbols, called **flowlines**, show the progression in which the steps take place. Flowcharts should "flow" from the top of the page to the bottom. Although the symbols used in flowcharts are standardized, no standards exist for the amount of detail required within each symbol.

Symbol	Name	Meaning
⟶	*Flowline*	Used to connect symbols and indicate the flow of logic.
⬭	*Terminal*	Used to represent the beginning (Start) or the end (End) of a task.
▱	*Input/Output*	Used for input and output operations. The data to be input or output is described in the parallelogram.
▭	*Processing*	Used for arithmetic and data-manipulation operations. The instructions are listed inside the rectangle.
◇	*Decision*	Used for any logic or comparison operations. Unlike the input/output and processing symbols, which have one entry and one exit flowline, the decision symbol has one entry and two exit paths. The path chosen depends on whether the answer to a question is "yes" or "no."
◯	*Connector*	Used to join different flowlines.
⊣	*Annotation*	Used to provide additional information about another flowchart symbol.

The table of the flowchart symbols has been adopted by the American National Standards Institute (ANSI). Figure 1.4 shows the flowchart for the postage-stamp problem.

The main advantage of using a flowchart to plan a task is that it provides a graphical representation of the task, thereby making the logic easier to follow. We can clearly see every step and how each is connected to the next. The major disadvantage is that when a program is very large, the flowcharts may continue for many pages, making them difficult to follow and modify.

■ Pseudocode

Pseudocode is an abbreviated plain English version of actual computer code (hence, *pseudocode*). The geometric symbols used in flowcharts are replaced by English-like statements that outline the process. As a result, pseudocode looks more like computer code than does

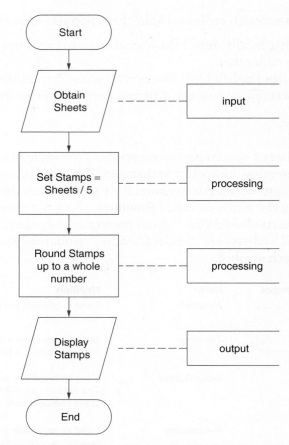

FIGURE 1.4 **Flowchart for the postage-stamp problem.**

a flowchart. Pseudocode allows the programmer to focus on the steps required to solve a problem rather than on how to use the computer language. The programmer can describe the algorithm in Python-like form without being restricted by the rules of Python. When the pseudocode is completed, it can be easily translated into the Python language.

The pseudocode for the postage-stamp problem is shown in Fig. 1.5.

Program: Determine the proper number of stamps for a letter.
Obtain number of sheets (Sheets)   *(input)*
Set the number of stamps to Sheets / 5   *(processing)*
Round the number of stamps up to a whole number   *(processing)*
Display the number of stamps   *(output)*

FIGURE 1.5 **Pseudocode for the postage-stamp problem.**

Pseudocode has several advantages. It is compact and probably will not extend for many pages as flowcharts commonly do. Also, the pseudocode looks like the code to be written and so is preferred by many programmers.

■ Hierarchy Chart

The last programming tool we'll discuss is the **hierarchy chart**, which shows the overall program structure. Hierarchy charts are also called structure charts, HIPO (Hierarchy plus Input-Process-Output) charts, top-down charts, or VTOC (Visual Table of Contents) charts. All these names refer to planning diagrams that are similar to a company's organization chart.

Hierarchy charts depict the organization of a program but omit the specific processing logic. They describe what each part of the program does and they show how the parts relate to each other. The details on how the parts work, however, are omitted. The chart is read from top to bottom and from left to right. Each part may be subdivided into a succession of subparts that branch out under it. Typically, after the activities in the succession of subparts are carried out, the part to the right of the original part is considered. A quick glance at the hierarchy chart reveals each task performed in the program and where it is performed. Figure 1.6 shows a hierarchy chart for the postage-stamp problem.

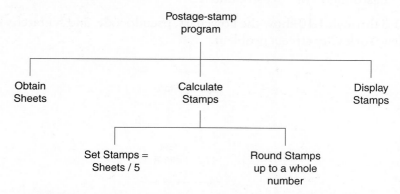

FIGURE 1.6 **Hierarchy chart for the postage-stamp problem.**

The main benefit of hierarchy charts is in the initial planning of a program. We break down the major parts of a program so we can see what must be done in general. From this point, we can then refine each part into more detailed plans using flowcharts or pseudocode. This process is called the **divide-and-conquer** method.

■ Decision Structure

The postage-stamp problem was solved by a series of instructions to obtain the data, perform calculations, and display the results. Each step was in a sequence, that is, we moved from one line to the next without skipping over any lines. This kind of structure is called a **sequence structure**. Many problems, however, require a decision to determine whether a series of instructions should be executed. If the answer to a question is "yes", then one group of instructions is executed. If the answer is "no", then another is executed. This structure is called a **decision structure**. Figure 1.7 contains the pseudocode and flowchart for a decision structure.

Sequence and decision structures are both used to solve the following problem.

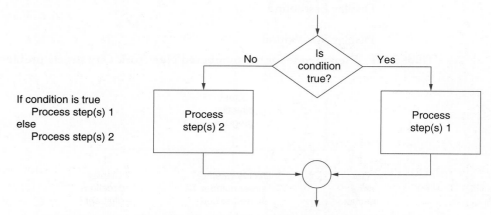

FIGURE 1.7 **Pseudocode and flowchart for a decision structure.**

■ Direction of Numbered NYC Streets Algorithm

Problem: Given a street number of a one-way street in New York City, decide the direction of the street, either eastbound or westbound.

Discussion: There is a simple rule to tell the direction of a one-way street in New York City: Even-numbered streets run eastbound.

Input: Street number.

Processing: Decide if the street number is divisible by 2.

Output: "Eastbound" or "Westbound".

Figures 1.8 through 1.10 show the flowchart, pseudocode, and hierarchy chart for the numbered New York City streets problem.

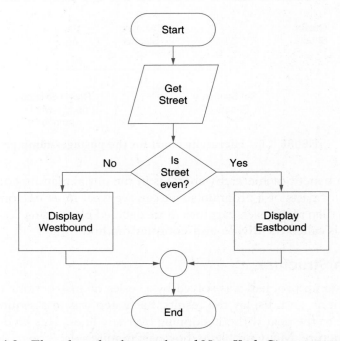

FIGURE 1.8 **Flowchart for the numbered New York City streets problem.**

Program: Determine the direction of a numbered NYC street.
Get street
if street is even
    Display Eastbound
else
    Display Westbound

FIGURE 1.9 **Pseudocode for the numbered New York City streets problem.**

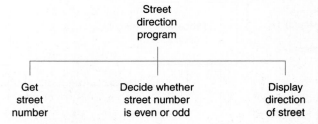

FIGURE 1.10 **Hierarchy chart for the numbered New York City streets problem.**

■ Repetition Structure

A programming structure that executes instructions many times is called a **repetition structure** or a **loop structure**. Loop structures need a test (or condition) to tell when the loop should end. Without an exit condition, the loop would repeat endlessly (an infinite loop). One way to control the number of times a loop repeats (often referred to as the number of passes or iterations) is to check a condition before each pass through the loop and continue executing the loop as long as the condition is true. See Fig. 1.11. The solution of the next problem requires a repetition structure.

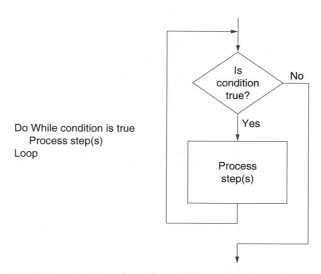

FIGURE 1.11   Pseudocode and flowchart for a loop.

■ Class Average Algorithm

Problem: Calculate and report the average grade for a class.

Discussion: The average grade equals the sum of all grades divided by the number of students. We need a loop to get and then add (accumulate) the grades for each student in the class. Inside the loop, we also need to total (count) the number of students in the class. See Figs. 1.12 to 1.14 on the next page.

Input: Student grades.

Processing: Find the sum of the grades; count the number of students; calculate average grade sum of grades / number of students.
Output: Average grade.

■ Comments

1. Tracing a flowchart is like playing a board game. We begin at the Start symbol and proceed from symbol to symbol until we reach the End symbol. At any time, we will be at just one symbol. In a board game, the path taken depends on the result of spinning a spinner or rolling a pair of dice. The path taken through a flowchart depends on the input.

2. The algorithm should be tested at the flowchart stage before being coded into a program. Different data should be used as input, and the output checked. This process is known as **desk checking**. The test data should include nonstandard data as well as typical data.

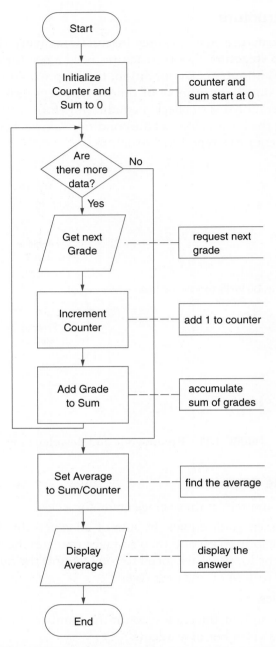

FIGURE 1.12 **Flowchart for the class average problem.**

Program: Calculate and report the average grade of a class.
Initialize Counter and Sum to 0
while there are more data
   Get the next Grade
   Increment the Counter
   Add the Grade to the Sum
Set Average to Sum / Counter
Display Average

FIGURE 1.13 **Pseudocode for the class average problem.**

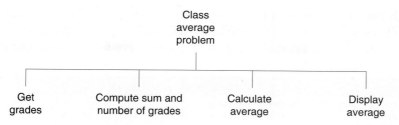

FIGURE 1.14   **Hierarchy chart for the class average problem.**

3. Flowcharts, pseudocode, and hierarchy charts are universal problem-solving tools. They can be used to plan programs for implementation in many computer languages, not just Python.

4. Flowcharts are time-consuming to write and difficult to update. For this reason, professional programmers are more likely to favor pseudocode and hierarchy charts. Because flowcharts so clearly illustrate the logical flow of programming techniques, they are a valuable tool in the education of programmers.

5. There are many styles of pseudocode. Some programmers use an outline form, whereas others use a form that looks almost like a programming language. Several Python keywords, such as "if", "else", and "while", are used extensively in pseudocode.

1.4   An Introduction to Python

The discussions in this book refer to IDLE, the editor that ships with Python. You should be able to carry out the tasks from the book with a different editor by making simple adjustments. We will assume that Python 3 is installed on your computer along with IDLE (or whatever editor you have decided to use). If necessary, see Appendix C for instructions on installing Python and IDLE.

■ Starting IDLE

WINDOWS: Depending on the version of Windows you are using, you should be able to invoke IDLE with a sequence like *Start/All Programs/Python 34/IDLE* or by clicking on a tile similar to the one in Fig. 1.15.

FIGURE 1.15   **IDLE tile from Windows.**

MAC: To invoke IDLE, open Finder, select *Applications*, select the *Python 3.x* folder, and run IDLE from there.

LINUX and UNIX: To invoke IDLE, run *idle3* from the folder */usr/bin*. IDLE can also be invoked by entering *idle3* into a terminal.

With any of the above operating systems, a window similar to the one in Fig. 1.16 should appear. This window is called the **Python shell**. The output of our programs will appear in the Python shell. The Python shell can also be used to immediately evaluate Python expressions.

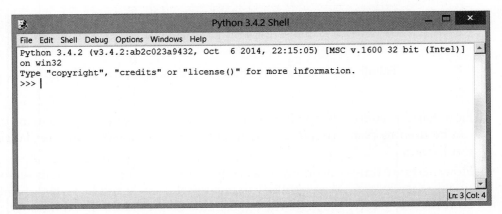

FIGURE 1.16   **The Python shell.**

VideoNote

IDLE
Walkthrough

■ A Python Shell Walkthrough

The three greater than signs (>>>) in Fig. 1.16 constitute the shell's prompt.

1. Type the expression **2 + 3** after the prompt and press the *Enter* (or *return*) key.

   The shell should appear as shown in Fig. 1.17. Notice that the expression has been evaluated and a second prompt has appeared.

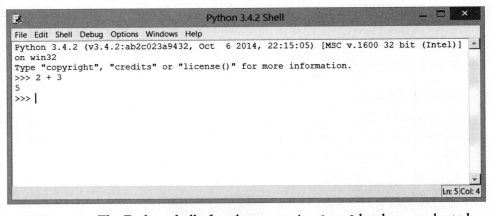

FIGURE 1.17   **The Python shell after the expression 2 + 3 has been evaluated.**

2. Type the statement **print("Hello World!")** after the second prompt and press the *Enter* (or *return*) key.

   The shell should appear as shown in Fig. 1.18. Notice that the words between the quotation marks have been displayed. The statement we entered is a valid Python instruction. If Fig. 1.18 were in color, we would see that the number 5 and the phrase *Hello World!* are colored blue, the word *print* is colored purple, and the characters inside the parentheses are colored green. IDLE uses color coding to differentiate the different types of program elements. For instance, the number 5 and the phrase *Hello World!* are outputs and IDLE colors all output blue.

   The two evaluations we performed in the shell are said to be executed by Python in **interactive mode**. The Python programs we will write in this book are created in a

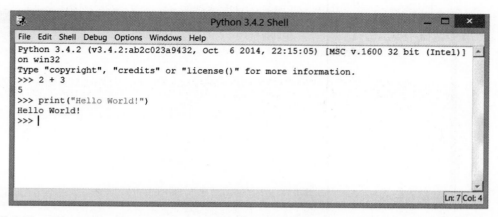

FIGURE 1.18   **The Python shell after the statement** `print("Hello World!")` **has been executed.**

different type of window, called a **code editor window**. However, the output of each program will be displayed in a Python shell.

■ A Python Code Editor Walkthrough

1. From the Python shell, click on *File* in the menu bar and then click on the top command in the drop-down list that appears. (The top command will be either *New File* or *New Window* depending on the version of Python.)

   See Figs. 1.19 and 1.20. Alternatively, the code editor window in Fig. 1.20 can be invoked directly by pressing Ctrl+N.

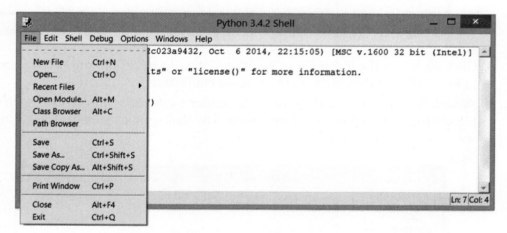

FIGURE 1.19   **The *File* drop-down list.**

2. Type the three lines shown in Fig. 1.21 on the next page into the code editor window.

   These instructions constitute a simple Python program. (The lines of instruction are also referred to as **source code**.) Be careful to type the three lines exactly as they appear in the figure. Notice that the first two lines begin at the left margin, that is, neither is indented. (If one of them were indented, the interpreter would reject the program.) However, the third line is indented by four spaces. Make sure to type the colon at the end of the second line. This program will display the sum of 2 and 3, and then display the phrase *Hello World!* four times. Python requires that all programs be saved as a file in a folder on a storage device (usually the computer's hard disk) before they can be executed.

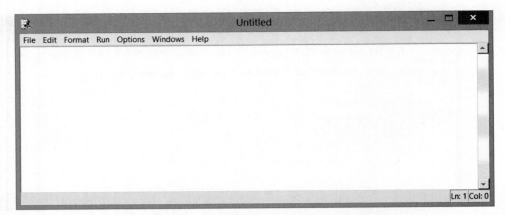

FIGURE 1.20 **The code editor window generated after *New File* (or *New Window*) is clicked on.**

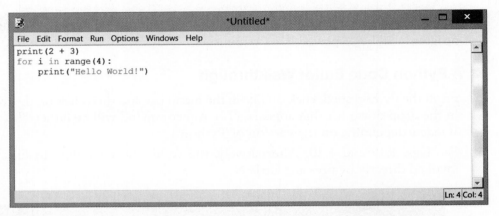

FIGURE 1.21 **The code editor window containing a three-line Python program.**

3. Click on *File* in the menu bar to reveal the drop-down list of commands shown earlier in Fig. 1.19, and then click on the *Save As* command.

A *Save As* dialog box will appear. It is similar to the ones you've used with other applications, such as your word processor. The dialog box will look something like the window shown in Fig. 1.22.

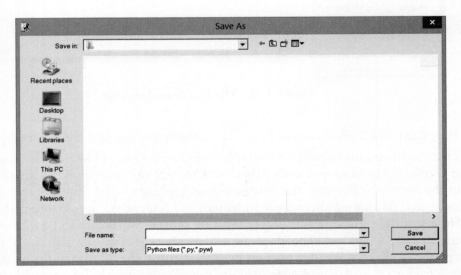

FIGURE 1.22 **A *Save* As dialog box.**

4. Click on the small down-arrow button to the right of the box labeled "Save in:" and navigate to the folder where you would like to save the program.

For right now, you can just use the default folder that appeared when you invoked the *Save As* dialog box. Very likely the folder will have a name such as *Python34*.

5. Type a file name, such as *MyFirstProgram*, into the "File name:" box near the bottom of the window. ***Note:*** The "Save as type:" box at the very bottom of the window contains the words "Python files (*.py.*.pyw)". This will cause ".py" to be added as an extension of the file name when the program is saved. All Python programs should have that extension.

6. Click on the *Save* button.

The code editor window will reappear with the name of the file in the title bar as shown in Fig. 1.23.

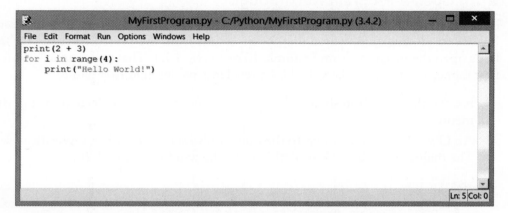

```
MyFirstProgram.py - C:/Python/MyFirstProgram.py (3.4.2)

File  Edit  Format  Run  Options  Windows  Help
print(2 + 3)
for i in range(4):
    print("Hello World!")

                                                          Ln: 5 Col: 0
```

FIGURE 1.23   The code editor window containing a three-line Python program.

7. Close the Python shell by clicking on the red *Close* button on the title bar.

This step is optional. However, by performing this step a new shell window will be created when the program is executed. The new shell will not contain the output from any prior programs.

8. Press the *F5* key (or click on *Run Module* in the *Run* drop-down menu) to execute the program.

The Python shell window in Fig. 1.24 will appear with the output of the program displayed in blue. ***Note:*** If we had neglected to save the program before executing it, the message box in Fig. 1.25 would have appeared and given us another chance to save the program.

```
Python 3.4.2 Shell

File  Edit  Shell  Debug  Options  Windows  Help
Python 3.4.2 (v3.4.2:ab2c023a9432, Oct  6 2014, 22:15:05) [MSC v.1600 32 bit (Intel)]
on win32
Type "copyright", "credits" or "license()" for more information.
>>> ============================ RESTART ============================
>>>
5
Hello World!
Hello World!
Hello World!
Hello World!
>>>

                                                          Ln: 10 Col: 4
```

FIGURE 1.24   The outcome of the Python program in Fig. 1.21.

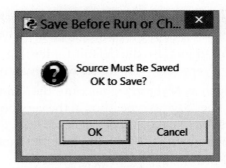

FIGURE 1.25 A *Save* message box.

■ An Open-a-Program Walkthrough

Beginning with Chapter 2, most examples contain a program. (See the discussion in the Preface for details on downloading the programs from the Pearson website for this book.) Let's open the program from Example 10 of Section 3.4. That program asks you to enter a first name, and then displays the U.S. presidents having that first name.

1. From either a Python shell or code editor window, click on *Open* in the *File* drop-down menu.

   An *Open* dialog box similar to the ones you've seen with other applications will appear. The dialog box will look something like the window in Fig. 1.26.

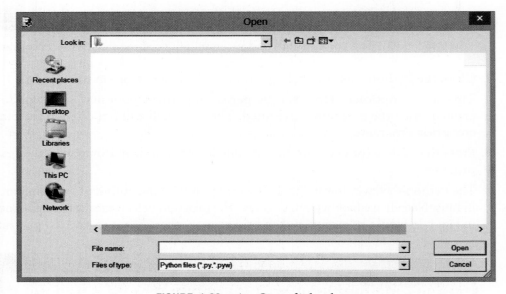

FIGURE 1.26 An *Open* dialog box.

2. Click on the small down-arrow button to the right of the box labeled "Look in:", navigate to the folder *Programs* downloaded from the Pearson website, and open the subfolder *Ch3*.

   The names of the files in the folder *Programs/Ch3* will appear in the large rectangular region in the center of the dialog box.

3. Double-click on 3-4-10.py.

   The Python code window in Fig. 1.27 will appear. The program is now open and can be altered or executed.

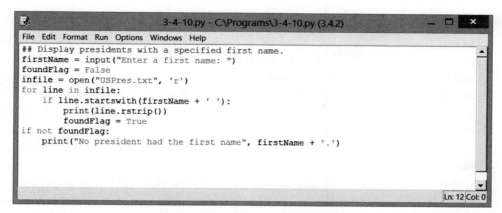

FIGURE 1.27   Example 10 of Section 3.4.

4. Press the *F5* key to run the program.

The Python shell in Fig. 1.28 will appear with the phrase "Enter a first name:" followed by a blinking cursor. *Note:* If you made any alterations to the program, you will be asked to save it after you press the *F5* key.

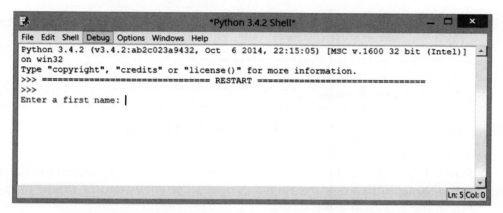

FIGURE 1.28   Request for input from Example 10 of Section 3.4.

5. Type in the name *John* and then press the *Enter* (or *return*) key.

6. The Python shell will now appear as shown in Fig. 1.29. You can close the shell by clicking on the red *Close* button on the title bar.

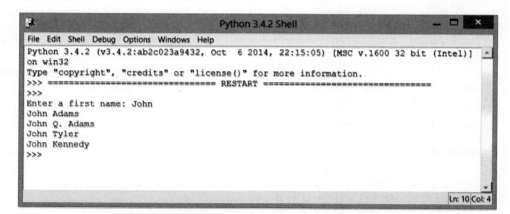

FIGURE 1.29   Complete output for Example 10 of Section 3.4.

■ Comments

1. Indentation is semantically meaningful in Python. For instance, consider the presidents program in Fig. 1.30. The indentation of the first line (the line beginning with ##) is not important since it is a comment statement that is ignored by the Python interpreter. However, the second-through-fifth lines must all begin at the left margin of the window with no indentation. If one of those lines were preceded with any spaces, the program would not run.

   Three of the lines end with a colon. Such lines are called **block headers** and are followed by a group of one or more lines called a **block**, each indented by four spaces. In our program, each block header is the beginning of a repetition or decision structure.

   Notice that each line of the block is indented four spaces from the beginning of the header. Since the level of indentation determines the extent of the block, it is essential that every line within the block have the same level of indentation. Due to this feature, Python is referred to as a **block-structured language**. Blocks can be nested within other blocks. In this particular program, the decision structure block is nested inside the repetition block.

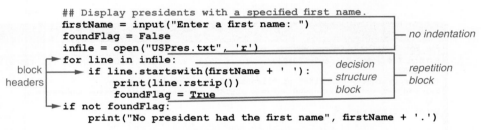

```
## Display presents with a specified first name.
firstName = input("Enter a first name: ")
foundFlag = False
infile = open("USPres.txt", 'r')
for line in infile:
    if line.startswith(firstName + ' '):
        print(line.rstrip())
        foundFlag = True
if not foundFlag:
    print("No president had the first name", firstName + '.')
```

FIGURE 1.30   **Example 10 of Section 3.4.**

2. Figure 1.31 explains the effects of the most useful commands from the *File* pull-down menu. **Note:** With some versions of Python 3, *New Window* will appear instead of *New File* in the *File* drop-down menu.

New File	Ctrl+N
Open...	Ctrl+O
Recent Files	▶
Open Module...	Alt+M
Class Browser	Alt+C
Path Browser	
Save	Ctrl+S
Save As...	Ctrl+Shift+S
Save Copy As...	Alt+Shift+S
Print Window	Ctrl+P
Close	Alt+F4
Exit	Ctrl+Q

SOME COMMANDS FROM THE *FILE* DROP-DOWN MENU.

COMMAND	EFFECT
New File	Create a new code editor window.
Open	Open a saved program.
Recent Files	Display a list of the most recently accessed programs.
Save	Save the current program.
Save As	Save the current program with a different name and possibly different location.
Print Window	Print a copy of the program on a printer.
Close	Close the current window.
Exit	Terminate Python.

FIGURE 1.31   **The *File* drop-down menu.**

3. The program **3-4-10.py** discussed above uses a text file named **USPres.txt** that is located in the *Programs/Ch3* folder downloaded from the Pearson website. To view the text file, navigate to it with your computer's file explorer and open the text file. The contexts of the text file will appear in a text editor such as *Notepad* (on a PC) or *TextEdit* (on a Mac). The first line of the file gives the name of the first president, the second line gives the name of the second president, and so on. To close the text file, click on the text editor's *Close* button.

4. When the program in a code editor window is first created or is altered, the name of the program in the title bar is surrounded by asterisks. See Fig. 1.21. The asterisks disappear when a newly created or altered program is saved. See Fig. 1.23.

2

Core Objects, Variables, Input, and Output

2.1   Numbers

Much of the data processed by computers consists of numbers. In programming terminology, numbers are called **numeric literals**. This section discusses the operations that are performed with numbers and the ways numbers are displayed.

■ Two Types of Numbers: *ints* and *floats*

A whole number written without a decimal point is called an **int** (short for *integer*) and a number written with a decimal point is called a **float** (short for *floating-point* number).

NUMBER	TYPE	NUMBER	TYPE
34	int	23.45	float
34.	float	−34	int

■ Arithmetic Operators

The five basic arithmetic operations are addition, subtraction, multiplication, division, and exponentiation. The addition, subtraction, and division operators are denoted in Python by the standard symbols $+$, $-$, and $/$, respectively. However, the notations for the multiplication and exponentiation operators differ from the customary mathematical notations.

MATHEMATICAL NOTATION	MEANING	PYTHON NOTATION
$a \cdot b$ or $a \times b$	a times b	a * b
a^r	a to the rth power	a ** r

The result of a division is always a float, even if the quotient evaluates to a whole number. The result of the other operations is a float if either of the numbers is a float and otherwise is an int.

■ The *print* Function

The **print function** is used to display numbers on the monitor. If n is a number, then the statement

```
print(n)
```

displays the number n. A combination of numbers, arithmetic operators, and parentheses that can be evaluated is called a **numeric expression**. The print function applied to an expression displays the result of evaluating the expression. A single print function can display several values. If $m, n, r, \ldots$ are numbers (or numeric expressions), then the statement

```
print(m, n, r, . . .)
```

displays the numbers (or values of the numeric expressions) one after another separated by spaces.

The print function invokes a **newline operation** that causes the next print function to display its output at the beginning of a new line.

 Example 1   Arithmetic Operations The following program applies each of the five standard arithmetic operations. [Run] indicates that the program should be executed (by pressing the F5 key or clicking on *Run Module* in the *Run* menu). The lines after [Run] show

the output of the program. In the evaluation of 2 * (3 + 4), the operation inside the parentheses was calculated first. (Expressions inside parentheses are *always* evaluated first.)

```
print(3 + 2, 3 - 2, 3 * 2)
print(8 / 2, 8 ** 2, 2 * (3 + 4))
```

[Run]

```
5 1 6
4.0 64 24
```

Note: All programs appearing in examples can be downloaded from the companion website for this book. See the discussion in the preface for details.

■ Variables

In mathematics problems, quantities are referred to by names. For instance, consider the following algebra problem: "If a car travels at 50 miles per hour, how far will it travel in 14 hours?" The solution to this problem uses the well-known formula

$$\text{distance} = \text{speed} \times \text{time elapsed}.$$

Example 2 shows how this problem would be solved with a Python program.

  Example 2   Distance Traveled   The following program uses the speed and the time elapsed to calculate the distance traveled. The names given to the values are called **variables**. The first line of the program is said to create (or declare) the variable *speed* and to assign it the value 50. Similarly, the second and third lines create and assign values to other variables.

```
speed = 50
timeElapsed = 14
distance = speed * timeElapsed
print(distance)
```

[Run]

```
700
```

Numeric expressions may also contain variables. Expressions are evaluated by replacing each variable by its value and then carrying out the arithmetic. Some examples of expressions containing variables are (2 * distance) + 7, n + 1, and (a + b)/3.

In general, a variable is a name that refers to an item of data stored in memory. In this section of the book, all data will be numbers. A statement of the form

$$variableName = numericExpression$$

VideoNote
Assignment
Statements

is called an **assignment statement**. The statement first evaluates the expression on the right and then assigns its value to the variable on the left. The variable is created the first time it appears on the left side of an assignment statement. Subsequent assignment statements for the variable alter the value assigned to the variable. Actually, each variable points to a location in memory that stores the value. A variable must first be created with an assignment statement before it can be used in an expression.

In Python, variable names must begin with a letter or an underscore, and can consist only of letters, digits, and underscores. (The shortest variable names consist of a single letter.) Descriptive variable names help others (and you at a later time) easily recall what the variable represents. Some examples of descriptive variable names are *totalSales*, *rateOfChange*, and *taxRate*. As a convention, we write variable names in lowercase letters except for the first letters of each additional word. This naming convention is called **camel casing** since the uppercase letters appear to create humps in the name.

Python is case-sensitive, that is, it distinguishes between uppercase and lowercase letters. Therefore, the variables *amount* and *Amount* are different variables.

There are 33 words, called **reserved words** (or **keywords**), that have special meanings in Python and cannot be used as variable names. Some examples of reserved words are *return*, *for*, *while*, and *def*. Appendix B lists the 33 reserved words. (**Note:** IDLE automatically color codes reserved words in the color orange.)

■ The *abs*, *int*, and *round* Functions

There are several common operations that can be performed on numbers other than the standard arithmetic operations. For instance, we may round a number or take its absolute value. These operations are performed by built-in functions. Functions associate with one or more values, called the *input*, a single value called the *output*. The function is said to **return** the output value. The three functions considered in the next paragraph have numeric input and output.

The absolute value function, `abs(x)`, is `|x|`. The function strips the minus signs from negative numbers while leaving other numbers unchanged. The int function leaves integers unchanged, and converts floating-point numbers to integers by discarding their decimal part. The value of `round(n, r)` is the number n rounded to r decimal places. The argument r can be omitted. If so, n is rounded to a whole number. Some examples are as follows:

EXPRESSION	VALUE	EXPRESSION	VALUE	EXPRESSION	VALUE
abs(3)	3	int(2.7)	2	round(2.7)	3
abs(0)	0	int(3)	3	round(2.317, 2)	2.32
abs(−3)	3	int(−2.7)	−2	round(2.317, 1)	2.3

The terms inside the parentheses can be numbers (as shown), numeric variables, or numeric expressions. Expressions are evaluated to produce the input.

✔ **Example 3** Functions The following program evaluates each of the preceding three functions at an expression:

```
a = 2
b = 3
print(abs(1 - (4 * b)))
print(int((a ** b) + .8))
print(round(a / b, 3))
```

[Run]

```
11
8
0.667
```

Note: Function names, like variable names, are case-sensitive. For instance, the round function cannot be written *Round*.

■ Augmented Assignments

Since the expression on the right side of an assignment statement is evaluated *before* the assignment is made, a statement such as

```
var = var + 1
```

is meaningful. It first evaluates the expression on the right (that is, it adds 1 to the value of the variable *var*) and then assigns this sum to the variable *var*. The effect is to increase the value of the variable *var* by 1. In terms of memory locations, the statement retrieves the value of *var* from *var*'s memory location, uses it to compute *var* + 1, and then places the sum into a memory location. This type of calculation is so common that Python provides a special operator to carry it out. The statement

```
var = var + 1
```

can be replaced with the statement

```
var += 1
```

In general, if *n* has a numeric value, then the statement

```
var += n
```

adds the value of *n* to the value of *var*. The operator += is said to perform an **augmented assignment**. Some other augmented assignment operators are −=, *=, /=, and **=.

✓ **Example 4** Augmented Assignments The following program illustrates the different augmented assignment operators.

```
num1 = 6
num1 += 1
num2 = 7
num2 -= 5
num3 = 8
num3 /= 2
print(num1, num2, round(num3))
num1 = 1
num1 *= 3
num2 = 2
num2 **= 3
print(num1, num2)
```

[Run]

```
7 2 4
3 8
```

■ Two Other Integer Operators

In addition to the five standard arithmetic operators discussed at the beginning of this section, the **integer division operator** (written //) and the **modulus operator** (written %) are also available in Python. Let *m* and *n* be positive whole numbers. When you use long division to divide *m* by *n*, you obtain an integer quotient and an integer remainder. In

Python, the integer quotient is denoted $m//n$, and the integer remainder is denoted $m \% n$. For instance,

$$4 \leftarrow 14 // 3$$
$$3\overline{)14}$$
$$\underline{12}$$
$$2 \leftarrow 14 \% 3$$

Essentially, $m//n$ divides two numbers and chops off the fraction part, and $m \% n$ is the remainder when m is divided by n. Some examples are as follows:

EXPRESSION	VALUE	EXPRESSION	VALUE
19 // 5	3	19 % 5	4
10 // 2	5	10 % 2	0
5 // 7	0	5 % 7	5

 Example 5 Convert Lengths The following program converts 41 inches to 3 feet and 5 inches:

```
totalInches = 41
feet = totalInches // 12
inches = totalInches % 12
print(feet, inches)
```

[Run]

```
3 5
```

■ Parentheses, Order of Precedence

Parentheses should be used to clarify the meaning of an expression. When there are insufficient parentheses, the arithmetic operations are performed in the following order of precedence:

1. terms inside parentheses (inner to outer)
2. exponentiation
3. multiplication, division (ordinary and integer), modulus
4. addition and subtraction.

In the event of a tie, the leftmost operation is performed first. For instance, 8 / 2 * 3 is evaluated as (8 / 2) * 3.

A good programming practice is to use parentheses liberally so that you *never* have to remember the order of precedence. For instance, write (2 * 3) + 4 instead of 2 * 3 + 4 and write 4 + (2 ** 3) instead of 4 + 2 ** 3.

■ Three Kinds of Errors

Grammatical and punctuation errors are called **syntax errors**. Some incorrect statements and their errors are shown in Table 2.1.

TABLE 2.1	Three syntax errors.
Statement	**Reason for Error**
`print(3))`	The statement contains an extraneous right parenthesis.
`for = 5`	A reserved word is used as a variable name.
`print(2; 3)`	The semicolon should be a comma.

If a syntax error is spotted when the code is analyzed by the interpreter (that is, before the program begins to execute), Python displays a message box similar to one of those in Fig. 2.1. After you click on the OK button, Python will display the program with a blinking cursor placed near the location of the error.

Windows   Macintosh   Linux

FIGURE 2.1   **Syntax error message boxes.**

Errors that are discovered while a program is running are called **runtime errors** or **exceptions**. Some incorrect statements and their errors are shown in Table 2.2.

TABLE 2.2	Three runtime errors.
Statement	**Reason for Error**
`primt(5)`	The function print is misspelled.
`x += 1`, when x has not been created	Python is not aware of the variable x.
`print(5 / 0)`	A number cannot be divided by zero.

The first two errors in Table 2.2 are said to be of the type *NameError*, and the third is said to be of the type *ZeroDivisionError*. When Python encounters an exception, Python terminates execution of the program and displays a message such as the one in Fig. 2.2. The last two lines of the error message identify the statement that caused the error and give its type.

```
Traceback (most recent call last):
  File "C:\test1.py", line 2, in <module>
    print(5 / 0) #ZeroDivisionError
ZeroDivisionError: division by zero
```

FIGURE 2.2   **An error message for an exception error.**

A third kind of error is called a **logic error**. Such an error occurs when a program does not perform the way it was intended. For instance, the statement

```
average = firstNum + secondNum / 2
```

is syntactically correct. However, an incorrect value will be generated, since the correct way to calculate an average is

```
average = (firstNum + second Num) / 2
```

Logic errors are the most difficult kind of error to locate.

■ Numeric Objects in Memory

Consider the following lines of code:

```
n = 5
n = 7
```

Figure 2.3 shows what happens in memory when the two lines of code are executed. When the first line of code is executed, Python sets aside a portion of memory to hold the number 5. The variable *n* is said to **reference** (or **point to**) the number 5 in the memory location. When the second line of code is executed, Python sets aside a new memory location to hold the number 7 and redirects the variable *n* to point to the new memory location. The number 5 in memory is said to be *orphaned* or *abandoned*. Python will eventually remove the orphaned number from memory with a process called *garbage collection*.

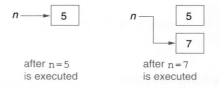

after n = 5
is executed

after n = 7
is executed

FIGURE 2.3   **Numeric objects in memory.**

■ Comments

1. Names given to variables are sometimes referred to as *identifiers*.

2. A numeric expression is any combination of literals, variables, functions, and operators that can be evaluated to produce a number. A single literal or variable is a special case of an expression.

3. Numeric literals used in expressions or assigned to variables must not contain commas, dollar signs, or percent signs. Also, mixed numbers, such as 8 1/2, are not allowed.

4. When the number *n* is halfway between two successive whole numbers (such as 1.5, 2.5, 3.5, and 4.5), the round function rounds it to the nearest even number. For instance, round(2.5) is 2 and round(3.5) is 4.

5. In scientific notation, numbers are written in the form $b \cdot 10^r$, where *b* is a number of magnitude from 1 up to (but not including) 10, and *r* is an integer. Python often displays very large and very small numbers in **scientific notation**, where $b \cdot 10^r$ is written as **be+r** or **be-r**. (The letter *e* is an abbreviation for *exponent*.) For instance, when the statement **print(123.8 * (10 ** 25))** is executed, 1.238e+27 is displayed.

6. The functions discussed in this section are referred to as **built-in functions** since they are part of the Python language. Chapter 4 shows how we can create our own functions. Such functions are commonly referred to as *user-defined functions*. The term

user-defined is a bit of a misnomer; such functions should really be called *programmer-defined functions*.

8. IDLE color codes the different types of elements. For instance, normal text is displayed in black and built-in functions (such as print, abs, int, and round) are displayed in purple.

9. The word "exception" is shorthand for "exceptional (that is, bad) event."

Practice Problems 2.1

1. Evaluate 7 − 4 % 3.

2. Explain the difference between the assignment statement

```
var1 = var2
```

and the assignment statement

```
var2 = var1
```

3. Complete the table by filling in the value of each variable after each line of code is executed.

	a	b	c
a = 5	5	does not exist	does not exist
b = 4	5	4	does not exist
c = a * b	5	4	20
a = c // a			
print((a - b) * c)			
b = b * b * b			

4. Write a statement that increases the value of the numeric variable *var* by 5%.

EXERCISES 2.1

In Exercises 1 through 12, evaluate the numeric expression without the computer, and then use Python to check your answer.

1. 1.7 * 8	**2.** 7 ** 2	**3.** 1 / (2 ** 3)
4. 3 + (4 * 5)	**5.** (8 + 6) / 5	**6.** 3 * ((−2) ** 5)
7. 7 // 3	**8.** 14 % 4	**9.** 9 % 3
10. 14 // 4	**11.** 2 ** 2	**12.** 5 % 5

In Exercises 13 through 18, determine whether the name is a valid variable name.

13. _salesman1	**14.** room&Board	**15.** fOrM_1040
16. 1040B	**17.** @variable	**18.** INCOME 2008

In Exercises 19 through 24, evaluate the numeric expression where $a = 5$, $b = 3$, and $c = 7$.

19. (a * b) + c	**20.** a * (b + c)	**21.** (1 + b) * c
22. a ** c	**23.** b ** (c - a)	**24.** (c - a) ** b

In Exercises 25 through 30, write lines of code to calculate and display the values.

25. $5 \cdot 3 + 3 \cdot 5$ **26.** $(3^4) \cdot (4^3)$ **27.** $200 + 10\%$ of 100

28. $(2^3 - 1) + 5$ **29.** $31 \cdot (2 + 28)$ **30.** $\frac{1}{2^4} \cdot 2^4$

In Exercises 31 and 32, complete the table by filling in the value of each variable after each line is executed.

31.

	x	y
`x = -2`		
`y = x + 5`		
`x = x ** y`		
`print((x/y) + 2)`		
`y = y % 2 + 0.6`		

32.

	bal	inter	withDr
`bal = 100`			
`inter = .05`			
`withDr = 25`			
`bal += (inter * bal)`			
`bal = bal - withDr`			

In Exercises 33 through 38, determine the output displayed by the lines of code.

33.
```
a = 3
b = 5
print(a * b ** 2)
```

34.
```
d = 5
d -= 1
print(d, d + 1, d - 2)
```

35.
```
n = 5
n ** = 2
print(n/5)
```

36.
```
points = 30
points += 20 * 10
print(points)
```

37.
```
totalBerries = 100
totalCost = 352
eachBerry = totalCost /
          totalBerries
print(eachBerry)
```

38.
```
totalMeters = 30255
kiloMeters = totalMeters // 1000
meters = totalMeters % 1000
print(kiloMeters, meters)
```

In Exercises 39 through 42, identify the errors.

39.
```
a = 2
b = 3
a + b = c
print(b)
```

40.
```
balance = 1,234
deposit = $100
print(Balance + Deposit)
```

41.
```
0.05 = interest
balance = 800
print(interest * balance)
```

42.
```
9W = 2 * 9W
print(9W)
```

In Exercises 43 through 48, find the value of the function.

43. `int(10.75)` **44.** `int(9 - 2)` **45.** `abs(3 - 10)`

46. `abs(10 ** (-3))` **47.** `round(3.1279, 3)` **48.** `round(-2.6)`

In Exercises 49 through 54, find the value of the function where $a = 6$ and $b = 4$.

49. `int(-a / 2)`   **50.** `round(a / b)`   **51.** `abs(a - 5)`

52. `abs(4 - a)`   **53.** `round(a + 0.5)`   **54.** `int(b * 0.5)`

In Exercises 55 through 60, rewrite the statements using augmented assignment operators.

55. `cost = cost + 5`   **56.** `sum = sum * 2`   **57.** `cost = cost / 6`

58. `sum = sum - 7`   **59.** `sum = sum % 2`   **60.** `cost = cost // 3`

In Exercises 61 through 68, write a program that has one line of code for each step.

61. Calculate Profit   The following steps calculate a company's profit.

(a) Create the variable *revenue* and assign it the value 98,456.
(b) Create the variable *costs* and assign it the value 45,000.
(c) Create the variable *profit* and assign it the difference between the values of the variables *revenue* and *costs*.
(d) Display the value of the variable *profit*.

62. Stock Purchase   The following steps calculate the amount of a stock purchase.

(a) Create the variable *costPerShare* and assign it the value 25.625.
(b) Create the variable *numberOfShares* and assign it the value 400.
(c) Create the variable *amount* and assign it the product of the values of *costPerShare* and *numberOfShares*.
(d) Display the value of the variable *amount*.

63. Discounted Price   The following steps calculate the price of an item after a 30% reduction.

(a) Create the variable *price* and assign it the value 19.95.
(b) Create the variable *discountPercent* and assign it the value 30.
(c) Create the variable *markdown* and assign it the value of (*discountPercent* divided by 100) times the value of *price*.
(d) Decrease the value of *price* by *markdown*.
(e) Display the value of *price* (rounded to two decimal places).

64. Break-Even Point   The following steps calculate a company's break-even point, the number of units of goods the company must manufacture and sell in order to break even.

(a) Create the variable *fixedCosts* and assign it the value 5,000.
(b) Create the variable *pricePerUnit* and assign it the value 8.
(c) Create the variable *costPerUnit* and assign it the value 6.
(d) Create the variable *breakEvenPoint* and assign it the value of *fixedCosts* divided by (the difference of the values of *pricePerUnit* and *costPerUnit*).
(e) Display the value of the variable *breakEvenPoint*.

65. Savings Account   The following steps calculate the balance after three years when $100 is deposited in a savings account at 5% interest compounded annually.

(a) Create the variable *balance* and assign it the value 100.
(b) Increase the value of the variable *balance* by 5%.
(c) Increase the value of the variable *balance* by 5%.

(d) Increase the value of the variable *balance* by 5%.

(e) Display the value of *balance* (rounded to two decimal places).

66. **Savings Account** The following steps calculate the balance at the end of three years when $100 is deposited at the beginning of each year in a savings account at 5% interest compounded annually.

(a) Create the variable *balance* and assign it the value 100.
(b) Increase the value of the variable *balance* by 5%, and add 100 to it.
(c) Increase the value of the variable *balance* by 5%, and add 100 to it.
(d) Increase the value of the variable *balance* by 5%.
(e) Display the value of *balance* (rounded to two decimal places).

67. **Savings Account** The following steps calculate the balance after 10 years when $100 is deposited in a savings account at 5% interest compounded annually.

(a) Create the variable *balance* and assign it the value 100.
(b) Multiply the value of the variable *balance* by 1.05 raised to the 10th power.
(c) Display the value of *balance* (rounded to two decimal places).

68. **Profit from Stock** The following steps calculate the percentage profit from the sale of a stock.

(a) Create the variable *purchasePrice* and assign it the value 10.
(b) Create the variable *sellingPrice* and assign it the value 15.
(c) Create the variable *percentProfit* and assign it 100 times the value of the difference between *sellingPrice* and *purchasePrice* divided by *purchasePrice*.
(d) Display the value of the variable *percentProfit*.

In Exercises 69 through 78, write a program to solve the problem and display the answer. The program should use variables for each of the quantities.

69. **Corn Production** Suppose each acre of farmland produces 18 tons of corn. How many tons of corn can be grown on a 30-acre farm?

70. **Projectile Motion** Suppose a ball is thrown straight up in the air with an initial velocity of 50 feet per second and an initial height of 5 feet. How high will the ball be after 3 seconds? **Note:** The height after *t* seconds is given by the expression $-16t^2 + v_0t + h_0$, where v_0 is the initial velocity and h_0 is the initial height.

71. **Distance Covered** If a car left the airport at 5 o'clock and arrived home at 9 o'clock, what was the distance covered? **Note:** Speed of the car is 81.34 km per hour.

72. **Gas Mileage** A motorist wants to determine her gas mileage. At 23,352 miles (on the odometer) the tank is filled. At 23,695 miles the tank is filled again with 14 gallons. How many miles per gallon did the car average between the two fillings?

73. **Power Usage** A survey showed that the average monthly electricity consumption for a city was 750 million watts per month. What was the daily power consumption in watts of each resident? **Note:** The city has a population of about 5 million people.

74. **Square Deck** José is building a square deck at the back of his house. José has a building permit for a 432-square-foot deck. How long will each side of the deck be?

75. **Banks** A bank offers 8.7% interest per year on all savings accounts. If a savings account initially contains $1000, how much money will the account hold two years later?

76. Population Increase You grew up in a tiny village and had to move to a nearby city for your undergraduate. When you left, the population was 845. You recently heard that the population of your village has grown by 6.5%. What is the present population of the village? Round the population to the nearest whole number.

77. Bacterial Growth Suppose a surface initially contained $2.19 \cdot 10^{14}$ bacterial cells. After some time, the surface contained $4.68 \cdot 10^{14}$ bacterial cells. Calculate the percentage of bacterial growth. Display the answer rounded to the nearest whole number.

78. Calories Estimate the number of calories in one cubic mile of chocolate ice cream. *Note:* There are 5,280 feet in a mile and one cubic foot of chocolate ice cream contains about 48,600 calories.

Solutions to Practice Problems 2.1

1. 6. Modulus operations are performed before subtractions. If the intent is for the subtraction to be performed first, the expression should be written $(7 - 4) \% 3$.

2. The first assignment statement assigns the value of the variable *var2* to the variable *var1*, whereas the second assignment statement assigns *var1*'s value to *var2*.

3.

	a	b	c
`a = 5`	5	does not exist	does not exist
`b = 4`	5	4	does not exist
`c = a * b`	5	4	20
`a = c // a`	4	4	20
`print((a - b)*c)`	4	4	20
`b = b * b * b`	4	64	20

Each time an assignment statement is executed, only one variable (the variable to the left of the equal sign) has its value changed.

4. Each of the following four statements increases the value of *var* by 5%.

```
var = var + (.05 * var)
var = 1.05 * var
var += .05 * var
var *= 1.05
```

2.2 Strings

The most common types of data processed by Python are strings and numbers. Sentences, phrases, words, letters of the alphabet, names, telephone numbers, addresses, and social security numbers are all examples of strings.

■ String Literals

A **string literal** is a sequence of characters that is treated as a single item. The characters in strings can be any characters found on the keyboard (such as letters, digits, punctuation marks, and spaces) and many other special characters.

In Python programs, string literals are written as a sequence of characters surrounded by either single quotes (') or double quotes ("). Some examples of strings are as follows:

"John Doe"
'5th Avenue'

'76'
"Say it ain't so, Joe!"

Opening and closing quotation marks must be the same type—either both double quotes or both single quotes. When a string is surrounded by double quotes, a single quote can appear directly in the string, but not a double quote. Similarly, a string surrounded by single quotes can contain a double quote, but not a single quote directly.[1]

■ Variables

Variables also can be assigned string values. As with variables assigned numeric values, variables assigned string values are created (that is, come into existence) the first time they appear in assignment statements. When an argument of a print function is a string literal or a variable having a string value, only the characters within the enclosing quotation marks (and not the quotation marks themselves) are displayed.

■ Indices and Slices

In Python, the **position** or **index** of a character in a string is identified with one of the numbers 0, 1, 2, 3, ... For instance, the first character of a string is said to have index 0, the second character is said to have index 1, and so on. If $str1$ is a string variable or literal, then str1[i] is the character of the string having index i. Figure 2.4 shows the indices of the characters of the string "spam & eggs".

FIGURE 2.4   **Indices of the characters of the string "spam & eggs".**

A **substring** or **slice** of a string is a sequence of consecutive characters from the string. For instance, consider the string "Just a moment". The substrings "Jus", "mom", and "nt" begin at positions 0, 7, and 11, and end at positions 2, 9, and 12, respectively. If $str1$ is a string, then **str1[m:n]** is the substring beginning at position m and ending at position $n - 1$. Figure 2.5 helps to visualize slices. Think of the indices of the characters pointing just to the left of the characters. Then "spam & eggs"[m:n] is the sequence of characters between the arrows labeled with the numbers m and n. For instance **"spam & eggs"[2:6]** is the substring **"am &"**; that is, the substring between the arrow labeled 2 and the arrow labeled 6.

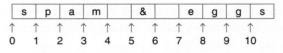

FIGURE 2.5   **Aid to visualizing slices.**

Note: If $m \geq n$, that is, if the character in position m is not to the left of the character in position n, then the value of **str1[m:n]** will be the **empty string ("")**, the string with no characters.

If $subStr$ is a string, then **str1.find(subStr)** is the positive index of the first appearance of $subStr$ in $str1$ with the search beginning at the left side of the string. The value of **str1.rfind(subStr)** is the positive index of the first appearance of $subStr$ in $str1$ with the search beginning at the right side of the string. If $subStr$ does not appear in $str1$, then the value returned by the **find** and **rfind** methods will be -1.

---

[1]In Section 2.3, we show how to use escape sequences to override this restriction.

Example 1 Indices The following program illustrates the use of indices.

```
print("Python")
print("Python"[1], "Python"[5], "Python"[2:4])
str1 = "Hello World!"
print(str1.find('W'))
print(str1.find('x'))
print(str1.rfind('l'))
```

[Run]

```
Python
y n th
6
-1
9
```

■ Negative Indices

The indices discussed above specify positions from the left side of the string. Python also allows strings to be indexed by their position with regards to the right side of the string by using negative numbers for indices. With negative indexing, the rightmost character is assigned index −1, the character to its left is assigned index −2, and so on. Figure 2.6 shows the negative indices of the characters of the string "spam & eggs".

FIGURE 2.6 **Negative indices of the characters of the string "spam & eggs".**

Example 2 Negative Indices The following program illustrates negative indices.

```
print("Python")
print("Python"[-1], "Python"[-4], "Python"[-5:-2])
str1 = "spam & eggs"
print(str1[-2])
print(str1[-8:-3])
print(str1[0:-1])
```

[Run]

```
Python
n t yth
g
m & e
spam & egg
```

■ Default Bounds for Slices

In the expression **str1[m:n]**, one or both of the bounds can be omitted. If so, the left bound *m* defaults to 0 and the right bound *n* defaults to the length of the string. That is, **str1[:n]** consists of all the characters from the beginning of the string to **str1[n-1]**, and

str1[m:] consists of all the characters from **str1[m]** to the end of the string. The slice **str1[:]** is the entire string *str1*.

Example 3   Default Bounds The following program illustrates default bounds.

```
print("Python"[2:], "Python"[:4], "Python"[:])
print("Python"[-3:], "Python"[:-3])
```

[Run]

```
·thon Pyth Python
hon Pyt
```

■ String Concatenation

Two strings can be combined to form a new string consisting of the strings joined together. This operation is called **concatenation** and is represented by a plus sign. For instance, "good" + "bye" is "goodbye". A combination of strings, plus signs, functions, and methods that can be evaluated to form a string is called a **string expression**. When a string expression appears in an assignment statement or a print function, the string expression is evaluated before being assigned or displayed.

■ String Repetition

The asterisk operator can be used with strings to repeatedly concatenate a string with itself. If *str1* is a string literal, variable, or expression and *n* is a positive integer, then the value of

str1 * n

is the concatenation of *n* copies of the value of *str1*.

EXPRESSION	VALUE	EXPRESSION	VALUE
"ha" * 4	"hahahaha"	'x' * 10	"xxxxxxxxxx"
"mur" * 2	"murmur"	("cha-" * 2) + "cha"	"cha-cha-cha"

VideoNote
String
Functions

■ String Functions and Methods

A string function operates much like a numeric function; it takes a string as input and returns a value. A string method is a process that performs a task on a string. We have already seen two examples of methods—the find and rfind methods. These methods perform the task of locating an index. The general form of an expression applying a method is

stringName.methodName()

where the parentheses might contain values. Like the numeric functions discussed in the previous section, string functions and methods also can be applied to literals, variables, and expressions. Table 2.3 below describes one string function and six additional string methods where *str1* is the string "Python". Some further string methods will be presented in subsequent chapters.

TABLE 2.3	String operations (str1 = "Python").		
Function or Method	Example	Value	Description
len	len(str1)	6	number of characters in the string
upper	str1.upper()	"PYTHON"	uppercases every alphabetical character
lower	str1.lower()	"python"	lowercases every alphabetical character
count	str1.count('th')	1	number of non-overlapping occurrences of the substring
capitalize	"coDE".capitalize()	"Code"	capitalizes the first letter of the string and lowercases the rest
title	"beN hur".title()	"Ben Hur"	capitalizes the first letter of each word in the string and lowercases the rest
rstrip	"ab ".rstrip()	"ab"	removes spaces from the right side of the string

■ Chained Methods

Consider the following two lines of code:

```
praise = "Good Doggie".upper()
numberOfGees = praise.count('G')
```

These two lines can be combined into the single line below that is said to **chain** the two methods.

```
numberOfGees = "Good Doggie".upper().count('G')
```

Chained methods are executed from left to right. Chaining often produces clearer code since it eliminates temporary variables, such as the variable *praise* above.

■ The *input* Function

The input function prompts the user to enter data. A typical input statement is

```
town = input("Enter the name of your city: ")
```

When Python reaches this statement, the string "Enter the name of your city: " is displayed and the program pauses. After the user types in the name of his or her city and presses the *Enter* (or *return*) key, the variable *town* is assigned the name of the city. (If the variable had not been created previously, it is created at this time.) The general form of an input statement is

```
variableName = input(prompt)
```

where *prompt* is a string that requests a response from the user.

 Example 4   Parse a Name   The following program requests a name from the user and then parses the name. When the program is run, the phrase "Enter a full name: " appears and execution of the program pauses. After the user types the words shown in black and presses the *Enter* (or *return*) key, the last two lines of output are displayed.

```
fullName = input("Enter a full name: ")
n = fullName.rfind(" ")
print("Last name:", fullName[n+1:])
print("First name(s):", fullName[:n])
```

[Run]

```
Enter a full name: Franklin Delano Roosevelt
Last name: Roosevelt
First name(s): Franklin Delano
```

■ The *int, float, eval,* and *str* Functions

If *str1* is a string containing a whole number, the **int** function will convert the string to an integer. If *str1* is a string containing any number, the **float** function will convert the string to a floating-point number. (The **float** function also converts an **integer** to a floating-point number.) If *str1* is a string consisting of a numeric expression, the **eval** function will evaluate the expression to an integer or floating-point number as appropriate.

✓   **Example 5**   Illustrate Functions The following program illustrates the use of the **int**, **float**, and, **eval** functions.

```
print(int("23"))
print(float("23"))
print(eval("23"))
print(eval("23.5"))
x = 5
print(eval("23 + (2 * x)"))
```

[Run]

```
23
23.0
23
23.5
33
```

The **input** function always returns a string. However, a combination of an **input** function and an **int**, **float**, or **eval** function allows numbers to be input into a program. For instance, consider the following three statements:

```
age = int(input("Enter your age: "))
age = float(input("Enter your age: "))
age = eval(input("Enter your age: "))
```

Suppose the user responds with an integer, say 25. Then, after each of the statements above has been responded to, the statement **print(age)** would display 25, 25.0, and 25, respectively. However, if the user was a youngster, he or she might respond with the number 3.5. With the first input statement, a Traceback error message would result. After either the second or third input statement was executed, the **print** function would display 3.5. The **eval** function produced good results with either age.

The **int** and **float** functions execute faster than the **eval** function and are preferred by many Python programmers when they can be used safely. In this book we will use all three functions, but will favor the **eval** function.

The **int** and **float** functions also can be applied to appropriate numeric expressions. If x is an integer, the value of int(x) is x. If x is a floating-point number, the **int** function removes the decimal part of the number. The **float** function operates as expected. The **eval** function cannot be applied to numeric literals, variables, or expressions.

EXAMPLE	VALUE		EXAMPLE	VALUE
int(4.8)	4		float(4.67)	4.67
int(−4.8)	4		float(−4)	−4.0
int(4)	4		float(0)	0.0

The **str** function converts a number to its string representation. For instance, the value of **str(5.6)** is **"5.6"** and the value of **str(5.)** is **"5.0"**.

A string cannot be concatenated with a number. However, the invalid statement

```
strVar = numVar + '%'
```

can be replaced with the valid statement

```
strVar = str(numVar) + '%'
```

that concatenates two strings.

■ Internal Documentation

Program documentation is the inclusion of **comments** that specify the intent of the program, the purpose of the variables, and the tasks performed by individual portions of the program. To create a comment statement, begin a line with a number sign (#). Such a statement is completely ignored when the program is executed. Comments are sometimes called *remarks*. A line of code can be documented by adding a number sign, followed by

Example 6 Parse a Name The following rewrite of Example 4 uses documentation. The first comment describes the entire program, the comment in the third line gives the meaning of a variable, and the final comment describes the purpose of the two lines that follow it.

```
## Break a name into two parts -- the last name and the first names.
fullName = input("Enter a full name: ")
n = fullName.rfind(" ")   # index of the space preceding the last name
# Display the desired information.
print("Last name:", fullName[n+1:])
print("First name(s):", fullName[:n])
```

the desired information, after the end of the line. Pressing Alt+3 and Alt+ 4 can be used in IDLE to comment and uncomment selected blocks of code.

Some of the benefits of documentation are as follows:

1. Other people can easily understand the program.

2. You can better understand the program when you read it later.

3. Long programs are easier to read because the purposes of individual pieces can be determined at a glance.

Good programming practice requires that programmers document their code while they are writing it. In fact, many software companies require a certain level of documentation before they release software and some judge a programmer's performance on how well their code is documented.

■ Line Continuation

A long statement can be split across two or more lines by ending each line (except the last) with a backslash character (\ ). For instance, the line

```
quotation = "Well written code is its own best documentation."
```

can be written as

```
quotation = "Well written code is its own " + \
            "best documentation."
```

Python has a feature that can be used to eliminate the need for line continuation with backslash characters. Any code enclosed in a pair of parentheses can span multiple lines. Since any expression can be enclosed in parentheses, this feature can nearly always be used. For instance, the statement above can be written as

```
quotation = ("Well written code is its own " +
             "best documentation.")
```

This method of line continuation has become the preferred style for most Python programmers and will be used whenever possible in this textbook.

■ Indexing and Slicing Out of Bounds

Python does not allow out of bounds indexing for individual characters of strings, but does allow out of bounds indices for slices. For instance, if

```
str1 = "Python"
```

then **print(str1[7])** and **print(str1[-7])** trigger the Traceback error message *IndexError*.
If the left index in a slice is too far negative, the slice will start at the beginning of the string, and if the right index is too large, the slice will go to the end of the string. For instance,

```
str1[-10:10] is "Python"
str1[-10:3]  is "Pyt"
str1[2:10]   is "thon"
```

■ Comments

1. In this textbook, we usually surround one-character strings with single quotation marks and all other strings with double quotation marks.

2. Since a string expression is any combination of literals, variables, functions, methods, and operators that can be evaluated to produce a string, a single string or variable is a special case of an expression.

3. Every character in a string has two indices—one positive and one negative. Therefore, the numbers m and n in an expression of the form strValue[m:n] can have opposite signs. If the character having index m is to the left of the character having index n, then the slice will consist of the substring beginning with the character having index m and

ending with the character to the left of the character having index n. For instance, the value of "Python"[−4:5] is "tho". Of course, if the character having index m is not to the left of the character having index n, then the slice will be the empty string.

4. Individual characters within a string cannot be changed directly. For instance, the code below, which intends to change the word *resort* to the word *report*, produces a Traceback error message.

```
word = "resort"
word[2] = 'p'
```

5. The operator += performs an augmented concatenation assignment for strings.

6. IDLE displays strings in the color green and comments in the color red.

7. Method names, like names of variables and functions, are case-sensitive.

8. For readability purposes, you should not chain more than three methods together.

9. Strings are said to have type str. The statement `print(dir(str))` displays all the string methods. (Ignore the items that begin and end with double underscore characters.)

Practice Problems 2.2

1. Assuming that $0 \leq m \leq n \leq$ len(*str*1), how many characters are in `str1[m:n]`?
2. What is displayed by the statement `print("Computer".find('E'))`?

EXERCISES 2.2

In Exercises 1 through 4, determine the output displayed by the lines of code.

1. `print("Python")`

2. `print("Hello")`

3. `var = "Ernie"`
   `print(var)`

4. `var = "Bert"`
   `print(var)`

In Exercises 5 through 46, determine the value of the expression.

5. `"Python"[4]`

6. `"Python"[-2]`

7. `"Hello Python!"[-9]`

8. `"Python"[5]`

9. `"Python"[0:3]`

10. `"Python"[2:2]`

11. `"Python"[:2]`

12. `"Python"[2:]`

13. `"Python"[-3:-2]`

14. `"Python"[-5:-1]`

15. `"Python"[2:-2]`

16. `"Python"[-4:4]`

17. `"Python"[:]`

18. `"Python"[-10:10]`

19. `"Python".find("tho")`

20. `"Python".find("ty")`

21. `"Python".find("oh")`

22. `"Python".find("Pyt")`

23. `"whizzbuzz".rfind("zz")`

24. `"whizzbuzz".find("zz")`

25. `" Python".lstrip()`

26. `"hello_world".startswith("hell")`

27. `"smallElements".capitalize()`

28. `"hello_python".rpartition('_')`

29. `"PyThOn".swapcase()`

30. `"python/java/c++".split('/')`

31. `"8 Ball".title()`

32. `len("brrr")`

33. `"8 Ball".upper()`

34. `"whippersnapper".count("pp")`

35. `"Python"[-1*len("Python")-1:3]`

36. `"Python".lower()`

37. `"the artist".title()`

38. `len("Gravity   ".rstrip())`

39. `len("Grand Hotel"[:6].rstrip())`

40. `"king lear".title()`

41. `"let it go".title().find('G')`

42. `"Hello World!".lower().find('wo')`

43. `"Amazon".lower().count('a')`

44. `"Python".upper().find("tho")`

45. `"john's school".capitalize()`

46. `"all clear".title().count('a')`

In Exercises 47 through 70, determine the output displayed by the lines of code.

47.
```
a = 4
b = 6
c = "Municipality"
d = "pal"
print(len(c))
print(c.upper())
print(c[a:b] + c[b + 4:])
print(c.find(d))
```

48.
```
m = 4
n = 3
s = "Microsoft"
t = "soft"
print(len(s))
print(s.lower())
print(s[m:m + 2])
print(s.find(t))
```

49. `print("f" + "lute")`

50. `print("a" + "cute")`

51. `print("Your age is " + str(21) + ".")`

52. `print("Fred has " + str(2) + " children.")`

53.
```
r = "A ROSE"
b = " IS "
print(r + b + r + b + r)
```

54.
```
sentence = "ALPHONSE TIPPYTOED AWAY."
print(sentence[12:15] + sentence[3:6])
```

55.
```
var = "WALLA"
var += 2 * var
print(var)
```

56.
```
str1 = "mur"
str1 += str1
print(str1)
```

57.
```
str1 = "good"
str1 += "bye"
print(str1)
```

58.
```
var = "eight"
var += "h"
print(var)
```

59. `print('M' + ('m' * 3) * 2 + '.')`

60. `print(('*' * 3) + "YES" + ('*' * 3))`

61. `print('a' + (" " * 5) + 'b')`

62. `print("spam" * 4)`

63.
```
s = "trom"
n = 76
print(n, s + "bones")
```

64.
```
str1 = "5"
num = 0.5 + int(str1)
print(num)
```

65.
```
num = input("Enter an integer: ")
print('1' + str(num))
```
(Assume the response is 7.)

66.
```
num = int(input("Enter an integer: "))
print(1 + num)
```
(Assume the response is 7.)

67.
```
num = float(input("Enter a number: "))
print(1 + num)
```
(Assume the response is 7.)

68.
```
num = eval(input("Enter a number: "))
print(1 + num)
```
(Assume the response is 7.)

69.
```
film = "the great gatsby".title()[:10].rstrip()
print(film, len(film))
```

70.
```
batmanAndRobin = "THE DYNAMIC DUO".lower().title()
print(batmanAndRobin)
```

71. Give a simple expression that lops off the last character of a string.

72. Give a simple expression that lops off the first character of a string.

73. What is the negative index of the first character in a string of eight characters?

74. What is the positive index of the last character in a string of eight characters?

75. (True or false) If *n* is the length of *str1*, then `str1[n - 1:]` is the string consisting of the last character of *str1*.

76. (True or false) If *n* is the length of *str1*, then `str1[n - 2:]` is the string consisting of the last two characters of *str1*.

77. (True or false) `str1[:n]` consists of the first *n* characters of *str1*.

78. (True or false) `str1[-n:]` consists of the last *n* characters of *str1*.

In Exercises 79 through 92, identify all errors.

79.
```
phoneNumber = 234-5678
print("My phone number is " + phoneNumber)
```

80.
```
quote = I came to Casablanca for the waters.
print(quote + ": " + "Bogart")
```

81.
```
for = "happily ever after."
print("They lived " + for)
```

82.
```
age = input("Enter your age: ")
print("Next year you will be " + (age + 1))
```

83. `print('Say it ain't so.')`

84. `print("George "Babe" Ruth")`

85. `print("Python".UPPER())`

86. `print("Python".lower)`

87.
```
age = 19
print("Age: " + age)
```

88.
```
num = 1234
print(num[3])
```

89.
```
num = '1234'
print(num.find(2))
```

90.
```
num = 45
print(len(num))
```

91.
```
language = "Python"
language[4] = 'r'
```

92.
```
show = "Spamalot"
print(show[9])
```

In Exercises 93 through 96, write a program having one line for each step. Lines that display data should use the given variable names.

93. Inventor   The following steps give the name and birth year of a famous inventor.

   (a) Create the variable *firstName* and assign it the value "Thomas".
   (b) Create the variable *middleName* and assign it the value "Alva".
   (c) Create the variable *lastName* and assign it the value "Edison".
   (d) Create the variable *yearOfBirth* and assign it the value 1847.
   (e) Display the phrase "The year of birth of" followed by the inventor's full name, followed by "is", and the inventor's year of birth.

94. Price of Ketchup   The following steps compute the price of ketchup.

   (a) Create the variable *item* and assign it the value "ketchup".
   (b) Create the variable *regularPrice* and assign it the value 1.80.
   (c) Create the variable *discount* and assign it the value .27.
   (d) Display the phrase "1.53 is the sale price of ketchup."

95. Copyright Statement   The following steps display a copyright statement.

   (a) Create the variable *publisher* and assign it the value "Pearson".
   (b) Display the phrase "(c) Pearson".

96. Advice   The following steps give advice.

   (a) Create the variable *prefix* and assign it the value "Fore".
   (b) Display the phrase "Forewarned is Forearmed."

Note: **For each of the following exercises, a possible output is shown in a shaded box. Responses to input statements appear underlined.**

97. Distance from a Storm   If *n* is the number of seconds between lightning and thunder, the storm is *n*/5 miles away. Write a program that requests the number of seconds between lightning and thunder and reports the distance from the storm rounded to two decimal places. See Fig. 2.7.

```
Enter number of seconds between
lightning and thunder: 1.25
Distance from storm: 0.25 miles.
```

```
Enter your age: 20
Enter your resting heart rate: 70
Training heart rate: 161 beats/min.
```

FIGURE 2.7   Possible outcome of Exercise 97.   **FIGURE 2.8   Possible outcome of Exercise 98.**

98. Training Heart Rate   The American College of Sports Medicine recommends that you maintain your *training heart rate* during an aerobic workout. Your training heart rate is computed as .7 * (220 − a) + .3 * r, where *a* is your age and *r* is your resting heart rate (your pulse when you first awaken). Write a program to request a person's age and resting heart rate and display their training heart rate. See Fig. 2.8.

99. Triathlon   The number of calories burned per hour by cycling, running, and swimming are 200, 475, and 275, respectively. A person loses 1 pound of weight for each 3,500 calories burned. Write a program to request the number of hours spent at each activity and then display the number of pounds worked off. See Fig. 2.9.

```
Enter number of hours cycling: 2
Enter number of hours running: 3
Enter number of hours swimming: 1
Weight loss: 0.6 pounds
```

```
Enter wattage: 100
Enter number of hours used: 720
Enter price per kWh in cents: 11.76
Cost of electricity: $6.12
```

FIGURE 2.9   Possible outcome of Exercise 99.   FIGURE 2.10   Possible outcome of Exercise 100.

100. **Cost of Electricity**   The cost of the electricity used by a device is given by the formula

$$\text{cost of electricity (in dollars)} = \frac{\text{wattage of device} \cdot \text{hours used}}{1{,}000 \cdot \text{cost per kWh (in cents)}}$$

where kWh is an abbreviation for "kilowatt hour." The cost per kWh of electricity varies with locality. Suppose the current average cost of electricity for a residential customer in the United States is 11.76¢ per kWh. Write a program that allows the user to calculate the cost of operating an electrical device. Figure 2.10 calculates the cost of keeping a light bulb turned on for an entire month.

101. **Baseball**   Write a program to request the name of a baseball team, the number of games won, and the number of games lost as input, and then display the name of the team and the percentage of games won. See Fig. 2.11.

```
Enter name of team: Yankees
Enter number of games won: 84
Enter number of games lost: 78
Yankees won 51.9% of their games.
```

```
Enter earnings per share: 5.25
Enter price per share: 68.25
Price-to-Earnings ratio: 13.0
```

FIGURE 2.11   Possible outcome of Exercise 101.   FIGURE 2.12   Possible outcome of Exercise 102.

102. **Price-to-Earnings Ratio**   Write a program that requests a company's earnings-per-share for the year and the price of one share of stock as input, and then displays the company's price-to-earnings ratio (that is, price ÷ earnings). See Fig. 2.12.

103. **Car Speed**   The formula $s = \sqrt{24d}$ gives an estimate of the speed in miles per hour of a car that skidded d feet on dry concrete when the brakes were applied. Write a program that requests the distance skidded and then displays the estimated speed of the car. See Fig. 2.13. **Note:** $\sqrt{x} = x^{.5}$.

```
Enter distance skidded: 54
Estimated speed: 36.0 miles per hour
```

```
Enter percentage: 125%
Equivalent decimal: 1.25
```

FIGURE 2.13   Possible outcome of Exercise 103.   FIGURE 2.14   Possible outcome of Exercise 104.

104. **Percentages**   Write a program that converts a percentage to a decimal. See Fig. 2.14.

105. **Convert Speeds**   On May 6, 1954, British runner Sir Roger Bannister became the first person to run the mile in less than 4 minutes. His average speed was 24.20 kilometers per hour. Write a program that requests a speed in kilometers per hour as

input and then displays the speed in miles per hour. See Fig. 2.15. **Note:** One kilometer is .6214 of a mile.

```
Enter speed in KPH: 24.20
Speed in MPH: 15.04
```

```
Enter amount of bill: 21.50
Enter percentage tip: 18
Tip: $3.87
```

FIGURE 2.15   Possible outcome of Exercise 105.   FIGURE 2.16   Possible outcome of Exercise 106.

106. Server's Tip   Write a program that calculates the amount of a server's tip, given the amount of the bill and the percentage tip as input. See Fig. 2.16.

107. Equivalent Interest Rates   Interest earned on municipal bonds from an investor's home state is not taxed, whereas interest earned on CDs *is* taxed. Therefore, in order for a CD to earn as much as a municipal bond, the CD must pay a higher interest rate. How much higher the interest rate must be depends on the investor's tax bracket. Write a program that requests a tax bracket and a municipal bond interest rate as input, and then displays the CD interest rate having the same yield. See Fig. 2.17. **Note:** If the tax bracket is expressed as a decimal, then

$$\text{CD interest rate} = \frac{\text{municipal bond interest rate}}{(1 - \text{tax bracket})}.$$

```
Enter tax bracket (as decimal): .37
Enter municipal bond interest rate (as %): 3.26
Equivalent CD interest rate: 5.175%
```

FIGURE 2.17   Possible outcome of Exercise 107.

108. Marketing Terms   The *markup* of an item is the difference between its *selling price* and its *purchase price*. Two other marketing terms are

$$\text{percentage markup} = \frac{\text{markup}}{\text{purchase price}} \quad and \quad \text{profit margin} = \frac{\text{markup}}{\text{selling price}}$$

where the quotients are expressed as percentages. Write a program that computes the markup, percentage markup, and profit margin of an item. See Fig. 2.18. Notice that when the purchase price is tripled, the percentage markup is 200%.

```
Enter purchase price: 215
Enter selling price: 645
Markup: $430.0
Percentage markup: 200.0%
Profit margin: 66.67%
```

```
Enter number: 123.45678
3 digits to left of decimal point
5 digits to right of decimal point
```

FIGURE 2.18   Possible outcome of Exercise 108.   FIGURE 2.19   Possible outcome of Exercise 109.

109. Analyze a Number   Write a program that requests a positive number containing a decimal point as input and then displays the number of digits to the left of the decimal point and the number of digits to the right of the decimal point. See Fig. 2.19.

110. Word Replacement Write a program that requests a sentence, a word in the sentence, and another word and then displays the sentence with the first word replaced by the second. See Fig. 2.20.

```
Enter a sentence: What you don't know won't hurt you.
Enter word to replace: know
Enter replacement word: owe
What you don't owe won't hurt you.
```

FIGURE 2.20 Possible outcome of Exercise 110.

111. Convert Months Write a program that asks the user to enter a whole number of months as input and then converts that amount of time to years and months. See Fig. 2.21. The program should use both integer division and the modulus operator.

```
Enter number of months: 234
234 months is 19 years and 6 months.
```

```
Enter number of inches: 185
185 inches is 15 feet and 5 inches.
```

FIGURE 2.21 Possible outcome of Exercise 111.   **FIGURE 2.22** Possible outcome of Exercise 112.

112. Convert Lengths Write a program that asks the user to enter a whole number of inches and then converts that length to feet and inches. See Fig. 2.22. The program should use both integer division and the modulus operator.

Solutions to Practice Problems 2.2

1. $n - m$. When $m = 0$ the number of characters in str1[0:n] is n. Increasing the number 0 to m, decreases the number of characters by m.

2. -1. There is no uppercase letter E in the string "Computer". The **find** method distinguishes between uppercase and lowercase letters.

2.3 Output

Enhanced output can be produced by the **print** function with two optional arguments and the use of the **format** method.

■ Optional *print* Argument *sep*

A statement of the form

```
print(value0, value1, . . ., valueN)
```

where the values are strings or numbers, displays the values one after another with successive values separated by a space. We say that the **print** function uses the string consisting of one space character as a **separator**. We can optionally change the separator to any string we like with the **sep argument**. If *sepString* is a string, then a statement of the form

```
print(value0, value1, . . ., valueN, sep=sepString)
```

displays the values with successive values separated by *sepString*. Some examples are as follows:

STATEMENT	OUTCOME
`print("Hello", "World!", sep="**")`	`Hello**World!`
`print("Hello", "World!", sep="")`	`HelloWorld!`
`print("1", "two", 3, sep="   ")`	`1   two   3`

■ Optional *print* Argument *end*

After any of the statements above are executed, the display of output on the current line comes to an end, and the next print statement will display its output on the next line. We say that the print statement ends by executing a **newline operation**. (We also say that the print statement moved the cursor to the beginning of the next line or that the print statement performed a "carriage return and line feed.") We can optionally change the ending operation with the **end argument**. If *endString* is a string, then a statement of the form

```
print(value0, value1, . . ., valueN, end=endString)
```

displays *value0* through *valueN* and then displays *endString* on the same line, without performing a newline operation. Here are some lines of code that use the end argument.

```
print("Hello", end=" ")
print("World!")
```

[Run]

```
Hello World!
```

```
print("Hello", end="")
print("World!")
```

[Run]

```
HelloWorld!
```

■ Escape Sequences

Escape sequences are short sequences that are placed in strings to instruct the cursor or to permit some special characters to be printed. The first character is always a backslash (\). The two most common cursor-instructing escape sequences are **\t** (induces a horizontal tab) and **\n** (induces a newline operation). By default, the tab size is eight spaces, but can be increased or decreased with the **expandtabs method**.

✓ **Example 1**   Escape Sequences The following program demonstrates the use of the escape sequences \t and \n.

```
## Demonstrate use of escape sequences.
print("01234567890123456")
print("a\tb\tc")
print("a\tb\tc".expandtabs(5))
print("Nudge, \tnudge, \nwink, \twink.".expandtabs(11))
```

[Run]

```
01234567890123456
a       b       c
a    b    c
Nudge,     nudge,
wink,      wink.
```

Each escape sequence is treated as a single character when determining the length of a string. For instance, `len("a\tb\tc")` has value 5. The backslash is not considered to be a character, but rather an indicator telling Python to treat the character following it in a special way. The escape sequence \n is often referred to as the **newline character**.

The backslash also can be used to treat quotation marks as ordinary characters. For instance, the statement `print('Say it ain\'t so.')` displays the third word as *ain't*. The backslash character tells Python to treat the quotation mark as an ordinary single quotation mark and not as a surrounding quotation mark. Two other useful escape sequences are \" and \\ which cause the print function to display a double quotation mark and a backslash character, respectively.

In future chapters we frequently encounter strings that end with a newline character. For instance, each line of a text file is a string ending with a newline character. The string method rstrip can be used to remove newline characters from the ends of strings. For instance, if *str1* has the value "xyz\n", then `str1.rstrip()` will have the value "xyz". Also, when the int, float, and eval functions are evaluated at a string ending with a newline character, they ignore the newline character. For instance, `int('7\n')` has the same value as `int('7')`.

■ Justifying Output in a Field

Programs often display output in columns of a fixed width. The methods **ljust(n)**, **rjust(n)**, and **center(n)** can be used to left-justify, right-justify, and center string output in a field of width *n*. If the string does not use the entire width of the field, the string is padded on the right, left, or both sides with spaces. If the string is longer than the allocated width, the justification method is ignored.

VideoNote
Print
Formatting

✔ **Example 2** Justifying Output The following program uses the three justification methods to create a table of the top three home run hitters in professional baseball. The first line was added to identify the columns of the table. The first five columns (columns 0 through 4) list the ranks of the top three hitters. The numbers 1, 2, and 3 are each centered in a field of width 5. The next 20 columns (columns 5 through 24) hold the names of the top three hitters, with each name left justified in a field of width 20. Each name is padded on the right with space characters. The last three columns (columns 25 through 27) hold the number of home runs hit by the players. Since each of the numbers is three digits long, they exactly fill the field of width 3 set aside for them. The output for this column would be the same even if the rjust method was not used.

```
## Demonstrate justification of output.
print("01234567890123456789012234567")
print("Rank".ljust(5), "Player".ljust(20), "HR".rjust(3), sep="")
print('1'.center(5), "Barry Bonds".ljust(20), "762".rjust(3), sep="")
print('2'.center(5), "Hank Aaron".ljust(20), "755".rjust(3), sep="")
print('3'.center(5), "Babe Ruth".ljust(20), "714".rjust(3), sep="")
```

[Run]

```
01234567890123456789012234567
Rank Player              HR
  1  Barry Bonds         762
  2  Hank Aaron          755
  3  Babe Ruth           714
```

■ Justifying Output with the *format* Method

The **format method** is a fairly recent addition to Python that can perform the same tasks as the justification methods and much more. For instance, it can place thousands separators in numbers, round numbers, and convert numbers to percentages. We will begin by demonstrating the method's justification capabilities and then present some of its other features.

If *str1* is a string and *w* is a field width, then statements of the forms

```python
print("{0:<ws}".format(str1))
print("{0:^ws}".format(str1))
print("{0:>ws}".format(str1))
```

produce the same output as the statements

```python
print(str1.ljust(w))
print(str1.center(w))
print(str1.rjust(w))
```

If *num* is a number and *w* is a field width, then statements of the forms

```python
print("{0:<wn}".format(num))
print("{0:^wn}".format(num))
print("{0:>wn}".format(num))
```

produce the same output as the statements

```python
print(str(num).ljust(w))
print(str(num).center(w))
print(str(num).rjust(w))
```

Notice that the format method accepts numbers directly; they do not have to be converted to strings. The symbols $<$, $^$, and $>$ that precede the width of each field instruct the print function to left-justify, center, and right-justify, respectively.

In each of the statements above containing the format method, there is a single argument (*num*) in the format method. Often there are several arguments, referred to by positions counting from zero. The 0 before the colon in the curly braces refers to the fact that *num* is in the 0th position. When there are several arguments, there are several pairs of curly braces, with each pair of curly braces associated with an argument. The numbers preceding the colons inside each pair of curly braces give the position of the argument it formats.

✓   **Example 3**   Justifying Output The following program produces the same output as Example 2, but using the format method. Consider the fourth line. The formatting braces {0:^5n}, {1:<20s}, and {2:>3n} determine the formatting of the number 1, the string "Barry Bonds", and the number 762, respectively.

```python
## Demonstrate justification of output.
print("0123456789012345678901234567")
print("{0:^5s}{1:<20s}{2:>3s}".format("Rank", "Player", "HR"))
print("{0:^5n}{1:<20s}{2:>3n}".format(1, "Barry Bonds", 762))
print("{0:^5n}{1:<20s}{2:>3n}".format(2, "Hank Aaron", 755))
print("{0:^5n}{1:<20s}{2:>3n}".format(3, "Babe Ruth", 714))
```

When numbers are being formatted, rather than using the letter *n* inside the curly braces, which corresponds to any type of number, we use the letter *d* for integers, the letter *f* for floating-point numbers, and the symbol % for numbers to be displayed as percentages. When *f* and % are used, they should be preceded by a period and a whole number. The whole number determines the number of decimal places to be displayed. In each of the three cases, we also can specify if we want thousands separators by inserting a comma after the field-width number.

When the **format** method is used to format a number, *right-justify* is the default justification. Therefore, when none of the symbols <, ^, or > are present, the number will be displayed right-justified in its field. Table 2.4 shows some statements and the outcomes they produce.

TABLE 2.4.   **Demonstrate number formatting.**

Statement	Outcome	Comment
`print("{0:10d}".format(12345678))`	12345678	number is an integer
`print("{0:10,d}".format(12345678))`	12,345,678	thousands separators added
`print("{0:10.2f}".format(1234.5678))`	1234.57	rounded
`print("{0:10,.2f}".format(1234.5678))`	1,234.57	rounded and separators added
`print("{0:10,.3f}".format(1234.5678))`	1,234.568	rounded and separators added
`print("{0:10.2%}".format(12.345678))`	1234.57%	changed to % and rounded
`print("{0:10,.3%}".format(12.34569))`	1,234.568%	%, rounded, separators

The field-width number following the colon can be omitted. If so, the number is displayed (without any alignment) as determined by the other specifiers following the colon.

So far, the string preceding "**.format**" has consisted of one or more pairs of curly braces. However, the string can be any string containing curly braces. In that case, the curly braces are placeholders telling Python where to insert the arguments from the **format** method.

Example 4   State Data   The following program demonstrates the use of placing curly braces inside a string.

```
## Demonstrate use of the format method.
print("The area of {0:s} is {1:,d} square miles.".format("Texas", 268820))
str1 = "The population of {0:s} is {1:.2%} of the U.S. population."
print(str1.format("Texas", 26448000 / 309000000))
```

[Run]

```
The area of Texas is 268,820 square miles.
The population of Texas is 8.56% of the U.S. population.
```

■ Comments

1. When the right side of the colon in a pair of curly braces is just the letter *s*, the colon and the letter *s* can be omitted. For instance, {0:s} can abbreviated to {0}. A placeholder such as {0} applies not only to strings, but also to numbers and expressions.

2. When the **format** method is used to format a string, left-justify is the default justification. Therefore, when a <, ^, or > symbol is not present, the string will be displayed left-justified in its field.

3. The **rstrip** method not only removes newline characters from the end of a string, but removes all ending spaces and escape sequences. When the **int**, **float**, or **eval** function is applied to a string, it ignores all spaces and escape sequences at the end of the string.

4. A common error is to write an escape sequence with a forward-slash (/) instead of the backslash (\), the proper character.

Determine the output displayed by the lines of code.

1. `print("{0:s} and {1:s}".format("spam", "eggs"))`

2. `str1 = "Ask not what {0:s} {1:s} you, ask what you {1:s} {0:s}."`
   `print(str1.format("your country", "can do for"))`

3. Rewrite the following statement without using escape sequences.
   `print("He said \"How ya doin?\" to me.")`

In Exercises 1 through 50, determine the output displayed by the lines of code.

1. `print("merry", " christmas", '!', sep="")`

2. `print("Price: ", '$', 23.45, sep="")`

3. `print("Portion: ", 90, '%', sep="")`

4. `print("Py", "th", "on", sep="")`

5. `print(1, 2, 3, sep=" x ")`

6. `print("tic", "tac", "toe", sep='-')`

7. `print("father", "in", "law", sep='-')`

8. `print("one", " two", " three", sep=',')`

9. `print("What is your name",`
   `   end = '?\n'))`
   `print("John")`

10. `print("spam", end=" and ")`
    `print("eggs")`

11. `print("Py", end="")`
    `print("thon")`

12. `print("on","site",sep='-',end="")`
    `print("repair")`

13. `print("Hello\n")`
    `print("World!")`

14. `print("Hello\n" , end = ',')`
    `print("World!")`

15. `print("One\t\tTwo\n--Three-Four")`

16. `print("1\t2\t3")`
    `print("\tDetroit\tLions")`
    `print("Indiana\t\tColts")`

17. `print("NUMBER\tSQUARE\tCUBE")`
    `print(str(2) + "\t" + str(2 ** 2) + "\t" + str(2 ** 3))`
    `print(str(3) + "\t" + str(3 ** 2) + "\t" + str(3 ** 3))`

18. `print("COUNTRY\t", "LAND AREA")`
    `print("India\t", 2.5, "million sq km")`
    `print("China\t", 9.6, "million sq km")`

19. `print("Hello\tWorld!")`
    `print("Hello\t\tWorld!".expandtabs(2))`

20. `print("STATE\tCAPITAL".expandtabs(15))`
    `print("North Dakota\tBismarck".expandtabs(15))`
    `print("South Dakota\tPierre".expandtabs(15))`

21.
```python
print("012345.67890")
print("A ".rjust(5), " B ".center(5)," C".ljust(5), sep="|")
```

22.
```python
print("0123456789012345")
print("one".center(7), "two".ljust(4), "three".rjust(6), sep="")
```

23.
```python
print("0123456789012345")
print("{0:^7s}{1:5s}{2:>7s}".format("one", "two", "three"))
```

24.
```python
print("01234567890")
print("{0:>5s}{1:^5s}{2:5s}".format("A", "B", "C"))
```

25.
```python
print("0123456789")
print("{0:10.1%}".format(.123))
print("{0:^10.1%}".format(1.23))
print("{0:<10,.1%}".format(12.3))
```

26.
```python
print("0123456789")
print("{0:10,d}".format(1234))
print("{0:^10,d}".format(1234))
print("{0:<10,d}".format(1234))
```

27.
```python
print("${0:,.1f}".format(1234.567))
```

28.
```python
print("{0:,.0f}".format(1234.567))
```

29.
```python
print("{0:,.1f}".format(1.234))
```

30.
```python
print("${0:,.2f}".format(1234))
```

31.
```python
print("{0:10s}{1:^16s} {2:s}".format("Team", "Fifa points",
                                      "% fans of World Pop."))
print("{0:10s}{1:^16,d}{2:10.2%}".format("Germany", 1725,.3412))
print("{0:10s}{1:^16,d}{2:10.2%}".format("Argentina", 1538,.25851))
print("{0:10s}{1:^16,d}{2:10.2%}".format("Columbia", 1450,.25523))
```

32.
```python
print("{0:14s}{1:s}".format("Major", "Percent of Students"))
print("{0:14s}{1:10.1%}".format("Biology", .062))
print("{0:14s}{1:10.1%}".format("Psychology", .054))
print("{0:14s}{1:10.1%}".format("Nursing", .047))
```

33.
```python
print("When nothing goes {0:s} go {1:s}.".format("right", "left"))
```

34.
```python
print("Plan {0:s}, code {1:s}.".format("first", "later"))
```

35.
```python
print("{0:s} are the {1:s} of {0:s}r own destiny".format("you","creator"))
```

36.
```python
print("And now for {0:s} completely {1:s}.".format("something",
"different"))
```

37.
```python
x=3
y = 4
print("The matrix of {0:d} and {1:d} has {2:d} elements.".format(x, y, x * y))
```

38.
```python
str1 = "{0:s} has {1:.1f} billion users in the world."
print(str1.format("Facebook", 1.3))
```

39.
```python
x = 2    # square root of 2 is 1.414213562 to 9 decimal places
print("The square root of {0:n} is about {1:.4f}.".format(x, x ** .5))
```

40.
```python
pi = 3.14159265898 # to 11 decimal places
print("Pi is approximately {0:.3f}.".format(pi))
```

41.
```
str1 = "In a randomly selected group of {0:d} people, the " + \
        "probability\nis {1:.2f} that 2 people have the same birthday."
print(str1.format(23, .507397))
```

42.
```
# Population Survey of Canada in 2014
areaOfCanada = 9984670
popOfCanada = 35344962 #35344962/9984670 is 3.539922902 to 9 decimal places
str1 = "The population of Canada is ${0:.3f} per km square."
print(str1.format(costOfCanada / areaOfCanada))
```

43.
```
str1 = "You miss {0:.0%} of the shots you never take. - Wayne Gretsky"
print(str1.format(1))
```

44.
```
str1 = "{0:.0%} of the members of the U.S. Senate are from {1:s}."
print(str1.format(12 / 100, "New England"))
```

45.
```
# 43/193 is .2227979275 to 10 decimal places
print("{0:.2%} of the UN nations are in {1:s}.".format(43/193, "Europe"))
```

46.
```
# 9984670/3794000 is 2.631700053 to 9 decimal places
str1 = "The area of {0:s} is {1:.1%} of the area of the U.S."
print(str1.format("Canada", 9984670 / 3794000))
```

47.
```
print("{0:s}{1:s}{0:s}".format("abra", "cad"))
```

48.
```
print("When you have {0:s} to {1:s}, {1:s} {0:s}.".format("nothing", "say"))
```

49.
```
str1 = "Be {0:s} whenever {1:s}. It is always {1:s}. - Dalai Lama"
print(str1.format("kind", "possible"))
```

50.
```
str1 = "If {0:s} dream it, {0:s} do it. - Walt Disney"
print(str1.format("you can"))
```

51. Do `print("Hello")` and `print("Hello", end="\n")` produce the same output?

52. Do `print("Hello\tWorld!")` and `print("Hello\tWorld!".expandtabs(8))` produce the same output?

In Exercises 53 through 58, write a program to carry out the stated task.[2]

53. Server's Tip Calculate the amount of a server's tip, given the amount of the bill and the percentage tip as input. See Fig. 2.23.

```
Enter amount of bill: 21.50
Enter percentage tip: 18
Tip: $3.87
```

```
Enter revenue: 550000
Enter expenses: 410000
Net income: $140,000.00
```

FIGURE 2.23 Possible outcome of Exercise 53.   **FIGURE 2.24** Possible outcome of Exercise 54.

54. Income Request a company's annual revenue and expenses as input, and display the company's net income (revenue minus expenses). See Fig. 2.24.

55. Change in Salary A common misconception is that if you receive a 10% pay raise and later a 10% pay cut, your salary will be unchanged. Request a salary as input and then display the salary after receiving a 10% pay raise followed by a 10% pay cut. The program also should display the percentage change in salary. See Fig. 2.25.

---

[2]For each of the following exercises, a possible output is shown in a shaded box. Responses to input statements appear underlined.

```
Enter beginning salary: 35000
New salary: $34,650.00
Change: -1.00%
```

```
Enter beginning salary: 35000
New salary: $40,516.88
Change: 15.76%
```

FIGURE 2.25 Possible outcome of Exercise 55. FIGURE 2.26 Possible outcome of Exercise 56.

56. Change in Salary A common misconception is that if you receive three successive 5% pay raises, then your original salary will have increased by 15%. Request a salary as input and then display the salary after receiving three successive 5% pay raises. The program also should display the percentage change in salary. See Fig. 2.26.

57. Future Value If P dollars (called the *principal*) is invested at r% interest compounded annually, then the future value of the investment after n years is given by the formula

$$\text{future value} = P\left(1 + \frac{r}{100}\right)^n.$$

Calculate the future value of an investment after the user enters the principal, interest rate, and number of years. Figure 2.27 shows that $1,000 invested at 5% interest will grow to $1,157.63 in 3 years.

```
Enter principal: 1000
Enter interest rate (as %): 5
Enter number of years: 3
Future value: $1,157.63
```

```
Enter future value: 10000
Enter interest rate (as %): 4
Enter number of years: 6
Present value: $7,903.15
```

FIGURE 2.27 Possible outcome of Exercise 57. FIGURE 2.28 Possible outcome of Exercise 58.

58. Present Value The present value of f dollars at interest rate r% compounded annually for n years is the amount of money that must be invested now in order to grow to f dollars (called the *future value*) in n years where the interest rate is r% per year. The formula for present value is

$$\text{present value} = \frac{f}{\left(1 + \frac{r}{100}\right)^n}.$$

Calculate the present value of an investment after the user enters the future value, interest rate, and number of years. Figure 2.28 shows that at 4% interest per year, $7,903.15 must be invested now in order to have $10,000 after 6 years.

Solutions to Practice Problems 2.3

1. spam and eggs. The **s** specifier in the curly braces is the default specifier. Therefore, the **print** statement could have been written

```
print("{0} and {1}".format("spam", "eggs"))
```

We will use the **s** specifier in our programs since it improves readability. It reminds the programmer that a string is required as the argument in the set of arguments.

2. Ask not what your country can do for you, ask what you can do for your country.

*The strings requested by the first two sets of curly braces are obvious. The third set of curly braces begins with **1** and therefore is requesting the argument in position 1, namely **"can do for"**. Similarly, the fourth set of curly braces is requesting the argument in position 0. The ability to use arguments more than once is a nice feature of the format method.*

3. `print('He said "How ya doin?" to me.')`

2.4 Lists, Tuples, and Files—An Introduction

The Python documentation and this textbook use the term **object** to refer to any instance of a data type. Python's core objects are numbers, strings, lists, tuples, files, sets, and dictionaries. We have already discussed numbers and strings. In this section we discuss lists, tuples, and files. Sets and dictionaries are discussed in Chapter 5.

VideoNote
The *list*
Object

■ The *list* Object

A **list** is an ordered sequence of Python objects. The objects can be of any type and do not have to all be the same type.

A list is constructed by writing its items enclosed in square brackets, with the items separated by commas. Some examples of lists are

```
["Seahawks", 2014, "CenturyLink Field"]
[5, 10, 4, 5]
["spam", "ni"]
```

Lists are usually assigned to a name. For instance, we might write

```
team = ["Seahawks", 2014, "CenturyLink Field"]
nums = [5, 10, 4, 5]
words = ["spam", "ni"]
```

TABLE 2.5 **List operations. (The lists *team*, *nums*, and *words* are given above.)**

Function or Method	Example	Value	Description
len	len(words)	2	number of items in list
max	max(nums)	10	greatest (items must have same type)
min	min(nums)	4	least (items must have same type)
sum	sum(nums)	24	total (items must be numbers)
count	nums.count(5)	2	number of occurrences of an object
index	nums.index(4)	2	index of first occurrence of an object
reverse	words.reverse()	["ni", "spam"]	reverses the order of the items
clear	team.clear()	[]	[] is the empty list
append	nums.append(7)	[5, 10, 4, 5, 7]	inserts object at end of list
extend	nums.extend([1, 2])	[5, 10, 4, 5, 1, 2]	inserts new list's items at end of list
del	del team[−1]	["Seahawks", 2014]	removes item with stated index
remove	nums.remove(5)	[10, 4, 5]	removes first occurrence of an object
insert	words.insert(1, "wink")	["spam", "wink", "ni"]	insert new item before item of given index
+	['a', 1] + [2, 'b']	['a', 1, 2, 'b']	concatenation; same as ['a', 1].extend([2,'b'])
*	[0] * 3	[0, 0, 0]	list repetition

Like the characters in a string, items in a list are indexed from the front with positive indices starting with 0, and from the back with negative indices starting with −1. The value of the item with index *i* is denoted *listName* [*i*]. For instance, the value of team[1] is 2014, and the value of words[−2] is "spam".

Some list functions and methods are shown in Table 2.5.

Note: After the del function or the **remove** method is executed, the items following the eliminated item are moved one position left in the list. After the **insert** method is executed, the items having index greater than or equal to the stated index are moved one position to the right in the list.

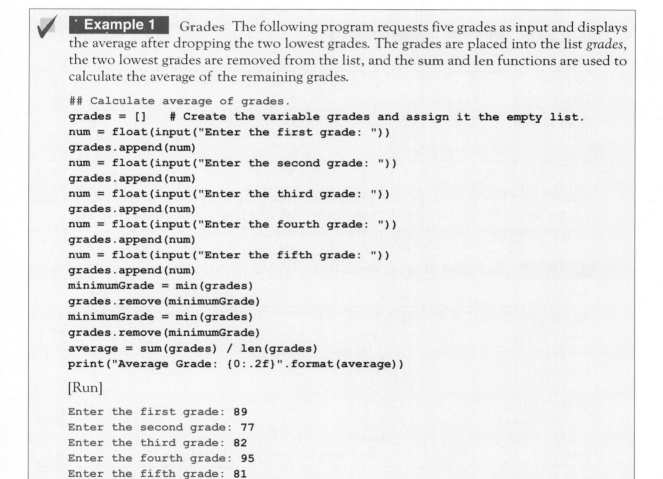

Example 1   Grades The following program requests five grades as input and displays the average after dropping the two lowest grades. The grades are placed into the list *grades*, the two lowest grades are removed from the list, and the **sum** and **len** functions are used to calculate the average of the remaining grades.

```
## Calculate average of grades.
grades = []    # Create the variable grades and assign it the empty list.
num = float(input("Enter the first grade: "))
grades.append(num)
num = float(input("Enter the second grade: "))
grades.append(num)
num = float(input("Enter the third grade: "))
grades.append(num)
num = float(input("Enter the fourth grade: "))
grades.append(num)
num = float(input("Enter the fifth grade: "))
grades.append(num)
minimumGrade = min(grades)
grades.remove(minimumGrade)
minimumGrade = min(grades)
grades.remove(minimumGrade)
average = sum(grades) / len(grades)
print("Average Grade: {0:.2f}".format(average))
```

[Run]

```
Enter the first grade: 89
Enter the second grade: 77
Enter the third grade: 82
Enter the fourth grade: 95
Enter the fifth grade: 81
Average Grade: 88.67
```

The value of the item having index *i* can be changed with a statement of the form

```
listName[i] = newValue
```

For instance, after the statement **words[1] = "eggs"** is executed, the value of *words* will be ["spam", "eggs"].

Note: In Section 2.2 we mentioned that any code enclosed in a pair of parentheses can span multiple lines. The same is true for code enclosed in a pair of square brackets. Therefore, the statement

```
team = ["Seahawks", 2014, "CenturyLink Field"]
```

can be written

```
team = ["Seahawks", 2014,
        "CenturyLink Field"]
```

■ Slices

A **slice** of a list is a sublist specified with colon notation. It is analogous to a slice of a string. Some slice notations are shown in Table 2.6.

TABLE 2.6	Meanings of slice notations.
Slice Notation	Meaning
list1[m:n]	list consisting of the items of *list1* having indices m through $n-1$
list1[:]	a new list containing the same items as *list1*
list1[m:]	list consisting of the items of *list1* from list1[m] through the end of *list1*
list1[:m]	list consisting of the items of *list1* from the beginning of *list1* to the element having index $m-1$

Note: The **del** function can be used to remove a slice from a list. Also, if the item of index m is not to the left of the item of index n, then list1[m:n] will be the empty list.

Some examples of slices are shown in Table 2.7.

TABLE 2.7	Examples of slices where list1 = ['a', 'b', 'c', 'd', 'e', 'f'].
Example	Value
list1[1:3]	['b', 'c']
list1[-4:-2]	['c', 'd']
list1[:4]	['a', 'b', 'c', 'd']
list1[4:]	['e', 'f']
list1[:]	['a', 'b', 'c', 'd', 'e', 'f']
del list1[1:3]	['a', 'd', 'e', 'f']
list1[2:len(list1)]	['c', 'd', 'e', 'f']
(list1[1:3])[1]	'c' (This expression is usually written as list1[1:3][1])
list1[3:2]	[], the list having no items; that is, the empty list

■ The *split* and *join* Methods

The **split** and **join methods** are extremely valuable methods that are inverses of each other. The **split** method turns a single string into a list of substrings and the **join** method turns a list of strings into a single string.

In general, if *strVar* has been assigned a string of the form "*value0,value1,value2, . . . , valueN*", then a statement of the form

```
L = strVar.split(",")
```

creates the list L containing the $N + 1$ string values as its items. That is, the first item of the list is the text preceding the first comma of strVar, the second item of the list is the text between the first and second commas, . . . , and the last item of the list is the text following the last comma. The string consisting of the comma character is called the **separator** for the statement above. Any string can be used as a separator. (Three common separators consisting of a single-character string are ",", "\n", and " ".) If no separator is specified, the split method uses whitespace as the separator, where **whitespace** is any string whose characters are newline, vertical tab, or space characters. The split method will play a vital role in Chapter 5.

The join method, which is the inverse of the split method, converts a list of strings into a string value consisting of the elements of the list concatenated together and separated by a specified string. The general form of a statement using join and having the string "," as separator is

```
strVar = ",".join(L)
```

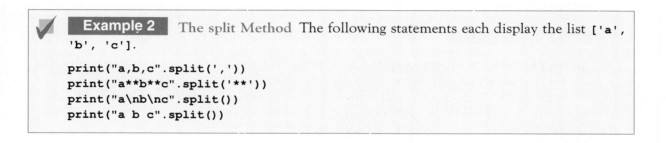

Example 2   The split Method   The following statements each display the list **['a',
'b', 'c']**.

```
print("a,b,c".split(','))
print("a**b**c".split('**'))
print("a\nb\nc".split())
print("a b c".split())
```

Example 3   The join Method   The following program shows how the join method can be used to display the items from a list of strings.

```
line = ["To", "be", "or", "not", "to", "be."]
print(" ".join(line))
krispies = ["Snap", "Crackle", "Pop"]
print(", ".join(krispies))
```

[Run]

```
To be or not to be.
Snap, Crackle, Pop
```

■ Text Files

Values used in a Python program reside in memory and are lost when the program terminates. However, if a program writes the values to a file on a storage device (such as a hard disk or a flash drive), any Python program can access the values at a later time. That is, files create long-term storage of data.

A **text file** is a simple file consisting of lines of text with no formatting (that is, no bold or italics) that can be created and read with Notepad (on a PC) or TextEdit (on a Mac). Usually, text files have the extension *txt*. A text file actually can be created with any word processor. For instance, after a document is created in Word, you can invoke *Save As* and then select "Save as type: Plain Text (*.txt)" to save the document as a text file. Also, any existing text file can be opened and edited in Word. Each line of a text file (except possibly the last line) ends with a newline character.

The lines of a text file (stripped of their newline characters) can be placed into a list with code of the form

```
infile = open("Data.txt", 'r')
listName = [line.rstrip() for line in infile]
infile.close()
```

The next three chapters explain how this statement carries out the task. For now, let's just assume it does the job.

If the data in a text file is all numbers, the process in the preceding paragraph produces a list consisting of strings, with each string holding a number. For a file of numbers, we can place the numbers into a list with code of the form

```
infile = open("Data.txt", 'r')
listName = [eval(line) for line in infile]
infile.close()
```

■ The *tuple* Object

Tuples, like lists, are ordered sequences of items. The main difference between tuples and lists are that tuples cannot be modified directly. That is, tuples have no append, extend, or insert methods. Also, the items of a tuple cannot be directly deleted or altered. All other list functions and methods apply to tuples, and its items can be accessed by indices. Tuples also can be sliced, concatenated, and repeated.

Tuples are written as comma-separated sequences enclosed in parentheses. However, they can often be written without the parentheses. For instance, the statements

```
t = ('a', 'b', 'c')  and  t = 'a', 'b', 'c'
```

create the tuple *t* and assign it the same value. However, print functions always display tuples enclosed in parentheses.

 Example 4   Tuple Functions The following program shows that tuples have several of the same functions as lists.

```
t = 5, 7, 6, 2
print(t)
print(len(t), max(t), min(t), sum(t))
print(t[0], t[-1], t[:2])
```

[Run]

```
(5, 7, 6, 2)
4 7 2 20
5 2 (5, 7)
```

A statement such as

```
(x, y, z) = (5, 6, 7)
```

creates three variables and assigns values to them. The statement also can be written

```
x, y, z = 5, 6, 7
```

which can be thought of as making three variable assignments with a single statement.

Example 5 Swap Values The following program swaps the values of two variables. In essence, the third line of the program is assigning the tuple (6, 5) to the tuple (x, y)

```
x = 5
y = 6
x, y = y, x
print(x, y)
```

[Run]

```
6 5
```

■ Nested Lists

So far, all items in lists and tuples have been numbers or strings. However, items also can be lists or tuples. Lists of tuples play a prominent role in analyzing data. If *L* is a list of tuples, then L[0] is the first tuple, L[0][0] is the first item of the first tuple, L[−1] (same as L[len(L)−1]) is the last tuple, and L[−1][−1] is the last item of the last tuple. An expression such as L[0][0] can be thought of as (L[0])[0].

Example 6 U.S. Regions The list *regions* contains four tuples, with each tuple giving the name and 2010 population (in millions) of a region of the United States. The following program displays the 2010 population of the Midwest and calculates the 2010 population of the United States.

```
regions = [("Northeast", 55.3), ("Midwest", 66.9),
           ("South", 114.6), ("West", 71.9)]
print("The 2010 population of the", regions[1][0], "was", regions[1][1],
    "million.")
totalPop = regions[0][1] + regions[1][1] + regions[2][1] + regions[3][1]
print("Total 2010 population of the U.S: {0:.1f} million.".format(totalPop))
```

[Run]

```
The 2010 population of the Midwest was 66.9 million.
Total 2010 population of the U.S: 308.7 million.
```

■ Immutable and Mutable Objects

An **object** is an entity that holds data and has operations and/or methods that can manipulate the data. Numbers, strings, lists, and tuples are objects. When a variable is created with an assignment statement, the value on the right side becomes an object in memory, and the variable references (that is, points to) that object. When a list is altered, changes are made to the object in the list's memory location. However, when a variable whose value is a number, string, or tuple, has its value changed, Python designates a new memory location to hold the new value and the variable references that new object. We say that lists can be changed in place, but numbers, strings, and tuples cannot. Objects that can be changed in place are called **mutable**, and objects that cannot be changed in place are called **immutable**. Figure 2.29 shows eight lines of code and the memory allocations after the first four lines of code have been executed and after all eight lines have been executed.

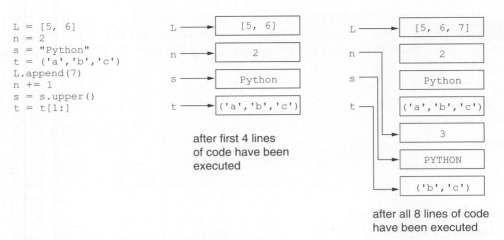

```
L = [5, 6]
n = 2
s = "Python"
t = ('a','b','c')
L.append(7)
n += 1
s = s.upper()
t = t[1:]
```

FIGURE 2.29   Memory allocation corresponding to a program.

■ Copying Lists

If the variable *var1* has a mutable value (such as a list), then a statement of the form **var2 = var1** results in *var2* referencing the same object as *var1*. Therefore, any change to the value of *var2* affects the value of *var1*. Consider the following four lines of code:

```
list1 = ['a', 'b']  # Lists are mutable objects.
list2 = list1       # list2 will point to the same memory location as list1
list2[1] = 'c'      # Changes the value of the second item in the list object
print(list1)
```

[Run]

```
['a', 'c']
```

In the second line of code, the variable *list2* references the same memory location as *list1*. Therefore, any changes to an item in *list2* produces the same change in the value of *list1*. This effect will not occur if the second line of code is changed to either **list2 = list(list1)** or **list2 = list1[:]**. In those cases, *list2* will point to an object in a different memory location containing the same value as *list1*. Then the third line of code will not affect the memory location pointed to by *list1* and so the output will be **['a', 'b']**.

■ Indexing, Deleting, and Slicing Out of Bounds

Python does not allow out of bounds indexing for individual items in lists and tuples, but does allow it for slices. For instance, if

```
list1 = [1, 2, 3, 4, 5]
```

then **print(list1[7])**, **print(list1[-7])**, and **del list1[7]** trigger the Traceback error message *IndexError*.

   If the left index in a slice is too far negative, the slice will start at the beginning of the list, and if the right index is too large, the slice will go to the end of the list. For instance,

   list1[-10:10] is **[1, 2, 3, 4, 5]**
   list1[-10:3] is **[1, 2, 3]**

```
list1[3:10] is [4, 5]
del list1[3:7] is [1, 2, 3]
```

■ Comments

1. When **max** and **min** are applied to lists containing strings, lexicographical order is used to compare two strings. Lexicographical ordering of strings is discussed in Section 3.1.

2. The empty tuple is written as an empty pair of parentheses.

3. A single-item tuple must have a trailing comma, such as (0,).

4. The **list** function converts tuples or strings to lists. For instance, the value of **list(('a', 'b'))** is ['a', 'b'], and the value of **list("Python")** is ['P', 'y', 't', 'h', 'o', 'n'].

5. The **tuple** function converts lists or strings to tuples. For instance, the value of **tuple(['a', 'b'])** is ('a', 'b'), and the value of **tuple("spam")** is ('s', 'p', 'a', 'm').

6. Tuples are more efficient than lists and should be used in situations where no changes will be made to the items. They execute faster, tie up less memory, and "write-protect" data. In Chapter 5 we discuss a powerful Python object called a *dictionary*. An important feature of dictionaries requires the use of tuples.

7. As we have seen, the values of an item in a list can be altered by using its index in a statement of the form **listName[i] = newValue**. Even though the characters in a string and the items in a tuple can be accessed with indices, statements such as **stringName[i] = newValue** and **tupleName[i] = newValue** are not valid.

8. The operator += performs an augmented assignment for lists and tuples.

9. We have discussed the core objects *numbers*, *strings*, *lists*, and *tuples*. Two other important core objects, *sets* and *dictionaries*, will be introduced in Chapter 5. Although they could have been presented in Section 2.4, we decided to postpone their presentation until they are needed.

Practice Problems 2.4

1. Determine the output of the following program.

```
companies = [("Apple", "Cupertino", "CA"), ("Amazon.com", "Seattle", "WA"),
             ("Google", "Mountain View", "CA")]
(name, city, state) = (companies[1][0], companies[1][1], companies[1][2])
print(name, " is located in ", city, ", ", state, '.',sep = "")
```

2. Determine the output of the following program.

```
a = 2
b = 3
print((a + b,))
print((a + b))
print(())
```

3. Do the statements **s = 'a' + 'b'** and **s = "".join(['a', 'b'])** assign the same value to the variable *s*?

EXERCISES 2.4

In Exercises 1 through 48, assume that the list countries contains the names of fifty countries in the world, and determine the output displayed by the lines of code.

countries = ["Japan", "India", "Algeria", "Brazil", "Angola", "England", "Argentina", "Portugal", "China", "Australia", "Austria", "Ghana", "Bahamas", "Bangladesh", "Belgium", "Bhutan", "Bosnia", "Cameroon", "Canada", "Denmark"]

1. ```
print(countries[2], countries[-1])
```

2. ```
print(countries[3],
        countries[-3])
```

3. ```
print(countries[18],
        countries[16])
```

4. ```
print(len(countries))
```

5. ```
print(countries[-1],
        countries[19])
```

6. ```
print(countries.
        index("Cameroon"))
```

7. ```
print(countries.index("Ghana")
```

8. ```
print(countries.
        index(countries[10]))
```

9. ```
print(countries[len(countries) - 1], countries[-1])
```

10. ```
print(countries[0].upper())
```

11. ```
countries[0] = countries[0].lower()
print(countries[0])
```

12. ```
countries.insert(5, "Germany")
print(countries[5])
```

13. ```
countries.append("Nigeria")
print(countries[20])
```

14. ```
countries.insert(11,"Nepal")
print(countries.index("Ghana"))
```

15. ```
del countries[4]
print(countries[4])
```

16. ```
del countries[3]
print(countries.index("Argentina"))
```

17. ```
print(countries[2:5])
```

18. ```
print(countries[-1:4])
```

19. ```
print(countries[-5:-2])
```

20. ```
print(countries[4:-1])
```

21. ```
print(countries[:10])
```

22. ```
print(countries[10:])
```

23. ```
print(countries[-3:])
```

24. ```
print(countries[:-1])
```

25. ```
print(countries[3:3])
```

26. ```
print(countries[-1:-4])
```

27. ```
print(countries[1:10][2]))
```

28. ```
print(countries[-
        2:len(countries)])
```

29. ```
print(countries[:][5])
```

30. ```
print(countries[-4][-4])
```

31. ```
print(len(countries[10:20]))
```

32. ```
print(len(countries[-20:]))
```

33. ```
print(len([]))
```

34. ```
print(len(countries[:]))
```

35. ```
print(len(countries[1:-1]))
```

36. ```
print(len(countries[2:-2]))
```

37. ```
countries.
        extend(["Algeria","Cuba"])
print(countries[-3:])
```

38. ```
countries.append(["New Zealand",
        "Norway"])
print(countries[-3:])
```

39. ```
del countries[-2]
countries.insert(-1, "Mangolia")
print(countries[-3:])
```

40. ```
countries[1] = "Poland"
print(countries[:3])
```

41. ```
    del countries[1]
    countries.insert(1, "Russia")
    print(countries[:3])
    ```

42. ```
    print(countries[-4].split())
    states.insert(-1, "Seward's Folly")
    print(states[-3:])
    ```

43. ```
    list2 = countries[2].split() +
    countries[-4].split()
    list2.remove("Algeria")
    print(list2)
    ```

44. ```
    print((',').join(countries[1:4]))
    ```

45. ```
    print(('-').
    join(countries[-10:-5]))
    ```

46. ```
    countries.remove(countries[-4])
    print(countries[-4])
    ```

47. ```
    print(('*').
    join(countries[-6:-3]))
    ```

48. ```
    countries[-1].append("Spain")
    print(countries[-1])
    ```

In Exercises 49 through 54, assume that *list1* contains 100 items. Determine the number of items in each of the slices.

49. `list1[-8:]`

52. `list1[-8:-1]`

50. `list1[:8]`

53. `list1[8:8]`

51. `list1[:]`

54. `list1[1:-1]`

In Exercises 55 through 58, assume that the list *nums* = [6, 2, 8, 0], and determine the output displayed by the line of code.

55. `print("Largest Number:", max(nums))`

56. `print("Length:", len(nums))`

57. `print("Total:", sum(nums))`

58. `print("Number lot", sum(nums) / list(nums))`

In Exercises 59 through 94, determine the output displayed by the lines of code.

59. ```
    L = ["sentence", "contains", "five", "words."]
    L.insert(0, "This")
    print(" ".join (L))
    del L[3]
    L.insert(3, "six")
    L.insert(4, "different")
    print(" ".join (L))
    ```

60. ```
    L = ["one", "for", "all"]
    L[0], L[-1] = L[-1], L[0]
    print(L)
    ```

61. ```
    name = input("Enter name with two parts: ")
    L = name.split()
    print("{0:s}, {1:s}".format(L[1], L[0]))
    ```
    (Assume the name entered is *Charles Babbage*.)

62. ```
    name = input("Enter name with three parts: ")
    L = name.split()
    print(L[0], L[2])
    ```
    (Assume the name entered is *Guido van Rossum*.)

63.
```python
name = input("Enter name with three parts: ")
L = name.split()
print("Middle Name:", L[1])
```
(Assume the name entered is *Guido van Rossum*.)

64.
```python
list1 = ['h', 'o', 'n', 'P', 'y', 't']
list2 = list1[3:] + list1[:3]
print(("").join(list2))
```

65.
```python
tuple1 = ("course", "of", "human", "events", "When", "in", "the")
tuple2 = tuple1[4:] + tuple1[:4]
print((" ".join(tuple2)))
```

66.
```python
list1 = ["is", "Less", "more."]
list1[0], list1[1] = list1[1], list1[0]
print(" ".join(list1))
```

67.
```python
headEditor = ["editor", "in", "chief"]
print(('-').join(headEditor))
```

68.
```python
carousel = ["merry", "go", "round"]
print(('-').join(carousel))
```

69.
```python
motto = ["e", "pluribus", "unum"]
print(("**").join(motto))
```

70.
```python
allDay = "around-the-clock"
print(allDay.split('-'))
```

71.
```python
state = "New York,NY,Empire State,Albany"
stateFacts = state.split(',')
print(stateFacts)
```

72.
```python
nations = "France\nEngland\nSpain"
countries = nations.split()
print(countries)
```

73.
```python
nations = "France\nEngland\nSpain\n"
countries = nations.split()
print(countries)
```

74.
```python
# The three lines of Abc.txt contain a b, c, d
infile = open("Abc.txt", 'r')
alpha = [line.rstrip() for line in infile]
infile.close()
word = ("").join(alpha)
print(word)
```

75.
```python
# The three lines of Dev.txt contain mer, gram, pro
infile = open("Dev.txt", 'r')
dev = [line.rstrip() for line in infile]
infile.close()
dev[0], dev[-1] = dev[-1], dev[0]
word = ("").join(dev)
print(word)
```

76.
```python
# The two lines of Live.txt contain Live, let
infile = open("Live.txt", 'r')
```

```
words = [line.rstrip() for line in infile]
infile.close()
words.append(words[0].lower())
quote = (" ").join(words) + '.'
print(quote)
```

77.
```
# The three lines of Star.txt contain your, own, star.
infile = open("Star.txt", 'r')
words = [line.rstrip() for line in infile]
infile.close()
words.insert(0, "Follow")
quote = (" ").join(words)
print(quote)
```

78.
```
nums = (6, 2, 8, 0)
print("Largest Number:", max(nums))
print("Length:", len(nums))
print("Total:", sum(nums))
print("Number list:", list(nums))
```

79.
```
phoneNumber = "9876543219"
list1 = list(phoneNumber)
list1.insert(3, '-')
list1.insert(7, '-')
phoneNumber = "".join(list1)
print(phoneNumber)
```

80.
```
word = "diary"
list1 = list(word)
list1.insert(3, list1[1])
del list1[1]
word = "".join(list1)
print(word)
```

81.
```
nums = (3, 9, 6)
print(list(nums))
```

82.
```
nums = [-5, 17, 123]
print(tuple(nums))
```

83.
```
word = "etch"
L = list(word)
L[1] = "a"
print("".join(L))
```

84.
```
t = (1, 2, 3)
t = (0,) + t[1:]
print(t)
```

85.
```
list1 = ["soprano", "tenor"]
list2 = ["alto", "bass"]
list1.extend(list2)
print(list1)
```

86.
```
list1 = ["soprano", "tenor"]
list2 = ["alto", "bass"]
print(list1 + list2)
```

87.
```
list1 = ["gold"]
list2 = ["silver", "bronze"]
print(list1 + list2)
```

88.
```
list1 = ["gold"]
list2 = ["silver", "bronze"]
list1.extend(list2)
print(list1)
```

89.
```
list1 = ["mur"] * 2
print("".join(list1))
```

90.
```
list1 = [0]
print(list1 * 4)
```

91.
```
t = ("Dopey", "Sleepy", "Doc", "Grumpy", "Happy", "Sneezy", "Bashful")
print(t[4:20])
```

92. ```
ships = ["Nina", "Pinta", "Santa Maria"]
print(ships[-5:2])
```

93. ```
answer = ["Yes!", "No!", "Yes!", "No!", "Maybe."]
num = answer.index("No!")
print(num)
```

94. ```
numbers = (3, 5, 7, 7, 3)
location = numbers.index(7)
print(location)
```

**In Exercises 95 through 100, identify all errors.**

95. ```
threeRs = ["reading", "riting", "rithmetic"]
print(threeRs[3])
```

96. ```
word = "sea"
location = numbers.index(7)
word[1] = 'p'
print(word)
```

97. ```
list1 = [1, "two", "three", 4]
print(" ".join(list1))
```

98. ```
# Four virtues presented by Plato
virtues = ("wisdom", "courage", "temperance", "justice")
print(virtues[4])
```

99. ```
title = ("The", "Call", "of", "the", "Wild")
title[1] = "Calm"
print(" ".join(title))
```

100. ```
words = ("Keep", "cool", "but", "don't")
words.append("freeze.")
print(words)
```

101. **Analyze a Sentence**   Write a program that counts the number of words in a sentence input by the user. See Fig. 2.30.

```
Enter a sentence: Know what I mean?
Number of words: 4
```

```
Enter a sentence: Reach for the stars.
First word: Reach
Last word: stars
```

FIGURE 2.30   Possible outcome of Exercise 101.   **FIGURE 2.31**   Possible outcome of Exercise 102.

102. **Analyze a Sentence**   Write a program that displays the first and last words of a sentence input by the user. See Fig. 2.31. Assume that the only punctuation is a period at the end of the sentence.

103. **Name**   Write a program that requests a two-part name and then displays the name in the form "*lastName, firstName*". See Fig. 2.32.

```
Enter a 2-part name: John Doe
Revised form: Doe, John
```

```
Enter a 3-part name: Michael Andrew Fox
Middle name: Andrew
```

FIGURE 2.32   Possible outcome of Exercise 103.

FIGURE 2.33   Possible outcome of Exercise 104.
```

104. Name   Write a program that requests a three-part name and then displays the middle name. See Fig. 2.33.

Solutions to Practice Problems 2.4

1. `Amazon.com is located in Seattle, WA.`

   The list *companies* is a list of tuples whose items can be referenced as companies[0], companies[1], and companies[2]. The program references companies[1], the tuple for Amazon. The Amazon tuple's three items are referenced as companies[1][0], companies[1][1], and companies[1][2]. *Note:* companies[1][0] can be thought of as (companies[1])[0], companies[1][1] can be thought of as (companies[1])[1], and companies[1][2] can be thought of as (companies[1])[2].

2. `(5,)`
   `5`
   `()`

   The arguments of the first and third print functions are tuples. The comma in the first print function indicates that the argument is a single-element tuple, and therefore the function displays a tuple. Since the argument in the second print function has no comma, the set of parentheses merely encloses an expression. The third print statement displays the empty tuple.

3. Yes. For performance purposes, the statement using join is superior.

CHAPTER 2 KEY TERMS AND CONCEPTS	EXAMPLES
2.1 Numbers	
int (integer) and **float** (floating point) are numeric data types.	**int:** $3, -7, 0$ **float:** $3., .025, -5.5$
A **variable** is a name that points to a location in memory that holds data. The data pointed to (called the *value* of the variable) can change during the execution of the program.	`price = 19.99` `numberOfGrades = 32`
The **print function** displays values of expressions separated by spaces.	`print(32, 3., .25, price)` displays `32 3.0 0.25 19.99`.
Arithmetic operators: $+, *, -, /, **, //$ (integer division), % (modulus).	$3 + 2 = 5, 3 * 2 = 6, 3 - 2 = 1, 3 / 2 = 1.5,$ $3 ** 2 = 8, 7 // 2 = 3, 7 \% 2 = 1, 4 ** .5 = 2$
Reserved words cannot be used as variable names.	*return, lambda, while,* and *if* are reserved words.
Mathematical Functions: abs, int, round.	$abs(-2) = 2, int(3.7) = 3, round(1.28, 1) = 1.3$
Python is **case-sensitive.**	*price* is a different variable than *Price.*
Augmented assignments combine an operator with an assignment statement.	Suppose n = 3. After **n += 2** is executed, the value of *n* is 5.
Errors: syntax (misuse of Python language), exception (error that occurs during runtime), logic (produces unintended result)	Syntax error: print((5) [should be print(5)] Exception error: num = 5 / 0 Logic error: average = 3 + 5 / 2

CHAPTER 2 KEY TERMS AND CONCEPTS	EXAMPLES
2.2 Strings	
A **string** is a data type consisting of a sequence of characters surrounded by quotation marks.	"Hello World!", 'x', "123-45-6789"
Each character of a string is identified by its relative position from the left with a non-negative **index** starting with 0 and its relative position from the right with a negative index starting with −1.	Suppose *s* has the value "Python". The value of s[3] is 'h' and the value of s[−4] is 't'. s[10] generates an *IndexError* exception.
A **slice** of a string is a substring denoted by square brackets containing a colon and possibly numbers.	Suppose *s* has the value "Python". s[2:5] is "tho", s[−3:] is "hon", and s[:] is "Python".
String functions and methods: len, find, upper, lower, count, title, rstrip.	len("ab") is 2, "ab".find('b') is 1, "ab".upper() is "AB", "Ab".lower() is "ab", "bob".count('b') is 2, "quo vadis".title() is "Quo Vadis", and "ab ".rstrip() is "ab".
Two **string operators** are concatenation (+) and repetition (*).	"ab" + 'c' is "abc" and "ha" * 3 is "hahaha".
The **input function** displays a prompt and then assigns data entered by the user to a variable.	```name = input("Enter name: ")``` ```age = int(input("Enter age: "))```
A **comment** is a statement preceded with a # character that documents a program.	```rate = 5 # interest rate``` ```# Find average grade.```
You can break a statement within parentheses or with the use of the **line-continuation** character (\).	```print("Hello", n = 2 +\``` ``` "World!") 3```
2.3 Output	

When a **horizontal tab character** (\t) or a **newline character** (\n) appears in a string, the **print** function displays the characters following it at the next tab stop or on the next line, respectively.	```print("spam\tand\neggs")```
	[Run]
	```spam and```
	```eggs```

print(val1,...,valN, sep=str1, end=str2) displays the N values separated by *str1* and ending with *str2*. The arguments **sep** and **end** are optional and have default values " " and "\n".	**print(1, 2, sep='*', end="")** displays **1*2** and suppresses moving cursor to a new line. **print(1, 2)** displays **1 2** and terminates printing on the current line.

CHAPTER 2 KEY TERMS AND CONCEPTS

EXAMPLES

The **expandtabs method** controls the number of positions between horizontal tab stops. (Default is 8.)

```
print("a\tbc\td".expandtabs(3))
```
displays `a  bc d`.

The **ljust**, **rjust**, and **center methods** control the justification of data in a field of a specified width.

```
print("01234567")
print("spam".center(8))
```
[Run]
```
01234567
  spam
```

The **format method** replaces numbered placeholders of the form {n:format specifier} in a string with comma-separated arguments of the method. Some common components of the format specifier are a number giving the width of the field in which the argument is to be displayed, a symbol giving the type of justification in the field, a comma to indicate that a number is to be displayed with thousands separators, .*r*f (where *r* is a whole number) to display a number as a **float** rounded to *r* decimal places, *d* to indicate that the argument is a number, and *s* to indicate that the argument is a string.

```
s = "{0:8s}{1:>10s}"
print(s.format("State", "Area"))
s = "{0:8s}{1:10,d}"
print(s.format("Ohio", 44830))
```
[Run]
```
State          Area
Ohio         44,830
```

```
print("{0:.1%}".format(.4568))
print("{0:9,.2f}".format(5876.237))
```
[Run]
```
45.7%
 5,876.24
```

2.4 Lists, Tuples, and Files—An Introduction

A **list** is an ordered sequence of items. Items are referred by their position (called their **index**) starting at 0 from the left end or their position (starting at −1) from their right end. **Slices** of lists are defined in much the same way as slices of strings.

L = ["spam", 35, 22.8]

The item "spam" can be referenced as L[0] or L[−3]. The values of both L[0:2] and L[:−1] are ["spam", 35].

List functions: del, len, max, min, sum. (The sum function applies only to lists of numbers.)

See Table 2.5.

List methods: append, clear, count, extend, index, insert, remove.

See Table 2.5.

CHAPTER 2 KEY TERMS AND CONCEPTS	EXAMPLES
| A **tuple** is a sequence similar to a list except that it cannot be altered in place. The list functions mentioned above (except for del) also apply to tuples. Of the list methods mentioned above, tuples support only count and index. Tuples support **concatenation** and **repetition**. | ```
t = (2, 3, 1, 3)
print(t[1], t.index(3), end=" ")
print(t.count(3), len(t), sum(t))
print(t + (7, 5))
print(t * 2)
```<br>[Run]<br>```
3 1 2 4 9
(2, 3, 1, 3, 7, 5)
(2, 3, 1, 3, 2, 3, 1, 3)
``` |
| The **split method** converts a string containing one or more instances of a separator (usually a comma or a blank space) to a list. The **join method** concatenates a list or tuple of strings into a single string with a specified separator inserted between each pair of items. | ```
print("spam,eggs".split(','))
print(", ".join(['spam','eggs']))
```<br>[Run]<br>```
['spam', 'eggs']
spam, eggs
``` |
| The **open function** can be used to fill a list with each line of a file as an item of the list. | ```
infile = open("fileName", 'r')
L = [line.rstrip() for line in
        infile]
```<br>`infile.close()` creates a list of strings consisting of the lines from the file. |
| When a list's items are all lists, the configuration is referred to as **nested lists**. | ```
L = [["Bonds", 762],["Aaron", 755]]
```<br>`L[0][1]` has the value **762**. |
An object whose data cannot be modified in place is said to be **immutable**.	Numbers, strings, and tuples are immutable. Lists are mutable.
Referencing an item of a list or tuple with an improper index generates an *IndexError* Traceback message	(5, 3, 2)[6] generates an *IndexError* Traceback message.
The **list** and **tuple functions** convert tuples to lists and vice versa.	`list(2, 3)` has value **[2, 3]**. `tuple[2, 3]` has value **(2, 3)**.

CHAPTER 2   PROGRAMMING PROJECTS

1. Make Change   Write a program to make change for an amount of money from 0 through 99 cents input by the user. The output of the program should show the number of coins from each denomination used to make the change. See Fig. 2.34.

```
Enter amount of change: 93
Quarters: 3    Dimes: 1
Nickels: 1    Cents: 3
```

FIGURE 2.34   Possible outcome of
                Programming Project 1.

```
Enter amount of loan: 12000
Enter interest rate (%): 6.4
Enter number of years: 5
Monthly payment: $234.23
```

FIGURE 2.35   Possible outcome of
                Programming Project 2.

2. Car Loan   If A dollars is borrowed at $r\%$ interest compounded monthly to purchase a car with monthly payments for n years, then the monthly payment is given by the formula

$$\text{monthly payment} = \frac{i}{1 - (1 + i)^{-12n}} \cdot A$$

where $i = \frac{r}{1200}$. Write a program that calculates the monthly payment after the user gives the amount of the loan, the interest rate, and the number of years. See Fig. 2.35.

3. Bond Yield   One measure of a bond's performance is its *Yield To Maturity* (YTM). YTM values for government bonds are complex to calculate and are published in tables. However, they can be approximated with the simple formula $\text{YTM} = \frac{intr + a}{b}$, where $intr$ is the interest earned per year, $a = \frac{\text{face value} - \text{current market price}}{\text{years until maturity}}$, and $b = \frac{\text{face value} + \text{current market price}}{2}$. For instance, suppose a bond has a face value of \$1,000, a coupon interest rate of 4%, matures in 15 years, and currently sells for \$1,180. Then $intr = .04 \cdot 1{,}000 = 40$, $a = \frac{1000 - 1180}{15} = -12$, $b = \frac{1000 + 1180}{2} = 1090$, and $\text{YTM} = \frac{40 - 12}{1090} \approx 2.57\%$. **Note:** The *face value* of the bond is the amount it will be redeemed for when it matures, and the *coupon interest rate* is the interest rate stated on the bond. If a bond is purchased when it is first issued, then the YTM is the same as the coupon interest rate. Write a program that requests the face value, coupon interest rate, current market price, and years until maturity for a bond, and then calculates the bond's YTM. See Fig. 2.36.

```
Enter face value of bond: 1000
Enter coupon interest rate: .04
Enter current market price: 1180
Enter years until maturity: 15
Approximate YTM: 2.57%
```

FIGURE 2.36   Possible outcome of
                Programming Project 3.

```
Enter price of item: 25.50
Enter weight of item in
pounds and ounces separately.
Enter pounds: 1
Enter ounces: 9
Price per ounce: $1.02
```

FIGURE 2.37   Possible outcome of
                Programming Project 4.

4. Unit Price   Write a program that requests the price and weight of an item in pounds and ounces, and then determines the price per ounce. See Fig. 2.37.

5. Stock Portfolio   An investor's stock portfolio consists of four Exchange Traded Funds (SPY, QQQ, EEM, and VXX). Write a program that requests the amount invested in each fund as input and then displays the total amount invested and each fund's percentage of the total amount invested. See Fig. 2.38.

```
Enter amount invested in SPY: 876543.21
Enter amount invested in QQQ: 234567.89
Enter amount invested in EEM: 345678.90
Enter amount invested in VXX: 123456.78

ETF      PERCENTAGE
------------------
SPY       55.47%
QQQ       14.84%
EEM       21.87%
VXX        7.81%

TOTAL AMOUNT INVESTED: $1,580,246.78
```

FIGURE 2.38   Possible outcome of Programming Project 5.

```
Enter number of miles: 5
Enter number of yards: 20
Enter number of feet: 2
Enter number of inches: 4
Metric length:
   8 kilometers
  65 meters
  73.5 centimeters
```

FIGURE 2.39   Possible outcome of Programming Project 6.

6. **Length Conversion**   Write a program to convert a U.S. Customary System length in miles, yards, feet, and inches to a Metric System length in kilometers, meters, and centimeters. A sample run is shown in Fig. 2.39. After the numbers of miles, yards, feet, and inches are entered, the length should be converted entirely to inches and then divided by 39.37 to obtain the value in meters. The **int** function should be used to break the total number of meters into a whole number of kilometers and meters. The number of centimeters should be displayed to one decimal place. The needed formulas are as follows:

$$\text{total inches} = 63{,}360 * \text{miles} + 36 * \text{yards} + 12 * \text{feet} + \text{inches}$$
$$\text{total meters} = \text{total inches}/39.37$$
$$\text{kilometers} = \text{int(meters}/1000)$$

3

Structures That Control Flow

VideoNote
Relational
and Logical
Operators

3.1 Relational and Logical Operators

In Chapter 1, we discussed the two logical programming constructs *decision* and *loop*. In this chapter, we learn how to implement decision and loop structures. In order to make decisions (and often in order to control loops), we must specify a condition that determines the course of action.

A **condition** (or **Boolean expression**) is an expression involving relational operators (such as $<$ and $>=$) and logical operators (such as *and*, *or*, and *not*). ASCII values determine the order used to compare strings with relational operators. A condition evaluates to either True or False (referred to as the **truth value** of the condition). True and False are reserved words.

■ ASCII Values

Each of the 47 keys in the center typewriter portion of the keyboard can produce two characters, for a total of 94 characters. Adding 1 for the character produced by the space bar makes 95 characters. Associated with these characters are numbers ranging from 32 to 126. These values, called the ASCII values of the characters, are given in Appendix A. Table 3.1 shows a few ASCII values.

TABLE 3.1   A few ASCII values.

32	(space)	48	0	66	B	122	z
33	!	49	1	90	Z	123	{
34	"	57	9	97	a	125	}
35	#	65	A	98	b	126	~

The ASCII standard also assigns characters to some numbers above 126. Table 3.2 shows a few of the higher ASCII values.

TABLE 3.2   A few higher ASCII values.

162	¢	177	±	181	μ	190	¾
169	©	178	²	188	¼	247	÷
176	°	179	³	189	½	248	ø

If n is a nonnegative number, then

```
chr(n)
```

is the single-character string consisting of the character with ASCII value n. If *str* is any single-character string, then

```
ord(str)
```

is the ASCII value of the character. For instance, the statement

```
print(chr(65))
```

displays the letter A, and the statement

```
print(ord('A'))
```

displays the number 65.

Concatenation can be used with `chr` to obtain strings using the higher ASCII characters. For instance, the statement

```
print("32" + chr(176) + " Fahrenheit")
```

displays **32° Fahrenheit**.

■ Relational Operators

The relational operator *less than* (<) can be applied to numbers, strings, and other objects. The number *a* is said to be less than the number *b* if *a* lies to the left of *b* on the number line. For instance, $2 < 5$, $-5 < -2$, and $0 < 3.5$.

The string *a* is said to be less than the string *b* if *a* precedes *b* when using the ASCII table to order their characters. Digits precede uppercase letters, which precede lowercase letters. Two strings are compared character by character (working from left to right) to determine which string should precede the other. Thus, "cat" < "dog", "cart" < "cat", "cat" < "catalog", "9W" < "bat", "Dog" < "cat", and "sales_99" < "sales_retail". This type of ordering is called **lexicographical ordering**. Table 3.3 shows the different relational operators and their meanings.

TABLE 3.3   Relational operators.

Python Notation	Numeric Meaning	String Meaning
==	equal to	identical to
!=	not equal to	different from
<	less than	precedes lexicographically
>	greater than	follows lexicographically
<=	less than or equal to	precedes lexicographically or is identical to
>=	greater than or equal to	follows lexicographically or is identical to
in		substring of
not in		not a substring of

 Example 1 Relational Operators Determine whether each of the following conditions evaluates to True or False.

(a) $1 <= 1$

(b) $1 < 1$

(c) "car" < "cat"

(d) "Dog" < "dog"

(e) "fun" in "refunded"

SOLUTION

(a) True. The notation <= means "less than *or* equal to." That is, the condition is true provided either of the two situations holds. The second one (equal to) holds.

(b) False. The notation < means "strictly less than" and no number can be strictly less than itself.

> **(c)** True. The characters of the strings are compared one at a time working from left to right. Because the first two characters match, the third character determines the order.
>
> **(d)** True. Because uppercase letters precede lowercase letters in the ASCII table, the first character of "Dog" precedes the first character of "dog".
>
> **(e)** True. The string "fun" is "refunded"[2:5], a substring of "refunded".

Conditions can also involve variables, numeric operators, and functions. To determine whether a condition is true or false, first evaluate the numeric or string expressions and then decide if the resulting assertion is true or false.

Example 2   Relational Operators Suppose the variables *a* and *b* have values 4 and 3, and the variables *c* and *d* have values "hello" and "bye". Are the following conditions true or false?

(a) $(a + b) < (2 * a)$

(b) $(len(c) - b) == (a/2)$

(c) $c < ("good" + d)$

SOLUTION

(a) True. The value of $a + b$ is 7 and the value of $2 * a$ is 8. Since $7 < 8$, the condition is true.

(b) True, because the value of len(c) − b is 2, the same as (a/2).

(c) False. The condition "hello" < "goodbye" is false, since *h* follows *g* in the alphabet.

An **int** can be compared to a **float**. Otherwise, values of different types cannot be compared. For instance, a string cannot be compared to a number.

The relational operators can be applied to lists or tuples. In order for two lists or two tuples to be equal, they must have the same length and corresponding items must have the same value. The truth value of the condition is determined by comparing successive corresponding items until the two items differ (or cannot be compared) or until one of the sequences runs out of items. The first pair of items that have different values determine the truth value of the condition. If one of the sequences runs out of items and all items pairs match, then the shorter sequence is said to be the lesser of the two. Some examples of comparisons having truth value **True** are as follows:

```
[3, 5] < [3, 7]
[3, 5] < [3, 5, 6]
[3, 5, 7] < [3, 7, 2]
[7, "three", 5] < [7, "two", 2]
```

When the **in** operator is applied to a list or tuple, it should be taken to mean *is an item of*. Two true examples are as follows:

```
'b' in ['a', 'b', 'c']
'B' not in ('a', 'b', 'c')
```

■ Sorting the Items in a List

The items in a list where every pair of items can be compared can be ordered with the sort method. The statement

```
list1.sort()
```

changes *list1* to a list having the same items, but in ascending order either numerically or lexicographically as appropriate.

Example 3   Sort a List   The following program illustrates how Python orders two simple lists.

```
list1 = [6, 4, -5, 3.5]
list1.sort()
print(list1)
list2 = ["ha", "hi", 'B', '7']
list2.sort()
print(list2)
```

[Run]

```
[-5, 3.5, 4, 6]
['7', 'B', 'ha', 'hi']
```

Example 4   Sort a List   The following program illustrates how Python orders the items in a complicated list of strings. **Note:** chr(177) is the ± character and chr(162) is the ¢ character.

```
list1 = [chr(177), "cat", "car", "Dog", "dog", "8-ball", "5" + chr(162)]
list1.sort()
print(list1)
```

[Run]

```
['5¢', '8-ball', 'Dog', 'car', 'cat', 'dog', '±']
```

Example 5   Sort a List   The following program orders the items in a list of tuples.

```
monarchs = [("George", 5), ("Elizabeth", 2), ("George", 6), ("Elizabeth", 1)]
monarchs.sort()
print(monarchs)
```

[Run]

```
[('Elizabeth', 1), ('Elizabeth', 2), ('George', 5), ('George', 6)]
```

■ Logical Operators

Programming often requires more complex conditions than those considered so far. For instance, suppose we would like to state that the value of the variable *str1* is a string of length 10 and contains the substring "gram". The proper Python condition is

```
(len(str1) == 10) and ("gram" in str1)
```

This condition is a combination of the condition `(len(str1) == 10)` and the condition `("gram" in str1)` with the logical operator and.

The three main logical operators are the reserved words and, or, and not. Conditions that use these operators are called **compound conditions**. If *cond1* and *cond2* are conditions, then the compound condition

`cond1` and `cond2`

is true if both of the conditions are true. Otherwise, it is false. The compound condition

`cond1` or `cond2`

is true if either (or both) of the two conditions are true. Otherwise, it is false. The compound condition

`not` `cond1`

is true if the condition is false, and is false if the condition is true.

 Example 6   Logical Operators Suppose the variable *n* has value 4 and the variable *answ* has value "Y". Determine whether each of the following conditions evaluates to True or False.

(a) (2 < n) and (n < 6)
(b) (2 < n) or (n == 6)
(c) not (n < 6)
(d) (answ == "Y") or (answ == "y")
(e) (answ == "Y") and (answ == "y")
(f) not (answ == "y")
(g) ((2 < n) and (n == 5 + 1)) or (answ == "No")
(h) ((n == 2) and (n == 7)) or (answ == "Y")
(i) (n == 2) and ((n == 7) or (answ == "Y"))

SOLUTION

(a) True, because the conditions (2 < 4) and (4 < 6) are both true.

(b) True, because the condition (2 < 4) is true. The fact that the condition (4 == 6) is false does not affect the conclusion. The only requirement is that at least one of the two conditions be true.

(c) False, because (4 < 6) is true.

(d) True, because the first condition becomes ("Y" == "Y") when the value of *answ* is substituted for *answ*.

(e) False, because the second condition is false. Actually, this compound condition is false for any value of *answ*.

(f) True, because ("Y" == "y") is false.

(g) False. In this logical expression, the compound condition ((2 < n) and (n == 5 + 1)) and the simple condition (answ == "No") are joined by the logical operator or. Because both these conditions are false, the total condition is false.

(h) True, because the condition following *or* is true.

(i) False, because the first condition is false. (Comparing (h) and (i) shows the necessity of using parentheses to specify the intended grouping.)

■ Short-Circuit Evaluation

When Python encounters the compound condition (*cond1* and *cond2*), it first evaluates *cond1*. If *cond1* is false, Python realizes that the compound condition is false and therefore does not bother to evaluate *cond2*. Similarly, when Python encounters the compound condition (*cond1* or *cond2*), it first evaluates *cond1*. If *cond1* is true, Python realizes that the compound condition is true and therefore does not bother to evaluate *cond2*. This process is called **short-circuit evaluation**.

Some programming languages evaluate both parts of a compound condition before assigning a value to the compound condition. If so, evaluation of the condition

```
(number != 0) and (m == (n / number))
```

will cause the program to crash and display an error message when *number* has the value 0. However, due to short-circuit evaluation, the evaluation of this compound condition will never cause a problem in Python.

Short-circuit evaluation sometimes improves the performance of a program. Such can be the case, for instance, when the evaluation of *cond2* is time-consuming.

■ The *bool* Data Type

A statement of the form

```
print(condition)
```

will display either True or False. The objects True and False are said to have **Boolean data type** or to be of data type bool. The following lines of code display False:

```
x = 5
print((3 + x) < 7)
```

The following lines of code display True:

```
x = 2
y = 3
var = x < y
print(var)
```

The answer to part (i) of Example 6 can be confirmed to be False by executing the following lines of code:

```
n = 4
answ = "Y"
print((n == 2) and ((n == 7) or (answ == "Y")))
```

■ Three Methods That Return Boolean Values

If *str1* and *str2* are strings, then the condition

```
str1.startswith(str2)
```

has the value **True** if and only if *str1* begins with *str2*, and the condition

```
str1.endswith(str2)
```

has the value **True** if and only if *str1* ends with *str2*.

For instance, the following two conditions are true:

```
"fantastic".startswith("fan")
"fantastic".endswith("stic")
```

If *var1* has the value "fantastic" and *var2* has the value "Fant", then the following two conditions are false:

```
var1.startswith(var2)
"elephant".endswith(var2)
```

If *item* is a literal or variable, then a condition of the form

```
isinstance(item, dataType)
```

has the value **True** if and only if the value of *item* has the specified data type, where *dataType* is any data type (such as int, float, str, bool, list, or tuple).

For example, the condition `isinstance("32", int)` has the value **False** and the condition `isinstance(32, int)` has the value **True**.

Table 3.4 shows several other string methods that return **Boolean** values. In the table, assume that *str1* is not the empty string. Each of the methods in the table returns **False** when *str1* is the empty string.

TABLE 3.4	Methods that return either True or False.
Method	**Returns True when**
str1.isdigit()	all of *str1*'s characters are digits
str1.isalpha()	all of *str1*'s characters are letters of the alphabet
str1.isalnum()	all of *str1*'s characters are letters of the alphabet or digits
str1.islower()	*str1* has at least 1 alphabetic character and all of its alphabetic characters are lowercase
str1.isupper()	*str1* has at least 1 alphabetic character and all of its alphabetic characters are uppercase
str1.isspace()	*str1* contains only whitespace characters

■ Simplifying Conditions

Lists or tuples can sometimes be used to simplify long compound conditions containing logical operators. For instance, the compound condition

```
(state == "MD") or (state == "VA") or (state == "WV") or (state == "DE")
```

can be replaced with the condition

```
state in ["MD", "VA", "WV", "DE"]
```

Sometimes compound conditions involving inequalities can be written in a clearer form. For instance, the condition

```
(x > 10) and (x <= 20)
```

can be replaced with the condition

```
10 < x <= 20
```

and the condition

```
(x <= 10) or (x > 20)
```

can be replaced with the condition

```
not(10 < x <= 20)
```

Two principles of logic, known as **De Morgan's Laws**, are as follows:

`not(`*cond1* `and` *cond2*`)` is the same as `not(`*cond1*`) or not(`*cond2*`)`

`not(`*cond1* `or` *cond2*`)` is the same as `not(`*cond1*`) and not(`*cond2*`)`

De Morgan's Laws can be applied from left to right or from right to left. For instance, according to De Morgan's Laws, the compound condition

```
not((temperature >= 80) and (humidity <= 60))
```

is the same as

```
(temperature < 80) or (humidity > 60))
```

and the compound condition

```
not(len(word) == 5) and not(word.startswith('A'))
```

is the same as

```
not((len(word) == 5) or (word.startswith('A')))
```

■ Comments

1. A condition involving numeric variables is different from an algebraic identity or inequality. The assertion $(a + b) < (2 * a)$ considered in Example 2 is not a valid algebraic inequality because it isn't true for all values of a and b. When encountered in a Python program, however, it will be considered true if it is true for the current values of the variables.

2. A common error is to replace the condition $(not\ (n < m))$ with the condition $(n > m)$. The correct replacement is $(n >= m)$.

3. The condition "three" $==$ 3 evaluates to False, but the condition "three" $<$ 3 triggers a Traceback error.

4. A common error is to use a single equal sign in a condition where a double equal sign is required.

5. The **sort** method cannot be used in an assignment statement. For instance, the statement **list2 = list1.sort()** is not valid because **sort** does not return a value; it just reorders the items in place. It can be replaced with the following pair of statements:

```
list1.sort()
list2 = list1
```

6. Since the words **and, or, not, True,** and **False** are reserved words, they are colorized orange by IDLE.

1. Does the condition `"Hello " == "Hello"` evaluate to True or False?
2. Explain why (27 > 9) evaluates to True, whereas ("27" > "9") evaluates to False.
3. Complete Table 3.5.

TABLE 3.5 **Truth values of logical operators.**

cond1	cond2	cond1 and cond2	cond1 or cond2	not cond2
True	True	True		
True	False		True	
False	True			False
False	False			

4. Consider Example 5. Suppose that *monarchs* had been a tuple instead of a list. Is there a way to order the items in *monarchs* even though tuples do not have a sort method?
5. What is displayed by the statement `print("Hello World".isalpha())`?
6. What is the difference between = and ==?

In Exercises 1 through 8, determine the output displayed.

1. `print(chr(42)*5)`

2. `print('Py'+chr(116)+'ho'+chr(110))`

3. `print("The upper case of letter g is " + chr((ord('g') - ord('a')) + ord('A') ) + '.')`

4. `print(chr(ord('B'))) # The ASCII value of B is 66`

5. ```
   list1 = [17, 3, 12, 9, 10]
   list1.sort()
   print("Minimum:", list1[0])
   print("Maximum:", list1[-1])
   ```

6. ```
   list1 = [17, 3, 12, 9, 10]
   list1.sort()
   print("Spread:", list1[-1] - list1[0])
   ```

7. ```
   letter = 'D'
   print(letter + " is 4 positions before " + chr(ord(letter) + 4) +
   " alphabetically.")
   ```

8. ```
   letter = 'D'
   spread = ord('a') - ord('A')
   print(chr(ord(letter) + spread))
   ```

In Exercises 9 through 20, assume the value of *a* is 1 and the value of *b* is 1.5, and determine whether the condition evaluates to True or False. Then, use a print function to confirm your answer.

9. `3 * a == 2 * b`

10. `((5 - a) * b) < 7`

11. `b <= 3`

12. `a ** b == b ** a`

13. `a ** (5 - 2) > 7`

14. `3e-2 < .01 * a`

15. `(a < b) or (b < a)`

16. `(a * a < b) or not(a * a < a)`

17. `not((a < b) and (a < (b + a)))`

18. `not(a < b) or not (a < (b + a))`

19. `((a == b) and (a * a < b * b)) or ((b < a) and (2 * a < b))`

20. `((a == b) or not (b < a)) and ((a < b) or (b == a + 1))`

In Exercises 21 through 44, determine whether the condition evaluates to True or False.

21. `9W <> "9w"`

22. `'Harry' > 'Mine'`

23. `''Ab' == 'aB'`

24. `'D' >= '//'`

25. `'a' == 'A'`

26. `'1' < 'one'`

27. `("Duck" < "pig") and ("pig" < "big")`

28. `"Duck" < "Duck" + "Duck"`

29. `not(('B' == 'b') or ("Big" < "big"))`

30. `"th" in "Python"`

31. `"ty" in "Python"`

32. `7 < 34 and (not ("7" > "34" or "7" == "34"))`

33. `isinstance(32, float)`

34. `isinstance(32., int)`

35. `isinstance(32., float)`

36. `isinstance(32, int)`

37. `"colonel".startswith('k')`

38. `"knight".startswith('n')`

39. `potato.endswith("o",2,4)`

40. `"flute".endswith('t')`

41. `True or False`

42. `True and False`

43. `not True`

44. `not False`

In Exercises 45 through 54, determine whether or not the two conditions are equivalent—that is, whether they will both evaluate to True or both evaluate to False for any values of the variables appearing in them.

45. `a <= b; (a < b) or (a == b)`

46. `not(a < b); a > b`

47. `(a == b) or (a < b); a != b`

48. `not((a == b) or (a == c)); (a != b) and (a != c)`

49. `not((a == b) and (a == c)); (a != b) or (a != c)`

50. `(a < b) and ((a > d) or (a > e));`
    `((a < b) and (a > d)) or ((a < b) and (a > e))`

51. `(a <= b) and (a <= c); not((a > b) or (a > c))`

52. `not(a >= b); (a <= b) and not(a == b)`

53. `ch in "abcdefghijklmnopqrstuvwxyz"; 97 <= ord(ch) <= 122`

54. `str1.upper() == str1; str1.isupper()` (Assume *str1* has at least 1 alphabetic character.)

In Exercises 55 through 60, write a condition equivalent to the negation of the given condition. (For example, a != b is equivalent to the negation of a == b.)

55. `a > b`

56. `(a == b) or (a == d)`

57. `(a < b) and (c != d)`

58. `not((a == b) or (a > b))`

59. `a <= b`

60. `(a != "") and (a < b) and (len(a) < 5)`

In Exercises 61 through 68, simplify the expression. (In Exercises 63 through 68, assume that the variable has an integer value.)

61. `(ans == 'Y') or (ans == 'y') or (ans == "Yes") or (ans == "yes")`

62. `(name == "Athos") or (name == "Porthos") or (name == "Aramis")`

63. `(year == 2010) or (year == 2011) or (year == 2012) or (year == 2013)`

64. `(n == 1) or (n == 2) or (n == 3) or (n == 4) or (n == 5) or (n == 6)`

65. `(n >= 3) and (n < 9)`

66. `(n <= 22) and (n > 1)`

67. `(n <= 10) and (n > -20)`

68. `(n <= 200) and (n >= 100)`

In Exercises 69 through 84, determine whether True or False is displayed.

69.
```
str1 = "target"
print(str1.startswith('t') and str1.endswith('t'))
```

70.
```
print("colonel".startswith('k'))
```

71.
```
str1 = "target"
print(str1.startswith('t') or str1.endswith('t'))
```

72.
```
str1 = "target"
str2 = "get"
print(str1.startswith(str2,3))
```

73.
```
str1 = "Teapot"
str2 = "Tea"
print(str1.startswith(str2))
```

74.
```
str1 = "Teapot"
print(str1.startswith(str1[0:4]))
```

75.
```
str1 = "tattarrattat"
print(str1.endswith(str1[::-1]))
```

76.
```
str1 = "spam and eggs"
print(str1.endswith(str1[10:len(str1)]))
```

77.
```
str1 = "spam and eggs"
print(str1.startswith(str1[:len(str1) - 1]))
```

78.
```
num = "1234.56"
print(isinstance(num, float))
```

79.
```
print(isinstance(25.0, int))
```

80.
```
num = object()
print(isinstance(num, int))
```

81.
```
char = chr(80)
print(isinstance(char, int))
```

82.
```
print(isinstance('34', str))
```

83.
```
str1 = "-123"
print(str1.isdigit())
```

84.
```
print("seven".isdigit())
```

85. Rewrite the following statement using the chr function instead of escape sequences.

```
print("He said \"How ya doin?\" to me.")
```

Solutions to Practice Problems 3.1

1. False. The first string has six characters, whereas the second string has five. Two strings must be 100% identical to be equal.

2. When 27 and 9 are compared as strings, their first characters, 2 and 9, determine their order. Since 2 precedes 9 in the ASCII table, "27" < "9".

3.

cond1	cond2	cond1 and cond2	cond1 or cond2	not cond2
True	True	True	True	False
True	False	False	True	True
False	True	False	True	False
False	False	False	False	True

4. Yes. Apply the list function to the tuple in order to create a list containing the items in *monarch*. Then, apply the sort method to the list and use the tuple function to convert the list back into a tuple.

5. False. The space is not an alphabetical character.

6. The symbol = is used for assignment, whereas the symbol == is used for comparison.

3.2   Decision Structures

Decision structures (also known as *branching structures*) allow a program to decide on a course of action based on whether a certain condition is true or false.

VideoNote

Decision Structures

■ *if-else* Statements

An **if-else statement** is a statement of the form

```
if condition:
    indented block of statements
else:
    indented block of statements
```

causes the program to execute the first block of statements when the condition is true and to execute the second block of statements when the condition is false. Each indented block consists of one or more Python statements. The reserved words if and else must be written entirely in lowercase letters and each line in the blocks of statements should be indented the same distance to the right. That is, they should be lined up vertically in columns. This physical indentation tells the interpreter and the human reader where the block starts and stops. (We will always indent blocks of statements by four spaces.)

 Example 1 Find the Larger Value The following program finds the larger of two numbers input by the user. The condition is

```
num1 > num2
```

and each block consists of a single assignment statement. With the inputs 3 and 7 for *num1* and *num2*, the condition is false, and so the second block is executed. Figure 3.1 shows the flowchart for the **if-else** part of the program.

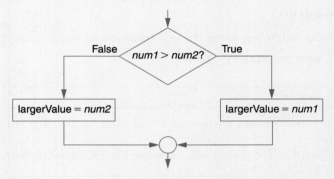

FIGURE 3.1 **Flowchart for the if-else statement in Example 1.**

```
## Determine the larger of two numbers.
# Obtain the two numbers from the user.
num1 = eval(input("Enter the first number: "))
num2 = eval(input("Enter the second number: "))
# Determine and display the larger value.
if num1 > num2:
    largerValue = num1  # execute this statement if the condition is true
else:
    largerValue = num2  # execute this statement if the condition is false
print("The larger value is", str(largerValue) + ".")
```

[Run]

```
Enter the first number: 3
Enter the second number: 7
The larger value is 7.
```

 Example 2 Volume of a Ten-Gallon Hat The **if-else** statement in the following program has relational operators in its condition.

```
## A quiz.
# Obtain answer to question.
answer = eval(input("How many gallons does a ten-gallon hat hold? "))
# Evaluate answer.
if (0.5 <= answer <= 1):
    print("Good, ", end="")
```

```
else:
    print("No, ", end="")
print("it holds about 3/4 of a gallon.")
```

[Run]

```
How many gallons does a ten-gallon hat hold? 10
No, it holds about 3/4 of a gallon.
```

■ *if* Statements

The else part of an if-else statement can be omitted. If so, when the condition is false execution continues with the line after the if statement block. This type of if statement appears twice in the next example.

Example 3   Find the Largest Value   The following program contains two if statements. Figure 3.2 shows the flowchart for the second part of the program. The value of *max* (largest value) is initially set to the first number input and is updated by the if statements when necessary.

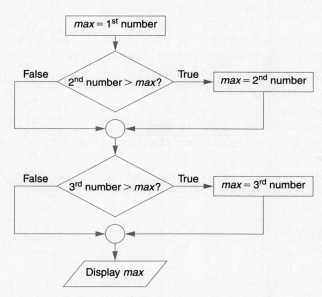

FIGURE 3.2   **Flowchart for Example 3.**

```
## Find the largest of three numbers.
# Input the three numbers.
firstNumber = eval(input("Enter first number: "))
secondNumber = eval(input("Enter second number: "))
thirdNumber = eval(input("Enter third number: "))
# Determine and display the largest value.
max = firstNumber
if secondNumber > max:
    max = secondNumber
if thirdNumber > max:
    max = thirdNumber
print("The largest number is", str(max) + ".")
```

[Run]

```
Enter first number: 3
Enter second number: 7
Enter third number: 4
The largest number is 7.
```

■ Nested *if-else* Statements

The indented blocks of **if-else** and if statements can contain other **if-else** and if statements. In this situation the statements are said to be **nested**. Examples 4 and 5 contain nested if-else statements.

 Example 4   Interpret Beacon The color of the beacon light atop Boston's old John Hancock building forecasts the weather according to the following rhyme:

> Steady blue, clear view.
> Flashing blue, clouds due.
> Steady red, rain ahead.
> Flashing red, snow instead.

The following program requests a color (Blue or Red) and a mode (Steady or Flashing) as input and then displays the weather forecast. Both courses of action associated with the main **if-else** statement consist of **if-else** statements.

```
## Interpret weather beacon.
# Obtain color and mode.
color = input("Enter a color (BLUE or RED): ")
mode = input("Enter a mode (STEADY or FLASHING): ")
color = color.upper()
mode = mode.upper()
# Analyze responses and display weather forecast.
result = ""
if color == "BLUE":
    if mode == "STEADY":
        result = "Clear View."
    else:  # mode is FLASHING
        result = "Clouds Due."
else:  # color is RED
    if mode == "STEADY":
        result = "Rain Ahead."
    else:  # mode is FLASHING
        result = "Snow Ahead."
print("The weather forecast is", result)
```

[Run]

```
Enter the color (BLUE or RED): RED
Enter the mode (STEADY or FLASHING): STEADY
The weather forecast is Rain Ahead.
```

Example 5 Evaluate Profit The following program requests the costs and revenue for a company and displays the message "Break even" if the costs and revenue are equal; otherwise, it displays the profit or loss. The indented block following the else header is another if-else statement.

```
## Evaluate profit.
# Obtain input from user.
costs = eval(input("Enter total costs: "))
revenue = eval(input("Enter total revenue: "))
# Determine and display profit or loss.
if costs == revenue:
    result = "Break even."
else:
    if costs < revenue:
        profit = revenue - costs
        result = "Profit is ${0:,.2f}.".format(profit)
    else:
        loss = costs - revenue
        result = "Loss is ${0:,.2f}.".format(loss)
print(result)
```

[Run]

```
Enter total costs: 9500
Enter total revenue: 8000
Loss is $1,500.00.
```

■ The *elif* Clause

An extension of the if-else statement allows for more than two possible alternatives with the inclusion of elif clauses. (elif is an abbreviation for "else if.") A typical compound statement containing elif clauses is as follows:

```
if condition1:
    indented block of statements to execute if condition1 is true
elif condition2:
    indented block of statements to execute if condition2 is true
    AND condition1 is not true
elif condition3:
    indented block of statements to execute if condition3 is true
    AND both previous conditions are not true
else:
    indented block of statements to execute if none of the above
    conditions are true
```

Python searches for the first true condition and carries out its associated block of statements. If none of the conditions are true, then else's block of statements is carried out. Execution then continues with the statement following the if-elif-else statement. In general, an if-elif-else statement can contain any number of elif clauses. As before, the else clause is optional.

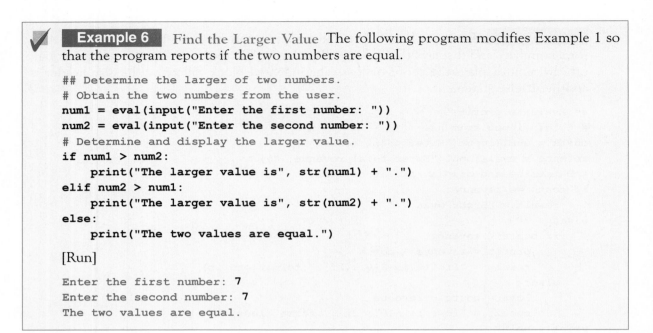

Example 6 Find the Larger Value The following program modifies Example 1 so that the program reports if the two numbers are equal.

```
## Determine the larger of two numbers.
# Obtain the two numbers from the user.
num1 = eval(input("Enter the first number: "))
num2 = eval(input("Enter the second number: "))
# Determine and display the larger value.
if num1 > num2:
    print("The larger value is", str(num1) + ".")
elif num2 > num1:
    print("The larger value is", str(num2) + ".")
else:
    print("The two values are equal.")
```

[Run]

```
Enter the first number: 7
Enter the second number: 7
The two values are equal.
```

The if-elif statement in Example 7 allows us to calculate values that are not determined by a simple formula.

Example 7 FICA Tax The Social Security or FICA tax has two components—the Social Security benefits tax, which in 2014 was 6.2% of the first $117,000 of earnings for the year, and the Medicare tax, which was 1.45% of earnings plus .9% of earnings above $200,000 (for unmarried employees). The following program calculates a single employee's FICA tax withheld for the current pay period.

```
## Calculate FICA tax for a single employee.
# Obtain earnings.
str1 = "Enter total earnings for this year prior to current pay period: "
ytdEarnings = eval(input(str1))  # year-to-date earnings
curEarnings = eval(input("Enter earnings for the current pay period: "))
totalEarnings = ytdEarnings + curEarnings
# Calculate the Social Security Benefits tax.
socialSecurityBenTax = 0
if totalEarnings <= 117000:
    socialSecurityBenTax = 0.062 * curEarnings
elif ytdEarnings < 117000:
    socialSecurityBenTax = 0.062 * (117000 - ytdEarnings)
# Calculate and display the FICA tax.
medicareTax = 0.0145 * curEarnings
if ytdEarnings >= 200000:
    medicareTax += 0.009 * curEarnings
elif totalEarnings > 200000:
    medicareTax += 0.009 * (totalEarnings - 200000)
ficaTax = socialSecurityBenTax + medicareTax
print("FICA tax for the current pay period: ${0:0,.2f}".format(ficaTax))
```

[Run]

```
Enter total earnings for this year prior to current pay period: 12345.67
Enter earnings for the current pay period: 543.21
FICA tax for current pay period: $41.56
```

The following example illustrates the fact that when a decision construct contains elif clauses, Python executes the block of statements corresponding to the first condition that is satisfied and ignores all subsequent elif clauses—even if they also satisfy the condition.

✓ **Example 8** Graduation Honors The program in Fig. 3.3 assumes that the user will graduate and determines if they will graduate with honors.

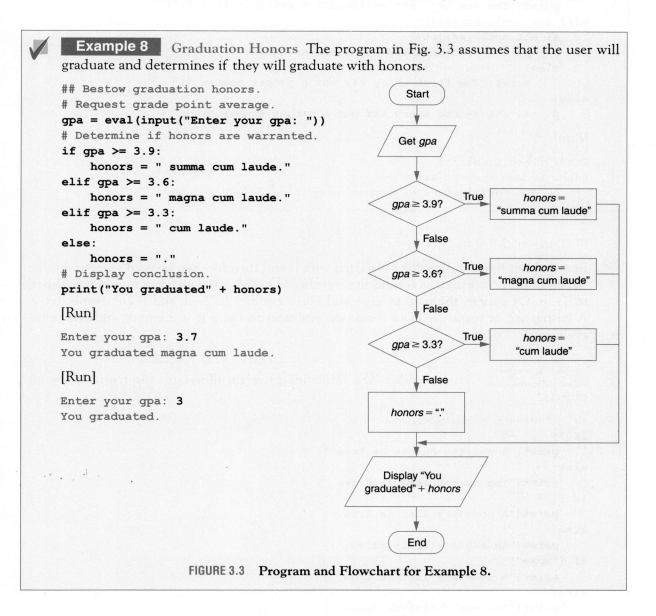

```
## Bestow graduation honors.
# Request grade point average.
gpa = eval(input("Enter your gpa: "))
# Determine if honors are warranted.
if gpa >= 3.9:
    honors = " summa cum laude."
elif gpa >= 3.6:
    honors = " magna cum laude."
elif gpa >= 3.3:
    honors = " cum laude."
else:
    honors = "."
# Display conclusion.
print("You graduated" + honors)
```

[Run]

```
Enter your gpa: 3.7
You graduated magna cum laude.
```

[Run]

```
Enter your gpa: 3
You graduated.
```

FIGURE 3.3 Program and Flowchart for Example 8.

■ Input Validation with *if-elif-else* Statements

Suppose a program asks the user to input a number, and then uses the number in a calculation. If the user does not enter a number or enters an inappropriate number, the program will crash. The Boolean-valued method isdigit can be used to prevent this from happening.

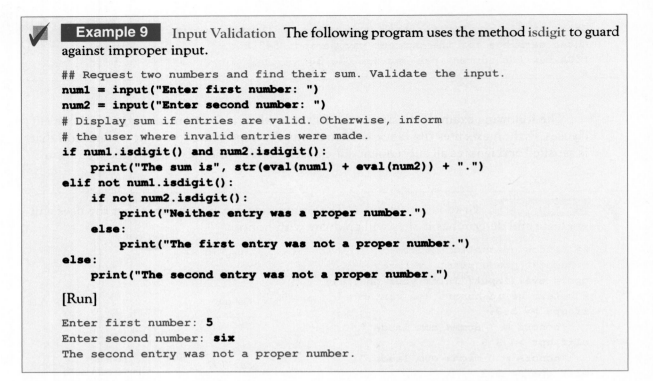

Example 9 Input Validation The following program uses the method isdigit to guard against improper input.

```
## Request two numbers and find their sum. Validate the input.
num1 = input("Enter first number: ")
num2 = input("Enter second number: ")
# Display sum if entries are valid. Otherwise, inform
# the user where invalid entries were made.
if num1.isdigit() and num2.isdigit():
    print("The sum is", str(eval(num1) + eval(num2)) + ".")
elif not num1.isdigit():
    if not num2.isdigit():
        print("Neither entry was a proper number.")
    else:
        print("The first entry was not a proper number.")
else:
    print("The second entry was not a proper number.")
```

[Run]

```
Enter first number: 5
Enter second number: six
The second entry was not a proper number.
```

■ True and False

Every object has a truth value associated with it and therefore can be used as a condition. When numbers are used as conditions, 0 evaluates to False and all other numbers evaluate to True. Of course, the objects True and False evaluate to True and False, respectively. A string, list, or tuple used as a condition evaluates to False if it is empty, and otherwise evaluates to True.

Example 10 True or False The following program illustrates the truth values of objects.

```
## Illustrate Boolean values.
if 7:
    print("A nonzero number is true.")
else:
    print("The number zero is false.")
if []:
    print("A nonempty list is true.")
else:
    print("An empty list is false.")
if ["spam"]:
    print("A nonempty list is true.")
else:
    print("The empty list is false.")
```

[Run]

```
A nonzero number is true.
An empty list is false.
A nonempty list is true.
```

■ Comments

1. A line of the form `if boolExp == True:` should be shortened to `if boolExp:`. Similarly, a line of the form `if boolExp == False:` should be shortened to `if not boolExp:`.

2. `if` statements can be used to guarantee that a number input by the user is in the proper range. For instance, when the user is asked to input an exam grade, a line such as

   ```
   if (0 <= grade <= 100):
   ```

   can be used to guarantee that the number entered is between 0 and 100.

3. The words `if`, `else`, and `elif` are reserved words and therefore are colorized orange by IDLE.

4. The use of indentation to mark blocks of code helps make Python code more readable. IDLE helps with indentation by automatically indenting code when required. For instance, when the *Enter* (or *return*) key is pressed after the colon is typed at the end of an `if`, `elif`, or `else` header, IDLE automatically indents the next line of code.

5. Statements consisting of a header followed by an indented block of code are called **compound statements**. Two other compound statements, the `while` statement and the `for` statement, are discussed in the next two sections.

6. The last six lines of Example 6 could have been written without `elif` as follows:

   ```python
   if num1 > num2:
       print("The larger value is", str(num1) + ".")
   if num2 > num1:
       print("The larger value is", str(num2) + ".")
   if num2 = num1:
       print("The two values are equal.")
   ```

   However, `elif` should always be used when the test conditions are mutually exclusive. In the code above, all three `if` statements are executed even if the first one is true.

Practice Problems 3.2

1. Suppose the user is asked to input a number for which the square root is to be taken. Complete the `if` statement so that the lines of code that follow will display either the message "Number can't be negative." or will display the square root of the number.

   ```python
   # Check reasonableness of input.
   number = eval(input("Enter a non-negative number: "))
   if
   ```

2. Improve the following code:

   ```python
   if a < b:
       if c < 5:
           print("hello")
   ```

3. Improve the following code:

   ```python
   if (name == "John") or (name == "George") or \
      (name == "Paul") or (name == "Ringo"):
       flag = True
   else:
       flag = False
   ```

4. Rewrite Example 5 using `elif`.

EXERCISES 3.2

In Exercises 1 through 14, determine the output displayed.

1.
```python
num = 4
if num <= 9:
    print("Less than ten.")
elif num == 4:
    print("Equal to four.")
```

2.
```python
gpa = 3.49
result = ""
if gpa >= 3.5:
    result = "Honors"
print(result + "Student")
```

3.
```python
print('a+b' < 'b+c')
```

4.
```python
print('a*b' < 'b*c')
```

5.
```python
a = 5
b = 7
sentence = ""
if ((5 * a) - 2*b + 4) <= (3*b-1):
    sentence = "Remember,"
print(sentence + "tomorrow is New Year's Day.")
```

6.
```python
change = 356
if change >= 100:
    print("Your change contains", change // 100, "dollars.")
else:
    print("Your change contains no dollars.")
```

7.
```python
a = 2
b = 3
c = 7
if (a * b) < c:
    b = a
else:
    c = a+b+c
print(a, b, c)
```

8.
```python
length = eval(input("Enter length of cloth in yards: "))
if length < 1:
    cost = 3.00     # cost in dollars
else:
    cost = 3.00 + ((length - 1) * 2.50)
result = "Cost of cloth is ${0:0.2f}.".format(cost)
print(result)
```
(Assume the response is 6.)

9.
```python
letter = input("Enter A, B, or C: ")
letter = letter.upper()
if letter == "A":
    print("A, my name is Alice.")
elif letter == "B":
    print("To be, or not to be.")
elif letter == "C":
    print("Oh, say, can you see.")
else:
    print("You did not enter a valid letter.")
```
(Assume the response is B.)

10.
```
isvowel = False
letter = input("Enter a letter: ")
letter = letter.upper()
if (letter in "AEIOU"):
    isvowel = True
if isvowel:
    print(letter, "is a vowel.")
elif (not(65 <= ord(letter) <= 90)):
    print("You did not enter a letter.")
else:
    print(letter, "is not a vowel.")
```
(Assume the response is *a*.)

11.
```
a = 5
if (a > 2) and ((a == 3) or (a < 7)):
    print("Hi")
```

12.
```
number = 5
if number < 0:
    print("negative")
else:
    if number == 0:
        print("zero")
    else:
        print("positive")
```

13.
```
if "spam":
    print("A nonempty string is true.")
else:
    print("A nonempty string is false.")
```

14.
```
if "":
    print("An empty string is true.")
else:
    print("An empty string is false.")
```

In Exercises 15 through 18, identify the errors, state the type of each error (syntax, runtime, or logic), and correct the block of code.

15.
```
n = eval(input("Enter a number: "))
if 'n'%2 = 0:
    print("The number is an even number.")
else:
    print("The number is an odd number.")
```

16.
```
number = 6
if number > 5 and < 9:
    print("Yes")
else:
    print("No")
```

17.
```
major = "Computer Science"
if major == "Business" Or "Computer Science":
    print("Yes" )
```

18.
```
if a not b:
    print("Both are unequal")

else:
    print("Both are equal")
```

In Exercises 19 through 24, simplify the code.

19.
```
if (a*3%3):
    a = (a*a)/(a+a)
else:
    a=5
```

20.
```
if (a == 7):
    print("seven")
elif (a != 7):
    print("eleven")
```

21.
```
if (j == 7):
    b = 1
else:
    if (j != 7):
        b = 2
```

22.
```
if state == "CA":
    if city == "LA" or city == "SD":
        print("Large city!")
```

23.
```
answer = input("Is the Indian Ocean bigger than the Pacific Ocean?")
if (answer[0]=="Y"):
    answer="YES"
elif (answer[0]=="y"):
    answer="YES"
if(answer=="YES"):
    print("Incorrect")
elif(answer=="NO"):
    print("Correct")
```

24.
```
feet = eval(input("How tall (in feet) is the Statue of Liberty? "))
if (feet <= 141):
    print("Nope")
if (feet > 141):
    if (feet < 161):
        print("Good")
    else:
        print("Nope")
print("The statue is 151 feet tall from base to torch.")
```

25. Restaurant Tip Write a program to determine how much to tip the server in a restaurant. The tip should be 15% of the check, with a minimum of $2. See Fig. 3.4.

```
Enter amount of bill: 25.98
Tip is $3.90
```

```
Enter number of bagels: 12
Cost is $7.20.
```

FIGURE 3.4 Possible outcome of Exercise 25.   **FIGURE 3.5** Possible outcome of Exercise 26.

26. Cost of Bagels A bagel shop charges 75 cents per bagel for orders of less than a half-dozen bagels and 60 cents per bagel for orders of a half-dozen or more. Write a program that requests the number of bagels ordered and displays the total cost. See Fig. 3.5.

27. Cost of Widgets A store sells widgets at 25 cents each for small orders or at 20 cents each for orders of 100 or more. Write a program that requests the number of widgets ordered and displays the total cost. See Fig. 3.6.

```
Enter number of widgets: 200
Cost is $40.00
```

```
Enter number of copies: 125
Cost is $5.75.
```

FIGURE 3.6 Possible outcome of Exercise 27. **FIGURE 3.7** Possible outcome of Exercise 28.

28. Cost of Copies   A copy center charges 5 cents per copy for the first 100 copies and 3 cents per copy for each additional copy. Write a program that requests the number of copies as input and displays the total cost. See Fig. 3.7.

29. Quiz   Write a quiz program to ask "Who was the first Ronald McDonald?" The program should display "You are correct." if the answer is "Willard Scott" and "Nice try." for any other answer. See Fig. 3.8.

```
Who was the first Ronald McDonald? Willard Scott
You are correct.
```

FIGURE 3.8 Possible outcome of Exercise 29.

30. Overtime Pay   Federal law requires that hourly employees be paid "time-and-a-half" for work in excess of 40 hours in a week. For example, if a person's hourly wage is $12 and he or she works 60 hours in a week, the person's gross pay should be

$$(40 * 12) + (1.5 * 12 * (60 - 40)) = \$840.$$

Write a program that requests the number of hours a person works in a given week and the person's hourly wage as input, and then displays the person's gross pay. See Fig. 3.9.

31. Compute an Average   Write a program that requests three scores as input and displays the average of the two highest scores. See Fig. 3.10.

```
Enter first score: 85
Enter second score: 93
Enter third score: 91
Average of two highest
scores is 92.00
```

```
Enter hourly wage: 12.50
Enter number of hours worked: 47
Gross pay for week is $631.25.
```

FIGURE 3.9 Possible outcome of Exercise 30. **FIGURE 3.10** Possible outcome of Exercise 31.

32. Pig Latin   Write a program that requests a word (in lowercase letters) as input and translates the word into Pig Latin. See Fig. 3.11. The rules for translating a word into Pig Latin are as follows:

(a) If the word begins with a group of consonants, move them to the end of the word and add *ay*. For instance, *chip* becomes *ipchay*.

(b) If the word begins with a vowel, add *way* to the end of the word. For instance, *else* becomes *elseway*.

```
Enter word to translate: chip
The word in Pig Latin is ipchay.
```

```
Enter weight in pounds: 6
Enter payment in dollars: 20
Your change is $5.00.
```

FIGURE 3.11 Possible outcome of Exercise 32. **FIGURE 3.12** Possible outcome of Exercise 33.

33. **Make Change**   A supermarket sells apples for $2.50 per pound. Write a cashier's program that requests the number of pounds and the amount of cash tendered as input and displays the change from the transaction. If the cash is not enough, the message "You owe $x.xx more." should be displayed, where $x.xx is the difference between the total cost and the cash. See Fig. 3.12 on the previous page.

34. **Savings Account**   Write a program to process a savings-account withdrawal. The program should request the current balance and the amount of the withdrawal as input and then display the new balance. If the withdrawal is greater than the original balance, the program should display "Withdrawal denied." If the new balance is less than $150, the message "Balance below $150" should also be displayed. See Fig. 3.13.

```
Enter current balance: 200
Enter amount of withdrawal: 25
The new balance is $175.00.
```

```
Enter a single uppercase letter: TEE
You did not comply with the request.
```

FIGURE 3.13   **Possible outcome of Exercise 34.**   **FIGURE 3.14**   **Possible outcome of Exercise 35.**

35. **Input Validation**   Write a program that asks the user to enter a single uppercase letter and then informs the user if they didn't comply with the request. See Fig. 3.14.

36. **Year**   The current calendar, called the Gregorian calendar, was introduced in 1582. Every year divisible by four was created to be a leap year, with the exception of the years ending in 00 (that is, those divisible by 100) and not divisible by 400. For instance, the years 1600 and 2000 are leap years, but 1700, 1800, and 1900 are not. Write a program that requests a year as input and states whether it is a leap year. See Fig. 3.15.

```
Enter a year: 2016
2016 is a leap year.
```

```
Enter a military time (0000 to
2359): 1532
The regular time is 3:32 pm.
```

FIGURE 3.15   **Possible outcome of Exercise 36.**   **FIGURE 3.16**   **Possible outcome of Exercise 37.**

37. **Military Time**   In military time, hours are numbered from 00 to 23. Under this system, midnight is 00, 1 a.m. is 01, 1 p.m. is 13, and so on. Time in hours and minutes is given as a four-digit string with minutes following hours and given by two digits ranging from 00 to 59. For instance, military time 0022 corresponds to 12:22 a.m. regular time, and military time 1200 corresponds to noon regular time. Write a program that converts from military time to regular time. See Fig. 3.16.

38. **Railroad Properties**   One of the four railroad properties in Monopoly is not an actual railroad. Write a program that displays the names of the four properties and asks the user to identify the property that is not a railroad. The user should be informed if the selection is correct or not. See Fig. 3.17.

```
The four railroad properties
are Reading, Pennsylvania,
B & O, and Short Line.
Which is not a railroad? Short Line
Correct.
Short Line is a bus company.
```

FIGURE 3.17   **Possible outcome of Exercise 38.**

39. Interest Rates Savings accounts state an interest rate and a compounding period. If the amount deposited is P, the stated interest rate is r, and interest is compounded m times per year, then the balance in the account after one year is $P \cdot \left(1 + \dfrac{r}{m}\right)^m$. For instance, if \$1,000 is deposited at 3% interest compounded quarterly (that is, four times per year), then the balance after one year is

$$1{,}000 \cdot \left(1 + \frac{.03}{4}\right)^4 = 1{,}000 \cdot 1.0075^4 = \$1{,}030.34.$$

Interest rates with different compounding periods cannot be compared directly. The concept of APY (annual percentage yield) must be used to make the comparison. The APY for a stated interest rate r compounded m times per year is defined by

$$\text{APY} = \left(1 + \frac{r}{m}\right)^m - 1.$$

(The APY is the simple interest rate that yields the same amount of interest after one year as the compounded annual rate of interest.) Write a program to compare interest rates offered by two different banks and determine the most favorable interest rate. See Fig. 3.18.

```
Enter annual rate of interest for Bank 1: 2.7
Enter number of compounding periods for Bank 1: 2
Enter annual rate of interest for Bank 2: 2.69
Enter number of compounding periods for Bank 2: 52
APY for Bank 1 is 2.718%.
APY for Bank 2 is 2.726%.
Bank 2 is the better bank.
```

FIGURE 3.18 **Possible outcome of Exercise 39.**

40. Graduation Honors Rewrite the program in Example 8 without elif clauses. That is, the task should be carried out with a sequence of simple if statements.

41. Graduation Honors Rewrite the program in Example 8 so that the GPA is validated to be between 2 and 4 before the if-elif-else statement is executed.

42. Second-Suit-Half-Off Sale A men's clothing store advertises that if you buy a suit, you can get a second suit at half-off. What they mean is that if you buy two suits, then the price of the lower-cost suit is reduced by 50%. Write a program that accepts the two costs as input and then calculates the total cost after halving the cost of the lowest price suit. See Fig. 3.19.

```
Enter cost of first suit: 378.50
Enter cost of second suit: 495.99
Cost of the two suits is $685.24
```

```
Enter your taxable income: 60000
Your tax is $1,500.
```

FIGURE 3.19 **Possible outcome of Exercise 42.**   FIGURE 3.20 **Possible outcome of Exercise 43.**

43. Income Tax The flowchart in Fig. 3.21 on the next page calculates a person's state income tax. Write a program corresponding to the flowchart. See Fig. 3.20.

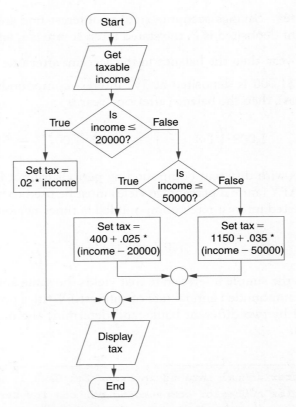

FIGURE 3.21 Flowchart for Exercise 43.

Solutions to Practice Problems 3.2

1.
```
# Check reasonableness of input.
number = eval(input("Enter a non-negative number: "))
if number >= 0:
    print("The square root of the number is", str(number ** .5)+ ".")
else:
    print("Number can't be negative.")
```

2. The word *hello* will be displayed when (a < b) is true and (c < 5) is also true. That is, it will be displayed when both of these two conditions are true. The clearest way to write the code is

```
if (a < b) and (c < 5):
    print("hello")
```

3.
```
flag = name in ["John", "George", "Paul", "Ringo"]
```

4.
```
## Evaluate profit.
# Obtain input from user.
costs = eval(input("Enter total costs: "))
revenue = eval(input("Enter total revenue: "))
# Determine and display profit or loss.
if costs == revenue:
    result = "Break even."
elif costs < revenue:
    profit = revenue - costs
    result = "Profit is ${0:,.2f}.".format(profit)
else:
```

```
        loss = costs - revenue
        result = "Loss is ${0:,.2f}.".format(loss)
    print(result)
```

3.3 The *while* Loop

A **loop**, one of the most important structures in programming, is a part of a program that can execute a block of code repeatedly.

■ The *while* Loop

The **while loop** repeatedly executes an indented block of statements as long as a certain condition is met. A while loop has the form

```
while condition:
    indented block of statements
```

The line beginning with while is called the **header** of the loop, the condition in the header is called the **continuation condition** of the loop, the indented block of code is called the **body** of the loop, and each execution of the body is called a **pass** through the loop. The continuation condition is a Boolean expression that evaluates to either **True** or **False**. Each line in the block of statements should be indented the same distance to the right. This physical indentation of the block tells the interpreter where the block starts and stops.

When Python encounters a while loop, it first checks the truth value of the continuation condition. If the condition evaluates to **False**, Python skips over the body of the loop and continues with the line (if any) after the loop. If the continuation condition evaluates to **True**, the body of the loop is executed. After each pass through the loop, Python rechecks the condition and proceeds accordingly. That is, the body will be continually executed until the continuation condition evaluates to **False**.

Example 1   Numbers The program in Fig. 3.22, in which the continuation condition is **num <= 5**, displays the numbers from 1 through 5. After the loop terminates, the value of *num* will be 6.

```
## Display the numbers from 1 to 5.
num = 1
while num <= 5:
    print(num)
    num += 1   # Increase the value of num by 1.
```

[Run]

```
1
2
3
4
5
```

FIGURE 3.22   Program and Flowchart for Example 1.

A while loop can be used to ensure that a proper response is received from a request for input. This process is called **input validation**.

Example 2   Movie Quotations The following program requires the user to enter a number from 1 through 3. The loop repeats the request until the user gives an acceptable response.

```
## Movie Quotations
print("This program displays a famous movie quotation.")
responses = ('1', '2', '3')
response = '0'
while response not in responses:
    response = input("Enter 1, 2, or 3: ")
    if response == '1':
        print("Plastics.")
    elif response == '2':
        print("Rosebud.")
    elif response == '3':
        print("That's all folks.")
```

[Run]

```
This program displays a famous movie quotation.
Enter 1, 2, or 3: one
Enter 1, 2, or 3: 5
Enter 1, 2, or 3: 2
Rosebud.
```

Example 3   Numbers The following program finds the minimum, maximum, and average of a sequence of nonnegative numbers entered by the user. The user is told to enter the number −1 to indicate the end of data entry. Since the first request for input appears before the loop is entered, there is the possibility that the entire loop will be skipped. The values of *min* and *max* are initially set to the first number input and are updated during each pass through the loop.

```
## Find the minimum, maximum, and average of a sequence of numbers.
count = 0  # number of nonnegative numbers input
total = 0  # sum of the nonnegative numbers input
# Obtain numbers and determine count, min, and max.
print("(Enter -1 to terminate entering numbers.)")
num = eval(input("Enter a nonnegative number: "))
min = num
max = num
while num != -1:
    count += 1
    total += num
    if num < min:
        min = num
    if num > max:
        max = num
    num = eval(input("Enter a nonnegative number: "))
```

```
# Display results.
if count > 0:
    print("Minimum:", min)
    print("Maximum:", max)
    print("Average:", total / count)
else:
    print("No nonnegative numbers were entered.")
```

[Run]

```
(Enter -1 to terminate entering numbers.)
Enter a nonnegative number: 3
Enter a nonnegative number: 7
Enter a nonnegative number: 2
Enter a nonnegative number: -1
Minimum: 2
Maximum: 7
Average: 4.0
```

In Example 3, the variable *count* is called a **counter variable**, the variable *total* is called an **accumulator variable**, the number −1 is called a **sentinel value**, and the loop is referred to as having **sentinel-controlled repetition**.

✔ **Example 4** Numbers The following program performs the same tasks as the program in Example 3. However, it first stores the numbers in a list, and then uses list methods and functions to determine the requested values.

```
## Find the minimum, maximum, and average of a sequence of numbers.
# Obtain list of numbers.
list1 = []
print("(Enter -1 to terminate entering numbers.)")
num = eval(input("Enter a nonnegative number: "))
while num != -1:
    list1.append(num)
    num = eval(input("Enter a nonnegative number: "))
# Display results.
if len(list1) > 0:
    list1.sort()
    print("Minimum:", list1[0])
    print("Maximum:", list1[-1])
    print("Average:", sum(list1) / len(list1))
else:
    print("No nonnegative numbers were entered.")
```

Loops allow us to calculate useful quantities for which we might not know a simple formula.

> ✓ **Example 5**   Compound Interest   Suppose you deposit money into a savings account and let it accumulate at 4% interest compounded annually. The following program determines when you will be a millionaire.
>
> ```python
> ## Calculate the number of years to become a millionaire.
> numberOfYears = 0
> balance = eval(input("Enter initial deposit: "))
> while balance < 1000000:
>     balance += .04 * balance
>     numberOfYears += 1
> print("In", numberOfYears, "years you will have a million dollars.")
> ```
>
> [Run]
>
> ```
> Enter initial deposit: 123456
> In 54 years you will have a million dollars.
> ```

■ The *break* Statement

The break statement causes an exit from anywhere in the body of a loop. When the statement

```python
break
```

is executed in the body of a while loop, the loop immediately terminates. Break statements usually appear in the bodies of if statements.

> ✓ **Example 6**   Numbers   The rewrite in Fig. 3.23 of the "Obtain list of numbers" code from Example 4 uses a break statement to avoid having two input statements. Many people find this rewrite easier to read.
>
> ```python
> # Obtain list of numbers.
> list1 = []
> print("(Enter -1 to terminate entering numbers.)")
> while True:
>     num = eval(input("Enter a nonnegative number: "))
>     if num == -1:
>         break    # Immediately terminate the loop.
>     list1.append(num)
> ```
>
>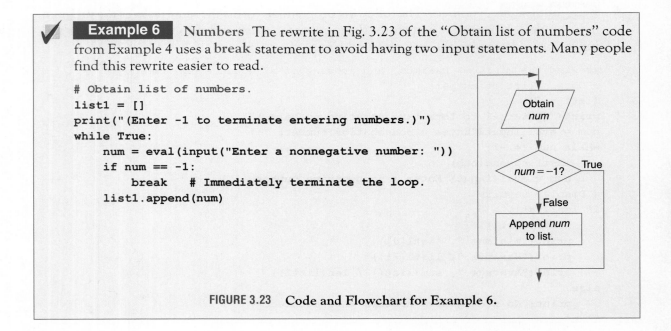
>
> **FIGURE 3.23**   Code and Flowchart for Example 6.

■ The *continue* Statement

When the statement

```python
continue
```

is executed in the body of a **while** loop, the current iteration of the loop terminates and execution returns to the loop's header. **Continue** statements usually appear inside **if** statements.

 Example 7 Integer Divisible by 11 The following program searches a list for the first **int** object that is divisible by 11. The variable *foundFlag* tells us if such an **int** has been found. (A **flag** is a Boolean-valued variable used to report whether a certain circumstance has occurred. The value of the flag is initially set to **False**, and then is changed to **True** if and when the circumstance occurs).

```
## Find first integer divisible by 11.
list1 = ["one", 23, 17.5, "two", 33, 22.1, 242, "three"]
i = 0
foundFlag = False
while i < len(list1):
    x = list1[i]
    i += 1
    if not isinstance(x, int):
        continue    # Skip to next item in list.
    if x % 11 == 0:
        foundFlag = True
        print(x, "is the first int that is divisible by 11.")
        break
if not foundFlag:
    print("There is no int in the list that is divisible by 11.")
```

[Run]

```
33 is the first int in the list that is divisible by 11.
```

■ Creating a Menu

Accessing menus is one of the fundamental tasks of interactive programs. The user makes choices until he or she decides to quit.

 Example 8 U.S. Facts The following program uses a menu to obtain facts about the United States.

```
## Display facts about the United States.
print("Enter a number from the menu to obtain a fact")
print("about the United States or to exit the program.\n")
print("1. Capital")
print("2. National Bird")
print("3. National Flower")
print("4. Quit\n")
while True:
    num = int(input("Make a selection from the menu: "))
    if num == 1:
        print("Washington, DC is the capital of the United States.")
```

```
        elif num == 2:
            print("The American Bald Eagle is the national bird.")
        elif num == 3:
            print("The Rose is the national flower.")
        elif num == 4:
            break
```

[Run]

```
Enter a number from the menu to obtain a fact
about the United States or to exit the program.

1. Capital
2. National Bird
3. National Flower
4. Quit

Make a selection from the menu: 3
The Rose is the national flower.
Make a selection from the menu: 2
The American Bald Eagle is the national bird.
Make a selection from the menu: 4
```

■ Infinite Loops

Be careful to avoid **infinite loops**; that is, loops that never end.

Example 9 Infinite Loop The program in Fig. 3.24 contains an infinite loop because the condition **number >= 0** will always be true. **Note:** While an infinite loop is executing, you can terminate the program by clicking on *Close* in the IDLE *File* menu.

```
## Infinite loop.
print("(Enter -1 to terminate entering numbers.)")
number = 0
while number >= 0:
    number = eval(input("Enter a number to square: "))
    number = number * number
    print(number)
```

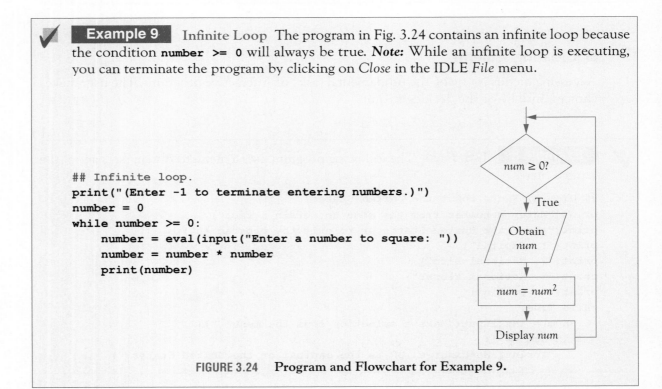

FIGURE 3.24 **Program and Flowchart for Example 9.**

Practice Problems 3.3

1. What is wrong with the following program?

```
initial_val = 10
while initial_val >0:
    print initial_val
    if initial_val == 5:
      break
    print initial_val
```

2. Change the following code segment so that the loop will execute at least once.

```
while answer.upper() != "SHAZAM":
    answer = input("Enter the password: "))
print("You may continue.")
```

3. How would you change the following code segment so that the word "Python" is displayed?

```
letters = ['P','y','t','h','o','n']
language = ""
i = 0
while letters: # This is the same as writing while letters != []
    language += letters [i]
    i = i+1
    letters = letters [i:]

print(language)
```

EXERCISES 3.3

In Exercises 1 through 8, determine the output displayed.

1.
```
num = 5
while True:
    num = 2 * num
    if num % 4 == 0:
        break
print(num)
```

2.
```
num = 3
while num < 15:
    num += 5
print(num)
```

3.
```
total = 0
num = 1
while True:
    total += num
    num += 1
    if num == 10:
        break
print(total)
```

4.
```
total = 0
num = 1
while num < 5:
    total += num
    num += 1
print(total)
```

5.
```
list1 = [2, 4, 6, 8]
total = 0
while list1: # same as while list1 != []:
    total += list1[0]
    list1 = list1[1:]
print(total)
```

6.
```python
oceans = ["Atlantic", "Pacific", "Indian", "Arctic", "Antarctic"]
i = len(oceans) - 1
while i >= 0:
    if len(oceans[i]) < 7:
        del oceans[i]
    i = i - 1
print(", ".join(oceans))
```

7.
```python
list1 = ['a', 'b', 'c', 'd']
i = 0
while True:
    print(list1[i]*i)
    i = i + 1
    if i == len(list1):
        break
```

8.
```python
numTries = 0
year = 0
while (numTries < 7) and (year != 1964):
    numTries += 1
    year = int(input("Try #" + str(numTries) + ": In what year " +
                     "did the Beatles invade the U.S.? "))
    if year == 1964:
        print("\nYes. They performed on the Ed Sullivan show in 1964.")
        print("You answered correctly in " + str(numTries) + " tries.")
    elif year < 1964:
        print("Later than", year)
    else: # year > 1964
        print("Earlier than", year)
if (numTries == 7) and (year != 1964):
    print("\nYour 7 tries are up. The answer is 1964.")
```
(Assume that the responses are 1950, 1970, and 1964.)

In Exercises 9 through 12, identify the errors.

9.
```python
q = 1
while q!= 0:
    q=q-2
    print(q)
```

10.
```python
## Display the numbers from 1 through 5.
num = 0
while True
    num = 1
    print(num)
    num += 1
```

11.
```python
## Display the elements of a list
list1 = ['H', 'e', 'l', 'l', 'o']
i = len(list1)
while i > 1:
    i - = 1
    print(list1[i])
```

12.
```
## Display the elements from a list.
list1 = ['a', 'b', 'c', 'd']
i = 0
while True:
    print(list1[i])
    if i = len(list1):
        break
    i = i + 1
```

In Exercises 13 and 14, write a simpler and clearer code that performs the same task as the given code.

13.
```
sum = int(input("Enter a number: "))
num = int(input("Enter a number: "))
sum = sum + num
num = int(input("Enter a number: "))
sum = sum + num
print(sum)
```

14.
```
L = [2, 4, 6, 8]
total = 0
while L != []:
    total += L[0]
    L = L[1:]
print(total)
```

15. **Temperature Conversions**   Write a program that displays a Celsius-to-Fahrenheit conversion table. Entries in the table should range from 10 to 30 degrees Celsius in increments of 5 degrees. See Fig. 3.25. **Note:** The formula $f = \left(\dfrac{9}{5} \cdot c\right) + 32$ converts Celsius degrees to Fahrenheit degrees.

Celsius	Fahrenheit
10	50
15	59
20	68
25	77
30	86

FIGURE 3.25   Outcome of Exercise 15.

```
Enter coefficient of restitution: .7
Enter initial height in meters: 8
Number of bounces: 13
Meters traveled: 44.82
```

FIGURE 3.26   Possible outcome of Exercise 16.

16. **Bouncing Ball**   The *coefficient of restitution* of a ball, a number between 0 and 1, specifies how much energy is conserved when the ball hits a rigid surface. A coefficient of .9, for instance, means a bouncing ball will rise to 90% of its previous height after each bounce. Write a program to input a coefficient of restitution and an initial height in meters, and report how many times a ball bounces when dropped from its initial height before it rises to a height of less than 10 centimeters. Also report the total distance traveled by the ball before this point. See Fig. 3.26. The coefficients of restitution of a tennis ball, basketball, super ball, and softball are .7, .75, .9, and .3, respectively.

In Exercises 17 and 18, write a program corresponding to the flowchart.

17. Greatest Common Divisor   The flowchart in Fig. 3.29 finds the greatest common divisor (GCD) of two nonzero integers input by the user. *Note:* The GCD of two numbers is the largest integer that divides both. See Fig. 3.27.

```
Enter value of M: 30
Enter value of N: 35
Greatest common divisor: 5
```

```
Enter a positive integer (>1): 2345
Prime factors are 5 7 67
```

FIGURE 3.27   Possible outcome of Exercise 17.   **FIGURE 3.28**   Possible outcome of Exercise 18.

18. Factorization   The flowchart in Fig. 3.30 requests a whole number greater than 1 as input and factors it into a product of prime numbers. *Note:* A number is *prime* if its only factors are 1 and itself. See Fig. 3.28.

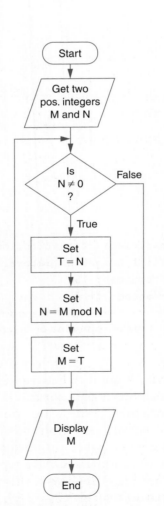

FIGURE 3.29   **Greatest common divisor.**

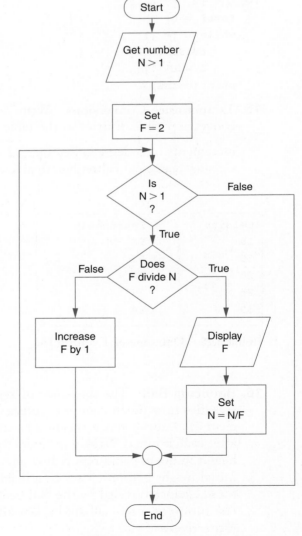

FIGURE 3.30   **Prime factors.**

In Exercises 19 through 31, write a program to answer the question.

19. Age   A person born in 1980 can claim, "I will be x years old in the year x squared." What is the value of x? See Fig. 3.31.

```
Person will be 45
in the year 2025.
```

FIGURE 3.31   Outcome of Exercise 19.

```
World population will be
8 billion in the year 2024.
```

FIGURE 3.32   Outcome of Exercise 20.

20. Population Growth   The world population reached 7 billion people on October 21, 2011, and was growing at the rate of 1.1% each year. Assuming that the population continues to grow at the same rate, approximately when will the population reach 8 billion? See Fig. 3.32.

21. Radioactive Decay   Strontium-90, a radioactive element that is part of the fallout from nuclear explosions, has a half-life of 28 years. This means that a given quantity of strontium-90 will emit radioactive particles and decay to one-half its size every 28 years. How many years are required for 100 grams of strontium-90 to decay to less than 1 gram? See Fig. 3.33.

```
The decay time is
196 years.
```

FIGURE 3.33   Outcome of Exercise 21.

```
Consumer prices will
double in 29 years.
```

FIGURE 3.34   Outcome of Exercise 22.

22. Consumer Price Index   The *consumer price index (CPI)* indicates the average price of a fixed basket of goods and services. It is customarily taken as a measure of inflation and is frequently used to adjust pensions. The CPI was 9.9 in July 1913, was 100 in July 1983, and was 238.25 in July 2014. This means that $9.90 in July 1913 had the same purchasing power as $100.00 in July 1983, and the same purchasing power as $238.25 in July 2014. In 2009, the CPI fell for the first time since 1955. However, for most of the preceding 15 years it had grown at an average rate of 2.5% per year. Assuming that the CPI will rise at 2.5% per year in the future, in how many years will the CPI have at least doubled from its July 2014 level? **Note:** Each year, the CPI will be 1.025 times the CPI for the previous year. See Fig. 3.34.

23. Car Loan   When you borrow money to buy a house or a car, the loan is paid off with a sequence of equal monthly payments with a stated annual interest rate compounded monthly. The amount borrowed is called the *principal*. If the annual interest rate is 6% (or .06), then the monthly interest rate is .06/12 = .005. At any time, the *balance* of the loan is the amount still owed. The balance at the end of each month is calculated as the balance at the end of the previous month, plus the interest due on that balance, and minus the monthly payment. For instance, with an annual interest rate of 6%,

[new balance] = [previous balance] + .005 · [previous balance] − [monthly payment]

= 1.005 · [previous balance] − [monthly payment].

Suppose you borrow $15,000 to buy a new car at 6% interest compounded monthly and your monthly payment is $290.00. After how many months will the car be half paid off? That is, after how many months will the balance be less than half the amount borrowed? See Fig. 3.35 on the next page.

```
Loan will be half paid
off after 33 months.
```

FIGURE 3.35 Outcome of Exercise 23.

```
Annuity will be worth more
than $3000 after 29 months.
```

FIGURE 3.36 Outcome of Exercise 24.

24. **Annuity** An *annuity* is a sequence of equal periodic payments. One type of annuity, called a *savings plan*, consists of monthly payments into a savings account in order to generate money for a future purchase. Suppose you decide to deposit $100 at the end of each month into a savings account paying 3% interest compounded monthly. The monthly interest rate will be .03/12 or .0025, and the balance in the account at the end of each month will be computed as

[balance at end of month] $= (1.0025) \cdot$ [balance at end of previous month] $+ 100.$

After how many months will there be more than $3,000 in the account? See Fig. 3.36.

25. **Annuity** An *annuity* is a sequence of equal periodic payments. For one type of annuity, a large amount of money is deposited into a bank account and then a fixed amount is withdrawn each month. Suppose you deposit $10,000 into such an account paying 3.6% interest compounded monthly, and then withdraw $600 at the end of each month. The monthly interest rate will be .036/12 or .003, and the balance in the account at the end of each month will be computed as

[balance at end of month] $= (1.003) \cdot$ [balance at end of previous month] $- 600.$

After how many months will the account contain less than $600, and what will be the amount in the account at that time? See Fig. 3.37.

```
Balance will be $73.91
after 17 months.
```

FIGURE 3.37 Outcome of Exercise 25.

```
Carbon-14 has a half-life
of 5776 years.
```

FIGURE 3.38 Outcome of Exercise 26.

26. **Radioactive Decay** Carbon-14 is constantly produced in Earth's upper atmosphere due to interactions between cosmic rays and nitrogen, and is found in all plants and animals. After a plant or animal dies, its amount of carbon-14 decreases by about .012% per year. Determine the half-life of carbon-14, that is, the number of years required for 1 gram of carbon-14 to decay to less than ½ gram. See Fig. 3.38.

27. **Same Birthday as You** Suppose you are in a large-lecture class with n other students. Determine how large n must be such that the probability that someone has the same birthday as you is greater than 50%? See Fig. 3.39. **Note:** Forgetting about leap years and so assuming 365 days in a year, the probability that no one has the same birthday as you is $\left(\dfrac{364}{365}\right)^n$.

```
With 253 students, the
probability is greater than
50% that someone has the same
birthday as you.
```

FIGURE 3.39 Outcome of Exercise 27.

```
Enter amount of deposit: 10000
Balance will be $73.19
after 17 months.
```

FIGURE 3.40 Possible outcome of Exercise 28.

28. **Annuity** Redo Exercise 25 with the amount of money deposited being input by the user. See Fig. 3.40.

29. **Population Growth** In 2014 China's population was about 1.37 billion and growing at the rate of .51% per year. In 2014 India's population was about 1.26 billion and growing at the rate of 1.35% per year. Determine when India's population will surpass China's population. Assume that the 2014 growth rates will continue. See Fig. 3.41.

```
India's population will exceed China's
population in the year 2025.
```

FIGURE 3.41 Outcome of Exercise 29.

```
The coffee will cool to below
150 degrees in 7 minutes.
```

FIGURE 3.42 Outcome of Exercise 30.

30. **Cooling** *Newton's Law of Cooling* states that when a hot liquid is placed in a cool room, each minute the decrease in the temperature is approximately proportional to the difference between the liquid's temperature and the room's temperature. That is, there is a constant k such that each minute the temperature loss is $k \cdot$ (liquid's temperature − room's temperature). Suppose a cup of 212°F coffee is placed in a 70°F room and that $k = .079$. Determine the number of minutes required for the coffee to cool to below 150°F. See Fig. 3.42.

31. **Saving Account** Write a menu-driven program that allows the user to make transactions to a savings account. Assume that the account initially has a balance of $1,000. See Fig. 3.43.

```
Options:
1. Make a Deposit
2. Make a Withdrawal
3. Obtain Balance
4. Quit
Make a selection from the options menu: 1
Enter amount of deposit: 500
Deposit Processed.
Make a selection from the options menu: 2
Enter amount of withdrawal: 2000
Denied. Maximum withdrawal is $1,500.00
Enter amount of withdrawal: 600
Withdrawal Processed.
Make a selection from the options menu: 3
Balance: $900.00
Make a selection from the options menu: 4
```

FIGURE 3.43 Possible outcome of Exercise 31.

Solutions to Practice Problems 3.3

1. initial_val will never change. To correct the program, add the statement initial_val −= 1

2. Either precede the loop with the statement **answer = " "**, or replace with the following loop.

```
while True:
    answer = input("Enter the password: ")
```

```
    if answer.upper() == "SHAZAM":
        break
print("You may continue.")
```

   3. Remove the statement i = i + 1 in the loop, and change the starting index to i + 1.

3.4   The *for* Loop

The for loop is used to iterate through a sequence of values. The general form of a for loop is

for *var* in *sequence*:
    indented block of statements

where *sequence* might be an arithmetic progression of numbers, a string, a list, a tuple, or a file object. The variable is successively assigned each value in the sequence and the indented block of statements is executed after each assignment. Each statement in the block is indented to the same indentation level. This physical indentation tells the interpreter where the block starts and stops.

■ Looping Through an Arithmetic Progression of Numbers

The range function is used to generate an arithmetic progression of numbers. If m and n have integer values and $m < n$, then the function

range(*m*, *n*)

generates the sequence of integers $m, m + 1, m + 2, \ldots, n - 1$.

That is, the sequence begins with m, and 1 is repeatedly added to m until the number just before n is reached. Some examples are as follows:

   range(3, 10) generates the sequence 3, 4, 5, 6, 7, 8, 9.

   range(0, 4) generates the sequence 0, 1, 2, 3.

   range(-4, 2) generates the sequence $-4, -3, -2, -1, 0, 1$.

The function **range(0, *n*)** can be abbreviated to **range(*n*)** and is usually written in that form.

The loop

for num in range(m, n):
    indented block of statements

executes the statement(s) in the block once for each integer in the sequence generated by range(m, n). The line beginning with for is called the **header** of the loop. The variable following the word for is called the **loop variable**, the indented block of statements is called the **body** of the loop, and each execution of the body is referred to as a **pass** through the loop. The header creates the loop variable and successively assigns it the numbers in the sequence, with each assignment followed by a pass through the loop. The most common single-letter names for loop variables are i, j, and k; however, when appropriate, the name should suggest the meaning of the numbers generated. For instance, we might write **for year in range(2000, 2015)**.

Example 1   Squares The following two lines of code display four integers and their squares. The loop variable *i* first assumes the value 2 and uses that value in the execution of the **print** statement. The variable then successively assumes and executes the **print** statement for each of the integers 3, 4, and 5.

```
for i in range(2, 6)
    print(i, i * i)
```

[Run]

```
2 4
3 9
4 16
5 25
```

 Example 2   Population Growth Suppose the population of a city was 300,000 in the year 2014 and is growing at the rate of 3% per year. The following program displays a table showing the population each year until 2018. Figure 3.44 shows the flowchart for the program.

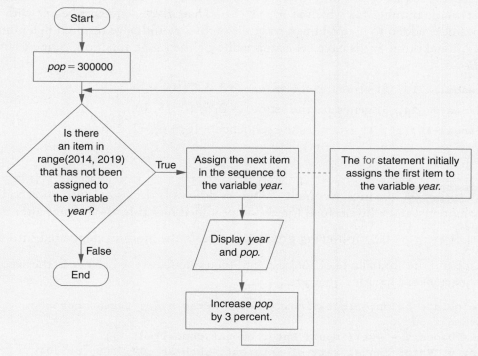

FIGURE 3.44   Flowchart for Example 2.

```
## Display population from 2014 to 2018.
pop = 300000
print("{0:10} {1}".format("Year", "Population"))
```

```
for year in range(2014, 2019):
    print("{0:<10d} {1:,d}".format(year, round(pop)))
    pop += 0.03 * pop     # Increase pop by 3 percent.
```

[Run]

```
Year  Population
2014  300,000
2015  309,000
2016  318,270
2017  327,818
2018  337,653
```

■ Step Values for the *range* Function

A variation of the **range** function generates a sequence of integers where successive integers differ by a value other than 1. If m, n, and s have integer values where $m < n$ and s is positive, then the function

```
range(m, n, s)
```

generates the sequence of integers m, $m + s$, $m + 2s$, $m + 3s$, ..., $m + r \cdot s$, where r is the largest whole number for which $m + r \cdot s < n$. That is, the sequence begins with m, and s is repeatedly added to m until the next addition of s would have resulted in a number $\geq n$. The optional number s is called the **step value** of the **range** function. Some examples are as follows:

> **range(3, 10, 2)** generates the sequence 3, 5, 7, 9.
>
> **range(0, 24, 5)** generates the sequence 0, 5, 10, 15, 20.
>
> **range(-10, 10, 4)** generates the sequence -10, -6, -2, 2, 6.

✓ **Example 3** Savings Account When A dollars is deposited into an account at the annual interest rate r (in decimal form) compounded monthly, the balance after m months is $A \cdot \left(1 + \dfrac{r}{12}\right)^{m}$. The following program requests the amount deposited into a savings account and the annual rate of interest, and then calculates the balance in the account after each quarter-year for four quarters.

```
## Calculate balance in savings account after every three months.
# Obtain input.
initialDeposit = eval(input("Enter amount deposited: "))
prompt = "Enter annual rate of interest; such as .02, .03, or .04: "
annualRateOfInterest = eval(input(prompt))
monthlyRateOfInterest = annualRateOfInterest / 12
# Display table.
print("{0}{1:>15}".format("Month", "Balance"))
for i in range(3, 13, 3):
    print("{0:2}              ${1:<15,.2f}".
        format(i, initialDeposit * (1 + monthlyRateOfInterest) ** i))
```

[Run]

```
Enter amount deposited: 1000
Enter annual rate of interest; such as .02, .03, or .04: .03
Month    Balance
  3      $1,007.52
  6      $1,015.09
  9      $1,022.73
 12      $1,030.42
```

In the **range** functions considered so far, the initial value was less than the terminating value and the step value was positive. However, if a negative step value is used and the initial value is greater than the terminating value, then the **range** function generates a decreasing sequence that begins with the initial value and decreases until just before reaching the terminating value. Some examples are as follows:

range(6, 0, -1) generates the sequence 6, 5, 4, 3, 2, 1.

range(5, 2, -3) generates the sequence 5.

range(10, -10, -4) generates the sequence 10, 6, 2, −2, −6.

■ Nested *for* Loops

The body of a **for** loop can contain any type of Python statement. In particular, it can contain another **for** loop. However, the second loop must be completely contained inside the first loop and must have a different loop variable. Such a configuration is called **nested for loops**.

✔ **Example 4** **Multiplication Table** The following program displays a multiplication table for the integers from 1 to 5. Here m denotes the left factors of the products, and n denotes the right factors. Each factor takes on a value from 1 to 5. The values are assigned to m in the outer loop and to n in the inner loop. Initially, m is assigned the value 1, and then the inner loop is traversed five times to produce the first row of products. At the end of these five passes, the value of m will still be 1, and the first execution of the inner loop will be complete. Following this, m assumes the next number in the sequence, 2. The header of the inner loop is then executed, and resets the value of n to 1. The second row of products is displayed during the next pass of the inner loop, and so on.

```
## Display a multiplication table for the numbers from 1 through 5.
for m in range(1, 6):
    for n in range(1, 6):
        print(m, 'x', n, '=', m * n, "\t", end="")
    print()
```

[Run]

```
1 x 1 = 1       1 x 2 = 2       1 x 3 = 3       1 x 4 = 4       1 x 5 = 5
2 x 1 = 2       2 x 2 = 4       2 x 3 = 6       2 x 4 = 8       2 x 5 = 10
3 x 1 = 3       3 x 2 = 6       3 x 3 = 9       3 x 4 = 12      3 x 5 = 15
4 x 1 = 4       4 x 2 = 8       4 x 3 = 12      4 x 4 = 16      4 x 5 = 20
5 x 1 = 5       5 x 2 = 10      5 x 3 = 15      5 x 4 = 20      5 x 5 = 25
```

Example 5 Triangle of Asterisks The following program uses nested for loops to display a triangle of asterisks.

```
## Display a triangle of asterisks.
numberOfRows = int(input("Enter a number from 1 through 20: "))
for i in range(numberOfRows):
    for j in range(i + 1):
        print("*", end="")
    print()
```

[Run]

```
Enter a number from 1 through 20: 5
*
**
***
****
*****
```

■ Looping Through the Characters of a String

If *str1* has a string value, then the loop

```
for ch in str1:
    indented block of statements
```

executes the statement(s) in the body once for each character of the string beginning with the first character. Therefore, there are `len(str1)` passes through the loop.

Example 6 Reverse Letters The following program requests a word as input and displays it backward. The program creates a string consisting of the first letter of the word, and then successively appends each subsequent letter to the front of the string.

```
## Reverse the letters in a word.
word = input("Enter a word: ")
reversedWord = ""
for ch in word:
    reversedWord = ch + reversedWord
print("The reversed word is " + reversedWord + ".")
```

[Run]

```
Enter a word: zeus
The reversed word is suez.
```

■ Looping Through the Items of a List or Tuple

If *listOrTuple* is a list or a tuple, then the loop

```
for item in listOrTuple:
    indented block of statements
```

executes the statement(s) in the body once for each item of the list or tuple beginning with the first item. Therefore, there are `len(listOrTuple)` passes through the loop.

Example 7 . R Months The following program displays the months whose names contain the letter *r*.

```
## Display months containing the letter "r".
months = ("January", "February", "March", "April", "May", "June",
          "July", "August", "September", "October", "November", "December")
for month in months:
    if 'r' in month.lower():
        print(month)
```

[Run]

```
January
February
March
April
September
October
November
December
```

The program in Example 6 would work exactly the same if a list was used instead of a tuple. We used a tuple since the sequence of items is fixed and not subject to change. Otherwise, we would have used a list. The program accessed every item of the sequence of months, but did not change any values in the sequence in place. A program that both accesses items and changes values in place not only must use a list, but must iterate over the index values of the list.

. Example 8 Abbreviate Months The following program replaces the name of each month with its three-letter abbreviation. **Note:** For any list, call it *list1*, the last item has index len(*list1*) – 1, and therefore range(len (*list1*)) generates the indices of the list.

```
## Replace each month with its three-letter abbreviation.
months = ["January", "February", "March", "April", "May", "June",
          "July", "August", "September", "October", "November", "December"]
for i in range(len(months)):
    months[i] = months[i][0:3]
print(months)
```

[Run]

```
['Jan', 'Feb', 'Mar', 'Apr', 'May', 'Jun', 'Jul', 'Aug', 'Sep', 'Oct', 'Nov',
'Dec']
```

Example 9 Deck of Cards The following program uses nested for loops with a list of ranks and a list of suits to create a list consisting of the 52 cards in a deck of cards. The cards are assigned their ranks in the outer loop and their suits in the inner loop. The first for statement iterates through the items in *ranks* until every item has been accessed. At each iteration of the outer loop, the second for statement iterates through the items of *suits* until all of those items have been accessed. Each pass of the inner loop appends the name of a

card to the list *deckOfCards*. Figure 3.45 shows a flowchart for the nested **for** loops portion of the program.

```
## Display the names of the 52 cards in a deck of cards.
ranks = ['2', '3', '4', '5', '6', '7', '8', '9',
         "10", "jack", "queen", "king", "ace"]
suits = ["spades", "hearts", "clubs", "diamonds"]
deckOfCards = []  # List to hold the names of the 52 cards in a deck.
# Use nested loops to fill the deckOfCards list.
for rank in ranks:
    for suit in suits:
        deckOfCards.append(rank + " of " + suit)
# Display the 52 cards.
for card in deckOfCards:
    print(card)
```

[Run]

```
2 of spades
2 of hearts
.
.
.
ace of clubs
ace of diamonds
```

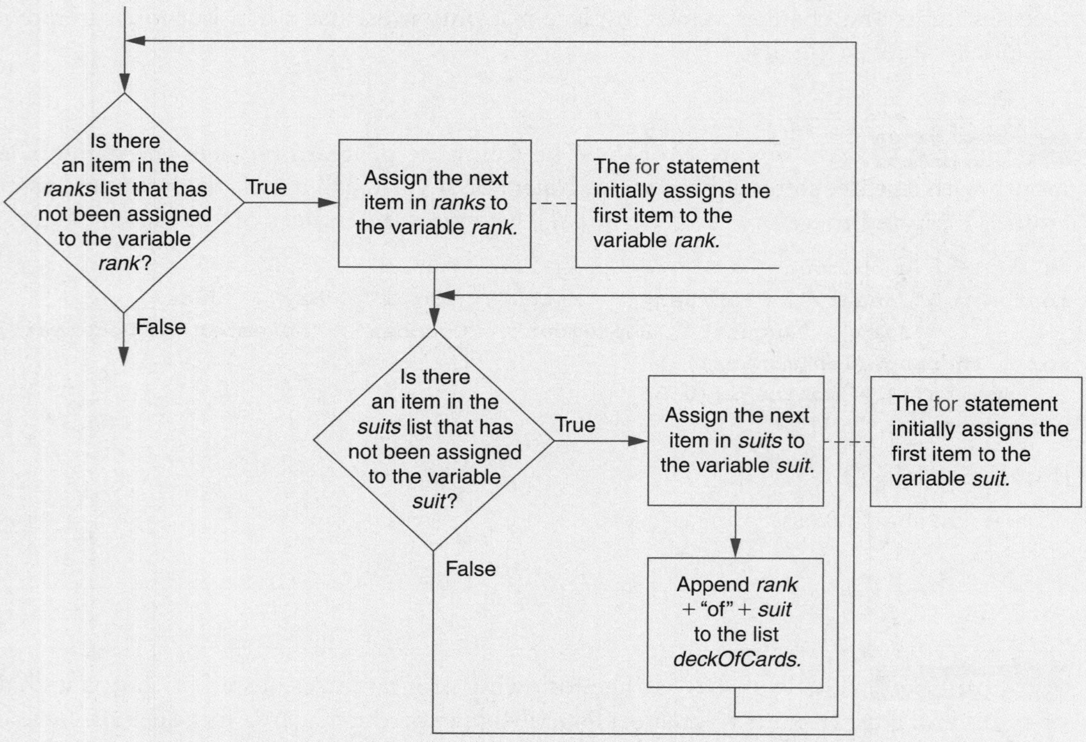

FIGURE 3.45 Flowchart of nested for loops for Example 9.

■ Looping Through the Lines of a Text File

If **fileName.txt** is a text file, then code of the form

```
infile = open("fileName.txt", 'r')
for line in infile:
    indented block of statements
infile.close()
```

reads each line of the file in succession beginning with the first line and executes the indented block of statement(s) for each line. The first statement establishes a connection between the program and the file that allows the program to read data from the file and the last statement terminates the connection. Throughout this textbook, we assume that the file is contained in the same folder as the program file. That way, we can just use the file name in the open function instead of giving a complete path leading to the file.

Example 10 U.S. Presidents The file **USPres.txt** contains the names of the first 44 U.S. presidents in the order in which they served. The following program requests a first name and then displays the names of the U.S. presidents having that first name. The variable *foundFlag* tells us if at least one president had the requested first name. Each line of a text file ends with a special newline character. The **rstrip** method removes that character.

```
## Display presidents with a specified first name.
firstName = input("Enter a first name: ")
foundFlag = False
infile = open("USPres.txt", 'r')
for line in infile:
    if line.startswith(firstName + ' '):
        print(line.rstrip())
        foundFlag = True
infile.close()
if not foundFlag:
    print("No president had the first name", firstName + '.')
```

[Run]

```
Enter a first name: John
John Adams
John Q. Adams
John Tyler
John Kennedy
```

■ The *pass* Statement

The header of a for loop must be followed by an indented block of at least one statement. However, there are times when you want the loop to cycle through a sequence and not do anything. In that case, the pass statement should be used. The pass statement is a do-nothing placeholder statement.

Example 11   Last Line of File The following program displays the last line of a file. After the **for** statement iterates through the entire file, the value of *line* will be the last line of the file. The **rstrip** method removes the newline character that is at the end of each line of a text file.

```
## Display the last line of a text file.
infile = open("aFile.txt", 'r')
for line in infile:
    pass
print(line.rstrip())
infile.close()
```

■ Populating a List with the Contents of a Text File

Sometimes the best way to analyze the data in a text file is to place the data into a list and make use of list functions and methods. The following lines of code show one way of placing the contents of a text file into a list.

```
dataList = []
infile = open("Data.txt", 'r')
for line in infile:
    dataList.append(line.strip())
infile.close()
```

However, a more efficient way (to be explained in the next two chapters) is

```
infile = open("Data.txt", 'r')
dataList = [line.rstrip() for line in infile]
infile.close()
```

In either case, each item in the list will be a string. If the file **Data.txt** contained only numbers, the items in the list can be converted from strings to numbers. The following two lines of code will not do the job:

```
for item in dataList:
    item = eval(item)
```

However, the task can be accomplished with

```
for i in range(len(dataList)):
    dataList[i] = eval(dataList[i])
```

A more efficient method (to be explained in the next two chapters) is

```
infile = open("Data.txt", 'r')
dataList = [eval(line) for line in infile]
infile.close()
```

■ Comments

1. The parentheses of the **range** function can contain one, two, or three values. When the parentheses contains two or three values, the first value is always the beginning of the sequence generated. When the parentheses contains a single number, call it *n*, no sequence will be generated when $n \leq 0$; otherwise the sequence of *n* numbers from 0 to $n - 1$ will be generated.

2. The values generated by the **range** function can be displayed by applying the **list** function. For instance, the statement `print(list(range(1, 8, 2)))` displays `[1, 3, 5, 7]`.

3. The function `range(m, n, s)` produces an empty sequence if $n \leq m$ and s is positive or if $m \leq n$ and s is negative.

4. When the statement

   ```
   continue
   ```

   is executed in the body of a **for** loop, the remaining statements in the body of the loop are skipped and execution continues with the next iteration of the loop.

5. When the statement

   ```
   break
   ```

   is executed in the body of a **for** loop, the loop is terminated and the loop variable keeps its current value. Both **break** and **continue** statements usually appear in the body of an **if** statement and provide an efficient way of transferring control.

6. *Any* type of loop can be nested inside another loop. For example, **for** loops can be nested inside **while** loops and vice versa.

7. The **pass** statement can be used in any compound statement, such as a **while** loop or an **if-elif-else** statement.

Practice Problems 3.4

1. What sequence is generated by the function `range(5)`?

2. Why won't the following lines of code work as intended?

   ```
   for i in range(15, 1):
       print(i)
   ```

3. Consider the 7th line of Example 10. How would the output change if `print(line.rstrip())` were changed to `print(line)`.

4. Simplify the following code:

   ```
   musketeers = ["Athos", "Porthos", "Aramis", "D'Artagnan"]
   i = 0
   while i < len(musketeers):
       print(musketeers[i])
       i += 1
   ```

5. What is the output of the following lines of code?

   ```
   n = 7
   for i in range(n):
       print(i, end=" ")
       n = 3
   ```

EXERCISES 3.4

In Exercises 1 through 8, determine the sequence generated by the range function.

1. `range(1, 10)`

2. `range(1, 10, -1)`

3. `range(10, 1, -1)`

4. `range(5)`

5. `range(5, -1)`

6. `range(-5, 1)`

7. `range(-1, 0)`

8. `range(10, 10)`

In Exercises 9 through 16, determine a range function that generates the sequence of numbers.

9. `4, 9, 14, 19`

10. `0, 1, 2, 3`

11. `-21, -20, -19, -18`

12. `4, 3, 2, 1`

13. `20, 17, 14`

14. `7`

15. `5, 4, 3, 2, 1, 0`

16. `-5, -3, -1, 1`

In Exercises 17 through 40, determine the output displayed.

17.
```
for i in range(1, 5):
    print("Pass #" + str(i))
```

18.
```
for i in range(3, 7):
    print(2 * i)
```

19.
```
num = 5
for i in range(num, 2 * num - 2):
    print(i)
```

20.
```
for i in range(-9, 0, 3):
    print(i)
```

21.
```
# chr(162) is a cents symbol
stringOfCents = ""
for i in range(1, 11):
    stringOfCents += chr(162)
print(stringOfCents)
```

22.
```
n = 3
total = 0
for i in range(1, n + 1):
    total += i
print(total)
```

23.
```
for j in range(2, 9, 2):
    print(j)
print("Who do we appreciate?")
```

24.
```
for countdown in range(10, 0, -1):
    print(countdown)
```

25.
```
number_of_sibilants = 0
word = "stargazers"
for ch in word:
    if (ch == 's') or (ch == 'z'):
        number_of_sibilants += 1
print(number_of_sibilants)
```

26.
```
numCaps = 0
name = "United States of America"
for ch in name:
    if ch.isupper():
        numCaps += 1
print(numCaps)
```

27.
```
word = "183651"
sumOfOddIndexes = 0
oddIndex = False
for ch in word:
    if oddIndex:
        sumOfOddIndexes += int(ch)
    oddIndex = not oddIndex
print(sumOfOddIndexes)
```

28.
```
word = "cloudier"
newWord = ""
evenIndex = True
for ch in word:
    if evenIndex:
        newWord += ch
    evenIndex = not evenIndex
print(newWord)
```

29.
```
for ch in "Python":
    continue
print(ch)
```

30.
```
for ch in "Python":
    break
print(ch)
```

31.
```
numEvens = 0
sumOfEvens = 0
list1 = [2, 9, 6, 7, 12]
```

```
    for num in list1:
        if num % 2 == 0:
            numEvens += 1
            sumOfEvens += num
    print(numEvens, sumOfEvens)
```

32.
```
list1 = [2, 9, 6, 7, 13, 3]
maxOfOdds = 0
for num in list1:
    if (num % 2 == 1) and (num > maxOfOdds):
        maxOfOdds = num
print(maxOfOdds)
```

33.
```
boroughs = ("Manhatten", "Bronx", "Brooklyn", "Queens", "Staten Island")
minLetters = 100
for borough in boroughs:
    if len(borough) < minLetters:
        minLetters = len(borough)
print("The shortest word has length", minLetters)
```

34.
```
numOfNumbers = 0
list1 = ["three", 4, 5.7, "six", "seven", 8, 3.1416]
for item in list1:
    if isinstance(item, str):
        continue
    numOfNumbers += 1
print(numOfNumbers)
```

35.
```
list1 = [1, 2, "three", 4, 5.7, "six", "seven", 8, 3.1416]
for item in list1:
    if isinstance(item, str):
        break
print(item)
```

36.
```
# I'm looking over a four leaf clover.
leaves = ("sunshine","rain", "the roses that bloom in the lane",
          "somebody I adore")
number = 1
for leaf in leaves:
    print("Leaf", str(number) + ':', leaf)
    number += 1
```

In Exercises 37 and 38, assume that the six lines of the file Numbers.txt contain the data 6, 9, 2, 3, 6, and 4.

37.
```
sumEvens = 0
infile = open("Numbers.txt", 'r')
for line in infile:
    if eval(line) % 2 == 0:
        sumEvens += eval(line)
    infile.close()
print(sumEvens)
```

38.
```
dataList = []
infile = open("Numbers.txt", 'r')
```

```
for line in infile:
    dataList.append(eval(line))
infile.close()
print(sum(dataList))
```

In Exercises 39 and 40, assume that the 50 lines of the file `States.txt` contain the names of the fifty states in the order they joined the union.

39.
```
infile = open("States.txt", 'r')
for line in infile:
    if line.startswith("North"):
        print(line, end="")
infile.close()
```

40.
```
infile = open("States.txt", 'r')
for line in infile:
    continue
infile.close()
print(line, end="")
```

In Exercises 41 through 46, identify all errors.

41.
```
for j in range(1, 26, -1):
    print(j)
```

42.
```
for i in range(1, 4):
    print(i + " " + 2 ** i)
```

43.
```
list1 = [2, 5, 7, 2, 7, 8]
list2 = []
for item in list1:
    if item not in list2:
        list2.append(item)
print list2
```

44.
```
list1 = ['a', 'b', 'c']
for letter in list1:
    letter = letter.upper()
print(list1)
```

45.
```
# Display all numbers from 0 through 19 except for 13
for i in range(20, 0):
    if i != 13:
print(i)
```

46.
```
list1 = ["one", "two", "three", "four"]
for item in list1:
    item = item.upper()
print(list1)
```

In Exercises 47 and 48, rewrite the program using a for loop.

47.
```
num = 1
while num <= 9:
    print(num)
    num += 2
```

48.
```
print("hello")
print("hello")
print("hello")
print("hello")
```

Simplify the programs in Exercises 49 and 50.

49.
```
lakes = ["Erie", "Huron", "Michigan", "Ontario", "Superior"]
result = ""
for i in range(len(lakes)):
    result += lakes[i]
    if i < len(lakes) - 1:
        result += ", "
print(result)
```

50.
```
lakes = ["Erie", "Huron", "Michigan", "Ontario", "Superior"]
for i in range(len(lakes)):
    print(lakes[i], end="")
```

```
if i < len(lakes) - 1:
    print(" | ", end="")
```

In Exercises 51 through 65, write a program to carry out the stated task.

51. Radioactive Decay   Cobalt-60, a radioactive form of cobalt used in cancer therapy, decays over a period of time. Each year, 12% of the amount present at the beginning of the year will have decayed. If a container of cobalt-60 initially contains 10 grams, determine the amount remaining after five years. Round the amount remaining to two decimal places. See Fig. 3.46.

```
The amount of cobalt-60 remaining
after five years is 5.28 grams.
```

FIGURE 3.46   Outcome of Exercise 51.

```
Enter a telephone number: 982-876-5432
Number without dashes is 9828765432.
```

FIGURE 3.47   Outcome of Exercise 52.

52. Phone Number   Remove the dashes from a telephone number input by the user. See Fig. 3.47.

53. Vowels   Count the number of vowels in a phrase input by the user. See Fig. 3.48.

```
Enter a phrase: Less is more.
The phrase contains 4 vowels.
```

```
Enter a number: 3.4
Enter a number: 9.3
Enter a number: 5.5
Largest number: 9.3
```

FIGURE 3.48   Possible outcome of Exercise 53.   **FIGURE 3.49**   Possible outcome of Exercise 54.

54. Largest Number   Without using a list, find the largest of three numbers obtained from the user. See Fig. 3.49.

55. Sum of Fractions   Find the value of $1 + 1/2 + 1/3 + 1/4 + \ldots + 1/100$ to five decimal places. See Fig. 3.50.

```
The sum 1 + 1/2 + 1/3 + ... + 1/100
is 5.18738 to five decimal places.
```

FIGURE 3.50   Outcome of Exercise 55.

```
The sum 1 + 2 + ... + 100
is 5050.
```

FIGURE 3.51   Outcome of Exercise 56.

56. Sum of Numbers   Find the sum of the first one hundred positive integers. See Fig. 3.51.

57. Alphabetical Order   Accept a word as input and determine if its letters are in alphabetical order. Some examples of words whose letters are in alphabetical order are *biopsy, adept, chintz,* and *lost.* See Fig. 3.52.

```
Enter a word: almost
Letters are in alphabetical order.
```

```
Enter a word: education
EDUCATION is a vowel word.
```

FIGURE 3.52   Possible outcome of Exercise 57.   **FIGURE 3.53**   Possible outcome of Exercise 58.

58. **Vowel Words**   A **vowel word** is a word that contains every vowel. Some examples of vowel words are *sequoia*, *facetious*, and *dialogue*. Determine if a word input by the user is a vowel word. See Fig. 3.53 on the previous page.

59. **Lifetime Earnings**   Estimate how much a young worker will earn before retiring at age 65, where the worker's name, age, and starting salary are input by the user. Assume the worker receives a 5% raise each year. See Fig. 3.54.

```
Enter name: Helen
Enter age: 25
Enter starting salary: 20000
Helen will earn about $2,415,995.
```

	Simple Interest	Compound Interest
1	$1,050.00	$1,050.00
2	$1,100.00	$1,102.50
3	$1,150.00	$1,157.62
4	$1,200.00	$1,215.51

FIGURE 3.54   Possible outcome of Exercise 59.   **FIGURE 3.55**   Outcome of Exercise 60.

60. **Simple versus Compound Interest**   When $1,000 is invested at 5% simple interest, the amount grows by $50 each year. When money is invested at 5% interest compounded annually, the amount at the end of each year is 1.05 times the amount at the beginning of that year. Display the amounts after the first four years for a $1,000 investment at 5% simple and compound interest. See Fig. 3.55.

61. **Car Loan**   Consider the car loan discussed in Exercise 23 of Section 3.3. The loan will be paid off after five years. Assume that the car was purchased at the beginning of January 2013, and display the balance at the end of each year for five years. See Fig. 3.56. **Note:** The last payment will be slightly less than the other payments, since otherwise the final balance would be a negative amount.

YEAR	AMOUNT OWED AT END OF YEAR
2013	$12,347.85
2014	$9,532.13
2015	$6,542.74
2016	$3,368.97
2017	$0.00

YEAR	BALANCE AT END OF YEAR
2014	$1,216.64
2015	$2,470.28
2016	$3,762.06
2017	$5,093.12
2018	$6,464.67

FIGURE 3.56   Outcome of Exercise 61.   **FIGURE 3.57**   Outcome of Exercise 62.

62. **Annuity**   Refer to the annuity discussed in Exercise 24 of Section 3.3. Assume that the first deposit is made at the end of January 2014, and display the balance in the account at the end of each year from 2014 to 2018. See Fig. 3.57.

63. **Average Grade**   Ask the user to enter three grades, and then compute the average after dropping the lowest grade. See Fig. 3.58.

64. **Automobile Depreciation**   A rule of thumb states that cars in personal use depreciate by 15% each year. Suppose a new car is purchased for $20,000. Produce a table showing the value of the car at the end of each of the next four years. See Fig. 3.59.

```
Enter a grade: 70
Enter a grade: 90
Enter a grade: 80
Average: 85
```

```
1        $17,000.00
2        $14,450.00
3        $12,282.50
4        $10,440.12
```

FIGURE 3.58   Possible outcome of Exercise 63.   FIGURE 3.59   Outcome of Exercise 64.

65. Supply and Demand   Each year's level of production and price (per bushel) for most agricultural products affects the level of production and price for the following year. Suppose the soybean crop in a country was 80 million bushels in 2014 and

$$[\text{price each year}] = 20 - .1 * [\text{quantity that year}]$$
$$[\text{quantity each year}] = 5 * [\text{price from the preceding year}] - 10,$$

where quantity is measured in units of millions of bushels. Generate a table to show the quantity and price from 2014 until 2018. See Fig. 3.60.

```
YEAR     QUANTITY     PRICE
2014     80.00        $12.00
2015     50.00        $15.00
2016     65.00        $13.50
2017     57.50        $14.25
2018     61.25        $13.88
```

```
How many numbers do you want to enter? 4
Enter a number: 9
Enter a number: 3
Enter a number: 6
Enter a number: 5
Median: 5.5
```

FIGURE 3.60   Outcome of Exercise 65.   FIGURE 3.61   Possible outcome of Exercise 66.

66. Median   The **median** of an ordered set of measurements is a number separating the lower half from the upper half. If the number of measurements is odd, the median is the middle measurement. If the number of measurements is even, the median is the average of the two middle measurements. Write a program that requests a number n and a set of n measurements (not necessarily ordered) as input and then displays the median of the measurements. See Fig. 3.61.

67. Salary Options   Suppose you are given the following two salary options:

Option 1: $20,000 per year, with a raise of $1,000 at the end of each year
Option 2: $10,000 per half-year, with a raise of $250 per half-year at the end of each half-year

Write a program to calculate the amount you would receive for the next ten years under each option to determine the best choice. See Fig. 3.62. (Many people are surprised at the answer.)

```
Option 1 earns $245,000.
Option 2 earns $247,500.
```

```
The value of the stock at the
end of the year was $9,483.48.
```

FIGURE 3.62   Outcome of Exercise 67.   FIGURE 3.63   Outcome of Exercise 68.

68. Misleading Percentages At the beginning of the year you purchased a stock for $10,000. At the end of the year you are told that your stock gained 18% during the past month and that the average monthly change was +1%. Sounds like good news, doesn't it? Later you learn that your stock lost 16% during each of the first six months of the year and gained 18% during each of the last six months of the year. Write a program to determine the value of the stock at the end of the year. See Fig. 3.63.

The file `ColoredBalls.txt` contains the sequence in which colored balls were drawn out of a bag. The file is available on the companion website. Use the file in Exercises 69 and 70.

69. Colored Balls Write a program to determine the number of red balls in the bag. See Fig. 3.64.

```
Number of red balls: 12
```

```
A red ball was first drawn in turn 2.
```

FIGURE 3.64 Outcome of Exercise 69. **FIGURE 3.65** Outcome of Exercise 70.

70. Colored Balls Write a program to determine the first turn in which a red ball was drawn from the bag. See Fig. 3.65.

71. Average Grade The file `Final.txt` contains student grades on a final exam. Write a program that displays the number of grades, the average grade, and the percentage of grades that are above the average grade. See Fig. 3.66.

```
Number of grades: 24
Average grade: 83.25
Percentage of grades above
average: 54.17%
```

```
Enter one of five grades: 84
Enter one of five grades: 96
Enter one of five grades: 88
Enter one of five grades: 77
Enter one of five grades: 90
Average grade: 91.33
```

FIGURE 3.66 Outcome of Exercise 71. **FIGURE 3.67** Possible outcome of Exercise 72.

72. Average Grade Write a program that requests five grades as input and then calculates the average after dropping the two lowest grades. See Fig. 3.67.

73. Number of Vowels Write a program that requests a word as input and counts the number of different vowels in the word. See Fig. 3.68.

```
Enter a word: successful
Number of different vowels: 2
```

```
Starting word: NAISNIENLGELTETWEORRSD
Crossed out letters: N I N E L E T T E R S
Remaining letters: A S I N G L E W O R D
```

FIGURE 3.68 Possible outcome of Exercise 73.

FIGURE 3.69 Outcome of Exercise 74.

74. A Puzzle The following puzzle is known as *The Big Cross-Out Swindle.* "Beginning with the word 'NAISNIENLGELTETWEORRSD,' cross out nine letters in such a way that the remaining letters spell a single word". Write a program that creates variables named *startingWord*, *crossedOutLetters*, and *remainingLetters*. The program should assign to *startingWord* the string given in the puzzle, assign to *crossedOutLetters* a list containing every other letter of *startingWord* beginning with the initial letter N, and assign to *remainingLetters* a list containing every other letter of *startingWord* beginning with the second letter, A. The program should then display the values of the three variables. See Fig. 3.69.

75. Same Birthday In a group of *r* people, the probability that at least two people have the same birthday is

$$1 - \left(\frac{n}{n} \times \frac{n-1}{n} \times \frac{n-2}{n} \times \cdots \times \frac{n-(r-1)}{n} \right)$$

where *n* is the number of days in the year. Write a program that calculates the probabilities for *r* = 21 through 25. Use *n* = 365. See Fig. 3.70.

NUMBER OF PEOPLE	PROBABILITY
21	0.444
22	0.476
23	0.507
24	0.538
25	0.569

FIGURE 3.70 Outcome of Exercise 75.

```
Connecticut
Delaware
Georgia
Maryland
Massachusetts
```

FIGURE 3.71 Partial Outcome of Exercise 76.

76. Original U.S. States The file **States.txt** contains the 50 U.S. states in the order in which they joined the union. Write a program to display the original 13 states in alphabetical order. Fig. 3.71 shows the first five lines of output.

77. Boston Accent Write a program that asks the user to input a sentence and then displays the sentence with all occurrences of the letter *r* removed. See Fig. 3.72.

```
Enter a sentence: Park the car in Harvard Yard.
Revised sentence: Pak the ca in Havad Yad.
```

FIGURE 3.72 Possible outcome of Exercise 77.

78. Special Number Write a program to find the four-digit number, call it *abcd*, whose digits are reversed when the number is multiplied by 4. That is, 4 × *abcd* = *dcba*. See Fig. 3.73.

```
Since 4 times 2178 is 8712,
the special number is 2178.
```

FIGURE 3.73 Outcome of Exercise 78.

In Exercises 79 and 80, use the file ICCWinners.txt provided on the companion website.

79. ICC Winners Write a program that places the names of the 11 winners of the ICC Cricket World Cup into a list and uses the list to determine the name of the sixth winner. See Fig 3.74.

```
The 6th winner was Sri Lanka.
```

FIGURE 3.74   Outcome of Exercise 79.

```
The 4th winner was Australia.
```

FIGURE 3.75   Outcome of Exercise 80.

80. **ICC Winners**   Write a program that determines the name of the 4th winner of the ICC Cricket World Cup. Do not use a list in the program. See Fig 3.75.

81. **Odometer Readings**   The numbers appearing on a car's odometer range from 000000 to 999999. Write a program to determine the number of readings that contain the digit 1. See Fig. 3.76.

```
468,559 numbers on the odometer
contain the digit 1.
```

FIGURE 3.76   Outcome of Exercise 81.

```
The sum of the digits in the numbers
from 1 to one million is 27,000,001.
```

FIGURE 3.77   Outcome of Exercise 82.

82. **Digit Sum**   Write a program to calculate the total sum of the digits in the integers from 1 to a million. See Fig. 3.77.

83. **Flowers and Vegetables**   The following list contains a mix of names of vegetables and flowers. Each name is followed by a letter about whether it is a vegetable or a flower.

```
mixed = ["Broccoli V", "Lily F", "Cucumber V", "Rose F", "Lotus
F", "Cabbage V", "Onion V", "Anemone F", "Aster F"]
```

Write a program that creates two lists (one of vegetables, and one of flowers) and uses the lists to produce the output shown in Fig 3.78.

```
Vegetables: Broccoli, Cucumber, Cabbage, Onion.
Flowers: Lily, Rose, Lotus, Anemone, Aster
```

FIGURE 3.78   Outcome of Exercise 83.

Solutions to Practice Problems 3.4

1. The sequence generated by **range(5)** is the same as the sequence generated by **range(0, 5)**, that is, 0, 1, 2, 3, 4.

2. The loop will never be entered because 15 is greater than 1. The intended first line might have been

   ```
   for i in range (15, 1, -1):
   ```
   or
   ```
   for i in range(2, 16):
   ```

3. Since each line of the file ends with a newline character, the names would have been displayed double-spaced.

4. ```
   musketeers = ["Athos", "Porthos", "Aramis", "D'Artagnan"]
   for name in musketeers:
       print(name)
   ```

   When no items of a list will be altered in place, use in instead of indices to iterate through the list.

5. 0 1 2 3 4 5 6. The header of the for loop generates a sequence of 7 numbers to be iterated over. That sequence is permanent. There will be 7 passes through the loop unless a break statement is encountered.
   ```

CHAPTER 3 KEY TERMS AND CONCEPTS	EXAMPLES

3.1 Relational and Logical Operators

The **Boolean data type** (or **bool**) has the two values True and False.

The **ASCII table** associates characters with nonnegative numbers. The value of **chr(n)** is the character associated with the number n. The function **ord** is the inverse of the chr function. The use of the ASCII table to order items of data is called **lexicographical ordering**.

chr(49) is '1', chr(65) is 'A', chr(97) is 'a'.
ord('9') is 57, ord('Z') is 90, ord('z') is 122.
"Spam" < "spa" lexicographically.
[8, 'X'] < [8, 'x'] has the value True.

The **relational operators** are <, > , ==, !=, <=, >=, *in*, and *not in*.

2 < 3, 2 != 3, 'a' in ['a', 'b'] have value True.
2 == 3, "spam"<="Spam" have value False.

The principal **logical operators** are *and*, *or*, and *not*.

(7 < 5) or (2 != 3) has value True.

A **condition** is an expression involving literals, variables, functions, and operators (arithmetic, relational, or logical) that can be evaluated as True or False.

Let a = 3 and b = "spam".
((5 < (2*a)) and (len(b) == 4)) has value True; not ((2*len(b)) == 8) has value False.

The list **sort method** lexicographically orders items.

['b', 'a', 'c'].sort() is ['a', 'b', 'c'].

The **startswith** and **endswith** methods return the values that their names imply.

"spam".startswith("sp") has value True.
"spam".endswith('m') has value True.

String methods that return Boolean values: isdigit, isalpha, isalnum, islower, isupper, isspace

"hi!".isalpha() has value False.
"ne1".isalnum() has value True.

The **in operator** can be used to simplify complex conditions.

(s == 'p') or (s == 'i') or (s == 'e') can be replaced with (s in "pie").

3.2 Decision Structures

An **if statement** has the form

```
if condition1:
    indented block of statements
elif condition2:
    indented block of statements
else:
    indented block of statements
```

It executes the first block whose associated condition is true. The elif and else clauses are optional and there may be multiple elif clauses.

```
n = int(input("Enter an int: "))
if n <= 0:
    print(n, "is neg or zero")
elif n % 2 == 0:
    print(n, "is pos and even")
else:
    print(n, "is pos and odd")
```

[Run]

```
Enter an int: 5
5 is pos and odd
```

CHAPTER 3 KEY TERMS AND CONCEPTS	EXAMPLES

3.3 The *while* Loop

A **while loop** has the form

```
while condition:
    indented block of statements
```

The loop repeatedly executes the block as long as the condition is true.

```
n = 1
while n < 6:
    print(n, end=" ")
    n += 1
```
[Run]
```
1 2 3 4 5
```

A while loop might use a **counter variable** to keep track of the number of times a certain event has occurred, an **accumulator variable** to hold a total, and a **sentinel value** to indicate the end of a sequence of inputs.

```
print("Enter -1 to end input.")
# -1 is the sentinel value
counter = 0
accumulator = 0
s = "Enter a positive integer: "
n = int(input(s))
while n != -1:
    counter += 1
    accumulator += n
    n = int(input(s))
print(counter, "ints entered")
print("Sum:", accumulator)
```
[Run]
```
Enter -1 to end input.
Enter a positive integer: 3
Enter a positive integer: 4
Enter a positive integer: -1
2 ints entered
Sum: 7
```

If a **break statement** is encountered during a pass through a while loop, the loop is immediately exited.

Can replace lines 6–10 with
```
while True:
    n = int(input(s))
    if n == -1:
        break
    counter += 1
    accumulator += n
```

If a **continue statement** is encountered in the block of a while loop, execution jumps back to the closest enclosing while loop header.

```
n = 9
while(n <= 15):
    n += 1
# skip unlucky number
    if n == 13:
        continue
    print(n, end=" ")
```
[Run]
```
10 11 12 14 15 16
```

CHAPTER 3 KEY TERMS AND CONCEPTS	EXAMPLES
3.4 The *for* Loop	
The **range function** generates an arithmetic progression of numbers.	range(5) generates 0, 1, 2, 3, 4 range(1, 9, 2) generates 1, 3, 5, 7

A **for loop** repeats a block of statements as its loop variable iterates through a sequence. The sequence can be an arithmetic progression, the items of a list or tuple, the characters of a string, or the lines of a file object. The statements **break** and **continue** have the same effect in **for** loops as they do in **while** loops.	```python
	list1 = []
	for i in range(9, 0, -1):
	    list1.append(i)
	for item in list1:
	    print(item, end="")
	``
	[Run]
	
	`987654321`

A **flag** is a variable used to indicate whether a certain event has occurred or a certain situation exists.	See Example 10.
The **pass statement** is a do-nothing placeholder that is sometimes used where the syntax requires a statement.	See Example 11.

CHAPTER 3   PROGRAMMING PROJECTS

1. **Car Loan**   Write a program to analyze a car loan. See Fig. 3.79. The user should enter the amount of the loan, the annual percentage rate of interest, and the duration of the loan in months. After each piece of data is entered, the data should be checked to make sure it is reasonable. If bad data has been supplied, the user should be so advised. Otherwise, the monthly payment and the total amount of interest paid should be displayed. The formula for the monthly payment is

$$\text{monthly payment} = \frac{p \cdot r}{1 - (1 + r)^{-n}},$$

where p is the amount of the loan, r is the monthly interest rate (annual rate divided by 12) given as a number between 0 (for 0%) and 100 (for 100%), and n is the duration of the loan in months. The formula for the total interest paid is

$$\text{total interest} = n \cdot [\text{monthly payment}] - p.$$

```
Enter the amount of the loan: 18000
Enter the interest rate: 5.25
Enter the duration in months: 60
Monthly payment: $341.75
Total interest paid: $2,505.00
```

FIGURE 3.79   Possible outcome of Programming Project 1.

```
Enter a: 1
Enter b: -11
Enter c: 28
Solutions: 7 and 4
```

FIGURE 3.80   Possible outcome of Programming Project 2.

2. **Quadratic Equation**   Write a program to determine the real roots of the quadratic equation $ax^2 + bx + c = 0$ (where $a \neq 0$) after requesting the values of a, b, and c. Before finding the roots, ensure that a is nonzero. [**Note:** The equation has 2, 1, or 0 solutions depending on whether the value of $b^2 - 4ac$ is positive, zero, or negative. In the first two cases, the solutions are given by the quadratic formula $(-b \pm (b^2 - 4ac)^{.5})/2a$.] See Fig. 3.80 on the previous page.

3. **Caffeine Absorption**   After caffeine is absorbed into the body, 13% is eliminated from the body each hour. Assume a person drinks an 8-oz cup of brewed coffee containing 130 mg of caffeine, and that the caffeine is absorbed immediately into the body. Write a program to calculate the following values. See Fig. 3.81.

   (a) The number of hours required until less than 65 mg (one-half the original amount) remain in the body.

   (b) The amount of caffeine in the body 24 hours after the person drinks the coffee.

   (c) Suppose the person drinks a cup of coffee at 7 a.m. and then drinks a cup of coffee at the end of each hour until 7 a.m. the next day. How much caffeine will be in the body at the end of the 24 hours?

```
CAFFEINE VALUES
One cup: less than 65 mg. will remain after 5 hours.
One cup: 4.60 mg. will remain after 24 hours.
Hourly cups: 969.24 mg. will remain after 24 hours.
```

FIGURE 3.81   **Outcome of Programming Project 3.**

4. **Rule of 72**   This rule is used to approximate the time required for prices to double due to inflation. If the inflation rate is $r\%$, then the Rule of 72 estimates that prices will double in $72/r$ years. For instance, at an inflation rate of 6%, prices double in about 72/6 or 12 years. Write a program to test the accuracy of this rule. For each interest rate from 1% to 20%, the program should display the rounded value of $72/r$ and the actual number of years required for prices to double at an $r\%$ inflation rate. (Assume prices increase at the end of each year.) Fig. 3.82 shows the first five sets of values.

Interest Rate	Rule of 72 Doubling Time (in years)	Actual Doubling Time (in years)
1%	72	70
2%	36	36
3%	24	24
4%	18	18
5%	14	15

FIGURE 3.82   **Partial Outcome of Programming Project 4.**

5. **Individual Retirement Accounts**   Money earned in an ordinary savings account is subject to federal, state, and local income taxes. However, a special type of retirement savings account, called a **traditional individual retirement account** (traditional IRA), allows these taxes to be deferred until after retirement. IRAs are highly touted by financial planners. The purpose of this programming project is to show the value of starting an IRA early. Earl and Larry each begin full-time jobs in January 2015 and

plan to retire in January 2063 after working for 48 years. Assume that any money they deposit into IRAs earns 4% interest compounded annually. Earl opens a traditional IRA account immediately and deposits $5,000 into his account at the end of each year for fifteen years. After that he plans to make no further deposits and just let the money earn interest. Larry plans to wait fifteen years before opening his traditional IRA and then deposit $5,000 into the account at the end of each year until he retires. Write a program that calculates the amount of money each person has deposited into his account and the amount of money in each account upon retirement. See Fig. 3.83.

```
                    AMOUNTS DEPOSITED
Earl: $75,000.00              Larry: $165,000.00
          AMOUNTS IN IRA UPON RETIREMENT
Earl: $365,268.39             Larry: $331,047.64
```

FIGURE 3.83   Outcome of Programming Project 5.

6. **Soundex System**   Soundex is a system that encodes a word into a letter followed by three numbers that roughly describe how the word sounds. Similar sounding words have the same four-character codes. For instance, the words Carrot and Caret are both coded as C123. A slight variation of the Soundex coding algorithm is as follows:

1. Retain the first letter.

2. For the remaining letters, delete all occurrences of a, e, i, o, u, h, y, and w.

3. Assign numbers to the other letters that remain so that

   (a) b, f, p, and v become 1
   (b) c, g, j, k, q, s, x, and z become 2
   (c) d and t both become 3
   (d) l (i.e., el) becomes 4
   (e) m and n become 5
   (f) r becomes 6

4. If two or more letters that have been replaced by the same number were next to each other in the original full word, keep only the first of them.

5. Keep only the first four characters of what you have left. If you have fewer than four, then add zeros on the end to make the string have length four.

Write a program that carries out the algorithm. See Fig. 3.84.

```
Enter a word to code: Robert
The coded word is R163.
```

FIGURE 3.84   Possible outcome of Programming Project 6.

7. **Error Detection**   Suppose you type a 14-digit credit card number into a Web site, but mistype one of the digits or inadvertently interchange two adjacent digits. The Web site will perform a validation check that always detects the first type of error and nearly always detects the second type of error. The validation check is as follows:

1. Starting with the leftmost digit, double it and then double every other digit after it. However, if any of the doubled digits is a two-digit number, subtract 9 from it. Then sum these new digits. For instance, if the credit card number is 58667936100244, then the digits considered are 5, 6, 7, 3, 1, 0, 4, their new replacements are 1, 3, 5, 6, 2, 0, 8, and the sum of the replacements is 25.

2. Sum together the remaining seven digits from the credit card number. That is, the digits in the odd-numbered positions. With the credit card number above, we obtain $8 + 6 + 9 + 6 + 0 + 2 + 4 = 35$.

3. Add together the two sums. If the result is a multiple of 10, then accept the credit card number. Otherwise, reject it. We accept the credit card number above since $25 + 35 = 60$, a multiple of 10.

Write a program that performs data validation on a credit card number. See Fig. 3.85.

```
Enter a credit card number: 58667936100244
The number is valid.
```

FIGURE 3.85   Possible outcome of Programming Project 7.

8. Palindrome   A *palindrome* is a word or phrase that reads the same forward and backward, character for character, disregarding punctuation, case, and spaces. Some examples are "racecar", "Madam, I'm Adam", and "Was it a cat I saw?". Write a program that asks the user to input a word or phrase and then determines if it is a palindrome. See Fig. 3.86. **Note:** Remove all spaces and punctuation before analyzing the word or phrase.

```
Enter a word or phrase: A man, a plan, a canal: Panama.
A MAN, A PLAN, A CANAL: PANAMA. is a palindrome.
```

FIGURE 3.86   Possible outcome of Programming Project 8.

4

Functions

4.1 Functions, Part 1

Functions are used to break complex problems into small problems to be solved one at a time. Functions allow us to write and read a program in such a way that we first focus on the tasks and later on how to accomplish each task. They also eliminate repetitive code and can be reused in other programs.

There are two types of functions—those that are designed to return values and those that execute lines of code without the intent to return a value. The second type of function often displays output with **print** statements or creates a file. We will begin by discussing functions designed to return a value.

■ Built-In Functions

Python has many built-in functions. In one respect, functions are like miniature programs. They receive input, they process the input, and they produce output. Some built-in functions we encountered earlier are listed in Table 4.1.

TABLE 4.1 Some Python built-in functions.

Function	Example	Input	Output
int	int(2.6) is 2	number	number
chr	chr(65) is 'A'	number	string
ord	ord('A') is 65	string	number
round	round(2.34, 1) is 2.3	number, number	number

The output for each of the four functions in the table above is a single value. A function is said to **return** its output. For instance, in the first example of Table 4.1, we say that the **int** function returns the value 2. The items inside the parentheses are called **arguments**. The first three functions in Table 4.1 have one argument and the fourth function has two arguments. Arguments can be literals (as in Table 4.1), variables, or any other type of expression. The following lines of code illustrate the use of literals, variables, and expressions as arguments for the **int** function. The third line of code is said to **call** (or, **invoke**) the **int** function and to **pass** the value of *num1* to the function.

```
num = int(3.7)          # literal as an argument

num1 = 2.6
num2 = int(num1)        # variable as an argument

num1 = 1.3
num2 = int(2 * num1)    # expression as an argument
```

■ User-Defined Functions

VideoNote

User-
Defined
Functions

In addition to using built-in functions, we can define functions of our own (called **user-defined functions**) that return values. Such functions are commonly defined by statements of the form

```
def functionName(par1, par2, ...):
    indented block of statements
    return expression
```

where *par1*, *par2* are variables (called **parameters**) and the expression evaluates to a literal of any type. (**Note:** *def* is an abbreviation of *define*.) As is the case with the control-flow statements discussed in Chapter 3, the function header must end with a colon, and each statement in the block below the header (including the **return** statement) must be indented by the same number of spaces (usually four spaces). The indentation delimits the body of the function definition. The IDLE editor helps with the indentation. Often there is more than one **return** statement. If so, the function terminates as soon as the first **return** statement is executed. The **return** statement(s) can appear anywhere in the block.

There are three ways to pass arguments to parameters: *pass by position*, *pass by keyword*, and *pass by default value*. In this section we consider only *passing by position*. The other two types of passing will be discussed in the next section. When arguments are passed by position, the arguments in the calling statement are matched to the parameters in the function header based on their order. That is, the 1st argument is passed to the 1st parameter, the 2nd argument is passed to the 2nd parameter, and so on. **Note:** When an argument is an expression, the expression is first evaluated and then its value is passed to a parameter.

Parameters and **return** statements are optional in function definitions. However, initially we will consider only functions having both.

Function names should describe the role performed by the function and must conform to the rules for naming variables. Initially, we will place all function definitions at the top of the editor and follow each function definition with a blank line.

■ Functions Having One Parameter

The following two functions have just one parameter. Figure 4.1 identifies the different parts of the first function's header.

```
def fahrenheitToCelsius(t):
    ## Convert Fahrenheit temperature to Celsius.
    convertedTemperature = (5 / 9) * (t - 32)
    return convertedTemperature

def firstName(fullName):
    ## Extract the first name from a full name.
    firstSpace = fullName.index(" ")
    givenName = fullName[:firstSpace]
    return givenName
```

keyword signifying
function definition   function name   parameter

```
def fahrenheitToCelsius(t):
```

FIGURE 4.1 Header of the **fahrenheitToCelsius** function.

Example 1   **Temperature Conversion** The following program uses the function *fahrenheitToCelsius*. The next to last line of the program, **celsiusTemp = fahrenheitToCelsius(fahrenheitTemp)**, calls (that is, executes) the function. The value of the argument *fahrenheitTemp* is assigned to the parameter *t* in the function header. (We say that the value of *fahrenheitTemp* is **passed** to the parameter *t*.) After the function does a calculation using the value of the parameter *t*, the **return** statement specifies that the calculated value is the output of the function *fahrenheitToCelsius*. That value is assigned to the variable *celsiusTemp*. The program then uses the value of the variable when displaying the output.

```
def fahrenheitToCelsius(t):
    ## Convert Fahrenheit temperature to Celsius.
    convertedTemperature = (5 / 9) * (t - 32)
    return convertedTemperature

fahrenheitTemp = eval(input("Enter a temperature in degrees Fahrenheit: "))
celsiusTemp = fahrenheitToCelsius(fahrenheitTemp)
print("Celsius equivalent:", celsiusTemp, "degrees")
```

[Run]

```
Enter a temperature in degrees Fahrenheit: 212
Celsius equivalent: 100.0 degrees
```

Note 1: Function definitions must have been processed by the Python interpreter before they can be called.

Note 2: The last two lines of the program above could have been replaced with the single line
print("Celsius equivalent:", fahrenheitToCelsius(fahrenheitTemp), "degrees")

   Example 2   Extract First Name The following program uses the function *firstName*. The last line of the program, **print("First name:", firstName(fullName))**, passes the value of the argument *fullName* to the parameter *fullName* in the function. Although the parameter in the function has the same name as the argument passed to it, they are not the same variable.

```
def firstName(fullName):
    firstSpace = fullName.index(" ")
    givenName = fullName[:firstSpace]
    return givenName

## Extract the first name from a full name.
fullName = input("Enter a person's full name: ")
print("First name:", firstName(fullName))
```

[Run]

```
Enter a person's full name: Franklin Delano Roosevelt
First name: Franklin
```

■ Passing a Value to a Function

If the argument in a function call is a variable, the *object* pointed to by the argument variable (not the argument variable itself) is passed to a parameter variable. Therefore, if the object is immutable and the function changes the value of the parameter variable, no change will occur in the object pointed to by the argument variable. Even if the two variables have the same name, they are treated as entirely different variables. Therefore, when the argument variable points to a numeric, string, or tuple object, there is no possibility what-so-ever that the value of the argument variable will be changed by a function call.

Example 3   Passing a Value to a Function The following program shows that even though the value of the parameter *num* in the function definition is changed, there is no change in the value of the argument *num* in the part of the program that called the function.

```
def triple(num):
    num = 3 * num
    return num

num = 2
print(triple(num))
print(num)
[Run]
6
2
```

Figure 4.2 shows the status of the memory locations as the program in Example 3 executes. The variable *num* inside the function is colored blue and the variable *num* outside the function is colored black. The memory location holding the object 6, comes into existence in part (c). It still exists in part (d), but is abandoned;—that is, no variable points to it.

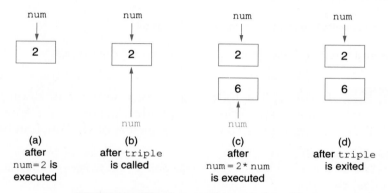

FIGURE 4.2   Passing a value to a function.

Some programmers feel that function definitions are easier to read if they never change the values of function parameters. They would write the function definition in Example 3 as

```
def triple(num):
    product = 3 * num
    return product
```

■ Functions Having Several Parameters

The following two functions have more than one parameter. In the function *futureValue*, one-letter names have been used for the parameters so that the mathematical formulas will look familiar and be easy to read. However, since the names are not descriptive, the meanings of these parameters are spelled out in comments. **Note:** The formula for the future value is $p\left(1 + \dfrac{r}{m}\right)^{mt}$.

```
def pay(wage, hours):
    ## Calculate weekly pay with time-and-a-half for overtime.
    if hours <= 40:
        amount = wage * hours
    else:
        amount = (wage * 40) + ((1.5) * wage * (hours - 40))
    return amount
```

```
def futureValue(p, r, m, t):
    ## Find the future value of a savings account deposit.
    # p   principal, the amount deposited
    # r   annual rate of interest in decimal form
    # m   number of times interest is compounded per year
    # t   number of years
    i = r / m    # interest rate per period
    n = m * t    # total number of times interest is compounded
    amount = p * ((1 + i) ** n)
    return amount
```

Although Python allows functions to receive a varying number of arguments, initially we will only consider functions that must receive a fixed number of arguments. When calling a function and passing arguments by position, there must be the same number of arguments as parameters. Also, the data types of the arguments' values must be compatible with (and in the same order) as the data types expected by the parameters. For instance, in a statement of the form

```
numVar = futureValue(arg1, arg2, arg3, arg4)
```

the arguments must all have values that are numeric data types.

Example 4 Earnings The following program uses the function *pay*. Here the arguments have different names than the corresponding parameters. Figure 4.3 shows how the values of the arguments are passed to the parameters of the function by position.

```
def pay(wage, hours):
    ## Calculate weekly pay with time-and-a-half for overtime.
    if hours <= 40:
        amount = wage * hours
    else:
        amount = (wage * 40) + ((1.5) * wage * (hours - 40))
    return amount

## Calculate a person's weekly pay.
hourlyWage = eval(input("Enter the hourly wage: "))
hoursworked = eval(input("Enter the number of hours worked: "))
earnings = pay(hourlyWage, hoursWorked)
print("Earnings: ${0:,.2f}".format(earnings))
```

[Run]

```
Enter the hourly wage: 24.50
Enter the number of hours worked: 45
Earnings: $1,163.75
```

FIGURE 4.3 **Passing arguments to a function.**

Example 5   Future Value of a Bank Deposit The following program uses the function *futureValue*. The function computes the balance in a savings account given the amount deposited (*p*), the annual rate of interest (*r*), the number of times interest is compounded per year (*m*), and the number of years that interest accrues (*t*).

```
def futureValue(p, r, m, t):
    # p  principal, the amount deposited
    # r  annual rate of interest in decimal form
    # m  number of times interest is compounded per year
    # t  number of years
    i = r / m   # interest rate per period
    n = m * t   # total number of times interest is compounded
    amount =  p * ((1 + i) ** n)
    return amount

## Find the future value for a saving account deposit.
p = eval(input("Enter amount deposited: "))
r = eval(input("Enter annual rate of interest in decimal form: "))
m = eval(input("Enter number of times interest is compounded per year: "))
t = int(input("Enter number of years: "))
balance = futureValue(p, r, m, t)
print("Balance after", t, "years: ${0:,.2f}".format(balance))
```

[Run]

```
Enter amount deposited: 1000
Enter annual rate of interest in decimal form: .04
Enter number of times interest is compounded per year: 4
Enter number of years: 5
Balance after 5 years: $1,220.19
```

■ Boolean- and List-Valued Functions

So far, the values returned by functions have been numbers or strings. However, a function can return any type of value. The following two programs use a function that returns a Boolean value and a function that returns a list.

Example 6   Vowel Words A **vowel word** is a word that contains every vowel. Some examples of vowel words are *sequoia*, *facetious*, and *dialogue*. The following program uses a Boolean-valued function to determine whether a word input by the user is a vowel word. The function *isVowelWord* examines the word for vowels one at a time and terminates when a vowel is found to be missing or after all vowels have been considered.

```
def isVowelWord(word):
    word = word.upper()
    vowels = ('A', 'E', 'I', 'O', 'U')
    for vowel in vowels:
        if vowel not in word:
            return False
    return True
```

```
## Determine if a word contains every vowel.
word = input("Enter a word: ")
if isVowelWord(word):
    print(word, "contains every vowel.")
else:
    print(word, "does not contain every vowel.")
```

[Run]

```
Enter a word: Education
Education contains every vowel.
```

Example 7 Included Vowels The following program displays the vowels contained in a word input by the user. The program uses a list-valued function.

```
def occurringVowels(word):
    word = word.upper()
    vowels = ('A', 'E', 'I', 'O', 'U')
    includedVowels = []
    for vowel in vowels:
        if (vowel in word) and (vowel not in includedVowels):
            includedVowels.append(vowel)
    return includedVowels

## Display the vowels appearing in a word.
word = input("Enter a word: ")
listOfVowels = occurringVowels(word)
print("The following vowels occur in the word: ", end="")
stringOfVowels = " ".join(listOfVowels)
print(stringOfVowels)
```

[Run]

```
Enter a word: important
The following vowels occur in the word: A I O
```

■ Functions That Do Not Return Values

Functions that do not return values look like the functions discussed above with the exception that they do not contain any return statements. They may or may not have parameters and are called by placing their names (along with their arguments) as a statement on a single line.

Example 8 Old McDonald's Farm The following program displays three verses of a well-known children's song. In this case, the function prevents having to write repetitive code.

```
def oldMcDonald(animal, sound):
    print("Old McDonald had a farm. Eyi eyi oh.")
    print("And on his farm he had a", animal + ".", "Eyi eyi oh.")
```

```
    print("With a", sound, sound, "here, and a", sound, sound, "there.")
    print("Here a", sound + ",", "there a", sound + ",",
          "everywhere a", sound, sound + ".")
    print("Old McDonald had a farm. Eyi eyi oh.")

## Old McDonald Had a Farm
oldMcDonald("lamb", "baa")
print()
oldMcDonald("duck", "quack")
print()
oldMcDonald("cow", "moo")
```

[Run]

```
Old McDonald had a farm. Eyi eyi oh.
And on his farm he had a lamb. Eyi eyi oh.
With a baa baa here, and a baa baa there.
Here a baa, there a baa, everywhere a baa baa.
Old McDonald had a farm. Eyi eyi oh.

Old McDonald had a farm. Eyi eyi oh.
And on his farm he had a duck. Eyi eyi oh.
With a quack quack here, and a quack quack there.
Here a quack, there a quack, everywhere a quack quack.
Old McDonald had a farm. Eyi eyi oh.

Old McDonald had a farm. Eyi eyi oh.
And on his farm he had a cow. Eyi eyi oh.
With a moo moo here, and a moo moo there.
Here a moo, there a moo, everywhere a moo moo.
Old McDonald had a farm. Eyi eyi oh.
```

■ Functions Without Parameters

In the following rewrite of the program from Example 2, the leading function (named *main*) has no parameters and no **return** statement.

```
def main():
    ## Extract the first name from a full name.
    fullName = input("Enter a person's full name: ")
    print("First name:", firstName(fullName))

def firstName(fullName):
    firstSpace = fullName.index(" ")
    givenName = fullName[:firstSpace]
    return givenName

main()
```

In this format, the program consists of a sequence of two functions beginning with the function directing the program and appropriately named *main*. The final line of the program calls the function *main* and thereby initiates the tasks to be performed. From now on, most of our programs will be written in this style.

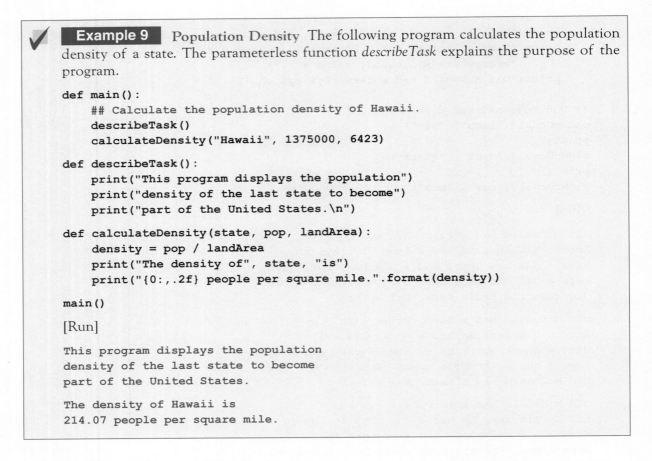

Example 9   Population Density The following program calculates the population density of a state. The parameterless function *describeTask* explains the purpose of the program.

```python
def main():
    ## Calculate the population density of Hawaii.
    describeTask()
    calculateDensity("Hawaii", 1375000, 6423)

def describeTask():
    print("This program displays the population")
    print("density of the last state to become")
    print("part of the United States.\n")

def calculateDensity(state, pop, landArea):
    density = pop / landArea
    print("The density of", state, "is")
    print("{0:,.2f} people per square mile.".format(density))

main()
```

[Run]

```
This program displays the population
density of the last state to become
part of the United States.

The density of Hawaii is
214.07 people per square mile.
```

VideoNote
Scope of
Variables

■ Scope of Variables

A variable created inside a function can only be accessed by statements inside that function, and ceases to exist when the function is exited. (The variable is recreated each time the function is called.) The variable is said to be **local** to the function or to have **local scope**. The same is true for the function's parameters.

Therefore, if variables created in two different functions have the same name, they have no relationship to each other; they are treated as completely different variables. The same is true for the parameters of functions.

Example 10   Scope of Variables The following program illustrates the fact that variables are local to the function in which they reside. The variable *x* in the function *main* and the variable *x* in the function *trivial* are different variables. Python deals with them as if their names were something like *main_x* and *trivial_x*.

```python
def main():
    ## Demonstrate the scope of variables.
    x = 2
    print(str(x) + ": function main")
    trivial()
    print(str(x) + ": function main")

def trivial():
    x = 3
    print(str(x) + ": function trivial")
```

```
main()
```

[Run]

```
2: function main
3: function trivial
2: function main
```

 Example 11   Local Variables The following program generates a *NameError* Traceback error message. The variable *x* created in the function *main* is not recognized by the function *trivial*.

```
def main():
    ## Demonstrate the scope of local variables.
    x = 5
    trivial()

def trivial():
    print(x)

main()
```

In general, the **scope** of a variable is the portion of the program that can refer to it. Python provides a way to make a variable recognized everywhere in a program. Such a variable is called a **global variable**. One way to make a variable global is to place the assignment statement that creates it at the top of the program.

Any function can read the value of a global variable—however, the value cannot be altered inside a function unless the altering statement is preceded by a statement of the form

```
global globalVariableName
```

The global statement affects only the statements following it in its function block. It does not allow the global variable to be altered inside other functions.

Example 12   Global Variable The following program contains a global variable.

```
x = 0    # Declare a global variable.

def main():
    ## Demonstrate the scope of a global variable.
    print(str(x) + ": function main")
    trivial()
    print(str(x) + ": function main")

def trivial():
    global x
    x += 7
    print(str(x) + ": function trivial")

main()
```

[Run]

```
0: function main
7: function trivial
7: function main
```

Many programmers limit the use of global variables; especially in large programs. They can make a program difficult to follow and can easily cause errors. However, there is one type of global variable, called a *named constant* that is quite useful and is frequently used.

■ Named Constants

A program sometimes employs a special constant that will be used several times in the program. Such a constant might refer to an interest rate or a minimum age. One convention programmers use is to create a global variable whose name is written in uppercase letters with words separated by underscore characters, and assign the constant to it. Some examples are as follows:

```
INTEREST_RATE = 0.04
MINIMUM_VOTING_AGE = 18
BOOK_TITLE = "Programming with Python"
```

The special naming convention reminds the programmer that no reassignments to the variable should be made during the execution of the program. Since Python allows reassignments to any variable, the programmer is responsible for not changing the value of the variable. Such constants are called **named constants**.

Some examples of statements using named constants are

```
interestEarned = INTEREST_RATE * amountDeposited

if (age >= MINIMUM_VOTING_AGE):
    print("You are eligible to vote.")

print("The title of the book is", BOOK_TITLE + ".")
```

Although the value of a named constant such as *INTEREST_RATE* will not change during the execution of a program, the value may need to be changed at a later time. The programmer can adjust to this change by altering just one line of code at the top of the program instead of searching through the entire program for each occurrence of the old interest rate.

■ Library Modules

Python facilitates the reuse of functions with a file called a **library module**. A library module is a file with the extension .py containing functions and variables that can be used (we say *imported*) by any program. The library module can be created in IDLE or any text editor and looks like an ordinary Python program. For instance, we might create a file containing the two functions *pay* and *futureValue*, and name the file **finance.py**. Then, assuming that **finance.py** is located in the same folder as Examples 4 and 5, Example 4 could be rewritten as

```
import finance

## Calculate a person's weekly pay.
hourlyWage = eval(input("Enter the hourly wage: "))
hoursworked = eval(input("Enter the number of hours worked: "))
earnings = finance.pay(hourlyWage, hoursWorked)
print("Earnings: ${0:,.2f}".format(earnings))
```

and Example 5 could be rewritten as

```
import finance

## Find the future value for a saving account deposit.
p = eval(input("Enter amount deposited: "))
```

```
r = eval(input("Enter annual rate of interest in decimal form: "))
m = eval(input("Enter number of times interest is compounded per year: "))
t = int(input("Enter number of years: "))
balance = finance.futureValue(p, r, m, t)
print("Balance after", t, "years: ${0:,.2f}".format(balance))
```

The only changes in the two programs were the replacement of the functions with the import statement and the replacement of **pay** and **futureValue** in the print statements with **finance.pay** and **finance.futureValue**.

Python comes with a collection of library modules referred to as the **standard library**. Table 4.2 shows the modules from the standard library that will be used in later chapters.

TABLE 4.2　**Several modules from the standard library.**

Module	Some Tasks Performed by Its Functions
os	delete and rename files
os.path	determine whether a file exists in a specified folder. This module is a submodule of os
pickle	store objects (such as dictionaries, lists, and sets) in files and retrieve them from files
random	randomly select numbers and subsets
tkinter	enable programs to have a graphical user interface
turtle	enable turtle graphics

To gain access to the functions and variables of a library module, place a statement of the form

import *moduleName*

at the beginning of the program. Then, any function from the module can be used in the program by prepending the function name with the module name followed by a period.

A variation of the import statement is

from *moduleName* import *

After such a statement has been executed, any function from the module can be used directly without having to prepend it with the module name and a period. This variation is most often employed when a program uses many functions from the module. For instance, in the program appearing on the previous page, if the statement **import finance** were replaced with **from finance import ***, then the *balance* assignment statement could have been written **balance = futureValue(p, r, m, t)**. Programmers prefer the other import statement when several library modules are being used since it gives explicit information about where a particular function comes from.

■ Comments

1. Functions name code segments in much the way that variables name numbers, strings, and lists. Functions allow programmers to focus on the main flow of a complex task and defer the details of implementation. Modern programs use them liberally. This method of program construction is known as **modular** or **top-down** design. As a rule, a function should perform only one task, or several closely related tasks, and should be kept relatively small.

2. Functions are used to break complex problems into small problems, to eliminate repetitive code, and to make a program easier to read by separating it into logical units. Also, functions can be reused in other programs.

3. IDLE displays the names of user-defined functions in the color blue.

4. The parameters in a function definition are also called *formal parameters* and the arguments in a function call are also called *actual parameters*.

5. Some programmers prefer that functions have at most one **return** statement. They feel this makes functions easier to understand and debug. Multiple **return** statements can be avoided by assigning the different function values to a variable and then returning the value of the variable at the end of the function block. For instance, the function on the left below can be replaced with the function on the right.

```
def parityOfNumber(num):          def parityOfNumber(num):
    if num % 2:                       if num % 2:
        return "odd"                      parity = "odd"
    else:                             else:
        return "even"                     parity = "even"
                                      return parity
```

6. Python has an object called None that is used to denote a lack of value, and has no methods. The None object is returned by functions that have no **return** statement as illustrated by the following program.

```
def f():
    pass

print(f())
```

[Run]

None

7. As mentioned earlier, from now on most programs in this book will be written as a sequence of functions. The first function will be named *main* and sometimes will be preceded by **import** statements and global variables. All programs will end with the statement **main()** to call the program's *main* function.

8. The function *main* should not perform lengthy computations. Ideally, *main* should be a supervisory function calling other functions according to the application's logic.

9. The standard library module **math** contains trigonometric, exponential, and logarithmic functions, and is regularly used in mathematics, science, and engineering applications.

Practice Problems 4.1

1. Can the third line of Example 6 be replaced with **vowels = "AEIOU"**?

2. The program on the left below displays the number 7, but the program on the right produces an error message. What is wrong with the program on the right?

```
x = 7                             x = 7

def main():                       def main():
    print(x)                          x += 1
                                      print(x)
main()
                                  main()
```

3. Simplify the following function.

```python
def f(x):
    if x > 0:
        return True
    else:
        return False
```

In Exercises 1 through 24, give the output of the program.

1.
```python
def main():
    print(uc('h'))
    print(uc('w'))

def uc(letter):
    if letter == 'h':
        return 'H'
    else:
        return letter

main()
```

2.
```python
def main():
    acres = 5  # number of acres in a parking lot
    print("You can park around", cars(acres), "cars on a five-acre lot.")

def cars(n):
    numberOfCars = 100 * n
    return numberOfCars

main()
```

3.
```python
def main():
    t = float(input("Enter the time in which you want to double
    your money: "))
    print("To double your money in",t,"years, ", end="")
    print("get an interest rate of about {0:.2f}
    %.".format(doublingRate(t)))

def doublingRate(x):
  ## Estimate interest rate required for money
  ## to double in a time of t years.
  rate = 72 / x
  return rate

main()
```
(Assume the response is 2.)

4.
```python
def main():
    num = 27
    if isEven(num):
        print(num, "is an even number.")
    else:
        print(num, "is an odd number.")
```

```
    def isEven(n):
        if n // 2 == 0:
            return True
        else:
            return False

main()
```

5.
```
def main():
    taxableIncome = 16000
    print("Your income tax is ${0:,.2f}".format(stateTax(taxableIncome)))

def stateTax(income):
    ## Calculate state tax for a single resident of Kansas
    if income <= 15000:
        return .03 * income
    else:
        return 450 + (.049 * (income - 15000))

main()
```

6.
```
def main():
    massKg = 50
    # since one stone is equal to 14 pounds
    massStone(massKg * 2.2 / 14 )

def massStone(num):
    print("You weigh", num, "stone.")

main()
```

7.
```
def main():
    question()
    answer()

def answer():
    print("Because they were invented in the northern")
    print("hemisphere where sundials go clockwise.")

def question():
    print("Why do clocks run clockwise?")
    print()

main()
```

8.
```
def main():
    ## Beginning of Tale of Two Cities
    times("best")
    times("worst")

def times(word):
    ## Display sentence
    print("It was the", word, "of times.")

main()
```

9.
```
import datetime as dt
def main():
    log_time("Message 1")
    log_time("Message 2", dt.datetime.now())
def log_time(message, time=dt.datetime.now()):
```

```
        print("{0}: {1}".format(message, time.isoformat()))
    main()
```

10.
```
def main():
    ## The fates of Henry the Eighth's six wives
    commonFates()
    print("died")
    commonFates()
    print("survived")

def commonFates():
    ## The most common fates
    print("divorced")
    print("beheaded")

main()
```

11.
```
def main():
    winner = "Kailash Satyarthi"
    field = "Peace"
    nobelPrizeWinner(winner,field)
    winner = "Patrick Modiano"
    field = "Literature"
    nobelPrizeWinner(winner,field)

def nobelPrizeWinner(winner,field):
    print(winner,"won the Nobel", field, "prize.")
main()
```

12.
```
def main():
    listPlayers = getListOfPlayers()
    num = int(input("Enter a number from 1 through 50: "))
    print("The world's number ",num,"football player is ",listPlayers[num
    - 1].split()[0], "and he has scored ",listPlayers[num - 1].split()[1],
    "goals.")

def getListOfPlayers():
  # The file FootballPlayers.txt contains the names of
  # the top 50 footballers and the goals they've scored.
    infile = open("FootballPlayers.txt", 'r')
    listPlayers = [line.rstrip() for line in infile]
    infile.close()
    return listPlayers
main()
```
(Assume the response is 1.)

13.
```
x = 7

def main():
    x = 5
    f()
    print(x)

def f():
    print(x)

main()
```

14.
```
x = 7

def main():
    global x
    x = 5
    f()
    print(x)

def f():
    print(x)

main()
```

15.
```python
name = "Fred"

def main():
    global name
    otherName = getName()
    name += otherName
    print(name)

def getName():
    name = "rick"
    return name

main()
```

16.
```python
word = "spam"

def main():
    f()
    print(word)

def f():
    global word
    word = word.upper()

main()
```

17.
```python
PLANE_RIDE_COST = 200

def main():
    noOfDays = 3
    cost = PLANE_RIDE_COST + noOfDays * 20
    print("Total cost: ${0:,.2f}".format(cost))
main()
```

18.
```python
ESTATE_TAX_EXEMPTION = 1000000
TAX_RATE = .45

def main():
    valueOfEstate = 3000000
    tax = TAX_RATE * (valueOfEstate - ESTATE_TAX_EXEMPTION)
    print("You owe ${0:,.2f} in estate taxes.".format(tax))

main()
```

19.
```python
def main():
    num = 5
    triple(num)
    print(num)

def triple(num):
    num = 3 * num

main()
```

20.
```python
def main():
    word = "garb"
    reverseWord(word)
    print(word)

def reverseWord(word):
    list1 = list(word)
    list1.reverse()
    word = "".join(list1)
    print(word)

main()
```

21.
```python
def main():
    # The file Independence.txt contains seven lines.
    # Each line contains one of the following words:
    # When, in, the, course, of, human, events
    independenceList = obtainList("Independence.txt")
    print(" ".join(independenceList))

def obtainList(file):
    infile = open(file, 'r')
    independenceList = [line.rstrip() for line in infile]
    infile.close()
    return independenceList

main()
```

22.
```python
def main():
    grades = [80, 75, 90, 100]
    grades = dropLowest(grades)
    average = sum(grades) / len(grades)
    print(round(average))

def dropLowest(grades):
    lowestGrade = min(grades)
    grades.remove(lowestGrade)
    return grades

main()
```

23.
```python
def main():
    ## Determine semester grade.
    grade = getAverageGrade()
    typeOfStudent = getTypeOfStudent()
    if typeOfStudent == "PASS/FAIL":
        semesterGrade = calculatePFgrade(grade)
    else:
        semesterGrade = calculateLetterGrade(grade)
    print("Semester grade:", semesterGrade)

def getAverageGrade():
    midtermGrade = int(input("Enter grade on midterm exam: "))
    finalExamGrade = int(input("Enter grade on final exam: "))
    return round((midtermGrade + finalExamGrade) / 2)

def getTypeOfStudent():
    prompt = "Enter type of student (Pass/Fail) or (Letter Grade): "
    typeOfStudent = input(prompt)
    return typeOfStudent.upper()

def calculatePFgrade(grade):
    if grade >= 60:
        return "Pass"
    else:
        return "Fail"

def calculateLetterGrade(grade):
    if grade >= 90:
        return "A"
    elif grade >= 80:
        return "B"
    elif grade >= 70:
        return "C"
    elif grade >= 60:
        return "D"
    else:
        return "F"

main()
```

(Assume each of the following responses: "85, 94, Letter Grade"; "50, 62, Pass/Fail"; "56, 67, Letter Grade".)

24.
```
def main():
    ## Analyze a quotation.
    quotation = input("Enter a quotation: ")
    print("\nMENU")
    print("  1. Count number of vowels in the quotation.")
    print("  2. Count number of uppercase letters in the quotation.")
    choice = int(input("Select 1 or 2 from menu: "))
    if choice == 1:
        print("Number of vowels:", calculateNumberOfVowels(quotation))
    else:
        print("Number of uppercase letters:",
            calculateNumberOfCaps(quotation))

def calculateNumberOfVowels(quotation):
    numberOfVowels = 0
    for ch in quotation:
        if ch.upper() in "AEIOU":
            numberOfVowels += 1
    return numberOfVowels

def calculateNumberOfCaps(quotation):
    numberOfCaps = 0
    for ch in quotation:
        if 'A' <= ch <= 'Z':
            numberOfCaps += 1
    return numberOfCaps

main()
```
(Assume the quotation is "You miss 100% of the shots you never take.—Wayne Gretsky" and execute with each choice from the menu.)

25. Max Function   Suppose the max function for a list didn't exist. Define a function that returns the maximum value in a list of numbers.

26. Count Function   Suppose the count function for a string didn't exist. Define a function that returns the number of non-overlapping occurrences of a substring in a string.

27. Qwerty Word   The keyboard in use on nearly all computers is known as the Qwerty keyboard, since the letters in the top letter line read QWERTYUIOP. A word is called a Qwerty word if all its letters appear on the top letter line of the keyboard. Some examples are *typewriter*, *repertoire*, and *treetop*. Write a program that requests a word as input and then determines whether or not it is a Qwerty word. Use a Boolean-valued function named *isQwerty* that evaluates the word. See Fig. 4.4.

```
Enter a word: TRY
TRY is a Qwerty word.
```

```
Enter a positive integer: 5
5! is 120
```

FIGURE 4.4   Possible outcome of Exercise 27.   **FIGURE 4.5**   Possible outcome of Exercise 28.

28. Factorial   The factorial of a positive integer n (written $n!$) is the product $1 \cdot 2 \cdot 3 \ldots \cdot n$. Write a program that asks the user to input a positive integer and then calculates and displays the factorial of the number. The program should call a function named *getN* that gets the input and guarantees that the input is a positive integer. Also, the factorial of the number input should be calculated with a function named *fact*. See Fig. 4.5.

29. **Salary Options** You are offered two salary options for 10 days of work. Option 1: $100 per day. Option 2: $1 the first day, $2 the second day, $4 the third day, and so on, with the amount doubling each day. Determine which option pays better. Use functions named *option1* and *option2* to calculate the amounts of money earned under the two options. See Fig. 4.6.

```
Option 1 pays $1,000.00
Option 2 pays $1,023.00
Option 2 is better.
```

FIGURE 4.6 **Possible outcome of Exercise 29.**

```
Enter first name: John
Enter last name: Doe
Enter current salary: 48000
New salary for John Doe: $50,160.00
```

FIGURE 4.7 **Possible outcome of Exercise 30.**

30. **Pay Raise** Write a pay-raise program that requests a person's first name, last name, and current annual salary, and then displays the person's salary for next year. People earning less than $40,000 will receive a 5% raise, and those earning $40,000 or more will receive a raise of $2,000 plus 2% of the amount over $40,000. Use functions for input and output, and a function to calculate the new salary. See Fig. 4.7.

31. **FICA Taxes** Rewrite Example 7 of Section 3.2 with **WAGE_BASE**, **SOCIAL_SECURITY_TAX_RATE**, and **MEDICARE_RATE** as named constants. The function *main* should call functions to process the input and to display the output.

32. **R Months** The file **Months.txt** has 12 lines with each line containing one of the months of the year.[1] Write a program that displays the months containing the letter *r*. The program should use a global variable *months* that is initialized as the empty list. The function *main* should call three functions, one to fill the list *months* with the contents of the text file, one to delete from the list *months* the months that do not contain the letter *r*, and one to display the names of the months remaining in the list. See Fig. 4.8.

```
The R months are:
January, February, March, April, September, October, November, December
```

FIGURE 4.8 **Outcome of Exercise 32.**

33. **Crayon Colors** The file **Colors.txt** contains the names (beginning with uppercase letters) of 123 crayon colors with one color per line. Write a program that requests a letter of the alphabet as input and then displays the colors beginning with that letter. The program should use a global variable *colors* that is initialized as an empty list. The function *main* should call three functions, one to request the initial letter, one to fill the list *colors* with the colors having the requested initial letter, and one to display the names of the colors in the list. See Fig. 4.9.

---

[1] The file **Months.txt** is located in the folder *Programs/Ch4* of the material downloaded from the Pearson website. All text files required for exercises in this chapter are located in that folder.

```
Enter a letter: D
   Dandelion
   Denim
   Desert Sand
```

FIGURE 4.9   **Possible outcome of Exercise 33.**

```
Enter your age: 65
Enter number of months of service: 448
Enter first of three highest salaries: 123456.78
Enter second of three highest salaries: 119876.55
Enter third of three highest salaries: 107546.45
Annual pension: $82,944.08
```

FIGURE 4.10   **Possible outcome of Exercise 34.**

34. Pensions   A person in the Civil Service Retirement System can retire at age 55 with at least 20 years of service. A simplified variation for the computation of the amount of their pension is as follows:

1. Calculate the average annual salary for the person's best three years; call it *ave*.

2. Calculate $\left(\dfrac{\text{number of months}}{12}\right)$ and call it *yrs*.

3. Calculate percentage rate: 1.5% for first five years, 1.75% for next five years, 2% for each additional year. Call it *perRate*.

4. Take the minimum of *perRate* and 80%; call it *p*.

5. The amount of the pension is *p* * *ave*.

Write a program that requests the input as shown in Fig. 4.10, and calculates the amount of the pension. The values of *ave* and *p* should be computed in functions.

Solutions to Practice Problems 4.1

1. Yes.

2. The statement **x += 1** changes the value of the global variable *x*. The values of global variables can be accessed in any function, but only can be changed if the altering statement is preceded with the statement **global x**.

3. ```
   def f(x):
       return (x > 0)
   ```

4.2   **Functions, Part 2**

■ Functions Calling Other Functions

A function can call another function. If so, when the called function terminates (that is, after a return statement or the last statement of the called function is executed), the control returns to the place in the calling function just after where the function call occurred.

> ✔ **Example 1**   Function Calls   In the following program, the function *firstPart* calls the function *secondPart*. After the statements in *secondPart* are executed, the execution continues with the remaining statements in the function *firstPart* before returning to the function *main*.
>
> ```
> def main():
>     ## Demonstrate functions calling other functions.
>     firstPart()
>     print(str(4) + ": from function main")
> ```
   ```

```
def firstPart():
    print(str(1) + ": from function firstPart")
    secondPart()
    print(str(3) + ": from function firstPart")

def secondPart():
    print(str(2) + ": from function secondPart")

main()
```

[Run]

```
1: from function firstPart
2: from function secondPart
3: from function firstPart
4: from function main
```

■ Functions Returning Multiple Values

Functions can return any type of object, not just a number, string, or Boolean value. For instance, a function can return a tuple.

Example 2   Savings Account   The *balanceAndInterest* function in the following program returns a tuple giving values associated with a deposit into a savings account.

```
INTEREST_RATE = .04     # annual rate of interest

def main():
    ## Calculate the balance and interest earned from a savings account.
    principal = eval(input("Enter the amount of the deposit: "))
    numberOfYears = eval(input("Enter the number of years: "))
    (bal, intEarned) = balanceAndInterest(principal, numberOfYears)
    print("Balance: ${0:,.2f}    Interest Earned: ${1:,.2f}".
          format(bal, intEarned))

def balanceAndInterest(prin, numYears):
    balance = prin * ((1 + INTEREST_RATE) ** numYears)
    interestEarned = balance - prin
    return (balance, interestEarned)

main()
```

[Run]

```
Enter the amount of the deposit: 10000
Enter the number of years: 10
Balance: $14,802.44   Interest Earned: $4,802.44
```

In Example 2, the return statement can be written

```
return balance, interestEarned
```

and the fifth line of the function *main* can be written

```
bal, intEarned = balanceAndInterest(principal, numberOfYears)
```

If so, the function *balanceAndInterest* appears to be returning two values. However, it is actually returning just one value—a single tuple containing two values.

By using functions that return multiple values, we can perform the three basic parts of a program (*input*, *processing*, and *output*) with three functions called from the *main* function.

✔ **Example 3** Savings Account The following variation of Example 2 has the input, processing, and output performed individually by three functions.

```
INTEREST_RATE = .04    # annual rate of interest

def main():
    ## Calculate the balance and interest earned from a savings account.
    (principal, numberOfYears) = getInput()
    bal, intEarned = balanceAndInterest(principal, numberOfYears)
    displayOutput(bal, intEarned)

def getInput():
    principal = eval(input("Enter the amount of the deposit: "))
    numberOfYears = eval(input("Enter the number of years: "))
    return (principal, numberOfYears)

def balanceAndInterest(prin, numYears):
    balance = prin * ((1 + INTEREST_RATE) ** numYears)
    interestEarned = balance - prin
    return (balance, interestEarned)

def displayOutput(bal, intEarned):
    print("Balance: ${0:,.2f}    Interest Earned: ${1:,.2f}".
            format(bal, intEarned))

main()
```

■ List Comprehension

When we want to apply a certain function to each item of a list, an ordinary for loop will do the job. However, a simpler way is to use **list comprehension**. If *list1* is a list, then the following statement creates a new list, *list2*, and places *f(item)* into the list for each *item* in *list1*, where *f* is either a Python built-in function or a user-defined function.

```
list2 = [f(x) for x in list1]
```

For instance, if `list1 = ['2', '5', '6', '7']`, then

```
[int(x) for x in list1]
```

will be the list

```
[2, 5, 6, 7].
```

That is, the int function will be applied to each item of *list1*.

If the function *g* is defined by

```
def g(x):
    return(int(x) ** 2)
```

then

```
[g(x) for x in list1]
```

will be the list

```
[4, 25, 36, 49].
```

The **for** clause in a list comprehension can optionally be followed by an if clause. For instance, with g and *list1* as above, then

```
[g(x) for x in list1 if int(x) % 2 == 1]
```

will be the filtered list

```
[25, 49].
```

That is, only the squares of the odd numbers will appear in the new list.

Note: There is nothing special about using x as the variable in the list comprehensions above or the use of a variable for the list name. For instance, we could have written the first list comprehension as

```
[int(num) for num in ['2', '5', '6', '7']].
```

List comprehension can be applied to objects other than lists, such as, strings, tuples, and arithmetic progressions generated by **range** functions. Some other examples of list comprehension are shown in Table 4.3.

TABLE 4.3 **Examples of list comprehension.**

List Comprehension	Result
`[ord(x) for x in "abc"]`	`[97, 98, 99]`
`[x ** .5 for x in (4, -1, 9) if x >= 0]`	`[2.0, 3.0]`
`[x ** 2 for x in range(3)]`	`[0, 1, 4]`

■ Default Values

Some (or all) of the parameters of a function can have **default values**—values that are assigned to them when no values are passed to them. That is, if the corresponding arguments are omitted when the function is called, the default values are assigned to the parameters. A typical format for a function definition using default values is

```
def functionName(par1, par2, par3=value3, par4=value4):
```

Then, a function call of the form functionName(*arg1*, *arg2*) will assign the value of *arg1* to *par1*, the value of *arg2* to *par2*, *value3* to *par3*, and *value4* to *arg4*. The assignment of values to par3 and par4 is optional. For instance, consider the function *total* defined by

```
def total(w, x, y=10, z=20):
    return (w ** x) + y + z
```

Table 4.4 shows the values of three function calls and how they will be calculated.

TABLE 4.4 **Three function calls.**

Function Call	Value	Calculated As
`total(2, 3)`	38	$2^3 + 10 + 20$
`total(2, 3, 4)`	32	$2^3 + 4 + 20$
`total(2, 3, 4, 5)`	17	$2^3 + 4 + 5$

Important note: In a function definition, the parameters without default values must precede the parameters with default values. For instance, a header such as

```
def func(par1, par2=value2, par3):
```

is not valid.

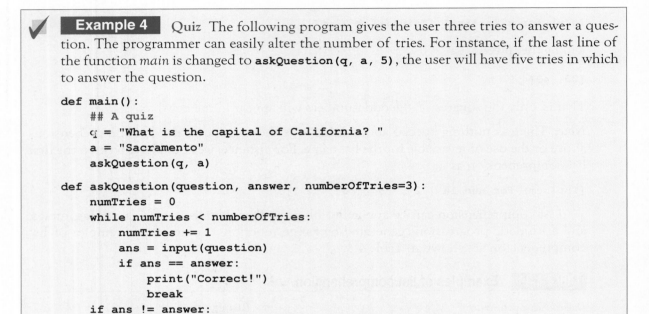

Example 4 Quiz The following program gives the user three tries to answer a question. The programmer can easily alter the number of tries. For instance, if the last line of the function *main* is changed to **askQuestion(q, a, 5)**, the user will have five tries in which to answer the question.

```
def main():
    ## A quiz
    q = "What is the capital of California? "
    a = "Sacramento"
    askQuestion(q, a)

def askQuestion(question, answer, numberOfTries=3):
    numTries = 0
    while numTries < numberOfTries:
        numTries += 1
        ans = input(question)
        if ans == answer:
            print("Correct!")
            break
    if ans != answer:
        print("You have used up your allotment of guesses.")
        print("The correct answer is", answer + '.')

main()
```

■ Passing by Parameter Name

Arguments can be passed to functions by using the names of the corresponding parameters instead of relying on position. This method of passing values to functions is called **keyword passing**. For instance, the first function call in Table 4.4 can be written

```
total(w=2, x=3)
```

or

```
total(x=3, w=2)
```

The second function call in Table 4.4 can be written several ways. Three possibilities are

```
total(y=4, x=3, w=2), total(2, y=4, x=3), and total(2, 3, y=4)
```

Note: Arguments passed by position must precede arguments passed by keyword. (Similarly for parameters.) For instance, the following function call is not valid.

```
total(w=2, 3, y=4)
```

 Example 5 Passing Values The following program shows several ways to pass values when calculating the balance in a savings account given the principal, number of years, and the annual rate of interest, with interest compounded annually. The formula used is

$$\text{balance} = \text{principal} \cdot (1 + \text{interest rate})^{\text{number of years}}.$$

```
def main():
    ## Demonstrate the passing of values.
    print("Balance:")
    print("${0:,.2f}".format(balance(1000, 5)))
    print("${0:,.2f}".format(balance(1000, 5, .04)))
    print("${0:,.2f}".format(balance(1000, intRate=.04, numYears=5)))
    print("${0:,.2f}".format(balance(numYears=5, prin=1000)))
    print()
    print("${0:,.2f}".format(balance(1000, 5, .03)))
    print("${0:,.2f}".format(balance(1000, intRate=.03, numYears=5)))
    print("${0:,.2f}".format(balance(intRate=.03, numYears=5, prin=1000)))
    print("${0:,.2f}".format(balance(numYears=5, intRate=.03, prin=1000)))

def balance(prin, numYears, intRate=.04):
    return prin * ((1 + intRate) ** numYears)

main()

[Run]

Balance:
$1,216.65
$1,216.65
$1,216.65
$1,216.65

$1,159.27
$1,159.27
$1,159.27
$1,159.27
```

Note: The program above shows that both positional passing and keyword passing can be used in the same function call.

■ Custom Sorting

We have used the **sort** method to place the items of a list into ascending order. However, functions can be used to order the items by any criteria we choose. For instance, starting with a list of strings, we can sort them by their length, by their last characters, by the number of vowels they contain, or by many other properties.

To create a custom sort, we use a function that takes each item of the list as input and returns the value of the property we want to sort on. For instance, if we wanted to sort a list of strings by the number of vowels in each string, we would define a function, call it *numberOfVowels*, that accepts a string as input and returns the number of vowels in the string. Then we would add the argument **key=numberOfVowels** to the **sort** method. The argument **reverse=True** can be added to sort in descending order.

> **Example 6** Sort Words The following program sorts a list of words using each of the three properties cited above.
>
> ```
> def main():
>     ## Custom sort a list of words.
>     list1 = ["democratic", "sequoia", "equals", "brrr", "break", "two"]
>     list1.sort(key=len)
>     print("Sorted by length in ascending order:")
> ```

```
        print(list1, '\n')
        list1.sort(key=lastCharacter)
        print("Sorted by last character in ascending order:")
        print(list1, '\n')
        list1.sort(key=numberOfVowels, reverse=True)
        print("Sorted by number of vowels in descending order:")
        print(list1)

def lastCharacter(word):
    return word[-1]

def numberOfVowels(word):
    vowels = ('a', 'e', 'i', 'o', 'u')
    total = 0
    for vowel in vowels:
        total += word.count(vowel)
    return total

main()

[Run]

Sorted by length in ascending order:
['two', 'brrr', 'break', 'equals', 'sequoia', 'democratic']

Sorted by last character in ascending order:
['sequoia', 'democratic', 'break', 'two', 'brrr', 'equals']

Sorted by number of vowels in descending order:
['sequoia', 'democratic', 'equals', 'break', 'two', 'brrr']
```

Suppose we wanted to display the words in *list1* above that contained the most and least number of vowels. We could sort the list using **key=numberOfVowels** and then obtain the first and last items in the custom-sorted list. However, the following extensions of the **max** and **min** functions accomplish the task more easily.

```
maxValue = max(list1, key=numberOfVowels)
minValue = min(list1, key=numberOfVowels)
```

VideoNote

Lambda
Expressions

■ Lambda Expressions

Lambda expressions are one-line mini-functions that can often be used where a simple function is required. They compute a single expression and cannot be used as a replacement for complex functions. Lambda expressions have the form

```
lambda par1, par2, ...: expression
```

where the expression is the value to be returned. For instance, the line

```
list1.sort(key=lastCharacter)
```

in Example 6 can be replaced with

```
list1.sort(key=lambda x: x[-1])
```

In this case there is no need to define the function *lastCharacter*. (**Note:** The function *numberOfVowels* in Example 6 is too complex to be replaced by a lambda expression.) One useful feature of lambda expressions is that they make use of variables from the function in which they are coded. This feature will be most helpful in the next chapter in the discussion of dictionaries.

 Example 7.   Sort Names   The following program sorts names by their surnames. The second line sorts the list of names, and the last two lines display the contents of the sorted list.

```
names = ["Dennis Ritchie", "Alan Kay", "John Backus", "James Gosling"]
names.sort(key=lambda name: name.split()[-1])
nameString = ", ".join(names)
print(nameString)
```

[Run]

```
John Backus, James Gosling, Alan Kay, Dennis Ritchie
```

■ The *sorted* Function

Whereas the sort method alters the order of the items in a list, the sorted function returns a new ordered list. In particular, after the statement

```
list2 = sorted(list1)
```

is executed, *list2* will contain the same elements as *list1*, but ordered.

Both the sort method and the sorted function can make use of the optional arguments key and reverse. Whereas the sort method only can be used with lists, the sorted function also can be used with lists, strings, and tuples. When used with strings, it produces an ordered list consisting of the characters of the string. Table 4.5 shows the output of several sorted statements.

TABLE 4.5   Values produced by sorted function (list1 = ["white", "blue", "red"]).

Statement	Output of print(list2)
`list2 = sorted(list1)`	`['blue', 'red', 'white']`
`list2 = sorted(list1, reverse=True)`	`['white', 'red', 'blue']`
`list2 = sorted(list1, key=len)`	`['red', 'blue', 'white']`
`list2 = sorted("spam")`	`['a', 'm', 'p', 's']`

■ Comments

1. Summary: There are two types of parameters that a function can have—*positional parameters* (also called *non-default parameters*) and *default parameters*. Default parameters have the form **param=defaultValue**, where *defaultValue* is usually a literal, but can be an expression. Positional parameters are not followed by an equal sign and a default value. If a function has both types of parameters, the positional parameters must precede the default parameters.

2. Summary: There are two types of arguments that can appear in a function call—*positional arguments* (also called *non-keyword arguments*) and *keyword arguments*. Keyword arguments have the form **parameterName=value**, where *value* is an expression. Positional arguments consist solely of an expression. If a function call has both types of

arguments, the positional arguments must precede the keyword arguments. The number of positional arguments in the function call must equal or exceed the number of positional parameters in the function definition. If the number of positional arguments in the function call exceeds the number of positional parameters in the function definition, the values of the extra arguments are passed to the remaining parameters in the order of their appearance in the function definition. Default parameters that do not have values passed to them assume their default values. The order of positional arguments is most important; order is not important for keyword arguments.

3. *List construction* might be a better name for the process called *list comprehension*.

4. Since lambda expressions are functions without a name, they are often referred to as *anonymous functions*.

Practice Problems 4.2

1. Rewrite the *main* function in Example 4 so that the body of the function consists of just one statement—a function call that uses keyword passing.

2. Could the *main* function in Example 4 be written as follows?

```
def main():
    a = "Sacramento"
    askQuestion(question="What is the capital of California? ", a)
```

3. Rewrite the *main* function of Example 4 so that just one argument is passed by keyword.

4. If `list1 = ['c', 'D', 'a', 'B']`, the statement `print(sorted(list1))` produces the output `['B', 'D', 'a', 'c']`. Add a lambda expression to the sorted function so that the list will appear alphabetized as `['a', 'B', 'c', 'D']`; that is, without regard to case.

5. Suppose the file `Countries.txt` contains the name of 20 countries , with one country on each line. What is displayed by the following line of code?

```
infile = open("countries.txt", 'r')
print([line.rstrip() for line in infile if line.startswith("Aust")])
infile.close()
```

EXERCISES 4.2

In Exercises 1 through 24, determine the output of the program.

1.
```
def main():
    howMany(24)
    print("a pie.")

def howMany(num):
    what(num)
    print("baked in", end=" ")

def what(num):
    print(num, "blackbirds", end = " ")

main()
```

2.
```python
def main():
    ## Good advice to follow
    advice()

def advice():
    print("Keep cool, but don't freeze.")
    source()

def source():
    print("Source: A jar of mayonnaise.")

main()
```

3.
```python
def main():
    cost = 250
    displayBill(cost, shippingCost(cost))

def shippingCost(costOfGoods):
    if costOfGoods < 100:
        return 10
    elif costOfGoods < 500:
        return 15
    else:
        return 20

def displayBill(cost, addedCost):
    print("Cost: ${0:.2f}".format(cost))
    print("Shipping cost: ${0:.2f}".format(addedCost))
    print("Total cost: ${0:.2f}".format(cost + addedCost))

main()
```

4.
```python
def main():
    grade = int(input("Enter your numeric grade: "))
    showResult(grade)

def showResult(grade):
    if passedExam(grade):
        print("You passed with a grade of", str(grade) + '.')
    else:
        print("You failed the exam.")

def passedExam(grade):
    if grade >= 60:
        return True
    else:
        return False

main()
```
(Assume the response is 92.)

5.
```python
def main():
    gradeList = list(getThreeGrades())
    gradeList.sort()
    print(gradeList)
```

```
def getThreeGrades():
    x = int(input(("Enter first grade: ")))
    y = int(input(("Enter second grade: ")))
    z = int(input(("Enter third grade: ")))
    return x, y, z

main()
```

(Assume the three responses are 88, 99, and 92.)

6.
```
def main():
    n, yob = getNameAndYOB()
    print(n, "will be", 2020 - yob, "years old in 2020.")

def getNameAndYOB():
    name = input("Enter a name: ")
    yearOfBirth = int(input("Enter a year of birth: "))
    return name, yearOfBirth

main()
```

(Assume the two responses are *Fred* and *1995*.)

7.
```
list1 = ["pear", "Banana", "apple"]
list1.sort()
print(list1)
list1.sort(key=lambda x: x.upper())
print(list1)
```

8.
```
list1 = ["pear", "Banana", "apple"]
list1.sort(reverse=True)
print(list1)
list1.sort(key=lambda x: len(x), reverse=True)
print(list1)
```

9.
```
def main():
    display("nudge ")
    display("nudge ", 4)

def display(x, times=2):
    print(x * times)

main()
```

10.
```
def main():
    for i in range(3):
        print(func())

def func(x=[]):
    x.append("wink")
    return x

main()
```

11.
```
def main():
    display("spam", "and", "eggs", 5)
    display("spam", "and", "eggs")

def display(x, y, z, spacing=1):
    print(x + (" " * spacing) + y + (" " * spacing) + z)

main()
```

12.
```python
def main():
    x, y = getTwoIntegers()
    x, y = calculateSumAndProduct(x, y)
    displaySumAndProduct(x, y)

def getTwoIntegers():
    a = int(input("Enter first integer: "))
    b = int(input("Enter second integer: "))
    return a, b

def calculateSumAndProduct(x, y):
     return x + y, x * y

def displaySumAndProduct(x, y):
    print("Sum" + ':', x)
    print("Product" + ':', y)

main()
```
(Assume the two responses are 4 and 25.)

13.
```python
presidents = [("John Adams", 61), ("George Washington", 57)]
presidents.sort(key=lambda pres: pres[1])
for pres in presidents:
    print(pres[0])
```

14.
```python
def main():
    composers = ["Johann Sebastian Bach", "Wolfgang Amadeus Mozart",
                "Franz Joseph Haydn", "Ralph Vaughan Williams"]
    composers.sort(key=lengthOfLastName)
    for composer in composers:
        print(composer)

def lengthOfLastName(composer):
    compList = composer.split()
    return len(compList[-1])

main()
```

15.
```python
def main():
    composers = ["Johann Sebastian Bach", "Wolfgang Amadeus Mozart",
                "Franz Joseph Haydn", "Ralph Vaughan Williams"]
    composers.sort(key=middleName)
    for composer in composers:
        print(middleName(composer))

def middleName(composer):
    compList = composer.split()
    return compList[1]

main()
```

16.
```python
def main():
    list1 = ["e", "pluribus", "unum"]
    list2 = sorted(list1, key=numberOfVowels)
    print(list2)

def numberOfVowels(word):
    return len([ch for ch in word if (ch in "aeiou")])

main()
```

17.
```
def main():
    list1 = sorted("alMoSt")
    print(list1)
    list2 = sorted("alMoSt", key=f)
    print(list2)

def f(letter):
    return letter.lower()

main()
```

18.
```
popularLanguages = ["Python", "Java", "C", "C++", "Ruby", "VB", "PHP"]
for item in sorted(popularLanguages):
    print(item, end = "   ")
```

19.
```
popularLanguages = ["Python", "Java", "C", "C++", "Ruby", "VB", "PHP"]
for item in sorted(popularLanguages, reverse=True):
    print(item, end = "   ")
```

20.
```
popularLanguages = ["Python", "Java", "C", "C++", "Ruby", "VB", "PHP"]
for item in sorted(popularLanguages, key=len):
    print(item, end = "   ")
```

21.
```
popularLanguages = ["Python", "Java", "C", "C++", "Ruby", "VB", "PHP"]
for item in sorted(popularLanguages, key=len, reverse=True):
    print(item, end = "   ")
```

22.
```
numbers = [4, 6, -2, -3, 5]
for num in sorted(numbers, key=abs):
    print(num, end = "   ")
```

23.
```
numbers = [4, 6, -2, -3, 5]
for num in sorted(numbers, key=lambda x: x ** 3):
    print(num, end = "   ")
```

24.
```
popLanguages = ["Python", "Java", "C", "C++", "Ruby", "VB", "PHP"]
sentence = "I program in VB, Python, and Ruby."
list1 = sentence.split()
myLanguages = [word[:-1] for word in list1 if word[:-1] in popLanguages]
for language in myLanguages:
    print(language, end = "   ")
```

In Exercises 25 through 30, determine the value of *list2*, where

```
list1 = ["democratic", "sequoia", "equals", "brrr", "break", "two"].
```

25. `list2 = [len(word) for word in list1]`

26. `list2 = [word.capitalize() for word in list1]`

27. `list2 = [word.upper() for word in list1 if len(word) < 5]`

28. `list2 = [word for word in list1 if numberOfVowels(word) > 3]`, where *number-OfVowels* is the function defined in Example 6.

29. `list2 = [x[-1] for x in list1 if numberOfVowels(x) > 3]`, where *numberOfVowels* is the function defined in Example 6.

30. `list2 = [x[0:2] for x in list1 if len(x) % 2 == 1]`

In Exercises 31 and 32 use list comprehension to simplify the code.

31.
```python
names = ["George Boole", "Charles Babbage", "Grace Hopper"]
lastNames = []
for name in names:
    lastNames.append(name.split()[-1])
```

32.
```python
numbers = [9, -5, 4, 1, -7]
newList = []
for num in numbers:
    if num >= 0:
        newList.append(num ** .5)    # square root
print(newList)
```

In Exercises 33 through 36, describe the output displayed by the lines of code, where the file `Countries.txt` contains 20 countries in alphabetical order.

33.
```python
infile = open("countries.txt", 'r')
print([line.rstrip().upper() for line in infile])
```

34.
```python
infile = open("countries.txt", 'r')
print(sorted([line.rstrip() for line in infile]))
```

35.
```python
infile = open("countries.txt", 'r')
print(sorted([line.rstrip() for line in infile], key=len))
```

36.
```python
infile = open("countries.txt", 'r')
print([line.rstrip() for line in infile if len(line.rstrip()) == 6])
```

In Exercises 37 through 42, determine whether the calling statement is valid where the function definition has the header `def bestFilm(year, film, star):`.

37. `bestFilm(2012,"Argo", "Ben Affleck")`

38. `bestFilm(2012, star="Ben Affleck", film="Argo")`

39. `bestFilm(star="Ben Affleck", film="Argo", year=2012)`

40. `bestFilm(star="Ben Affleck", 2012, film="Argo")`

41. `bestFilm()`

42. `bestFilm(2012, director="Ben Affleck", film="Argo")`

In Exercises 43 through 46, determine whether the calling statement is valid where the function definition has the header `def breakfast(toast, coffee, spam=0, eggs=0):`.

43. `breakfast(2, spam=1, eggs=1, coffee=1)`   **44.** `breakfast(2, 1, 1, 1)`

45. `breakfast(spam=1, 1, eggs=1, toast=2)`   **46.** `breakfast(2, 1, 1)`

In Exercises 47 and 48, determine the output displayed by the statement.

47. `print("".join(sorted("stomal")))`

48. `print("".join(sorted("pengos", reverse=True)))`

49. Cost of Postage   The original postage cost of airmail letters was 5 cents for the first ounce and 10 cents for each additional ounce. Write a program to compute the cost of a letter whose weight is given by the user. See Fig. 4.11. The cost should be calculated by a function named *cost*. The function *cost* should call a function named *ceil* that rounds noninteger numbers up to the next integer.

```
Enter the number of ounces: 4
Cost: $0.35
```

```
Enter grade on midterm: 88
Enter grade on final exam: 91
Semester Grade: A
```

FIGURE 4.11 Possible outcome of Exercise 49. **FIGURE 4.12** Possible outcome of Exercise 50.

50. **Semester Grade**   Write a program that requests the numeric grades on a midterm and a final exam and then uses a function named *semesterGrade* to assign a semester grade (A, B, C, D, or F). The final exam should count twice as much as the midterm exam, the semester average should be rounded up to the nearest whole number, and the semester grade should be assigned by the following criteria: 90–100 (A), 80–89 (B), ... See Fig. 4.12. The function *semesterGrade* should call a function named *ceil* that rounds noninteger numbers up to the next integer.

51. **Anagrams**   An *anagram* of a word or phrase is another word or phrase that uses the same letters with the same frequency. Punctuation marks, case, and spaces are ignored. Some examples of anagram pairs are "angered"/"enraged" and "A gentleman"/"Elegant man". Write a program that requests two words or phrases as input and determines if they are anagrams of each other. See Fig. 4.13. The program should use a Boolean-valued function with header

```
def areAnagrams(string1, string2):
```

that returns **True** when the two strings are anagrams, and otherwise returns **False**.

```
Enter grade 1: 90
Enter grade 2: 75
Enter grade 3: 85
Enter grade 4: 72
Enter grade 5: 80
Range: 10
Average: 85
```

```
Enter the first word or phrase: Elvis
Enter the second word or phrase: lives
Are anagrams.
```

FIGURE 4.14 Possible outcome of Exercise 52.

FIGURE 4.13 Possible outcome of Exercise 51.

52. **Grades**   Write a program that requests five grades as input, drops the lowest two grades, and displays the range and average of the remaining three grades. See Fig. 4.14. *Note:* The *range* of a set of numbers is the difference between the highest and lowest numbers. The program should use a function that returns two values.

53. **Programming Languages**   Consider the list

```
programmingLanguages =[[("Dennis Ritchie", "C"), ("Bjarne Stroustrup",
"C++"), ("Guido van Rossum", "Python")]
```

Write a program using the line above that displays the three programming languages ordered by their chief developer name and then secondarily ordered by the name of the langauge. *Note:* The code should use the **sort** function twice.

```
C, Dennis Ritchie
C++, Bjarne Stroustrup
Python, Guido van Rossum
```

FIGURE 4.15 Outcome of Exercise 53.

In Exercises 54 through 57, use the following list of tuples, where each tuple contains the name of a planet, its surface area in million square kilometers (approx.) and its position relative to the sun.

Planets = [("Mercury", 75, 1), ("Venus", 460, 2), ("Mars", 140, 4), ("Earth", 510, 3), ("Jupiter", 62000, 5), ("Neptune", 7640, 8), ("Saturn", 42700, 6), ("Uranus", 8100, 7)]

54. Planets   Write a program that displays the names of the planets in the list *Planets* in descending order by surface area. See Fig. 4.16.

```
Sorted by surface area in descending order:
Jupiter  Saturn  Uranus  Neptune  Earth  Venus  Mars  Mercury
```

FIGURE 4.16 Outcome of Exercise 54.

55. Planets   Write a program that displays the names of the planets in the list *Planets* in descending order by their position from the Sun. See Fig. 4.17.

```
Sorted by position from Sun in descending order:
Neptune  Uranus  Saturn  Jupiter  Mars  Earth  Venus  Mercury
```

FIGURE 4.17 Outcome of Exercise 55.

56. Planets   Write a program that displays the names of the planets in the list *Planets* in ascending order by the length of the name of the planets. See Fig. 4.18.

```
Sorted by length of name of planet in ascending order:
Mars  Venus  Earth  Saturn  Uranus  Mercury  Jupiter  Neptune
```

FIGURE 4.18 Outcome of Exercise 56.

57. Planets   Write a program that displays the names of the planets in the list *Planets* in ascending order by number of vowels in planet name. See Fig. 4.19.

```
Sorted by number of vowels in name in ascending order:
Mars  Mercury  Venus  Earth  Saturn  Jupiter  Neptune  Uranus
```

FIGURE 4.19 Outcome of Exercise 57.

In Exercises 58 through 61, use the following list: numbers = [865, 1169, 1208, 1243, 329].

58. Numbers   Write a program that displays the values in the list *numbers* in ascending order sorted by the sum of their digits. See Fig. 4.20.

```
Sorted by sum of digits:
[1243, 1208, 290, 1169, 865]
```

FIGURE 4.20   Outcome of Exercise 58.

```
Sorted by largest prime factor:
[290, 1243, 1208, 1169, 865]
```

FIGURE 4.21   Outcome of Exercise 59.

59. **Numbers**   Write a program that displays the values in the list *numbers* in ascending order sorted by their largest prime factor. Consult the flowchart in Fig. 3.30 of Section 3.3. See Fig. 4.21.

60. **Numbers**   Write a program that displays the values in the list *numbers* in descending order sorted by their last digit. See Fig. 4.22.

```
Sorted by last digit:
[1169, 1208, 865, 1243, 290]
```

FIGURE 4.22   Outcome of Exercise 60.

```
Sorted by sum of odd digits:
[1169, 290, 865, 1243, 1208]
```

FIGURE 4.23   Outcome of Exercise 61.

61. **Numbers**   Write a program that displays the values in the list *numbers* in descending order sorted by the sum of their digits that are odd numbers. See Fig. 4.23.

62. **World Countries**   The file **Countries.txt** contains the names of 20 countries. Write a program that places the countries names in a list, sorts the list alphabetically, and displays the names of the first six countries. See Fig. 4.24.

```
Algeria
Angola
Argentina
Australia
Austria
Bahamas
```

FIGURE 4.24   Outcome of Exercise 62.

```
India
China
Ghana
Japan
Brazil
Angola
```

FIGURE 4.25   Outcome of Exercise 63.

63. **World Countries**   The file **Countries.txt** contains the names of 20 countries. Write a program that places the names in a list, sorts the list by the length of the country name, and displays the names of the first six countries in the list. See Fig. 4.25.

64. **World Countries**   The file **Countries.txt** contains the names of 20 countries. Write a program that places the names of the countries in a list, sorts the list by the length of the countries in descending order, and display the names of the first six countries in the list. See Fig. 4.26.

```
China
Ghana
India
Japan
Angola
Brazil
```

FIGURE 4.26   Outcome of Exercise 64.

```
New Zealand
Australia
Argentina
Portugal
Algeria
Austria
```

FIGURE 4.27   Outcome of Exercise 65.

65. World Countries   The file **Countries.txt** contains the names of 20 countries. Write a program that places the names of the countries in a list, sorts the list by the number of vowels in their names in descending order, and displays the names of the first six countries in the list. See Fig 4.27.

66. Pay Raise   Write a pay-raise program that requests a person's first name, last name, and current annual salary, and then displays the person's salary for next year. People earning less than $40,000 will receive a 5% raise, and those earning $40,000 or more will receive a raise of $2,000 plus 2% of the amount over $40,000. The *main* function should call three functions—one (multi-valued) for input, one to calculate the new salary, and one for output. See Fig. 4.28.

```
Enter first name: John
Enter last name: Doe
Enter current salary: 48000
New salary for John Doe: $50,160.00.
```

```
Enter old balance: 200
Enter charges for month: 150
Enter credits: 100
New balance: $253.00.
Minimum payment: $43.30
```

FIGURE 4.28   Possible outcome of Exercise 66.   **FIGURE 4.29   Possible outcome of Exercise 67.**

67. Credit Card Payment   Write a program to calculate the balance and minimum payment for a credit card statement. See Fig. 4.29. The finance charge is 1.5% of the old balance. If the new balance is $20 or less, the minimum payment should be the entire new balance. Otherwise, the minimum payment should be $20 plus 10% of the amount of the new balance above $20. The *main* function should call three functions—one (multi-valued) for input, one (multi-valued) to calculate the new balance and minimum payment, and one for output.

68. Mortgage Calculations   Write a program to calculate three monthly values associated with a mortgage. See Fig. 4.30. The interest paid each month is the monthly rate of interest (annual rate of interest / 12) applied to the balance at the beginning of the month. Each month the reduction of principal equals the monthly payment minus the interest paid. At any time, the balance of the mortgage is the amount still owed—that is, the amount required to pay off the mortgage. The end of month balance is calculated as [beginning of month balance] − [reduction of principal]. The *main* function should call three functions—one (multi-valued) for input, one (multi-valued) to calculate the values, and one for output.

```
Enter annual rate of interest: 5
Enter monthly payment: 1932.56
Enter beg. of month balance: 357819.11
Interest paid for the month: $1,490.91
Reduction of principal: $441.56
End of month balance: $357,377.46
```

FIGURE 4.30   Possible outcome of Exercise 68.

```
Enter hours worked: 42
Enter hourly pay: 10.00
Week's pay: $430.00
```

FIGURE 4.31   Possible outcome of Exercise 69.

69. Earnings   Write a program to determine a person's weekly pay, where he or she receives time-and-a-half for overtime work beyond 40 hours. See Fig. 4.31. The *main* function should call three functions—one (multi-valued) for input, one to calculate the value, and one for output.

70. Wilson's Theorem   A number is *prime* if its only factors are 1 and itself. Write a program that determines whether a number is prime by using the theorem "The number *n* is a prime number if and only if *n* divides $(n-1)! + 1$." [See Exercise 28 of Section 4.1 for the definition of factorial (!).] The program should define a Boolean-valued function named *isPrime* that calls a function named *factorial*. See Fig. 4.32.

```
Enter an integer greater than 1: 37
37 is a prime number.
```

FIGURE 4.32   Possible outcome of Exercise 70.

Solutions to Practice Problems 4.2

1. ```
def main():
    askQuestion(question="What is the capital of California? ",
                answer="Sacramento")
```

2. No. Arguments passed by position must precede arguments passed by keyword.

3. ```
def main():
    q = "What is the capital of California? "
    askQuestion(q, answer="Sacramento")
```

4. Change the print statement to

   ```
print(sorted(list1, key=lambda letter: letter.upper()))
```

5. **[North Carolina, North Dakota].** Since North Carolina was one of the original 13 states, it precedes North Dakota.

4.3   Program Design

■ Top-Down Design

Full-featured software usually requires large programs. One method programmers use to make a complicated problem more understandable is to divide it into smaller, less complex subproblems. Repeatedly using a "divide-and-conquer" approach to break up a large problem into smaller subproblems is called **stepwise refinement**. Stepwise refinement is part of a larger methodology of writing programs known as **top-down design**, in which the more general tasks occur near the top of the design and tasks representing their refinement occur below. Top-down design and structured programming emerged as techniques to enhance programming productivity. Their use leads to programs that are easier to read and maintain. They also produce programs containing fewer initial errors, with these errors being easier to find and correct. When such programs are later modified, there is a much smaller likelihood of introducing new errors.

The goal of top-down design is to break a problem into individual subtasks that can easily be transcribed into pseudocode, flowcharts, or a function. Any subtasks that remain too complex are broken down further. The process of refining subtasks continues until the smallest subtasks can be coded directly. Each stage of refinement adds a more complete specification of what tasks must be performed. The main idea in top-down design is to go from the general to the specific. This process of dividing and organizing a problem into tasks can be pictured using a hierarchy chart. When using top-down design, certain criteria should be met:

1. The design should be easily readable and emphasize small function size.
2. Tasks proceed from general to specific as you read down the chart.
3. The subtasks, as much as possible, should be single-minded. That is, they should perform only a single well-defined job.
4. Subtasks should be independent of each other as much as possible, and any relationships among subtasks should be specified.

The following example illustrates this process.

 Example 1   Car Loan   Figure 4.33 is the beginning of a hierarchy chart for a program that gives information about a car loan. The inputs are the amount of the loan, the duration (in years), and the interest rate. The output consists of the monthly payment and the amount of interest paid for the first month. In the broadest sense, the program calls for obtaining the input, making calculations, and displaying the output.

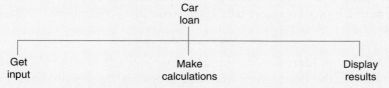

FIGURE 4.33   **Beginning of a hierarchy chart for the car loan program.**

Each task can be refined into more specific subtasks. (See Fig. 4.34 for the final hierarchy chart.) Most of the subtasks in the third row are straightforward and do not require further refinement. For instance, the first month's interest is calculated by multiplying the amount of the loan by one-twelfth of the annual rate of interest. The most complicated subtask, the computation of the monthly payment, has been broken down further. This task is carried out by applying a standard formula found in finance books—however, the formula requires the number of payments.

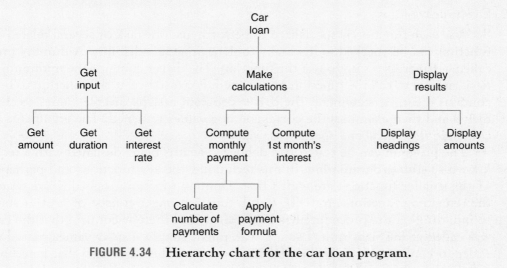

FIGURE 4.34   **Hierarchy chart for the car loan program.**

It is clear from the hierarchy chart that the top tasks manipulate the subtasks beneath them. While the higher-level tasks control the flow of the program, the lower-level tasks do the actual work. By designing the top modules first, we can delay specific processing decisions.

■ Structured Programming

A program is said to be **structured** if it meets modern standards of program design. Although there is no formal definition of the term **structured program**, computer scientists agree that such programs should use top-down design and use only the three types of logical structures discussed in Chapter 1: sequences, decisions, and loops.

> *Sequences:*   Statements are executed one after another.
>
> *Decisions:*   One of several blocks of program code is executed based on a test for some condition.
>
> *Loops (iteration):*   One or more statements are executed repeatedly as long as a specified condition is true.

■ Advantages of Structured Programming

The goal of structured programming is to create correct programs that are easy to write, debug, understand, and change. Let us now take a closer look at the way structured programming, along with a limited number of logical structures, contributes to attaining these goals.

1. *Easy to write.*

Structured design increases the programmer's productivity by allowing the programmer to look at the big picture first and focus on the details later. During the actual coding, the programmer works with a manageable chunk of the program and does not have to think about an entire complex program. Several programmers can work on a single large program, each taking responsibility for a specific task.

Studies have shown that structured programs require significantly less time to write than unstructured programs.

Often, functions written for one program can be reused in other programs requiring the same task. Not only is time saved in writing a program, but reliability is enhanced, because reused functions will already be tested and debugged. A function that can be used in many programs is said to be **reusable**.

2. *Easy to debug.*

Because each function is specialized to perform just one task or several related tasks, a function can be checked individually to determine its reliability. A dummy program, called a **driver**, is set up to test the function. The driver contains the minimum definitions needed to call the function to be tested. For instance, if the function to be tested contains a **return** statement, the driver program assigns diverse values to the arguments and then examines the corresponding values returned. The arguments should contain both typical and special-case values.

The program can be tested and debugged as it is being designed with a technique known as **stub programming**. In this technique, the key functions and perhaps some of the smaller functions are coded first. Dummy functions, or stubs, are written for the remaining functions. Initially, a stub function might consist of a **print** statement to indicate that the procedure has been called, and thereby confirm that the function was called at the right time. Later, a stub might simply display values passed to it in order to confirm not only that the function was called, but also that it received the correct values from the calling function. A stub also can assign new values to one or more of its parameters to simulate either input or computation. This provides greater control of the conditions being tested. The stub function is always simpler than the actual function it represents. Although the stub program is only a skeleton of the final program, the program's structure can still be debugged and tested. (The stub program consists of some coded functions and the stub functions.)

Old-fashioned unstructured programs consist of a linear sequence of instructions that are not grouped for specific tasks. The logic of such a program is cluttered with details and therefore difficult to follow. Needed tasks are easily left out and crucial details easily neglected. Tricky parts of the program cannot be isolated and examined. Bugs are difficult to locate because they might be present in any part of the program.

3. *Easy to understand.*

The interconnections of the functions reveal the structured design of the program.

The meaningful function names, along with relevant comments, identify the tasks performed by the functions.

The meaningful variable names help the programmer recall the purpose of each variable.

4. *Easy to change.*

Because a structured program is self-documenting, it can easily be deciphered by another programmer.

Modifying a structured program often amounts to inserting or altering a few functions rather than revising an entire complex program. The programmer does not even have to look at most of the program. This is in sharp contrast to the situation with unstructured programs, where one must understand the entire logic of the program before any changes can be made with confidence.

■ Object-Oriented Programming

An object is an encapsulation of data and code that operates on the data. Objects have properties and respond to methods. The most effective type of programming for complex problems is called **object-oriented** design. An object-oriented program can be viewed as a collection of cooperating objects. Many modern programmers use a blend of traditional structured programming along with object-oriented design. Python is an object-oriented programming language—in fact, every structure, such as a list or a string is actually an object. This book illustrates the building blocks of Python in the early chapters and then puts them together using object-oriented techniques in Chapter 7.

■ A Relevant Quote

We end this section with a few paragraphs from *Dirk Gently's Holistic Detective Agency*, by Douglas Adams, Simon & Schuster, 1987:

"What really is the point of trying to teach anything to anybody?" This question seemed to provoke a murmur of sympathetic approval from up and down the table.

Richard continued, "What I mean is that if you really want to understand something, the best way is to try and explain it to someone else. That forces you to sort it out in your own mind. And the more slow and dim-witted your pupil, the more you have to break things down into more and more simple ideas. And that's really the essence of programming. By the time you've sorted out a complicated idea into little steps that even a stupid machine can deal with, you've certainly learned something about it yourself. The teacher usually learns more than the pupil. Isn't that true?"

CHAPTER 4 KEY TERMS AND CONCEPTS

EXAMPLES

4.1 Functions, Part 1

A function definition begins with a header of the form def *functionName*(*par1*, *par2*, . . ., *parN*): followed by an indented block of statements. The optional **parameters**, *par1*, *par2*, . . ., *parN*, are variables. Optional **return** statements in the block allow the function to pass values back to calling statements. A statement containing an expression of the form *functionName*(*arg1*, *arg2*, . . ., *argN*), where the arguments *arg1*, *arg2*, . . ., *argN* are expressions, assigns the values of the arguments to the corresponding parameters of the function and causes the function block to be executed. The statement is said to **call** the function. **Positional passing** passes the value of the first argument to the first parameter, the value of the second argument to the second parameter, and so on.

```
def main():
    invented("browser", 1990)
def invented(what, when):
    print("The", what,
        "was invented in", when)
main()
```
[Run]
```
The browser was invented in 1990
```
```
def main():
    what = getInvention()
    invented(what, 1959)
def getInvention():
    s = "Enter an invention: "
invention = input(s)
    return invention
def invented(what, when):
    print("The", what,
        "was invented in", when)
main()
```
[Run]
```
Enter an invention: chip
The chip was invented in 1959
```

When a variable is passed to a parameter, and the value of the parameter is an immutable object, then any change to the parameter by the function block has no effect on the argument.

```
def main():
    what = "computer"
    alter(what)
    print(what)
def alter(what):
    what = "typewriter"
main()
```
[Run]
```
computer
```

The **scope** of a variable is the portion of the program that can refer to it. A variable created in a function block can be referred to only inside the block and is said to be a **local variable**. A variable created outside of any function block can be referred to anywhere in the program and is said to be a **global variable**. However, its value only can be altered in a function block if the altering statement is preceded with a statement in the function block of the form global *variableName*.

```
(x, y) = (2, 3)
def main():
    z = 5
    global y
    y += 1  # x += 1 is an error
    display()
    print(x, y, z)
def display():
    print(x, y, end="    ")
    z = 8
main()
```

CHAPTER 4 KEY TERMS AND CONCEPTS	EXAMPLES
	[Run] `2 4   2 4 5`
Named constants are global variables that are intended to never be altered by any function.	`INTEREST_RATE = .04`
Library modules facilitate the reuse of functions created by the programmer and the standard libraries give the programmer access to a wide variety of functions that are not built into Python.	`import finance`

4.2 Functions, Part 2

A function can **call other functions**.

```
def main():
    str1 = getInput()
    str2 = precessInput(str1)
    displayOutput(str2)
```

A function can **return more than one value** by returning a record.

```
def main():
    x, y = returnTwoValues()
    print(", ".join((x, y)))
def returnTwoValues():
    return ("spam", "eggs")
main()
```
[Run]
```
spam, eggs
```

The **sorted function** creates a new ordered list from a list, tuple, or string.

```
print(sorted(("MBA","MA")))
```
displays `['MA', 'MBA']`.

Custom sorting can be accomplished by assigning a function name or a lambda expression to the **key argument** and a value to the **reverse argument** of a sort method or sorted function.

```
print(sorted(["MA", "MBA"],
    key=lambda x: len(x),
    reverse=True))
```
displays `['MBA', 'MA']`.

List comprehension creates a list by carrying out whatever function precedes a for clause to each item in the for clause (provided that the item satisfies an optional condition specified by an if clause).

```
L=[ord(x) for x in ['1','A','a']
        if x.isalpha()]
print(L)
```
[Run]
```
[65, 97]
```

Keyword passing allows an argument to be passed to a parameter by writing the argument in the form `parameterName=value`. If a parameter in a function header has the form `par=defaultValue`, the default value will be assigned to the parameter when no argument in the calling statement is assigned to the parameter.

```
def main():
    invented(what="Web")
def invented(what, when=1989):
    print("The", what,
        "was invented in", when)
main()
```
[Run]
```
The Web was invented in 1989
```

CHAPTER 4 KEY TERMS AND CONCEPTS	EXAMPLES
4.3 Program Design	
Structured programming uses top-down design to refine large problems into smaller subproblems.	See Section 4.3.

CHAPTER 4   PROGRAMMING PROJECTS

1. Projectile Motion   Write a program to provide information on the height of a ball thrown straight up into the air. The program should request as input the initial height, h feet, and the initial velocity, v feet per second. The height of the ball after t seconds is $h + vt - 16t^2$ feet. The program should perform the following two calculations:

   (a) Determine the maximum height of the ball. **Note:** The ball will reach its maximum height after $v/32$ seconds.

   (b) Determine approximately when the ball will hit the ground. **Hint:** Calculate the height after every .1 second and determine when the height is no longer a positive number.

   A function named *getInput* should be used to obtain the values of h and v and that function should call a function named *isValid* to ensure that the input values are positive numbers. Each of the tasks (a) and (b) should be carried out by functions. See Fig. 4.35.

   ```
   Enter the initial height of the ball: 5
   Enter the initial velocity of the ball: 34
   The maximum height of the ball is 23.06 feet.
   The ball will hit the ground after approximately 2.27 seconds.
   ```

   FIGURE 4.35   Possible outcome of Programming Project 1.

2. Prime Factors   Write a program that requests a positive integer greater than 1 as input and displays the largest and smallest prime factors of the number. Refer to Exercise 18 of Section 3.3 for a discussion of prime factorization. See Fig. 4.36. The program should use a function that returns two values.

   ```
   123 septillion
     0 sextillion
     4 quintillion
    56 quadrillion
   777 trillion
   888 billion
   999 million
    12 thousand
   345
   ```

   ```
   Enter a positive integer > 1: 2345
   Largest prime factor: 67
   Smallest prime factor: 5
   ```

   FIGURE 4.36   Possible outcome of Programming Project 2.

   FIGURE 4.37   Outcome of Programming Project 3.

3. **Verbalize a Number**   Write a function with header `def verbalizeNumber(number):` that accepts a positive whole number with at most 27 digits as input and then displays a verbalization of the number. Figure 4.37 shows the output of `verbalizeNumber(123000004056777888999012345)`.

4. **Depreciation**   For tax purposes an item may be depreciated over a period of several years, n. With the *straight-line* method of depreciation, each year the item depreciates by (1/n)th of its original value. With the *double-declining-balance* method of depreciation, each year the item depreciates by (2/n)ths of its value at the beginning of that year. (In the final year it is depreciated by its value at the beginning of the year.) Write a program that performs the following tasks:

(a) Request a description of the item, the year of purchase, the cost of the item, the number of years to be depreciated (estimated life), and the method of depreciation.

(b) Display a year-by-year description of the depreciation. See Fig. 4.38.

```
Enter name of item purchased: computer
Enter year purchased: 2012
Enter cost of item: 2000
Enter estimated life of item (in years): 5
Enter method of depreciation (SL or DDB): DDB

Description: computer
Year of purchase: 2012
Cost: $2,000.00
Estimated life: 5 years
Method of depreciation: double-declining balance

          Value at     Amount Deprec    Total Depreciation
          Beg of Yr.    During Year       to End of Year
2012      2,000.00         800.00               800.00
2013      1,200.00         480.00             1,280.00
2014        720.00         288.00             1,568.00
2015        432.00         172.80             1,740.80
2016        259.20         259.20             2,000.00
```

FIGURE 4.38   Possible outcome of Programming Project 4.

5. **Alphabetical Order**   The following words have three consecutive letters that are also consecutive letters in the alphabet: THIRSTY, NOPE, AFGHANISTAN, STUDENT. Write a program that accepts a word as input and determines whether or not it has three consecutive letters that are consecutive letters in the alphabet. The program should use a Boolean-valued function named *isTripleConsecutive* that accepts an entire word as input. **Hint:** Use the ord function. See Fig. 4.39.

```
Enter a word: HIJACK
HIJACK contains three successive letters
in consecutive alphabetical order.
```

FIGURE 4.39   Possible outcome of Programming Project 5.

6. **ISBN Validator**   Every book is identified by a 10-character International Standard Book Number (ISBN), which is usually printed on the back cover of the book.

The first nine characters are digits and the last character is either a digit or the letter X (which stands for ten). Three examples of ISBNs are 0-13-030657-6, 0-32-108599-X, and 0-471-58719-2. The hyphens separate the characters into four blocks. The first block usually consists of a single digit and identifies the language (0 for English, 2 for French, 3 for German, etc.). The second block identifies the publisher. The third block is the number the publisher has chosen for the book. The fourth block, which always consists of a single character called the *check digit*, is used to test for errors. Let's refer to the 10 characters of the ISBN as $d_1, d_2, d_3, d_4, d_5, d_6, d_7, d_8, d_9$, and d_{10}. The check digit is chosen so that the sum

$$10 \cdot d_1 + 9 \cdot d_2 + 8 \cdot d_3 + 7 \cdot d_4 + 6 \cdot d_5 + 5 \cdot d_6 + 4 \cdot d_7 + 3 \cdot d_8 + 2 \cdot d_9 + 1 \cdot d_{10} \ (*)$$

is a multiple of 11. (**Note:** A number is a multiple of 11 if it is exactly divisible by 11.) If the last character of the ISBN is an X, then in the sum (*), d_{10} is replaced with 10. For example, with the ISBN 0-32-108599-X, the sum would be

$$10 \cdot 0 + 9 \cdot 3 + 8 \cdot 2 + 7 \cdot 1 + 6 \cdot 0 + 5 \cdot 8 + 4 \cdot 5 + 3 \cdot 9 + 2 \cdot 9 + 1 \cdot 10 = 165$$

Since 165/11 is 15, the sum is a multiple of 11. This checking scheme will detect every single digit and transposition-of-adjacent-digits error. That is, if while copying an IBSN number you miscopy a single character or transpose two adjacent characters, then the sum (*) will no longer be a multiple of 11.

Write a program to accept an ISBN type number (including the hyphens) as input, calculate the sum (*), and tell if it is a valid ISBN. See Fig. 4.40. (**Hint:** The number n is divisible by 11 if n % 11 is 0.) Before calculating the sum, the program should check that each of the first nine characters is a digit and that the last character is either a digit or an X.

```
Enter an ISBN: 0-13-030657-6
The number is valid.
```

FIGURE 4.40 Possible outcome of Programming Project 6.

5

Processing Data

5.1   Processing Data, Part 1

So far, the output of our programs has been displayed on the screen and eventually lost. In most real-life applications, we want the output to be preserved in files in permanent storage (such as on a hard drive) that will be available for later use. Word processors and spreadsheets are two types of programs whose output must be preserved and accessed at a later time. We have already seen how data from text files can be retrieved. In this section we will expand our ability to read data from text files, and will show how to write programs that create new text files.

In Chapter 2 we discussed the core objects *numbers*, *strings*, *lists*, and *tuples*. In this chapter we will present two other core objects—*sets* and *dictionaries*. Sets will be introduced in this section and used to manage text files. Dictionaries will be introduced in Section 5.3 and used to efficiently access large quantities of data. **Note:** In this textbook, we assume that all files referred to by a program reside in the same folder as the program.

■ Reading Text Files

VideoNote

Reading
Text Files

In previous chapters we showed how to access every line of a text file successively with a for loop, and how to place all the lines of a text file into a list using list comprehension.

A statement of the form

```
infile = open(fileName, 'r')
```

establishes a connection between the program and the file that allows the program to read data from the file. The file is said to be **opened for reading** (or **opened for input**). The open function is said to return a **file object**. The variable *infile* is used to read lines from the file and to eventually terminate the connection to the file. After a text file is opened for reading, a for loop with header

```
for line in infile:
```

accesses the lines of the file in succession, and the statement

```
listVar = [line.rstrip() for line in infile]
```

creates a list of strings where each item of the list is a line of the file minus its newline character.

Note: With the pure for loop, the newline character (\n) appears at the end of each line (except possibly the last line).

At any time, the connection from the program to the file can be terminated with the statement

```
infile.close()
```

Files are usually automatically closed when the functions in which they were opened terminate. However, we will explicitly close all files when we have finished using them.

Note: Most text files have a newline character at the end of their last line—however, some do not. For instance, if the text file was created in a text editor such as Notepad or TextEdit, the presence of the final endline character depends on whether the person who created the file pressed the *Enter* (or *return*) key after typing the last line. We have written our programs so that they run as intended with both types of text files.

✓ **Example 1** First Three Presidents The three lines of the file **FirstPresidents.txt** contain the names of the first three U.S. presidents. The following program shows two ways to display the contents of the file.

```
def main():
    ## Display the names of the first three presidents.
    file = "FirstPresidents.txt"
    displayWithForLoop(file)
    print()
    displayWithListComprehension(file)

def displayWithForLoop(file):
    infile = open(file, 'r')
    for line in infile:
        print(line, end="")
    infile.close()

def displayWithListComprehension(file):
    infile = open(file, 'r')
    listPres = [line.rstrip() for line in infile]
    infile.close()
    print(listPres)

main()
```

[Run. Assume the file ends with a newline character.]

```
George Washington
John Adams
Thomas Jefferson

['George Washington', 'John Adams', 'Thomas Jefferson']
```

A file that is open for reading can also be accessed with the **read** and **readline** methods. A statement of the form

```
strVar = infile.read()
```

places the entire contents of the file into a single string.

When a text file is opened for input, a pointer is set to the beginning of the first line of the file. Each time a statement of the form

```
strVar = infile.readline()
```

is executed, the current line is assigned to *strVar* and the pointer advances to the end of that line. After all the lines of the file have been read, the **readline** method returns the empty string. The following function could be added to Example 1 as another way to display the contents of the file **FirstPresidents.txt**.

```
def displayWithReadline(file):
    infile = open(file, 'r')
    line = infile.readline()
```

```
while line != "":
    print(line, end="")
    line = infile.readline()
infile.close()
```

Figure 5.1 shows the successive positions of the pointer during the execution of the *displayWithReadline* function. After the third **readline** method is executed, the pointer will be at the end of the file and therefore the fourth **readline** method will return the empty string. The values of *line* after each of the **readline** methods are **George Washington\n**, **John Adams\n**, **Thomas Jefferson\n**, and **""**, respectively. *Note:* The **newline** character (\n) serves to separate lines.

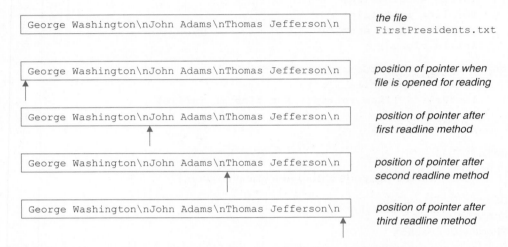

FIGURE 5.1   Pointer positions during the execution of the *displayWithReadline* function.

■ Creating Text Files

A statement of the form

***outfile* = open(*fileName*, 'w')**

creates a new text file with the specified name. The file is said to be **opened for writing**. The variable *outfile* is used to write lines to the file and to eventually close the file. If *list1* is a list of strings, where each string ends with a newline character (\n), then the statement

outfile.writelines(list1)

writes each item of the list into the file as a line. If the value of *strVar* is a string, the statement

outfile.write(strVar)

adds the value of *strVar* to the file.

Since memory access is much faster than disk access, Python sets aside a portion of memory called a **buffer** as a temporary holding place for data to be written to the disk. The contents of the buffer are written to the disk whenever the buffer is full or when the file is closed. Therefore, after all **write** and **writelines** statements have been executed, the file must be closed to guarantee that all data has been physically transferred to the disk.

Example 2 U.S. Presidents The following program shows two ways to create files identical to **FirstPresidents.txt**. Figure 5.2 shows the contents of the buffer during the execution of the last two lines of the *main* function. After the **close** method is executed, the three lines will be written to the disk and no variable will reference the buffer. For all practical purposes, the buffer no longer exists.

```python
def main():
    ## Create two files containing the first three presidents.
    outfile = open("FirstPresidents2.txt", 'w')
    createWithWritelines(outfile)
    outfile = open("FirstPresidents3.txt", 'w')
    createWithWrite(outfile)

def createWithWritelines(outfile):
    list1 = ["George Washington", "John Adams", "Thomas Jefferson"]
    # Append endline characters to the list's items.
    for i in range(len(list1)):
        list1[i] = list1[i] + "\n"
    # Write the list's items to the file.
    outfile.writelines(list1)
    outfile.close()

def createWithWrite(outfile):
    outfile.write("George Washington\n")
    outfile.write("John Adams\n")
    outfile.write("Thomas Jefferson\n")
    outfile.close()

main()
```

[Run. Each of the newly created files will look as follows when opened in a text editor.]

```
George Washington
John Adams
Thomas Jefferson
```

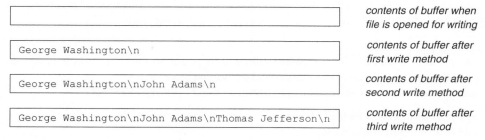

FIGURE 5.2 Contents of the buffer after execution of the second open statement and the *createWithWrite* function in Example 2.

 Example 3 U.S. States The file **States.txt** contains the names of the U.S. states in the order they joined the union. The following program uses this file to create a text file named **StatesAlpha.txt** containing the states in alphabetical order.

```
def main():
    ## Create a text file containing the 50 states in alphabetical order.
    statesList = createListFromFile("States.txt")
    createSortedFile(statesList, "StatesAlpha.txt")

def createListFromFile(fileName):
    infile = open(fileName, 'r')
    desiredList = [line.rstrip() for line in infile]
    infile.close()
    return desiredList

def createSortedFile(listName, fileName):
    listName.sort()
    for i in range(len(listName)):
        listName[i] = listName[i] + "\n"
    outfile = open(fileName, 'w')
    outfile.writelines(listName)
    outfile.close()

main()
```

[Run. The newly created file **StatesAlpha.txt** will look as follows when opened in a text editor.]

```
Alabama
Alaska
Arizona
   :
   :
West Virginia
Wisconsin
Wyoming
```

✓   **Example 4**   U.S. Presidents The file **USPres.txt** contains the U.S. presidents in the order they served and the file **VPres.txt** contains the names of the people who served as vice presidents of the U.S. The following program creates a file named **Both.txt** containing the names of the presidents who also served as vice president.

```
def main():
    ## Create a file of the presidents who also served as vice-presidents.
    vicePresList = createListFromFile("VPres.txt")
    createNewFile(vicePresList, "USPres.txt", "Both.txt")

def createListFromFile(fileName):
    infile = open(fileName, 'r')
    desiredList = [line.rstrip() for line in infile]
    infile.close()
    return desiredList

def createNewFile(listName, oldFileName, newFileName):
    infile = open(oldFileName, 'r')
    outfile = open(newFileName, 'w')
    for person in infile:
        if person.rstrip() in listName:
            outfile.write(person)
```

```
        infile.close()
        outfile.close()

main()
```

[Run. The newly created file **Both.txt** will look as follows when opened in a text editor.]

```
John Adams
Thomas Jefferson
Martin Van Buren
    ⋮
Richard Nixon
Gerald Ford
George H. W. Bush
```

■ Adding Lines to an Existing Text File

A statement of the form

```
outfile = open(fileName, 'a')
```

allows the program to add lines to the end of the specified file. Then the writelines and write methods can be used to add new lines. The file is said to be **opened for append**.

Example 5   After the following program is executed, the file **FirstPresidents.txt** will contain the names of the first six U.S. presidents.

```
def main():
    ## Add next three presidents to the file containing first three presidents.
    outfile = open("FirstPresidents.txt", 'a')
    list1 = ["James Madison\n", "James Monroe\n"]
    outfile.writelines(list1)
    outfile.write("John Q. Adams\n")
    outfile.close()

main()
```

[Run. The file **FirstPresidents.txt** will now look as follows when opened in a text editor.]

```
George Washington
John Adams
Thomas Jefferson
James Madison
James Monroe
John Q. Adams
```

■ Altering Items in a Text File

There is one file-management operation that we have yet to discuss—altering, inserting, or deleting a line of a text file. These types of changes cannot be made directly. A new file must be created by reading each item from the original file and recording it, with the changes, into the new file. The old file is then erased, and the new file is renamed with the name of the original file. In order to gain access to the functions needed for these tasks, we must first import the standard library module *os* with the statement

import os

This statement is customarily placed at the top of the program before the *main* function. Then the statement

os.remove(*fileName*)

will delete the specified file, and the statement

os.rename(*oldFileName*, *newFileName*)

will change the name and possibly the path of a file. **Notes:** The **remove** and **rename** functions cannot be used with open files; doing so generates an error message. Also, the second argument of the **rename** function cannot be the name of an existing file.

An error message is generated if the file to be removed, renamed, or opened for reading does not exist. The function

os.path.isfile(*fileName*)

that returns **True** if the specified file exists and **False** otherwise, can be used to verify that a file exists before attempts are made to rename, delete, or read it.

We will now change the subject and discuss a new data type called a *set*. Then we will show how sets provide a powerful tool for refining text files and for extracting data from pairs of related text files.

VideoNote

Sets

■ Sets

A list is an *ordered* collection of items, possibly with repetitions. A **set** is an *unordered* collection of items (referred to as **elements**) with no duplicates. Whereas the items in a list are delimited with square brackets, the elements in a set are delimited with braces. Sets can contain numbers, strings, tuples, and Boolean values. However, sets cannot contain lists or other sets. Some examples of sets are {"spam", "ni"}, {3, 4, 7}, {True, 7, "eleven"}, and {'a', 'b', (3, 4)}.

Many **list** and **tuple** operations (like **in**, **len**, **max**, **min**, **sum**, and **writelines**) and being able to use a **for** loop to iterate over all of their elements, also apply to sets. The main differences between sets and lists (or tuples) are that no items in a set can appear twice and the elements in a set have no order. Since the elements have no order, they cannot be indexed and therefore slicing and list methods such as **sort** and **reverse** are meaningless with regards to sets. Table 5.1 contains a few basic elementary methods and functions for sets. (Note that when the set function is applied to a list or record, duplicate items only appear once in the set.) Two sets are equal if they contain the same elements.

TABLE 5.1	**Set operations (words = {"spam", "ni"}).**			
Methods and Functions	Example	Value of Set	Description	
add	words.add("eggs")	{"spam", "ni", "eggs"}	adds item to set	
discard	words.discard{"ni"}	{"spam"}	removes specified item	
clear	words.clear()	set()	set() is the empty set	
set	set([3, 7, 3])	{3, 7}	convert a list to a set	
	set((3, 7, 3))	{3, 7}	convert a tuple to a set	

Although the elements of a set cannot be ordered, they can be placed into a list in a customized order with a statement of the form

```
sorted(set1, key=f, reverse=BooleanValue)
```

✓ **Example 6** The following program illustrates several set operations.

```python
def main():
    # Use a set to remove the duplicates from a list.
    words = ["nudge", "nudge", "wink", "wink"]
    terms = set(words)
    print(terms)
    words = list(terms)
    print(words)
    # Demonstrate the effect of the add method.
    terms.add("nudge")   # Has no effect since 'nudge' was already in the set.
    terms.add("maybe")
    print(terms)
    # Demonstrate the effect of the discard method.
    terms.discard("nudge")
    print(terms)   # The word 'nudge' was removed from the set.
    # Convert the set to a tuple.
    words = tuple(terms)
    print(words)

main()
```

[Run]

```
{'nudge', 'wink'}
['nudge', 'wink']
{'nudge', 'wink', 'maybe'}
{'wink', 'maybe'}
('wink', 'maybe')
```

■ Set Comprehension

Like lists, sets can be created with **comprehension**. For instance, the statement

```
{x * x for x in range(-3, 3)}
```

creates the set {0, 1, 4, 9}.

■ Set-Theoretic Methods

Python has methods that create new sets from two existing sets. For instance, we might want to merge the two sets. Or, we might want a new set to contain the items that appear in both of the existing sets. Or, we might want to alter one set by deleting the items that also appear in the other set. The three methods used to carry out such operations are as follows:

set1.union(set2) is the set containing the elements in either *set1* or *set2*, without duplications.

set1.intersection(set2) is the set containing the elements that are in both *set1* and *set2*.

set1.difference(set2) is the set containing the elements of *set1* with the elements of *set2* removed.

■ Using Set-Theoretic Methods with Files

Three steps for extracting information from two related text files are as follows:

1. Create two sets, each containing the contents of one of the two text files.
2. Apply a set operation, such as **union**, **intersection**, or **difference**, to the sets.
3. Write the resulting set into a new text file.

 Example 7   Set-Theoretic Methods   The following program demonstrates the use of the three set-theoretic operations with two simple text files whose contents are shown below. The program combines these two files in three ways. In the fifth and eighth lines, precaution is taken in case the last line of the file does not end with a newline character.

File1.txt	File2.txt
Alpha	Bravo
Bravo	Delta
Charlie	

```
def main():
    ## Demonstrate set-theoretic methods.
    # Use the two files to create two sets.
    infile = open("File1.txt", 'r')
    firstSet = {line.rstrip() + "\n" for line in infile}
    infile.close()
    infile = open("File2.txt", 'r')
    secondSet = {line.rstrip() + "\n" for line in infile}
    infile.close()
    # Create files containing the union, intersection, and difference of
    # the original two files.
    outfile = open("Union.txt", 'w')
    outfile.writelines(firstSet.union(secondSet))
    outfile.close()
    outfile = open("Intersection.txt", 'w')
    outfile.writelines(firstSet.intersection(secondSet))
    outfile.close()
    outfile = open("Difference.txt", 'w')
    outfile.writelines(firstSet.difference(secondSet))
    outfile.close()

main()
```

[Run, and then look at the three new text files.]

The file **Union.txt** contains the four words Alpha, Bravo, Charlie, and Delta.
The file **Intersection.txt** contains the single word Bravo.
The file **Difference.txt** contains the two words Alpha and Charlie.

 Example 8   U.S. Presidents   The following rewrite of Example 4 uses set methods to create a file containing the names of vice presidents who became presidents.

```
def main():
    ## Create a file of the presidents who also served as vice-presidents.
    vicePresSet = createSetFromFile("VPres.txt")
```

```
        presSet = createSetFromFile("USPres.txt")
        bothPresAndVPresSet = createIntersection(vicePresSet, presSet)
        writeNamesToFile(bothPresAndVPresSet, "PresAndVPres.txt")

def createSetFromFile(fileName):
    # Assume that the last line of the file ends with a newline character.
    infile = open(fileName, 'r')
    namesSet = {name for name in infile}
    infile.close()
    return namesSet

def createIntersection(set1, set2):
    return set1.intersection(set2)

def writeNamesToFile(setName, fileName):
    outfile = open(fileName, 'w')
    outfile.writelines(setName)
    outfile.close()

main()
```

[Run. The file **PresAndVPres.txt** will resemble the file below when opened in a text editor. (Assume both files end with a newline character.)]

```
Theodore Roosevelt
Andrew Johnson
    .
    .
George H. W. Bush
Martin Van Buren
```

■ Comments

1. We have been using the variable names *infile* and *outfile* since they are suggestive of the roles the variables play. However, any valid variable names can be used. Two other suggestive names are *fin*, an abbreviation for "file input," and fout, an abbreviation for "file output."

2. An attempt to open a nonexistent file for input generates a runtime error. If a file that already exists is opened for writing, the contents of the file will be erased. One way to prevent these two unwanted events from happening is to use the Boolean-valued **os.path.isfile** function. Another way to prevent these events from happening is to use a **try** statement. The **try** statement is discussed in Chapter 6.

3. If the file specified in an "open for append" statement does not exist, the **open** statement will create a new file with the specified name. That is, in that case the append mode will perform the same as the "open for writing" mode.

4. "Open for reading" is the default mode for opening a file. Therefore, a statement of the form

   ```
   infile = open(fileName, 'r')
   ```

   can be abbreviated to

   ```
   infile = open(fileName)
   ```

5. Only strings can be written to text files. Therefore a statement such as **outfile.write(7)** is not valid.

6. The value of **set1.union(object1)**, where *object1* is a list or tuple, is the same as the value of **set1.union(set(object1))**. Similarly for the **intersection** and **difference** methods.

7. If *s* is a string, the value of **set(s)** is the set containing the characters of the string without repetition. For instance, **print(set("Mississippi"))** displays **{'M', 's', 'p', 'i'}**.

8. The value of **set()** is the empty set.

Practice Problems 5.1

1. Suppose the file **Words.txt** contains words written in lowercase letters, with some words appearing more than once. What is the effect of the following lines of code?

```
infile = open("Words.txt", 'r')
wordList = [line.rstrip() for line in infile]
infile.close()
wordSet = set(wordList)
outfile = open("Words.txt", 'w')
for word in sorted(wordSet):
    outfile.write(word + "\n")
outfile.close()
```

2. What would happen if the argument **end=""** was omitted from the *displayWithReadline* function discussed earlier?

3. Suppose *listNumbers* is a list of numbers. Write lines of code to place the contents of *listNumbers* into the file **SomeNumbers.txt**.

4. The statement **list2 = list(set(list1))** creates a list with all duplicates from *list1* removed. Write code that accomplishes the same task without using a set function.

EXERCISES 5.1

In Exercises 1 through 12, determine the output displayed by the lines of code.

1.
```
outfile = open("Greetings.txt", 'w')
outfile.write("Hello\n")
outfile.write("Aloha\n")
outfile.close()
infile = open("Greetings.txt", 'r')
for line in infile:
    text = infile.readline().rstrip()
infile.close()
print(text)
```

2.
```
outfile = open("Greetings.txt", 'w')
outfile.write("Hello\n")
outfile.write("Aloha\n")
outfile.close()
infile = open("Greetings.txt", 'r')
text = infile.readline().rstrip()
infile.close()
print(text)
```

3.
```
list1 = ["Hello\n", "Aloha\n"]
outfile = open("Greetings.txt", 'w')
```

```
outfile.writelines(list1)
outfile.close()
infile = open("Greetings.txt", 'r')
text = infile.read()
infile.close()
print(text.rstrip())
```

4. ```
list1 = ["Hello", "Aloha\n"]
outfile = open("Greetings.txt", 'a')
outfile.writelines(list1)
outfile.close()
infile = open("Greetings.txt", 'r')
text = infile.read().rstrip()
infile.close()
print(text)
```

5. ```
print(len(set("Bookkeeper")))
```

6. ```
print(sorted(set([3, 4, 1, 4, 3])))
```

7. ```
print([x ** 2 for x in range(-2, 3)])
```

8. ```
print(sorted({x ** 2 for x in range(-2, 3)}))
```

9. ```
s = {"Believe", "yourself."}
s.add("in")
print(" ".join(sorted(s)))
```

10. ```
s = {"Always", "up.", "give", "Never"}
s.discard("Always")
print(" ".join(sorted(s, key=len, reverse=True)))
```

11. ```
s = set("cat")
s.add('t')
print(sorted(s))
```

12. ```
s = set("dozen")
s.discard('d')
print(sorted(s, reverse=True))
```

In Exercises 13 through 22, identify any errors in the code segments. Assume that the file ABC.txt has three lines containing the data A, B, and C.

13. ```
infile = open("ABC.txt", 'w')
line = infile.readline()
infile.close()
```

14. ```
outfile = open(ABC.txt, 'a')
outfile.write("D\n")
outfile.close()
```

15. ```
infile = open("ABC.txt", 'r')
line = infile.readline()
"ABC.txt".close()
```

16. ```
outfile = open("ABC.txt", 'r')
outfile.write("D\n")
outfile.close()
```

17. ```
outfile = open("Data.txt", 'w')
for i in range(5):
    outfile.write(i)
outfile.close()
```

18. ```
list1 = ["spam\n", "eggs\n"]
outfile = open("Data.txt", 'w')
outfile.writelines(list1)
print(len(outfile))
outfile.close()
```
```

19.
```
list1 = ["Hello\n", "Aloha"]
outfile = open("Greet.txt", 'w')
outfile.writelines(list1)
infile = open("Greet.txt", 'r')
text = infile.read()
outfile.close()
print(text)
```

20.
```
list1 = ["spam", "and", "eggs"]
outfile = open("Data.txt", 'w')
for word in list1:
    outfile.write(word + "\n")
    outfile.write((len(word))
outfile.close()
```

21.
```
infile = open("ABC.txt", 'r')
infile.close()
line = infile.readline()
```

22.
```
set1 = {"xyz", 5, [3, 4]}
list1 = list(set1)
```

Exercises 23 and 24 refer to the following program. (Assume that the current folder does not contain a file named ABC.txt.)

```
import os.path
if os.path.isfile("ABC.txt"):
    print("File already exists.")
else:
    infile = open("ABC.txt", 'w')
    infile.write("a\nb\nc\n")
    infile.close()
```

23. What happens the first time the program is run?

24. What happens the second time the program is run?

In Exercises 25 through 28, use sets to simplify the function. There is no need to maintain the order of the items in the lists.

25.
```
def removeDuplicates(list1):
    list2 = []
    for item in list1:
        if item not in list2:
            list2.append(item)
    return list2
```

26.
```
def findItemsInBoth(list1, list2):
    list3 = []
    for item in list1:
        if (item in list2) and (item not in list3):
            list3.append(item)
    return list3
```

27.
```
def findItemsInEither(list1, list2):
    list3 = []
    for item in list1:
        if (item not in list3):
            list3.append(item)
    for item in list2:
        if (item not in list3):
            list3.append(item)
    return list3
```

28. Use set comprehension to simplify the following lines of code.

```
names = ["Donald Shell", "Harlan Mills", "Donald Knuth", "Alan Kay"]
setLN = set()    # empty set
```

```
for name in names:
    setLN.add(name.split()[-1])
print(setLN)
```

29. **Gettysburg Address** The file `Gettysburg.txt` contains the entire Gettysburg Address as a single line.[1] Write lines of code that display the first 89 characters of the Gettysburg Address, the number of words in the Gettysburg Address, and the number of different words. See Fig. 5.3.

```
Four score and seven years ago, our fathers brought
forth on this continent a new nation:
The Gettysburg Address contains 268 words.
The Gettysburg Address contains 139 different words.
```

FIGURE 5.3   Outcome of Exercise 29.

In Exercises 30 through 32, describe the new file created by the code. Assume the file `NYTimes.txt` contains the names of subscribers to the *New York Times* and the file `WSJ.txt` contains the names of the subscribers to the *Wall Street Journal*.

30.
```
infile = open("NYTimes.txt", 'r')
timesList = [line.rstrip() for line in infile]
infile.close()
timesSet = set(timesList)
infile = open("WSJ.txt", 'r')
wsjList = [line.rstrip() for line in infile]
infile.close()
wsjSet = set(wsjList)
combinationSet = timesSet.union(wsjSet)
combinationList = list(combinationSet)
combinationString = ('\n').join(combinationList)
outfile = open("NewFile.txt", 'w')
outfile.write(combinationString)
outfile.close()
```

31. Rework Exercise 30 with the word *union* in the ninth line changed to *intersection*.

32. Rework Exercise 30 with the word *union* in the ninth line changed to *difference*.

33. **Crayon Colors** At the beginning of 1990, a complete box of Crayola[2] crayons had 72 colors (in the file `Pre1990.txt`). During the 1990s, 8 colors were retired (in the file `Retired.txt`) and 56 new colors were added (in the file `Added.txt`). Write a program that creates a text file containing the post-1990s set of 120 colors in alphabetical order. *Note:* The first four lines of the new text file will contain the colors Almond, Antique Brass, Apricot, and Aquamarine.

The file `Numbers.txt` contains the integers 6, 9, 2, 3, 6, 4 with each integer on a separate line. In Exercises 34 through 42, write a program that uses the file to carry out the task without using lists.

34. **Numbers** Display the number of numbers in the file `Numbers.txt`. See Fig. 5.4.

35. **Numbers** Display the largest number in the file `Numbers.txt`. See Fig. 5.5.

---

[1]The file `Gettysburg.txt` is located in the folder *Programs/Ch5* of the material downloaded from the Pearson website. All files required for exercises in this chapter are located in that folder.

[2]Crayola is a registered trademark of Binney & Smith.

```
The file Numbers.txt
contains 6 numbers.
```

FIGURE 5.4 Outcome of Exercise 34.

```
The largest number in the
file Numbers.txt is 9.
```

FIGURE 5.5 Outcome of Exercise 35.

36. Numbers Display the smallest number in the file **Numbers.txt**. See Fig. 5.6.

```
The smallest number in the
file Numbers.txt is 2.
```

FIGURE 5.6 Outcome of Exercise 36.

```
The sum of the numbers in
the file Numbers.txt is 30.
```

FIGURE 5.7 Outcome of Exercise 37.

37. Numbers Display the sum of the numbers in the file **Numbers.txt**. See Fig. 5.7.

38. Numbers Display the average of the numbers in the file **Numbers.txt**. See Fig. 5.8.

```
The average of the numbers in
the file Numbers.txt is 5.0.
```

FIGURE 5.8 Outcome of Exercise 38.

```
The last number in the
file Numbers.txt is 4.
```

FIGURE 5.9 Outcome of Exercise 39.

39. Numbers Display the last number in the file **Numbers.txt**. See Fig. 5.9.

40. Months The file **SomeMonths.txt** initially contains the names of the 12 months. Write a program that deletes all months from the file that do not contain the letter *r*.

41. Crayon Colors The file **ShortColors.txt** initially contains the names of all the colors in a full box of Crayola crayons. Write a program that deletes all colors from the file whose name contains more than six characters.

42. Players The files **SomePlayers.txt** initially contains the names of 30 football players. Write a program that deletes those players from the file whose names do not begin with a vowel.

43. Students The file **AllStudents.txt** contains the names and final grades of all 30 students in a class, arranged in alphabetical order. The file **PassedStudents.txt** contains the names of the 17 students who passed. Create a text file that contains the alphabetized names of the remaining 13 students who did not pass.

44. States The 44 lines of the file **PresStates.txt** contain the names of the states that produced each of the first 44 presidents. The first four lines of the file contain the states Virginia, Massachusetts, Virginia, and Virginia. Write a program that deletes all duplications from the file and also displays the number of states that have produced presidents. See Fig. 5.10.

```
Enter the lower number for the range: 10
Enter the upper number for the range: 14
   10 John Tyler
   11 James Polk
   12 Zachary Taylor
   13 Millard Fillmore
   14 Franklin Pierce
```

```
18 different states have
produced presidents of the
United States.
```

FIGURE 5.10 Outcome of Exercise 44.

FIGURE 5.11 Outcome of Exercise 45.

45. U.S. Presidents   The file **USPres.txt** contains the names of the first 44 U.S. presidents in the order they served. Write a program (without using a list) that requests a range of numbers and displays all presidents whose number is in that range. Figure 5.11 shows one possible outcome. (John Tyler was the tenth president, James Polk was the eleventh president, and so on.)

46. File of Names   The file **Names.txt** contains a list of first names in alphabetical order. Write a program that requests a name from the user and inserts the name into the file in its proper location. If the name is already in the file, it should not be inserted.

Solutions to Practice Problems 5.1

1. A new file is created with all the words from the old file in alphabetical order and with no duplicates.

2. The names would be displayed double-spaced.

3.
```
# Convert each number in the list to a string with "\n" appended to it.
for i in range(len(listNumbers)):
    listNumbers[i] = str(listNumbers[i]) + "\n"
# Write the list to a file.
outfile = open("SomeNumbers.txt", 'w')
outfile.writelines(listNumbers)
outfile.close()
```

or

```
# Write the list of numbers to a file. Convert to strings while writing.
outfile = open("SomeNumbers.txt", 'w')
for num in listNumbers:
    outfile.write(str(num) + "\n")
outfile.close()
```

4.
```
list2 = []
for x in list1:
    if x not in list2:
        list2.append(x)
```

5.2   Processing Data, Part 2

Data to be processed usually comes in files containing large tables. This section shows how to analyze such tables. It also shows how to obtain data from the Web.

■ CSV Files

The text files considered so far had a single piece of data per line. For instance, each line of the file **States.txt** contained the name of a state, and each line of the file **USPres.txt** contained the name of a president. Another type of text file, called a **CSV-formatted file**, has several items of data on each line with the items separated by commas. (CSV stands for *Comma-Separated Values*.) An example is the file **UN.txt** that gives data about the 193 members of the United Nations with the countries listed in alphabetical order. Each line of the file gives four pieces of data about a country—*name*, *continent*, *population* (in millions), and *land area* (in square miles). Some lines of the file are

```
Canada,North America,34.8,3855000
France,Europe,66.3,211209
New Zealand,Australia/Oceania,4.4,103738
Nigeria,Africa,177.2,356669
Pakistan,Asia,196.2,310403
Peru,South America,30.1,496226
```

Each line of this text file is called a **record** and each record is said to contain four **fields**—a name field, a continent field, a population field, and an area field. The data in the fields of each record are related—they apply to the same country.

VideoNote

Accessing
Data in a
CSV File

■ Accessing the Data in a CSV File

The split method is used to access the fields of CSV-formatted files. For instance, if the variable *line* holds the first record shown above and the value of the variable *data* is the list line.split(","), then the value of **data[0]** is **Canada**, the value of **data[1]** is **North America**, the value of **eval(data[2])** is the number **34.8**, and the value of **eval(data[3])** is the number **3855000**.

✔ **Example 1**   United Nations The following program requests the name of a continent and then displays the names of the U.N. member countries located on that continent.

```
def main():
    ## Display the countries in a specified continent.
    continent = input("Enter the name of a continent: ")
    continent = continent.title()   # Allow for all lowercase letters.
    if continent != "Antactica":
        infile = open("UN.txt", 'r')
        for line in infile:
            data = line.split(',')
            if data[1] == continent:
                print(data[0])
    else:
        print("There are no countries in Antarctica.")

main()
```

[Run]

```
Enter the name of a continent: South America
Argentina
Bolivia
Brazil
  ⋮
Uruguay
Venezuela
```

■ Analyzing the Data in a CSV File with a List

The data in a CSV file can be analyzed by placing the data into a list. The items of the list are other lists holding the contents of a single line of the file.

Example 2   United Nations   The following program places the contents of the file **UN.txt** into a list of 193 items, where each item is a list containing the four pieces of data for a single country. Since all data in text files is stored as strings, the values for population and area must be converted to numbers. **Note:** After the third line of the *placeRecordsIntoList* function is executed, the first item in *listOfRecords* will be

"Afghanistan,Asia,31.8,251772"

After the **split** method is applied to this item in the sixth line of *placeRecordsIntoList*, the item will be replaced with the four-item list

["Afghanistan", "Asia", "31.8", "251772"]

After the **eval** function is applied to the last two entries in this list, the four-item list becomes

["Afghanistan", "Asia", 31.8, 251772].

The program then returns to the *main* function, where it sorts the countries by area in descending order and calls a function to display the names and areas of the five largest countries. Finally the program calls a function to create a new CSV file containing the names and areas of all the countries in descending order by area.

```python
def main():
    ## Create a file containing all countries and areas, ordered by area.
    ## Display first five lines of the file.
    countries = placeRecordsIntoList("UN.txt")
    countries.sort(key=lambda country: country[3], reverse=True) #sort by area
    displayFiveLargestCountries(countries)
    createNewFile(countries)  # Create file of countries and their areas.

def placeRecordsIntoList(fileName):
    infile = open(fileName, 'r')
    listOfRecords = [line.rstrip() for line in infile]
    infile.close()
    for i in range(len(listOfRecords)):
        listOfRecords[i] = listOfRecords[i].split(',')
        listOfRecords[i][2] = eval(listOfRecords[i][2])  # population
        listOfRecords[i][3] = eval(listOfRecords[i][3])  # area
    return listOfRecords

def displayFiveLargestCountries(countries):
    print("{0:20}{1:9}".format("Country", "Area (sq. mi.)"))
    for i in range(5):
        print("{0:20}{1:9,d}".format(countries[i][0], countries[i][3]))

def createNewFile(countries):
    outfile = open("UNbyArea.txt", 'w')
    for country in countries:
        outfile.write(country[0] + ',' + str(country[3]) + "\n")

main()
```

[Run]

```
Country             Area (sq. mi.)
Russian Federation  6,592,800
Canada              3,855,000
United States       3,794,066
```

```
China                  3,696,100
Brazil                 3,287,597
```

The first three lines of the CSV file **UNbyArea.txt** are

```
Russian Federation,6592800
Canada,3855000
United States,3794066
```

Note: In Example 2, the individual pieces of data, such as a county's name or a country's area, are accessed by a doubly-indexed variable. For instance, *country*[0][0] holds the name of the first country and *country*[0][3] holds the area of the first country. The first index determines the four-item list for the country, and the second index identifies one of the four fields for the country. The population of the last country in the list can be accessed as *country*[−1][2] or *country*[len(countries) − 1][2].

■ Analyzing Numeric Data

Suppose we wanted to do a statistical analysis of the areas of the 193 countries. For instance, we might want to calculate their average, median, and standard deviation. These tasks would be most easily accomplished by placing the 193 numbers into a list.

Example 3 United Nations The following program carries out a statistical analysis of the areas of the countries in the United Nations. (See Exercise 66 in Section 3.4 and Programming Project 2 of Chapter 5 for the definitions of *median* and *standard deviation*.)

```python
def main():
    ## Do statistical analysis of country's areas.
    areasAsStrings = extractField("UN.txt", 4)    # Place areas into a list.
    areas = [eval(num) for num in areasAsStrings]
    displaySomeStatistics(areas)

def extractField(fileName, n):
    ## Extract the nth field from each record of a CSV file
    ## and place the data into a list.
    infile = open(fileName, 'r')
    return [line.rstrip().split(',')[n - 1] for line in infile]

def displaySomeStatistics(listOfNumbers):
    ## Display the average, median, and standard deviation of the areas.
    average = sum(listOfNumbers) / len(listOfNumbers)
    median = calculateMedian(listOfNumbers)
    standardDeviation = calculateStandardDeviation(listOfNumbers, average)
    print("Average area: {0:,.2f} square miles".format(average))
    print("Median area: {0:,d} square miles".format(median))
    print("Standard deviation: {0:,.2f} square miles".format(standardDeviation))

def calculateMedian(listOfNumbers):
    listOfNumbers.sort()
    if len(listOfNumbers) % 2 == 1:
        median = listOfNumbers[int(len(listOfNumbers) / 2)]  # middle number
```

```
    else:
        # Median will be the average of the two middle numbers.
        m = int(len(listOfNumbers) / 2)
        median = (listOfNumbers[m] + listOfNumbers[m + 1]) / 2
    return median

def calculateStandardDeviation(listOfNumbers, average):
    m = average
    n = len(listOfNumbers)
    listOfSquaresOfDeviations = [0] * n
    for i in range(n):
        listOfSquaresOfDeviations[i] = (listOfNumbers[i] - m) ** 2
    standardDeviation = (sum(listOfSquaresOfDeviations) / n) ** .5
    return standardDeviation

main()
```

[Run]

```
Average area: 268,550.96 square miles
Median area: 46,528 square miles
Standard deviation: 741,598.06 square miles
```

■ Excel and CSV Files

CSV files can be converted to Excel spreadsheets and vice versa. For instance, consider the CSV file **UN.txt**. If you open the file in Excel and select comma when asked for the delimiter, Excel will create a spreadsheet with 193 lines and 4 columns. Figure 5.12 shows the first four lines of the spreadsheet.

	A	B	C	D
1	Afghanistan	Asia	31.8	251772
2	Albania	Europe	3	11100
3	Algeria	Africa	38.3	919595
4	Andorra	Europe	0.085	181

FIGURE 5.12   **Spreadsheet created from UN.txt.**

Conversely, a spreadsheet you create or download from the Internet can be converted to a CSV file. After clicking on "Save As" from the FILE menu, choose "CSV (Comma delimited)(*.csv)" in the "Save as type" dropdown box.

■ Comments

1. The function *extractField* from Example 3 is a good all-purpose function that will be useful, with slight modifications, in several of the exercises in this book. Also, the functions *calculateMedian* and *calculateStandardDeviation* come in handy whenever statistics are needed.

2. In Example 2, we used a long list of four-item lists to hold the data. The information in each four-item list was referenced by a pair of index numbers. In the next section, we will discuss a structure that allows us to access data with meaningful names such as *popl* and *area* instead of with index numbers.

Practice Problems 5.2

1. Describe the output of the following program.

```
def main():
    continents = extractField("UN.txt", 2)    # Place continents into a set.
    displayElementsOfSet(continents)

def extractField(fileName, n):
    ## Extract the nth field from each record of a CSV file
    ## and place the data into a set.
    infile = open(fileName, 'r')
    return {record.rstrip().split(',')[n - 1] for record in infile}

def displayElementsOfSet(setName):
    ## Display ordered elements.
    for element in sorted(setName):
        print(element)

main()
```

2. Describe the output of the following program.

```
def main():
    list1 = extractFields("UN.txt", 1, 4)
    for pair in list1:
        pair[1] = eval(pair[1])
    for pair in list1:
        print(pair[0], pair[1])

def extractFields(fileName, m, n):
    ## Extract the mth and nth fields of each record.
    infile = open(fileName, 'r')
    return [[record.rstrip().split(',')[m - 1],
            record.rstrip().split(',')[n - 1]] for record in infile]

main()
```

EXERCISES 5.2

Exercises 1 through 6 refer to the file UN.txt that gives data about the 193 members of the United Nations with the countries listed in alphabetical order. Each line of the file gives four pieces of data about a single country—*name*, *continent*, *population* (in millions), and *land area* (in square miles). The first two lines of the file are as follows:

```
Afghanistan,Asia,31.8,251772
Albania,Europe,3.0,11100
```

In Exercises 1 through 4, determine the first two lines of the new file created by the code.

1.
```
infile = open("UN.txt", 'r')
outfile = open("NewFile.txt", 'w')
for line in infile:
    line = line.rstrip()
    data = line.split(',')
```

```
        data[3] = eval(data[3])
        outfile.write("The area of {0} is {1:,.0f} sq. miles.".format(data[0],
                    data[3]) + '\n')
    infile.close()
    outfile.close()
```

2.
```
infile = open("UN.txt", 'r')
outfile = open("NewFile.txt", 'w')
for line in infile:
    data = line.split(',')
    outfile.write(data[0] + " is in " + data[1] + '.\n')
infile.close()
outfile.close()
```

3.
```
infile = open("UN.txt", 'r')
outfile = open("NewFile.txt", 'w')
for line in infile:
    data = line.split(',')
    country = data[0]
    continent = data[1]
    area = data[3]
    outfile.write(country + ',' + continent + ',' + area)
infile.close()
outfile.close()
```

4.
```
infile = open("UN.txt", 'r')
outfile = open("NewFile.txt", 'w')
for line in infile:
    data = line.split(',')
    country = data[0]
    pop = 1000000 * eval(data[2])
    area = eval(data[3])
    popDensity = pop / area
    outfile.write("{0}'s pop. density is {1:0,.2f}".format(country,
                popDensity) + " people per sq. mile.\n")
infile.close()
outfile.close()
```

In Exercises 5 and 6, describe the new file created by the program.

5.
```
def main():
    countries = placeDataIntoList("UN.txt")
    countries.sort(key=byPop, reverse=True)
    createFile(countries)

def placeDataIntoList(fileName):
    countries = []
    infile = open(fileName, 'r')
    for line in infile:
        line = line.split(',')
        if line[1] == "Europe":
            countries.append(list((line[0], eval(line[2]))))
```

```
    infile.close()
    return countries

def byPop(country):
    return country[1]

def createFile(countries):
    outfile = open("EuropeByPop.txt", 'w')
    for country in countries:
        outfile.write(country[0] + ',' + str(country[1]) + "\n")
    outfile.close()

main()
```

6.
```
def main():
    countries = placeDataIntoList("UN.txt")
    countries.sort(key=byContinent)
    createFile(countries)

def placeDataIntoList(fileName):
    listOfInfo = []
    infile = open(fileName, 'r')
    line = infile.readline()
    while line.startswith('A'):
        line2 = line.split(',')
        listOfInfo.append(list((line2[0], line2[1])))
        line = infile.readline()
    infile.close()
    return listOfInfo

def byContinent(country):
    return country[1]

def createFile(countries):
    outfile = open("CountriesByContinent.txt", 'w')
    for country in countries:
        outfile.write(country[0] + ',' + str(country[1]) + "\n")

main()
```

In Exercises 7 through 10, use the file DOW.txt that contains the name, symbol, exchange, industry, price at the end of trading on 12/31/2012, price at the end of trading on 12/31/2013, 2013 earnings per share, and the dividend paid in 2013 for each of the 30 stocks in the Dow Jones Industrial Average. The first three lines of the file are

```
American Express,AXP,NYSE,Consumer finance,57.48,90.73,4.88,.89
Boeing,BA,NYSE,Aerospace & Defense,75.36,136.49,5.96,2.19
Caterpillar,CAT,NYSE,Construction & Mining Equipment,89.61,90.81,5.75,2.32
```

7. DOW   Write a program that displays the symbols for the 30 DOW stocks in alphabetical order. When the user enters one of the symbols, the information shown in Fig. 5.13 should be displayed. The Price/Earnings ratio should be calculated as the price of a share of stock on 12/31/2013 divided by the 2013 earnings per share.

```
Symbols for the Thirty DOW Stocks
AXP     BA      CAT     CSCO    CVX     DD      DIS     GE      GS      HD
IBM     INTC    JNJ     JPM     KO      MCD     MMM     MRK     MSFT    NKE
PFE     PG      T       TRV     UNH     UTX     V       VZ      WMT     XOM

Enter a symbol: CSCO
Company: Cisco Systems
Industry: Computer networking
Exchange: NASDAQ
Growth in 2013: 14.15%
Price/Earning ratio in 2013: 15.05
```

FIGURE 5.13   Outcome of Exercise 7.

8. DOW   Write a program that determines the best and worst performing stock(s) in 2013 with regards to percentage growth. See Fig. 5.14.

```
Best performing stock: Boeing 81.12%
Worst performing stock: International Business Machines -2.08%
```

FIGURE 5.14   Outcome of Exercise 8.

9. Dogs of the DOW   A simple investment strategy known as "Dogs of the DOW" has performed well in many years. An investor employing this strategy maintains a portfolio of 10 DOW stocks. At the beginning of each year, the portfolio is readjusted so that it contains equal amounts of money invested in the 10 stocks having the highest dividend yields, that is, the highest ratios of dividend in 2013 to price at the end of the year. Write a program to determine the 10 stocks that should be in the portfolio at the beginning of 2014. See Fig. 5.15.

```
Company                 Symbol      Yield as of 12/31/2013
AT&T                    T           5.15%
Verizon                 VZ          4.19%
Intel                   INTC        3.47%
Merck                   MRK         3.46%
McDonald's              MCD         3.22%
Cisco Systems           CSCO        3.21%
Chevron Corporation     CVX         3.20%
Pfizer                  PFE         3.20%
Procter & Gamble        PG          3.06%
Microsoft               MSFT        2.86%
```

FIGURE 5.15   Outcome of Exercise 9.

10. Small Dogs of the DOW   An investment strategy known as "Small Dogs of the DOW" has also performed well in many years. An investor employing this strategy maintains a portfolio of the five lowest-priced DOW stocks. The portfolio is readjusted at the beginning of each year. Write a program to determine the five stocks that should be in the portfolio at the beginning of 2014. See Fig. 5.16.

Company	Symbol	Price on 12/31/2013
Cisco Systems	CSCO	$22.43
Intel	INTC	$25.95
General Electric	GE	$28.03
Pfizer	PFE	$30.63
AT&T	T	$35.16

FIGURE 5.16   Outcome of Exercise 10.

In Exercises 11 through 14, use the file `Justices.txt` that contains data about the Supreme Court justices, past and present as of January 2015. Each record of the file contains six fields—*first name, last name, appointing president, the state from which they were appointed, year appointed,* and *the year the justice left the court.* (For current justices, the last field is set to 0.) The first five lines of the file are as follows:

```
Samuel,Alito,George W. Bush,NJ,2006,0
Henry,Baldwin,Andrew Jackson,PA,1830,1844
Philip,Barbour,Andrew Jackson,VA,1836,1841
Hugo,Black,Franklin Roosevelt,AL,1937,1971
Harry,Blackman,Richard Nixon,MN,1970,1994
```

11. Supreme Court   Write a program that requests the name of a president as input and then displays the justices appointed by that president. The justices should be ordered by the length of time they served on the court in descending order. (**Note:** For current justices, use **2015 − yrAppointed** as their time of service. Otherwise, use **yrLeft − yrAppointed**.) See Fig. 5.17.

```
Enter the name of a president: George W. Bush
Justices Appointed:
   John Roberts
   Samuel Alito
```

FIGURE 5.17   Possible outcome of Exercise 11.

12. Supreme Court   Write a program that displays the current justices ordered by the year they joined the Supreme Court. See Fig. 5.18.

Current Justices:
Antonin Scalia
Anthony Kennedy
Clarence Thomas
Ruth Ginsburg
Stephen Breyer
John Roberts
Samuel Alito
Sonia Sotomayor
Elena Kagen

FIGURE 5.18   Outcome of Exercise 12.

Justice	Appointing President
William Brennan	Dwight Eisenhower
Potter Stewart	Dwight Eisenhower
Byron White	John Kennedy
Thurgood Marshall	Lyndon Johnson
Warren Burger	Richard Nixon
Harry Blackman	Richard Nixon
Lewis Powell	Richard Nixon
William Rehnquist	Richard Nixon
John Stevens	Gerald Ford

FIGURE 5.19   Outcome of Exercise 13.

13. **Supreme Court** Write a program that displays the composition of the Supreme Court at the beginning of 1980. The justices should be ordered by the year they were appointed, and the names of the appointing presidents should be displayed. See Fig. 5.19.

14. **Supreme Court** Write a program that requests a state abbreviation as input and displays the justices appointed from that state. The justices should be ordered by their years served. The output should also display the last name of the appointing president and the length of time served. (*Note:* For current justices, use **2015 − yrAppointed** as their time of service. Otherwise, use **yrLeft − yrAppointed**.) Also, the program should inform the user if no justices have been appointed from the requested state. See Fig. 5.20.

```
Enter a state abbreviation: NH

Justice             Appointing Pres    Yrs Served
David Souter        Bush               19
Levi Woodbury       Polk               6
```

FIGURE 5.20 Possible outcome of Exercise 14.

15. **The 12 Days of Christmas** Each year, PNC Advisors of Pittsburgh publishes a Christmas price index. See Table 5.2. Write a program that requests an integer from 1 through 12 and then lists the gifts for that day along with that day's cost. On the nth day, the n gifts are 1 partridge in a pear tree, 2 turtle doves, . . . , n of the nth gift. The program should also give the total cost up to and including that day. As an example, Fig. 5.21 shows the output when the user enters 3. The contents of Table 5.2, along with the day corresponding to each gift, are contained in the file **Gifts.txt**. The first three lines of the file are as follows:

```
1,partridge in a pear tree,207.68
2,turtle doves,62.50
3,French hens,60.50
```

TABLE 5.2 Christmas price index for 2014.

Item	Cost	Item	Cost
partridge in a pear tree	207.68	swan-a-swimming	1000.00
turtle dove	62.50	maid-a-milking	7.25
French hen	60.50	lady dancing	839.20
calling bird	149.99	lord-a-leaping	534.82
gold ring	150.00	piper piping	239.56
goose-a-laying	60.00	drummer drumming	237.83

```
Enter a number from 1 through 12: 3
The gifts for day 3 are
1 partridge in a pear tree
2 turtle doves
3 French hens

Cost for day 3: $514.18
Total cost for the first 3 days: $1,054.54
```

FIGURE 5.21 Possible output of Exercise 15.

16. Computer Pioneers The file `Pioneers.txt` contains some computer pioneers and their accomplishments. The first three records in the file are

```
Charles Babbage,is called the father of the computer.
Augusta Ada Byron,was the first computer programmer.
Alan Turing,was a prominent computer science theorist.
```

Write a program that displays the names. When a name is entered as input, the person's accomplishment should be displayed. See Fig. 5.22.

```
Charles Babbage      Augusta Ada Byron    Alan Turing          John V. Atanasoff
Grace M. Hopper      John Mauchley        J. Presper Eckert    John von Neumann
John Backus          Reynold B. Johnson   Harlan B. Mills      Donald E. Knuth
Ted Hoff             Stan Mazer           Robert Noyce         Federico Faggin
Douglas Engelbart    Bill Gates           Paul Allen           Stephen Wozniak
Stephen Jobs         Dennis Ritchie       Ken Thompson         Alan Kay
Tim Berners-Lee      Charles Simonyi      Bjarne Stroustrup    Richard M. Stallman
Marc Andreessen      James Gosling        Linus Torvalds       Guido van Rossum

Enter the name of a computer pioneer:  Augusta Ada Byron
Augusta Ada Byron was the first computer programmer.
```

FIGURE 5.22 Possible outcome of Exercise 16.

In Exercises 17 and 18, use the file `Colleges.txt` that contains data (*name, state,* and *year founded*) about colleges founded before 1800. The first four lines of the file are

```
Harvard University,MA,1636
William and Mary College,VA,1693
Yale University,CT,1701
University of Pennsylvania,PA,1740
```

17. Earliest Colleges Write a program that requests a state abbreviation as input and then displays the colleges alphabetically ordered (along with their year founded) in that state. If there are no early colleges in the state, so inform the user. See Fig. 5.23.

```
Enter a state abbreviation: PA
Dickinson College 1773
Moravian College 1742
University of Pennsylvania 1740
University of Pittsburgh 1787
Washington & Jefferson 1781
```

FIGURE 5.23 Possible outcome of Exercise 17.

```
Enter a state abbreviation: PA
Last college in PA founded before 1800:
University of Pittsburgh
```

FIGURE 5.24 Possible outcome of Exercise 18.

18. Earliest Colleges Write a program that requests a state abbreviation as input and then displays the last college in that state founded before 1800. See Fig. 5.24.

In Exercises 19 and 20, use the file `StatesANC.txt` that contains the name, abbreviation, nickname, and capital of each state in the United States. The states are listed in alphabetical order. The first three lines of the file are

```
Alabama,AL,Cotton State,Montgomery
Alaska,AK,The Last Frontier,Juneau
Arizona,AZ,Grand Canyon State,Phoenix
```

19. State Capitals   Write a program that displays the states (and their capitals) for which the name of the state and its capital begin with the same letter. See Fig. 5.25.

```
Dover, Delaware
Honolulu, Hawaii
Indianapolis, Indiana
Oklahoma City, Oklahoma
```

```
Enter the name of a state: Ohio
Abbreviation: OH
Nickname: Buckeye State
Capital: Columbus
```

FIGURE 5.25   Outcome of Exercise 19.   FIGURE 5.26   Possible outcome of Exercise 20.

20. State Data   Write a program that requests the name of a state as input and displays the abbreviation, nickname, and capital of the state. See Fig. 5.26.

In Exercises 21 and 22, use the file `Oscars.txt` that contains the names and genres of each film that won an Oscar for best picture of 1928 through 2013. The films are listed in the order they received the award. The first three lines of the file are

```
Wings,silent
The Broadway Melody,musical
All Quiet on the Western Front,war
```

21. Academy Awards   Write a program that displays the different film genres, requests a genre as input, and then displays the Oscar-winning films of that genre. See Fig. 5.27.

```
The different film genres are as follows:
adventure   bioptic    comedy    crime     drama
epic        fantasy    musical   romance   silent
sports      thriller   war       western

Enter a genre: silent

The Academy Award winners are
  Wings
  The Artist
```

FIGURE 5.27   Possible outcome of Exercise 21.

22. Academy Awards   Write a program that requests a year from 1928 through 2013 and then displays the name and genre of that year's best picture winner. See Fig. 5.28.

```
Enter year from 1928-2013: 2012
Best Film: Argo
Genre: drama
```

FIGURE 5.28   Possible outcome of Exercise 22.

Exercises 23 through 26 are related and use the data in Table 5.3. The file created in Exercise 23 should be used in Exercises 24 through 26.

23. Cowboys   Write a program to create the file `Cowboy.txt` containing the information in Table 5.3 on the next page.

TABLE 5.3	Prices paid by cowboys in mid-1800s.
Item	Price ($)
Colt Peacemaker	12.20
Holster	2.00
Levi Strauss jeans	1.35
Saddle	40.00
Stetson	10.00

24. Cowboys   Suppose the price of saddles is reduced by 20%. Use the file **Cowboy.txt** to create a file, **Cowboy2.txt**, containing the new price list.

25. Cowboys   Suppose an order is placed for 3 Colt Peacemakers, 2 Holsters, 10 pairs of Levi Strauss jeans, 1 Saddle, and 4 Stetsons. Write a program to perform the following tasks:

    (a) Create the file **Order.txt** to hold the numbers 3, 2, 10, 1, and 4 on five separate lines.
    (b) Use the files **Cowboy.txt** and **Order.txt** to display a sales receipt giving the quantity, name, and cost for each item ordered. See Fig. 5.29.
    (c) Compute the total cost of the items and display it at the end of the sales receipt.

```
3 Colt Peacemaker: $36.60

2 Holster: $4.00

10 Levi Strauss jeans: $13.50

1 Saddle: $40.00

4 Stetson: $40.00

TOTAL: $134.10
```

FIGURE 5.29   Outcome of Exercise 26.

26. Cowboys   Write a program to add the line **Winchester Rifle,20.50** to the end of the file **Cowboy.txt**.

27. **(a)** Calendar   Use Excel to create a spreadsheet of 365 rows and 2 columns, where the first column of each row contains a date in 2015 and the adjacent second column contains the corresponding day of the week. Figure 5.33 shows the first two rows of the spreadsheet. The remaining entries of the spreadsheet can be obtained by selecting the cells in Fig. 5.30 and dragging them down until 365 rows have been created.
    (b) Save the spreadsheet as a CSV file named **Calendar2015.csv**. *Note:* Select "CSV (Comma delimited)(*.csv)" in the "Save as type" dropdown box.
    (c) Change the file's name to **Calendar2015.txt**.
    (d) Use the text file in a program that requests a date in 2015 as input and then gives its day of the week. See Fig. 5.31.

◢	A	B
1	1/1/2015	Thursday
2	1/2/2015	Friday

FIGURE 5.30   Spreadsheet for Exercise 27.

```
Enter a date in 2015: 11/3/2015
11/3/2015 falls on a Tuesday
```

FIGURE 5.31   Possible outcome of Exercise 27.

Solutions to Practice Problems 5.2

1. The program displays the names of the six continents that contain countries. The first two lines of output will be as follows:

```
Africa

Asia
```

2. The program displays the name and area of every member country in the United Nations. The first two lines of output will be as follows:

```
Afghanistan 251772
Albania 11100
```

5.3   Dictionaries

VideoNote
Dictionaries

Consider the following function that translates certain English words to Spanish.

```
def translate(color):
    if color == "red":
        return "rojo"
    elif color == "blue":
        return "aloz"
    elif color == "green":
        return "verdi"
    elif color == "white":
        return "blanco"
```

This function is a mini English-Spanish dictionary. A function of this type is called a *mapping*. It maps English words to Spanish words. In mapping terminology, the words *red*, *blue*, *green*, and *white* are called **keys**, and the words *rojo*, *aloz*, *verdi*, and *blanco* are called **values**. The function, which could be extended to include thousands of words, associates a value with each key. Python has a much more efficient and flexible mapping device, called a **dictionary**. The dictionary that performs the same mapping as the function above is defined as follows:

```
translate = {"red":"rojo", "blue":"aloz", "green":"verdi", "white":"blanco"}
```

Then, the value of **translate["red"] is "rojo"**, the value of **translate["blue"] is "aloz"**, and so on. The dictionary is said to contain four **items**.

■ Dictionaries

In general, a Python dictionary is defined as a collection of comma-separated pairs of the form *"key:value"* enclosed in curly braces. The keys must be immutable objects (such as strings, numbers, or tuples), but the values can have any data types. The keys are unique, but the values needn't be unique.

The value associated with *key1* is given by the expression *dictionaryName*[*key1*]. Some examples of short programs using dictionaries are as follows:

```
bob = {"firstName":"Robert", "lastName":"Smith", "age":19}
print(bob["firstName"], bob["lastName"], "is", bob["age"], "years old.")
```

[Run]

```
Robert Smith is 19 years old.
```

```
phoneNum = {"Sam":2345678, "Ted":5436666, "Joe":4443456}
name = input("Enter a person's name: ")
print(name + "'s phone number is", phoneNum[name])
```

[Run]

```
Enter a person's name: Ted
Ted's phone number is 5436666
```

```
band = {6:"Six", "instrument":"Trombone", 7:"seventy"}
print(band[7].capitalize() + '-' + band[6], band["instrument"] + "s" )
```

[Run]

```
Seventy-Six Trombones
```

Table 5.4 shows functions and methods that can be applied to a dictionary.

TABLE 5.4   **Dictionary operations.**

Operation	Description
len(d)	number of items (that is, *key:value* pairs) in the dictionary
x in d	has value True if *x* is a key of the dictionary
x:y in d	has value True if *x:y* is an item of the dictionary. Otherwise, has value False
x:y not in d	has value True if *x:y* is not an item of the dictionary. Otherwise, has value False
d[*key1*] = *value1*	if *key1* is already a key in the dictionary, changes the value associated with *key1* to *value1*; otherwise, adds the item *key1:value1* to the dictionary
d[*key1*]	returns the value associated with *key1*. Raises an error if *key1* is not a key of d.
d.get(*key1*, *default*)	if *key1* is not a key of the dictionary, returns the default value. Otherwise, returns the value associated with *key1*
list(d.keys())	returns a list of the keys in the dictionary
list(d.values())	returns a list of the values in the dictionary
list(d.items())	returns a list of two-tuples of the form (*key, value*) where d(*key*) = *value*
list(d)	returns a list of the keys in the dictionary
tuple(d)	returns a tuple of the keys in the dictionary
set(d)	returns a set of the keys in the dictionary
c = {}	creates an empty dictionary
c = dict(d)	creates a copy of the dictionary d
del d[*key1*]	removes the item having *key1* as key; raises an exception if *key1* is not found
d.clear()	removes all items (that is, *key:value* pairs) from the dictionary
for k in d:	iterates over all the keys in the dictionary
d.update(c)	merges all of dictionary c's entries into dictionary d. If two items have the same key, the value from c replaces the value from d
max(d)	largest value of d.keys(), provided all keys have the same data type
min(d)	smallest value of d.keys(), provided all keys have the same data type

 Example 1   Dictionary Functions and Methods The following program illustrates many of the functions and methods for dictionaries. **Note:** When dictionaries are displayed by print functions, single quotation marks are used for strings and spaces are inserted after

the colons. Unlike lists, dictionaries are not ordered structures. Therefore, the order in which the pairs are displayed by print functions will not usually be the same as the order used when the dictionary was created.

```python
def main():
    ## Illustrate dictionary functions and methods.
    d = {}  # an empty dictionary
    d["spam"] = 3
    print(d)
    d.update({"spam":1, "eggs":2})
    print(d)
    print("d has", len(d), "items")
    print("eggs" in d)
    print("keys:", list(d.keys()))
    print("values:", list(d.values()))
    for key in d:
        print(key, d[key])
    print(d.get("toast", "not in dictionary"))
    del(d["eggs"])
    print(d)

main()
```

[Run]

```
{'spam': 3}
{'eggs': 2, 'spam': 1}
d has 2 items
True
keys: ['eggs', 'spam']
values: [2, 1]
eggs 2
spam 1
not in dictionary
{'spam': 1}
```

■ The *dict* Function

A list of two-item lists or two-item tuples can be converted to a dictionary with the dict function. For instance if

```python
list1 = [["one", 1], ["two", 2], ["three", 3]]
```

or

```python
list1 = [("one", 1), ("two", 2), ("three", 3)]
```

then the value of

```python
dict(list1)
```

will be the dictionary

```python
{"one":1, "two":2, "three":3}
```

■ Creating a Dictionary from a Text File

When a program incorporates a large dictionary, the dictionary is usually created from a file, such as a text file. Each line of the file **Textese.txt** contains a word and its translation into textese. The first five lines of the file are

```
anyone,ne1
are,r
ate,8
band,b&
be,b
```

 Example 2   Textese The following program translates simple sentences into textese. The function *createDictionary* first places the contents of the text file into a list of two-item lists and then uses the dict function to convert the list into a dictionary. Whenever a word in the original sentence is not a key in the dictionary, the get method places the word itself into the translated sentence.

```python
def main():
    ## Translate an English sentence into textese.
    texteseDict = createDictionary("Textese.txt")
    print("Enter a simple sentence in lowercase letters without")
    sentence = input("any punctuation: ")
    print()
    translate(sentence, texteseDict)

def createDictionary(fileName):
    infile = open(fileName, 'r')
    textList = [line.rstrip() for line in infile]
    infile.close()
    return dict([x.split(',') for x in textList])

def translate(sentence, texteseDict):
    words = sentence.split()
    for word in words:
        print(texteseDict.get(word, word) + " ", end="")

main()
```

[Run]

```
Enter a simple sentence in lowercase letters without
any punctuation: enjoy the excellent band tonight

njoy the xlnt b& 2nite
```

 Example 3   Admission Fee A program with a long if-elif statement can be simplified with the use of a dictionary. Consider the following program that calculates an admission fee.

```python
def main():
    ## Determine an admission fee based on age group.
    print("Enter the person's age group ", end="")
```

```
      ageGroup = input("(child, minor, adult, or senior): ")
      print("The admission fee is", determineAdmissionFee(ageGroup), "dollars." )

def determineAdmissionFee(ageGroup):
    if ageGroup == "child":      # age < 6
        return 0                 # free
    elif ageGroup == "minor":    # age 6 to 17
        return 5                 # $5
    elif ageGroup == "adult":    # age 18 to 64
        return 10
    elif ageGroup == "senior":   # age >= 65
        return 8

main()
```

[Run]

```
Enter the person's age group (child, minor, adult, or senior): adult
The admission fee is 10 dollars.
```

The rewrite of the *determineAdmissionFee* function below, replaces the **if-elif** statement with a dictionary.

```
def determineAdmissionFee(ageGroup):
    dict = {"child":0, "minor":5, "adult":10, "senior":8}
    return dict[ageGroup]
```

■ Using a Dictionary as a Frequency Table

✓ **Example 4**　Counting Words The file `Gettysburg.txt` contains the entire Gettysburg Address as a single line. The following program counts the number of words in the Gettysburg Address and displays the most frequently used words.

```
def main():
    ## Analyze word frequencies in the Gettysburg Address.
    listOfWords = formListOfWords("Gettysburg.txt")
    freq = createFrequencyDictionary(listOfWords)
    displayWordCount(listOfWords, freq)
    displayMostCommonWords(freq)

def formListOfWords(fileName):
    infile = open(fileName)
    originalLine = infile.readline().lower()
    # Remove punctuation marks from the line.
    line = ""
    for ch in originalLine:
        if ('a' <= ch <= 'z') or (ch == " "):
            line += ch
    # Place the individual words into a list.
    listOfWords = line.split()
    return listOfWords

def createFrequencyDictionary(listOfWords):
    ## Create dictionary with each item having the form word:word frequency.
    freq = {}  # an empty dictionary
```

```
        for word in listOfWords:
            freq[word] = 0
        for word in listOfWords:
            freq[word] = freq[word] + 1
        return freq

def displayWordCount(listOfWords, freq):
    print("The Gettysburg Address contains", len(listOfWords), "words.")
    print("The Gettysburg Address contains", len(freq), "different words.")
    print()

def displayMostCommonWords(freq):
    print("The most common words and their frequencies are:")
    listOfMostCommonWords = []  # an empty list
    for word in freq.keys():
        if freq[word] >= 6:
            listOfMostCommonWords.append((word, freq[word]))
    listOfMostCommonWords.sort(key=lambda x: x[1], reverse=True)
    for item in listOfMostCommonWords:
        print("   ", item[0] + ':', item[1])

main()
```

[Run]

```
The Gettysburg Address contains 268 words.
The Gettysburg Address contains 139 different words.
The most common words and their frequencies are:
    that: 13
    the: 11
    we: 10
    to: 8
    here: 8
    a: 7
    and: 6
```

■ Storing Dictionaries in Binary Files

Text files store data as a sequence of characters that can be read with a text editor such as Word or Notepad. Another file format, called a **binary format**, stores data as a sequence of bytes that can only be accessed by special readers. Python has functions that store dictionaries as binary files and retrieve dictionaries from binary files. These functions must be imported from a module named *pickle*. Although text files are adequate for simple dictionaries, binary files can handle the most complicated dictionaries with ease.

The following lines of code save a dictionary as a binary file, where the mode 'wb' states that the file is to be opened for writing as a binary file.

```
import pickle

outfile = open(fileName, 'wb')
pickle.dump(dictionaryName, outfile)
outfile.close()
```

The following lines of code create a dictionary from a binary file, where the mode 'rb' states that the binary file is to be opened for reading.

```
infile = open(fileName, 'rb')
dictionaryName = pickle.load(infile)
infile.close()
```

Note: In this book, we will use the extension "dat" for binary files that store dictionaries.

If the dictionary *texteseDict* from Example 2 had been saved as the binary file **TexteseDict.dat** and the *pickle* module had been imported, then the body of the function *createDictionary* could have been written

```
infile = open(fileName, 'rb')
dictionaryName = pickle.load(infile)
infile.close()
return dictionaryName
```

■ Dictionary-Valued Dictionaries

A dictionary's values can be any type of object, including a dictionary. Consider the CSV file **UN.txt** that was discussed in Section 5.2. Each line of the file gives the name, continent, population (in millions), and area (in square miles) of a member of the United Nations. Some lines of the file are

```
Canada,North America,34.8,3855000
France,Europe,66.3,211209
New Zealand,Australia/Oceania,4.4,103738
Nigeria,Africa,177.2,356669
Pakistan,Asia,196.2,310403
Peru,South America,30.1,496226
```

This data could be efficiently accessed if it was placed into the following dictionary:

```
nations = {"Canada":{"cont":"North America", "popl":34.8, "area":3855000},
          "France":{"cont":"Europe","popl":66.3},"area":211209} ...}
```

Then, the value of **nations["Canada"]** would be the dictionary

```
{"cont":"North America", "popl":34.8, "area":3855000}
```

The value of **nations["Canada"]["cont"]** would be **North America**, the value of **nations["Canada"]["popl"]** would be **34.8**, and the value of **nations["Canada"]["area]** would be **3855000**.

The complete dictionary *nations* containing data for the 193 member nations of the U.N. has been created and saved as the binary file **UNdict.dat**. This file will be used in the next two examples.

 Example 5. United Nations The following program displays the data for a requested nation.

```
import pickle

def main():
    ## Display the data for an individual country.
    nations = getDictionary("UNdict.dat")
    nation = inputNameOfNation(nations)
    displayData(nations, nation)
```

```
def getDictionary(fileName):
    infile = open(fileName, 'rb')
    nations = pickle.load(infile)
    infile.close()
    return nations

def inputNameOfNation(nations):
    nation = input("Enter the name of a UN member nation: ")
    while nation not in nations:
        print("Not a member of the UN. Try again.")
        nation = input("Enter the name of a UN member nation: ")
    return nation

def displayData(nations, nation):
    print("Continent:", nations[nation]["cont"])
    print("Population:", nations[nation]["popl"], "million people")
    print("Area:", nations[nation]["area"], "square miles")

main()
```

[Run]

```
Enter the name of a UN member nation: Canada
Continent: North America
Population: 34.8 million people
Area: 3855000 square miles
```

■ Extracting Ordered Data from a Dictionary

A dictionary is an unordered structure and therefore does not have a sort method. However, the items of the dictionary can be placed into a list as two-tuples in a customized order with a statement of the form

```
sorted(dict1.items(), key=f, reverse=BooleanValue):
```

✔ **Example 6**   United Nations The following program displays the U.N. member countries (and their populations) from a specified continent. The countries will be ordered by their populations.

```
import pickle

def main():
    ## Display countries (and their population) from a specified continent.
    nations = getDictionary("UNdict.dat")
    continent = input("Enter the name of a continent other than Antarctica: ")
    continentDict = constructContinentNations(nations, continent)
    displaySortedResults(continentDict)

def getDictionary(fileName):
    infile = open(fileName, 'rb')
    nations = pickle.load(infile)
    infile.close()
    return nations

def constructContinentNations(nations, continent):
    ## Reduce the full 193 item dictionary to a dictionary consisting
```

```
        ## solely of the countries in the specified continent.
        continentDict = {}  # an empty dictionary
        for nation in nations:
            if nations[nation]["cont"] == continent:
                continentDict[nation] = nations[nation]
        return continentDict

def displaySortedResults(dictionaryName):
    ## Display countries in descending order by population.
    continentList = sorted(dictionaryName.items(),
                    key=lambda k: k[1]["popl"], reverse=True)
    for k in continentList:
        print("   {0:s}: {1:,.2f}".format(k[0], k[1]["popl"]))

main()
```

[Run. The first six lines displayed are as follows:]

```
Enter the name of a continent other than Antarctica: Europe
  Russian Federation: 142.50
  Germany: 81.00
  United Kingdom: 66.70
  France: 66.30
  Italy: 61.70
```

■ Using a Dictionary with Tuples as Keys

The file **USpresStatesDict.dat** holds a dictionary giving the names of the presidents and their home states. Each key is a tuple of the form (last name, first name(s)). Two of the items in the dictionary are **('Kennedy', 'John'):'Massachusetts'** and **('Reagan', 'Ronald'):'California'**.

✔ **Example 7**   U.S. Presidents The following program requests the name of a state and then displays the presidents from that state ordered alphabetically by their last names. The use of tuples to store the names simplifies alphabetizing the names. Although the items of a dictionary cannot be ordered, they can be displayed in a specified order with statements such as **print(sorted(dictName))**.

```
import pickle

def main():
    presDict = createDictFromBinaryFile("USpresStatesDict.dat")
    state = getState(presDict)
    displayOutput(state, presDict)

def createDictFromBinaryFile(fileName):
    infile = open(fileName, 'rb')
    dictionaryName = pickle.load(infile)
    infile.close()
    return dictionaryName

def getState(dictName):
    state = input("Enter the name of a state: ")
```

```
        if state in dictName.values():
            return state
        else:
            return "There are no presidents from " + state + '.'
def displayOutput(state, dictName):
    if state.startswith("There"):
        print(state)
    else:
        print("Presidents from", state + ':')
        for pres in sorted(dictName):
            if dictName[pres] == state:
                print("   " + pres[1] + " " + pres[0])
main()
```

[Run]

```
Enter the name of a state: Virginia
Presidents from Virginia:
  Thomas Jefferson
  James Madison
  James Monroe
  John Tyler
  George Washington
```

■ Dictionary Comprehension

Dictionaries can be created with **dictionary comprehension**. For instance,

```
{x: x * x for x in range(4)}
```

creates the dictionary {0:0, 1:1, 2:4, 3:9}.

Dictionary comprehension can be used to extract a subset of a dictionary. Consider the dictionary *presDict* from Example 7. The following lines of code create the subset of *presDict* consisting of the presidents from New England states.

```
NE = ["Maine", "Connecticut", "New Hampshire",
      "Massachusetts", "Vermont", "Rhode Island"]
subSet = {key:presDict[key] for key in presDict if presDict[key] in NE}
```

The *createDictionary* function from Example 2 can be rewritten with dictionary comprehension as follows:

```
def createDictionary(fileName):
    infile = open(fileName, 'r')
    return {line.split(',')[0]:line.split(',')[1].rstrip()
            for line in infile}
```

■ Comments

1. Dictionary keys must be immutable objects. Therefore, lists and sets cannot serve as keys. Also, tuples whose items are lists or sets cannot serve as keys.
2. Strings, lists, tuples, and sets can also be saved as binary files using the *pickle* module.

Practice Problems 5.3

1. Modify the last two lines of the function *displaySortedResults* in Example 6 so that only the first five most populous countries will be displayed.

2. Which of the following statements are true?

   (a) Strings, numbers, tuples, and lists can be keys in a dictionary.
   (b) Strings, numbers, tuples, and lists can be values in a dictionary.
   (c) Two different keys can map to the same value.
   (d) Two different values can have the same key.

EXERCISES 5.3

In Exercises 1 through 20 , determine the output of the print function where the dictionary WF gives the heights of five waterfalls in feet.

```
WF = {"Angel Falls" : 3211.7, "Tugela Falls" : 3110.2, "Three Sisters
Fall" : 2998.5,"Olo'supena Falls": 2953.3, "Yumbilla Falls": 2940}
```

1. `print(WF["Tugela Falls"])`

2. `print(len(WF))`

3. `print(list(WF.keys()))`

4. `print(list(WF.values()))`

5. `print(list(WF.items()))`

6. `print("Three Sisters Fall" in WF)`

7. `print(WF .get("Vinnufossen", "absent"))`

8. `print(WF .get("Olo'supena Falls", "absent"))`

9. `print(max(WF))`

10. `print(min(WF))`

11. ```
WF["Tugela Falls"] += .4
print(round(WF["Tugela. Falls"]))
```

12. ```
del WF["Tugela Falls"]
print(len(WF))
```

13. ```
WF.update({"Tugela Falls":3110})
print(WF["Tugela Falls"])
```

14. ```
WF.clear()
print(WF)
```

15. ```
for x in WF:
    print(x + " ", end="")
```

16. ```
for x in sorted(WF):
    print(x + " ", end="")
```

17. ```
total = 0
for x in WF.values():
    total += x
print("{0:.1f}".format(total))
```

18. ```
total = 0
for x in WF:
    total += WF[x]
print("{0:.1f}".format(total))
```

19. ```
Waterfall = WF
del Waterfall["Angel Falls"]
print(len(WF))
```

20. ```
Waterfall = dict (WF)
del Waterfall["Angel Falls"]
print(len(WF))
```

In Exercises 21 through 44, determine the output of the print function where the dictionary studentData contains the names of students and their ages.

```
studentData = {'std1': 'John', 'std1_age': 20, 'std2': 'Harry', 'std2_
age': 21}
```

21. `print(len(studentData))`

22. `print( studentData['std1_age'])`

23. `print("John" in studentData)`

24. `print(list(studentData.items())[3])`

25. `print(min(studentData))`

26. `print('std1' in studentData)`

27. `print(list(studentData)[:-1])`

28. `print('std1_age' not in studentData)`

29. `print(studentData.setdefault('std1'))`

30. `print(list(studentData.values()))`

31. `print(studentData.get("John","None"))`

32. `print(studentData.get("A", "Not Found"))`

33.
```
del studentData["std2"]
print(studentData)
```

34.
```
studentData["std2"] = 'Smith'
print(studentData)
```

35.
```
studentData.clear()
print(len(studentData))
```

36.
```
studentData["std2_age"] += 4
print(studentData)
```

37.
```
for x in studentData:
    print(x)
```

38.
```
for x in studentData.values():
    print(x)
```

39.
```
for x in studentData.items():
    print(x[1])
```

40.
```
for x in sorted(studentData):
    print(x)
```

41.
```
dupData = dict(studentData)
dupData["std1_age"] *= 2
print(studentData["std1_age"])
```

42.
```
dupData = (studentData)
dupData["std1_age"] *= 2
print(studentData["std1_age"])
```

43.
```
studentData.update({"std1_age":30, "std2_age":45})
print(studentData)
```

44.
```
newData = {}
newData.update(studentData)
print(newData["std2"])
```

In Exercises 45 and 46, rewrite the code using a dictionary instead of an if statement.

45.
```
pres = input("Who was the youngest U.S. president? ")
pres = pres.upper()
if (pres == "THEODORE ROOSEVELT") or (pres == "TEDDY ROOSEVELT"):
    print("Correct. He became president at age 42 ")
    print("when President McKinley was assassinated.")
elif (pres=="JFK") or (pres=="JOHN KENNEDY") or (pres=="JOHN F. KENNEDY"):
    print("Incorrect. He became president at age 43. However,")
    print("he was the youngest person elected president.")
else:
    print("Nope")
```

46.
```
def determineRank(years):
    if years == 1:
        return "Freshman"
    elif years == 2:
        return "Sophmore"
    elif years == 3:
        return "Junior"
    else:
        return "Senior"
```

In Exercises 47 through 50, use the dictionary *topHitters* below.

```
topHitters = {"Gehrig":{"atBats":8061, "hits":2721},
              "Ruth":{"atBats":8399, "hits":2873},
              "Williams":{"atBats":7706, "hits":2654}}
```

47. Baseball   Write lines of code to produce Fig. 5.32 that shows the batting averages of the three baseball players.

```
Ruth        0.342
Williams    0.344
Gehrig      0.338
```

FIGURE 5.32   Outcome of Exercise 47.

```
del topHitters[max(topHitters)]
del topHitters[min(topHitters)]
print(topHitters)
```

FIGURE 5.33   Code for Exercise 48.

48. Baseball   What output is displayed by the code in Fig. 5.33.

49. Baseball   Write lines of code to produce Fig. 5.34 that shows the average number of hits by the three players.

```
The average number of hits by
the baseball players was 2749.3.
```

FIGURE 5.34   Outcome of Exercise 49.

```
The most hits by one of the
baseball players was 2873.
```

FIGURE 5.35   Outcome of Exercise 50.

50. Baseball   Write lines of code to produce Fig. 5.35 that shows the most hits by any of the three players. The code should use the **max** function.

In Exercises 51 through 54, use the file `JusticesDict.dat` that stores a dictionary containing data about the Supreme Court justices, past and present. Each item of the dictionary has the form "*name of justice:data dictionary*". The data dictionary for a justice contains their *appointing president, the state from which they were appointed, the year appointed*, and *the year they left the court*. (For current justices, the year they left the court is set to 0.) Three items from the dictionary are as follows:

```
'Earl Warren':{'pres':'Dwight Eisenhower','yrLeft':1969,'yrAppt':1953,'state':'CA'}
'Sonia Sotomayor':{'pres':'Barack Obama','yrLeft':0,'yrAppt':2009,'state':'NY'}
'Salmon Chase':{'yrAppt':1864,'pres':'Abraham Lincoln','state':'OH','yrLeft':1873}
```

51. Supreme Court   Write a program that requests the name of a president as input and then displays the names and years of the justices appointed by that president. See Fig. 5.36.

```
Enter a president: John Kennedy
   Arthur Goldberg  1962
   Byron White      1962
```

FIGURE 5.36   Possible outcome of Exercise 51.

```
Enter a state abbreviation: NH
   David Souter     1990
   Levi Woodbury    1845
```

FIGURE 5.37   Possible outcome of Exercise 52.

52. Supreme Court   Write a program that requests a state abbreviation as input and then displays the names and years of the justices appointed from that state. See Fig. 5.37.

53. Supreme Court   Write a program that requests the name of a justice and displays the justice's data. See Fig. 5.38.

```
Enter name of a justice: John Roberts
Appointed by George W. Bush
State: MD
Year of appointment: 2005
Currently serving on Supreme Court.
```

FIGURE 5.38   Possible outcome of Exercise 53.

```
31 states have produced justices.
   AL: 3
   AZ: 2
   CA: 5
   CO: 1
   CT: 3
```

FIGURE 5.39   First part of outcome of Exercise 54.

54. Supreme Court Write a program that displays the name of each state (alphabetically) that has produced a Supreme Court justice and the number of justices produced. Fig. 5.39 shows the first six lines displayed.

55. Letter Frequency Write a program that requests a sentence as input and then displays the letters in the sentence along with their frequencies. The letters should appear ordered by their frequencies. Fig. 5.40 shows the first five lines displayed.

```
Enter a sentence: Always look on the bright side of life.
  O: 4
  L: 3
  I: 3
  E: 3
```

FIGURE 5.40 Possible outcome of Exercise 55.

56. Rose Bowl The file `Rosebowl.txt` contains the names of the Rose Bowl winners (up through 2014) in the order the games were played. Write a program that displays the names of the teams that have won four or more Rose Bowls and the number of wins for each team. The teams should appear ordered by the number of wins. See Fig. 5.41.

```
Teams with four or more
Rose Bowl wins as of 2014:
  USC: 24
  Washington: 8
  Michigan: 8
  Ohio State: 7
  Stanford: 6
  UCLA: 5
  Alabama: 4
  Michigan State: 4
```

FIGURE 5.41 Outcome of Exercise 56.

```
States that produced three or
more presidents as of 2016:
  Ohio: 6
  New York: 6
  Virginia: 5
  Massachusetts: 4
  Tennessee: 3
  California: 3
  Texas: 3
  Illinois: 3
```

FIGURE 5.42 Outcome of Exercise 57.

57. U.S. Presidents Use the file `USpresStatesDict.dat` to obtain an ordered list of the states that were home to three or more presidents. Each state should be followed by the number of presidents from that state and the states should be ordered by the number of presidents they produced. See Fig. 5.42.

58. U.S. Presidents Use the file `USpresStatesDict.dat` to obtain a list of the presidents having a specified first name. See Fig. 5.43. If no president has the specified first name, that fact should be displayed.

```
Enter a first name: John
  John Adams
  John Q. Adams
  John Kennedy
  John Tyler
```

FIGURE 5.43 Possible outcome of Exercise 58.

59. Calendar   Redo Exercise 27 of Section 5.2 by placing the contents of the text file into a dictionary and using the dictionary to find the requested day of the week.

In Exercises 60 and 61, use the file `LargeCitiesDict.dat` that stores a dictionary giving the large cities (population > 250,000) for each state. Each item of the dictionary has the form *"name of state:list of large cities in that state"*. The first three items in the dictionary are as follows:

```
"Alabama":[],"Alaska":["Anchorage"],"Arizona":["Phoenix", "Tucson", "Mesa"]
```

60. Large Cities   Write a program that requests the name of a state as input and then displays the large cities in that state. See Figs. 5.44 and 5.45.

```
Enter the name of a state: Arizona
Large cities: Phoenix Tucson Mesa
```

```
Enter the name of a state: Alabama
There are no large cities in Alabama.
```

FIGURE 5.44   Possible outcome of Exercise 60.   **FIGURE 5.45**   Possible outcome of Exercise 60.

61. Large Cities   Write a program that requests an integer from 0 through 13 and then displays the names of the states (in alphabetical order) having exactly that many large cities. See Fig. 5.46.

```
Enter an integer from 0 to 13: 3
The following states have exactly 3 large cities:
Arizona  Colorado  Delaware  Florida  New York  North Carolina
```

FIGURE 5.46   Possible outcome of Exercise 61.

Solutions to Practice Problems 5.3

1. Change the last two lines of the function to the following:

```
for i in range(5):
    print("  " + continentList[i][0] + ':', continentList[i][1]["pop1"])
```

2. (b) and (c) are true.

CHAPTER 5 KEY TERMS AND CONCEPTS

CHAPTER 5 KEY TERMS AND CONCEPTS	EXAMPLES
5.1 Processing Data, Part 1 The functions **open(*fileName*,'r')**, **open(*fileName*,'w')**, and **open(*fileName*,'a')** create file objects connected to the named text file. These objects are used for reading content from the file, writing content to the file, and adding content to the file, respectively. After a file is opened for writing or appending, a statement of the form **write(str1)** writes *str1* to the	``` f = open("Python.txt", 'w') f.write("spam\n") f.close() f = open("Python.txt", 'a') f.write("eggs\n") f.close() f = open("Python.txt", 'r') L = [line.rstrip() for line in f] print(L) ```

CHAPTER 5 KEY TERMS AND CONCEPTS	EXAMPLES
file via a buffer. The **close method** makes sure that all data still in the buffer is written to the file and then terminates the connection.	[Run] ```['spam', 'eggs']```

Some other methods for file objects are **writelines** (writes all the items in a list of strings into the file), **read** (returns the entire contents of the file as a single string), and **readline** (reads the next line of the file).	```L = ["a\n", "b\n"]```
	```outfile = open("ab.txt", 'w')```
	```outfile.writelines(L)```
	```outfile.close()```
	```infile = open("ab.txt", 'r')```
	```print(infile.read(), end="")```
	```f = open("ab.txt", 'r')```
	```print(f.readline().rstrip(),end="")```
	```print(f.readline().rstrip(),end="")```
	[Run]
	```a```
	```b```
	```ab```

After the *os* module has been imported, a closed file can be renamed with a statement of the form **os.rename(*oldFileName*, *newFileName*)**, deleted with a statement of the form **os.remove(*fileName*)**, and have its existence verified with a Boolean function of the form **os.path.exists(*fileName*)**.	```import os```
	```# Assume "ab.txt" in current folder```
	```os.rename("ab.txt", "alpha.txt")```
	```print(os.path.exists("ab.txt"))```
	```print(os.path.exists("alpha.txt"))```
	```os.remove("alpha.txt")```
	```print(os.path.exists("alpha.txt"))```
	[Run]
	```False```
	```True```
	```False```

A **set** is an unordered collection of distinct objects. It can be created by listing its elements inside curly braces or by applying the **set function** to a list or tuple. Sets support the mathematical **union**, **intersection**, and **difference** methods. Sets support many list operations, but do not support the list operations that rely on indices or order.	```s1 = {1, "one"}```
	```s2 = set([2, "one"])```
	```print(s1.union(s2))```
	```print(s1.intersection(s2))```
	```print(s1.difference(s2))```
	[Run]
	```{1, 'one', 2}```
	```{'one'}```
	```{1}```

Sets can be created with **set comprehension**. Sets can be placed into an ordered list with the **sorted** function.	```s = {x * x for x in range(-2, 3)}```
	```print(s)```
	```L = sorted(s, reverse=True)```
	```print(L)```
	[Run]
	```{0, 1, 4}```
	```[4, 1, 0]```

CHAPTER 5 KEY TERMS AND CONCEPTS	EXAMPLES

5.2 Processing Data, Part 2

CSV files store tabular data with each line containing the same number of fields, where the fields are separated by commas. The text file **InaugAge.txt** gives the names of the U.S. presidents and their ages at inauguration. The first five lines of the file are shown in the right column.

```
George Washington,57
John Adams,61
Thomas Jefferson,57
James Madison,57
James Monroe,58
```

The **split** method is needed to extract information from a CSV file.

```
f = open("InaugAge.txt", 'r')
L = f.readline().split(',')
s = "{0} inaugurated at {1}"
print(s.format(L[0], L[1]))
```
[Run]
```
George Washington inaugurated at 57
```

The data from a CSV file can be placed into an **Excel spreadsheet** and analyzed with Excel; and data from an Excel spreadsheet can be transferred to a CSV file and analyzed with Python.

	A	B
1	George Washington	57
2	John Adams	61
3	Thomas Jefferson	57
4	James Madison	57
5	James Monroe	58

The contents of a CSV file can be placed into a list of lists (or tuples), and individual pieces of data accessed with doubly-indexed variables.

```
infile = open("InaugAge.txt", 'r')
L = [line.rstrip().split(',') for
     line in infile]
infile.close()
s = "{0} inaugurated at {1}"
print(s.format(L[4][0], L[4][1]))
```
[Run]
```
James Monroe inaugurated at 58
```

5.3 Dictionaries

A **dictionary** is an unordered collection of *key:value* pairs that map each key into its value. One way to create a dictionary is to place its *key:value* pairs (separated by commas) inside curly braces. *dictionaryName*[*key*] returns the value associated with the key.

```
# translate to Spanish
d={"red":"rojo", "balloon":"globo"}
print(d["red"], d["balloon"])
```
[Run]
```
rojo globo
```

Dictionary operations: len, in, get, keys, values, items, del, clear, update, list, tuple, set, max, min

See Table 5.4.

Numbers, strings, and tuples (but not lists) can serve as **keys** and all types of Python objects can serve as **values**.

```
d={("Blue","Green"):"Cyan"}  valid
d={["Blue","Green"]:"Cyan"}  invalid
```

CHAPTER 5 KEY TERMS AND CONCEPTS	EXAMPLES
| The **dump** and **load** functions from the **pickle module** can be used to store dictionaries as binary files and retrieve the dictionaries from the binary files. | ```
import pickle
d1 = {("Blue", "Yellow"):"Green"}
outfile = open("Colors.dat", 'wb')
pickle.dump(d1, outfile)
outfile.close()
infile = open("Colors.dat", 'rb')
d2 = pickle.load(infile)
print(d2)
```<br>[Run]<br>`{('Blue', 'Yellow'): 'Green'}` |

CHAPTER 5 PROGRAMMING PROJECTS

1. Unit Conversions   Table 5.5 contains some lengths in terms of feet. Write a program that displays the nine different units of measure; requests the unit to convert from, the unit to convert to, and the quantity to be converted; and then displays the converted quantity. A typical outcome is shown in Fig. 5.47. Use the file **Units.txt** to create a dictionary that provides the number of feet for a given unit of length. The first two lines of the file are **inches,.083333; furlongs,660**.

TABLE 5.5   **Equivalent lengths.**

1 inch = .083333 foot	1 rod = 16.5 feet
1 yard = 3 feet	1 furlong = 660 feet
1 meter = 3.28155 feet	1 kilometer = 3281.5 feet
1 fathom = 6 feet	1 mile = 5280 feet

```
UNITS OF LENGTH
inches        furlongs      yards
rods          miles         fathoms
meters        kilometers    feet

Units to convert from: yards
Units to convert to: miles
Enter length in yards: 555
Length in miles: 0.3153
```

FIGURE 5.47   **Possible outcome of Programming Project 1.**

2. Curve Grades   Statisticians use the concepts of mean and standard deviation to describe a collection of numbers. The **mean** is the average value of the numbers, and the **standard deviation** measures the spread or dispersal of the numbers about the mean. Formally, if $x_1, x_2, x_3, \ldots, x_n$ is a collection of numbers, then the mean is

$$m = \frac{x_1 + x_2 + x_3 + \cdots + x_n}{n}$$
```

and the standard deviation is

$$s = \sqrt{\frac{(x_1 - m)^2 + (x_2 - m)^2 + (x_3 - m)^2 + \cdots + (x_n - m)^2}{n}}$$

The file **Scores.txt** contains exam scores. The first four lines of the file hold the numbers 59, 60, 65, and 75. Write a program to calculate the mean and standard deviation of the exam scores, assign letter grades to each exam score, ES, as follows, and then display information about the exam scores and the grades, as shown in Fig. 5.48.

$ES \geq m + 1.5s$	A
$m + .5s \leq ES < m + 1.5s$	B
$m - .5s \leq ES < m + .5s$	C
$m - 1.5s \leq ES < m - .5s$	D
$ES < m - 1.5s$	F

```
Number of scores: 14
Average score: 71.0
Standard deviation of scores: 14.42
GRADE DISTRIBUTION AFTER CURVING GRADES.
A: 2    B: 1    C: 6    D: 4    F: 1
```

FIGURE 5.48   Outcome of Programming Project 2.

For instance, if m were 70 and s were 12, then grades of 88 or above would receive A's, grades between 76 and 87 would receive B's, and so on. A process of this type is referred to as *curving grades*.

3. **Baseball**   The file **ALE.txt** contains the information shown in Table 5.6. Write a program to use the file to produce a text file containing the information in Table 5.7. In the new file, the baseball teams should be in descending order by the percentage of games won.

TABLE 5.6   **American League East games won and lost in 2014.**

Team	Won	Lost
Baltimore	96	66
Boston	71	91
New York	84	78
Tampa Bay	77	85
Toronto	83	79

TABLE 5.7   **Final 2014 American League East standings.**

Team	Won	Lost	Pct
Baltimore	96	66	0.593
New York	84	78	0.519
Toronto	83	79	0.512
Tampa Bay	77	85	0.475
Boston	71	91	0.438

4. **U.S. Senate** The file **Senate113.txt** contains the members of the 113th U.S. Senate—that is, the Senate prior to the November 2014 election. Each record of the file consists of three fields—name, state, and party affiliation.[3] Some records in the file are as follows:

```
Richard Shelby,Alabama,R
Bernard Sanders,Vermont,I
Kristen Gillibrand,New York,D
```

The file **RetiredSen.txt** contains the records from the file **Senate113.txt** for senators who left the Senate after the November 2014 election due to retirement, defeat, death, or resignation. Some records in the file are as follows:

```
John Rockefeller,West Virginia,D
Tom Coburn,Oklahoma,R
Carl Levin,Michigan,D
```

The file **NewSen.txt** contains records for the senators who were newly elected in November 2014 or who were appointed to fill the seats of senators who left after the November 2014 election. Some records in the file are as follows:

```
Shelly Capito,West Virginia,R
Steve Daines,Montana,R
Gary Peters,Michigan,D
```

(a) Write a program that uses the three files above to create the file **Senate114.txt** that contains records (each consisting of three fields) for the members of the 114th Senate where the members are ordered by state. Use this file in parts (b), (c), and (d).

(b) Write a program that determines the number of senators of each party affiliation. See Fig. 5.49.

(c) Write a program that determines the number of states whose two senators have the same party affiliation.

(d) Write a program that asks the user to input a state, and then displays the two senators from that state. See Fig. 5.50.

```
Party Affiliations:
  Republicans: 54
  Democrats: 44
  Independents: 2
```

FIGURE 5.49 Outcome of Programming Project 4(b).

```
Enter the name of a state: Maryland
Benjamin Cardin
Barbara Mikulski
```

FIGURE 5.50 Outcome of Programming Project 4(d).

5. **Bachelor Degrees** Table 5.8 shows the number of bachelor degrees conferred in 1981 and 2010 in certain fields of study. Tables 5.9 and 5.10 show the percentage change and a histogram of 2010 levels, respectively. Write a program that allows the user to display any one of these tables as an option and to quit as a fourth option. Table 5.8 is ordered alphabetically by field of study, Table 5.9 is ordered by decreasing percentages, and Table 5.10 is ordered by increasing number of degrees. Use the file **DegreesDict.dat** that stores a dictionary where each field of study is a key and each value is a two-tuple of the form (*number of degrees in 1981*, *number of degrees in 2010*). One item of the dictionary is "Business":(200521,358293).

---

[3]We refer to anyone who is neither a Republican nor a Democrat as an Independent.

TABLE 5.8   Bachelor degrees conferred in certain fields.

Field of Study	1981	2010
Business	200,521	358,293
Computer and info. science	15,121	39,589
Education	108,074	101,265
Engineering	63,642	72,654
Social sciences and history	100,513	172,780

Source: National Center for Education Statistics.

TABLE 5.9   Percentage change in bachelor degrees conferred.

Field of Study	% Change (1981–2010)
Computer and info. science	161.8%
Business	78.7%
Social sciences and history	71.9%
Engineering	14.2%
Education	−6.3%

TABLE 5.10   Bachelor degrees conferred in 2010 in certain fields.

```
Computer and info. science **** 39,589
             Engineering ******* 72,654
               Education ********** 101,265
Social sciences and history ***************** 172,780
                Business *********************************** 358,293
```

6. **Fuel Economy**   A fuel-economy study was carried out for five models of cars. Each car was driven 100 miles, and then the model of the car and the number of gallons used were placed in a line of the file **Mileage.txt**. Table 5.11 shows the data for the entries of the file. Write a program to display the models and their average miles per gallon in decreasing order with respect to mileage. See Fig. 5.51. The program should create a dictionary of five items, with a key for each model, and a two-tuple for each value. Each two-tuple should be of the form (*number of test vehicles for the model*, *total number of gallons used by the model*).

TABLE 5.11   Gallons of gasoline used in 100 miles of driving.

Model	Gal	Model	Gal	Model	Gal
Prius	2.1	Accord	4.1	Accord	4.3
Camry	4.1	Camry	3.8	Prius	2.3
Sebring	4.2	Camry	3.9	Camry	4.2
Mustang	5.3	Mustang	5.2	Accord	4.4

```
Model     MPG
Prius     45.45
Camry     25.00
Sebring   23.81
Accord    23.44
Mustang   19.05
```

FIGURE 5.51   Outcome of Programming Project 6.

7. U.S. Cities The file `Cities.txt` contains information about the 25 largest cities in the United States. Each line of the file has four fields—*name*,*state*,*population in 2000* (in 100,000s), and *population in 2010* (in 100,000s). Write a program that creates a new file with each line containing the name of a city and its percentage population growth from 2000 to 2010. The cities should be in decreasing order by their percent population growth. The first four lines of the file `Cities.txt` are as follows:

```
New York,NY,80.1,82.7
Los Angeles,CA,36.9,38.84
Chicago,IL,29.0,28.7
Houston,TX,19.5,22.4
```

8. Exchange Rates The text file `Exchrate.txt` gives information about the currencies of 49 major countries. The first eight lines of the file are as follows:

```
America,Dollar,1
Argentina,Peso,8.405692
Australia,Dollar,1.070835
Austria,Euro,0.760488
Belgium,Euro,0.760488
Brazil,Real,2.237937
Canada,Dollar,1.086126
Chile,Peso,591.4077
```

Each line of the file gives the name of a country, the name of its currency, and the number of units of the currency that were equal to one American dollar (called the *exchange rate*[4]). For instance, one American dollar is equal to 591.4077 Chilean pesos. Use the text file `Exchrate.txt` in parts (a), (b), and (c).

(a) Write a program that requests the name of a county as input and then displays the name of its currency and its exchange rate. See Fig. 5.52.

```
Enter the name of a country: Chile
Currency: Peso
Exchange rate: 591.4077
```

FIGURE 5.52 Possible outcome of Programming Project 8(a).

```
Kuwait
United Kingdom
Australia
```

FIGURE 5.53 Outcome of Programming Project 8(b).

(b) Write a program that displays the names of the countries in ascending order determined by the number of units that can be purchased for one American dollar. Figure 5.53 shows the first three countries displayed.

(c) Write a program that requests the names of two countries and an amount of money, and then converts the amount from the first country's currency to the equivalent amount in the second country's currency. See Fig. 5.54.

```
Enter name of first country: America
Enter name of second country: Chile
Amount of money to convert: 100
100 dollars from America equals 59,140.77 pesos from Chile
```

FIGURE 5.54 Possible outcome of Programming Project 8(c).

---

[4]The text file gives the exchange rates in September 2014.

6

Miscellaneous Topics

6.1   Exception Handling

Python provides a mechanism called **exception handling** that allows the programmer to report and recover from errors that occur while a program is running.

■ Exceptions

Exceptions are runtime errors that usually occur due to circumstances beyond the programmer's control, such as when invalid data are input or when a file cannot be accessed. For example, if a user enters a word when the program prompts for a number, an exception is generated and the program terminates abruptly. In this situation, the programmer did not employ faulty logic or mistype. If the user had followed the directions, no problem would have occurred. Even though the user is at fault, however, it is still the programmer's responsibility to anticipate exceptions and to include code to work around their occurrence. This section describes techniques used to anticipate and deal with exceptions. Table 6.1 lists several exception types and some possible causes.

TABLE 6.1   **Some common exceptions.**

Exception name	Description and example
AttributeError	An unavailable functionality (usually a method) is requested for an object. `(2, 3, 1).sort()` or `print(x.endswith(3))   # where x = 23`
FileNotFoundError	Requested file doesn't exist or is not located where expected. `open("NonexistentFile.txt", 'r')`
ImportError	Import statement fails to find requested module. `import nonexistentModule`
IndexError	An index is out of range. `letter = "abcd"[7]`
KeyError	No such key in dictionary. `word = d['c']   # where d = {'a':"alpha", 'b':"bravo"}`
NameError	The value of a variable cannot be found. `term = word   # where word was never created`
TypeError	Function or operator receives the wrong type of argument. `x = len(23)` or `x = 6 / '2'` or `x = 9 + 'W'` or `x = abs(-3,4)`
ValueError	Function or operator receives right type of argument, but inappropriate value. `x = int('a')` or `L.remove(item)   # where item is not in list`
ZeroDivisionError	The second number in a division or modulus operation is 0. `num = 1 / 0` or `num = 23 % 0`

If the programmer does not explicitly include exception-handling code in a program, Python displays a Traceback error message and terminates the program when an exception occurs. Consider a program containing the following lines of code:

```
numDependents = int(input("Enter number of dependents: "))
taxCredit = 1000 * numDependents
print("Tax credit:", taxCredit)
```

A user with no dependents might not enter a number and just press the *Enter* (or *return*) key. If so, Python will terminate the program and display a Traceback error message whose last line reads

```
ValueError: invalid literal for int() with base 10: ''
```

The first word in the line gives the type of the error and the rest of the line provides details on the cause of the error. The exception was raised because the input value, the empty string, cannot be converted to an integer.

■ The *try* Statement

A more robust program explicitly handles the previous exception by protecting the code with a **try** statement. The following code shows one way to handle the exception. Python first attempts to execute the code in the **try** block. If a *ValueError* exception occurs, execution jumps to the **except** clause. Whether an exception occurred or not, the code in the last two lines will be executed.

VideoNote
Exception Handing

```
try:
    numDependents = int(input("Enter number of dependents: "))
except ValueError:
    print("\nYou did not respond with an integer value.")
    print("We will assume your answer is zero.\n")
    numDependents = 0
taxCredit = 1000 * numDependents
print("Tax credit:", taxCredit)
```

A **try** statement can contain several **except** clauses. There are three types of **except** clauses:

except:	(Its block is executed when any exception occurs.)
except *ExceptionType*:	(Its block is executed only when the specified type of exception occurs.)
except *ExceptionType* **as** *exp*:	(Its block is executed only when the specified type of exception occurs. Additional information about the problem is assigned to *exp*.)

In the **try** statement discussed earlier, had the **except** clause been

```
except ValueError as exc:
```

then the variable *exc* would have been assigned the type of exception—in this case *invalid literal for int() with base 10: "*.

✓ **Example 1**   Exception Handling We will run the following program with different assumptions.

```
def main():
    ## Display the reciprocal of a number in a file.
    try:
        fileName = input("Enter the name of a file: ")
        infile = open(fileName, 'r')
        num = float(infile.readline())
        print(1 / num)
    except FileNotFoundError as exc1:
        print(exc1)
    except ValueError as exc2:
        print(exc2)

main()
```

[Run assuming that **Numbers.txt** is not present.]

```
Enter the name of a file: Numbers.txt
[Errno 2] No such file or directory: 'Numbers.txt'
```

[Run assuming that **Numbers.txt** is present and the first line contains the word TWO.]

```
Enter the name of a file: Numbers.txt
could not convert string to float: 'TWO\n'
```

[Run assuming that **Numbers.txt** is present and the first line contains the number 2.]

```
Enter the name of a file: Numbers.txt
0.5
```

 Example 2 Phonetic Alphabet The following program uses exception handling to guarantee a proper response from the user.

```python
def main():
    ## Request that the user enter a proper response.
    phoneticAlphabet = {'a':"alpha", 'b':"bravo", 'c':"charlie"}
    while True:
        try:
            letter = input("Enter a, b, or c: ")
            print(phoneticAlphabet[letter])
            break
        except KeyError:
            print("Unacceptable letter was entered.")

main()
```

[Run]

```
Enter a, b, or c: d
Unacceptable letter was entered.
Enter a, b, or c: b
bravo
```

■ The *else* and *finally* Clauses

A try statement can also include a single else clause that follows the except clauses. Its block is executed when no exceptions occur and is a good place for code that does not need protection.

A try statement can end with a **finally clause**. Blocks for finally clauses are usually used to clean up resources such as files that were left open. A try statement must contain either an except clause or a finally clause.

Example 3 Calculate an Average and a Total The following program attempts to find the average and total of the numbers in a file. The program uses exception handling to cope with the possibilities that the file is not found, the file contains a line that is not a number, or the file is empty.

```python
def main():
    ## Calculate the average and total of the numbers in a file.
    total = 0
```

```
            counter = 0
            foundFlag = True
            try:
                infile = open("Numbers.txt", 'r')
            except FileNotFoundError:
                print("File not found.")
                foundFlag = False
            if foundFlag:
                try:
                    for line in infile:
                        counter += 1
                        total += float(line)
                    print("average:", total / counter)
                except ValueError:
                    print("Line", counter, "could not be converted to a float.")
                    if counter > 1:
                        print("Average so far:", total / (counter - 1))
                        print("Total so far:", total)
                    else:
                        print("No average can be calculated.")
                except ZeroDivisionError:
                    print("File was empty.")
                else:
                    print("Total:", total)
                finally:
                    infile.close()

main()
```

■ Comments

1. The words **try, except, else,** and **finally** are reserved words and therefore are colorized orange by IDLE. Error names are colorized purple by IDLE.

2. A program is said to be **robust** if it performs well under atypical situations. The **try** statement is one of the primary tools for creating robust programs.

3. A single **except** clause may refer to several types of errors. If so, the error names are listed in a tuple. For instance, a possible **except** clause is **except (ValueError, NameError) as exc:**.

Practice Problems 6.1

1. Rewrite the following lines of code without using a **try** statement.

```
phoneBook = {"Alice":"123-4567", "Bob":"987-6543"}
name = input("Enter a name: ")
try:
    print(phoneBook[name])
except KeyError:
    print("Name not found.")
```

2. Python will not delete a file that is open. Attempting to do so generates an exception. Write a short program that creates a file and uses exception handling to deal with such an exception.

EXERCISES 6.1

Each of the statements in Exercises 1 through 22 generates one of the Traceback error messages [labeled (a) through (t)] in Table 6.2. Determine the error message generated by each statement.

1. `x = str(asdf)`

2. `f = open("abc.txt", 'R')`

3. `str = abs("str")`

4. `total = ('2' * '3')`

5. `x = ['a', 'b', 'c'][]`

6. `x = list(range(1, 9, '1'))[8]`

7. `x = '23'`
   `print(x.startswith(2))`

8. `x = '8'`
   `x.append(2)`

9. `{'1':"uno", 2:"dos"}['2']`

10. `{"Mars":"War","Neptune":"Sea"}.values()[2]`

11. `num = [1, 3].remove(2)`

12. `num = ('1', '3').index(3)`

13. `letter = ("ha" * '5')[9]`

14. `s = ['s', 'e', 'd']['0']`

15. `x = {1, 2, 3}[1]`

16. `(2, 3, 1).insert(0)`

17. `num = eval('x = 3*3')`

18. `value = min(1, 'a')[1]`

19. `del ['11', '12', '13'][0][0]`

20. `print([2] in {1: [2], 2: [3], 3: [1]})`

21. `["air", "fire", "earth", "water"].sort()[2]`

22. `"1, 2, 3".find(1)`

TABLE 6.2   Error messages for Exercises 1 through 22.

(a) `ValueError: tuple.index(x): x not in tuple`

(b) `TypeError: 'dict_values' object does not support indexing`

(c) `AttributeError: 'str' object has no attribute 'append'`

(d) `SyntaxError: invalid syntax`

(e) `TypeError: 'str' object cannot be interpreted as an integer`

(f) `NameError: name 'asdf' is not defined`

(g) `TypeError: list indices must be integers, not str`

(h) `TypeError: 'str' object doesn't support item deletion`

(i) `TypeError: startswith first arg must be str or a tuple of str, not int`

(j) `TypeError: can't multiply sequence by non-int of type 'str'`

(k) `ValueError: invalid mode: 'R'`

(l) `TypeError: bad operand type for abs(): 'str'`

(m) `TypeError: unhashable type: 'list'`

(n) `TypeError: 'set' object does not support indexing`

(o) `ValueError: list.remove(x): x not in list`

(p) `TypeError: Can't convert 'int' object to str implicitly`

(q) `TypeError: unorderable types: str() < int()`

(r) `TypeError: 'NoneType' object is not subscriptable`

(s) `KeyError: '2'`

(t) `AttributeError: 'tuple' object has no attribute 'insert'`

In Exercises 23 through 28, determine the output displayed by the lines of code.

23.
```
# Assume the user enters a letter.
try:
    num = float(input("Enter a number: "))
    print("Your number is", num)
except:
    print("You must enter a number.")
```

24.
```
nafta = ["Canada", "United States", "Mexico"]
try:
    print("The third member of NAFTA is", nafta[3])
except IndexError:
    print("Error occurred.")
```

25.
```
flower = "Bougainvillea"
try:
    lastLetter = flower[13]
    print(lastLetter)
except TypeError:
    print("Error occurred.")
except IndexError as exc:
    print(exc)
    print("Oops")
```

26. Assume that the file **Ages.txt** is located in the current folder and the first line of the file is **Twenty-one\n**.

```
try:
    infile = open("Ages.txt", 'r')   # FileNotFound if fails
    age = int(infile.readline())      # ValueError if fails
    print("Age:", age)
except FileNotFoundError:
    print("File Ages.txt not found.")
except ValueError:
    print("File Ages.txt contains an invalid age.")
    infile.close()
else:
    infile.close()
```

27. Assume that the file **Salaries.txt** is located in the current folder and the first line of the file contains the string 20,000.

```
def main():
    try:
        infile = open("Salaries.txt", 'r')   # FileNotFound if fails
        salary = int(infile.readline())      # ValueError if fails
        print("Salary:", salary)
    except FileNotFoundError:
        print("File Salaries.txt not found.")
    except ValueError:
        print("File Salaries.txt contains an invalid salary.")
        infile.close()
    else:
        infile.close()
```

```
finally:
    print("Thank you for using our program.")

main()
```

28. Redo Exercise 26 with the assumption that the file **Ages.txt** is not located in the same folder as the program.

29. The following program will perform properly if the user enters 0 in response to the request for input. However, the program will crash if the user responds with "eight". Rewrite the program using a **try/except** statement so that it will handle both types of responses. See Fig. 6.1.

```
while True:
    n = int(input("Enter a nonzero integer: "))
    if n != 0:
        reciprocal = 1 / n
        print("The reciprocal of {0} is {1:,.3f}".format(n, reciprocal))
        break
    else:
        print("You entered zero. Try again.")
```

```
Enter a nonzero integer: 0
You entered zero. Try again.
Enter a nonzero integer: eight
You did not enter a nonzero integer. Try again.
Enter a nonzero integer: 8
The reciprocal of 8 is 0.125
```

FIGURE 6.1 Possible outcome of Exercise 29.

30. State Capitals   Assume that the list *stateCapitals* contains the names of the 50 state capitals. Write a robust code segment that requests the name of a capital and removes it from the list. See Fig. 6.2.

```
Enter a state capital to delete: Chicago
Not a state capital.
Enter a state capital to delete: Springfield
Capital deleted.
```

FIGURE 6.2 Possible outcome of Exercise 30.

31. Enter a Number   Write a robust program that requests an integer from 1 through 100. See Fig. 6.3.

```
Enter an integer from 1 to 100: 5.5
You did not enter an integer.
Enter an integer from 1 to 100: five
You did not enter an integer.
Enter an integer from 1 to 100: 555
Your number was not between 1 and 100.
Enter an integer from 1 to 100: 5
Your number is 5.
```

FIGURE 6.3 Possible outcome of Exercise 31.

Solutions to Practice Problems 6.1

1.
```python
phoneBook = {"Alice":"123-4567", "Bob":"987-6543"}
name = input("Enter a name: ")
print(phoneBook.get(name, "Name not found."))
```

2.
```python
import os

def main():
    createFile()
    infile = open("NewFile.txt", 'r')
    deleteFile("NewFile.txt")

def createFile():
    f = open("NewFile.txt", 'w')
    f.write("Hello, World!\n")
    f.close()

def deleteFile(fileName):
    try:
        os.remove(fileName)
    except:
        print("File is open and cannot be deleted.")

main()
```

6.2   Selecting Random Values

VideoNote
Random
Values

The **random** module contains functions that randomly select items from a list and randomly reorder the items in a list.

■ Functions from the *random* Module

If *L* is a list, then

`random.choice(L)`

will be a randomly selected item from *L*,

`random.sample(L, n)`

will be a list containing *n* randomly selected items from *L*, and

`random.shuffle(L)`

will randomly reorder the items in *L*.
    If *m* and *n* are integers with $m \leq n$, then

`random.randint(m, n)`

will return a randomly selected integer from *m* to *n*, inclusive.

Example 1   Random Functions The following program demonstrates functions from the *random* module.

```python
import random

elements = ["earth", "air", "fire", "water"]
print(random.choice(elements))
```

```
print(random.sample(elements, 2))
random.shuffle(elements)
print(elements)
print(random.randint(1, 5))
```

[Run. A possible outcome is shown below.]

```
fire
['air', 'earth']
['water', 'fire', 'earth', 'air']
5
```

■ Games of Chance

 Example 2 Poker Hand The file `DeckOfCardsList.dat` is a pickled binary file containing a list of the 52 cards in an ordinary deck of playing cards. The following program randomly selects five cards from the deck.

```
import random
import pickle

infile = open("DeckOfCardsList.dat", 'rb')
deckOfCards = pickle.load(infile)
infile.close()
pokerHand = random.sample(deckOfCards, 5)
print(pokerHand)
```

[Run. A possible outcome is shown below.]

```
['2♠', '2♦', '6♠', 'Q♠', '10♦']
```

Example 3 Roulette American roulette wheels have 38 numbers (1 through 36 plus 0 and 00). Many different types of bets are possible. We shall consider the "odd" bet. When you bet $1 on "odd", you win $1 if an odd number appears and you lose $1 otherwise. In the following program, the user specifies an amount of money, called the bankroll, to risk at the roulette table. He decides to bet $1 on each spin of the wheel and to quit when he doubles his bankroll or goes broke. The program simulates his session at the roulette table.

```
import random

def main():
    bankroll = int(input("Enter the amount of the bankroll: "))
    (amount, timesPlayed) = playDoubleOrNothing(bankroll)
    print("Ending bankroll:", amount, "dollars")
    print("Number of games played:", timesPlayed)

def isOdd(n):
    if (1 <= n <= 36) and (n % 2):
        return True
    else:
        return False

def profit(n):
    if isOdd(n):
        return 1
```

```
        else:
            return -1
def playDoubleOrNothing(bankroll):
    amount = bankroll
    timesPlayed = 0
    while 0 < amount < 2 * bankroll:
        # let 37 represent 00
        n = random.randint(0, 37)
        timesPlayed += 1
        amount += profit(n)
    return (amount, timesPlayed)

main()
```

[Run. A possible outcome is shown below.]

```
Enter the amount of the bankroll: 12
Ending bankroll: 24 dollars
Number of games played: 74
```

In the next example, items are selected from a list of six items. However, some items are more likely to be selected than others. In this case, we must use an if-elif-else statement to do a truly random selection.

Example 4 Slot Machine   A slot machine is operated by inserting a coin in a slot and pulling a lever. This causes three wheels containing pictures of cherries, oranges, plums, melons, bars, and bells to spin around and finally come to rest with one picture showing on each wheel. Certain combinations of pictures, such as three of a kind, produce a payoff to the player. Suppose each wheel contains five cherries, five oranges, five plums, three melons, one bell, and one bar. The following program simulates the outcome from pulling the lever. Each wheel contains 20 pictures, which we will associate with the numbers from 1 through 20.

```
import random

def main():
    for i in range(3):
        outcome = spinWheel()
        print(outcome, end="  ")

def spinWheel():
    n = random.randint(1, 20)
    if n > 15:
        return "Cherries"
    elif n > 10:
        return "Orange"
    elif n > 5:
        return "Plum"
    elif n > 2:
        return "Melon"
    elif n > 1:
        return "Bell"
    else:
        return "Bar"
```

```
main()
```

[Run. A possible outcome is shown below.]

```
Plum  Melon  Cherries
```

■ Comments

1. The numbers generated by the random module are said to be **pseudorandom**. They are generated by an algorithm that makes them appear to be random. The time on the system clock, which changes approximately every hundredth of a second, is used by the algorithm.

Practice Problems 6.2

1. Assuming that *list1* contains three or more items, the following lines of code will display a list of two randomly selected items from *list1*. Write some lines of code that will accomplish the same result without using the sample function.

```
import random
print(random.sample(list1, 2))
```

2. Assuming that *list1* contains two or more items, the following lines of code will display a randomly selected item from *list1*. Write some lines of code that will accomplish the same result without using the choice function.

```
import random
print(random.choice(list1))
```

EXERCISES 6.2

In Exercises 1 through 8, describe an event whose outcome could be simulated by the lines of code. Assume that the *random* module has been imported.

1. ```
freeHit = ['Hit', 'Miss', 'Miss', 'Hit']
print(random.choice(freeHit))
```

2. ```
result = ("Selected", "Rejected")
print(random.choice(result))
```

3. ```
hitStrength = random.randint(1, 100)
if hitPower >= 50:
    print("BROKE")
else:
    print("SAFE")
```

4. ```
player1 = random.randint(1, 6)
player2 = random.randint(1, 6)
print("palyer1: " + player1 + "player2: " + player2)
```

5. ```
colors = ['red', 'cyan', 'teal', 'yellow', 'black']
flagTriplet = random.sample(colors, 3)
print(flagTriplet)
```
```

6.
```
songs = ['song1.mp3', 'song2.mp3','song3.mp3', 'song4.mp3', 'song5.mp3',
    'song6.mp3']
print(random.shuffle(songs))
```

7.
```
presenters = {'Cheryll': 1, 'Rio': 2, 'Tim': 3, 'Miranda': 4, 'Paul': 5}
order = [1, 2, 3, 4, 5]
for person in presenters:
    c = random.choice(order)
    presenters[person] = c
    order.remove(c)
```

8.
```
ticketNumber = ['2', '4', '6', '1', '3', '5']
print(random.choice(ticketNumber))
```

In Exercises 9 through 14, write lines of code to carry out the stated task. Assume that the *random* module has been imported.

9. **Alphabet** Display three letters selected at random from the alphabet.

10. **Perfect Square** Display a perfect square integer between 1 and 10,000 (inclusive) selected at random.

11. **Even Numbers** Display two even numbers between 2 and 100 (inclusive) selected at random.

12. **Vowel** Display a vowel selected at random.

13. **Coin** Toss a coin 100 times and display the number of times that a "Heads" occurs.

14. **Dice** Roll a pair of dice 100,000 times and display the percentage of times the sum of the numbers is 7.

15. **U.S. States** The file **StatesAlpha.txt** contains the names of the 50 U.S. states in alphabetical order. Write a program that selects three states at random without placing them into a list.

16. **U.S. States** The file **StatesAlpha.txt** contains the names of the 50 U.S. states in alphabetical order. Write a program that creates a new file named **RandomStates.txt** that contains the names in a random order.

17. **Matching Cards** Suppose two shuffled decks of cards are placed on a table, and then cards are drawn from the tops of the decks one at a time and compared. On average, how many matches do you think will occur? Write a program to carry out this process 10,000 times and calculate the average number of matches that occur. See Fig. 6.4. (**Note:** This problem was first analyzed in 1708 by the French probabilist Pierre Remond de Montmort who determined that the theoretical answer is 1. There are many variations on the problem, and the theoretical answer is always 1 even when the number of items is other than 52. One variation of the problem is as follows: A typist types letters and envelopes to 20 different people. The letters are randomly put into the envelopes. On average, how many letters are put into the correct envelope?)

```
The average number of cards that
matched was 1.005659.
```

```
Player 1: paper
Player 2: scissors
Player 2 wins.
```

FIGURE 6.4 Possible outcome of Exercise 17.   **FIGURE 6.5** Possible outcome of Exercise 18.

18. Rock, Paper, Scissors Write a program to simulate a game of Rock, Paper, Scissors between two players and display the outcome. Assume the players randomly make their choices. See Fig. 6.5. (**Note:** Paper beats Rock (Paper can cover Rock), Scissors beats Paper (Scissors can cut Paper), and Rock beats Scissors (Rock can break Scissors).)

Exercises 19 and 20 refer to the Powerball lottery. In the Powerball lottery, five balls are randomly selected from a set of white balls numbered 1 through 59, and then a single ball, called the Powerball, is randomly selected from a set of red balls numbered 1 through 35.

19. Powerball Lottery Write a program to randomly produce a Powerball drawing. See Fig. 6.6.

```
White balls: 22 28 51 11 5
Powerball: 20
```

```
31% of the time there were at least
two consecutive numbers in the set
of five numbers.
```

FIGURE 6.6 Possible outcome of Exercise 19.   **FIGURE 6.7** Possible outcome of Exercise 20.

20. Powerball Lottery Often the five selected white balls contain two or more balls with consecutive numbers. Write a program that simulates 100,000 selections of white balls and displays the percentage of times the selection contains at least two consecutive numbers. See Fig. 6.7. Feel free to use the function **random.sample((range(1,60), 5))**.

21. Coin Toss Write a program to display the result of tossing a coin 32 times. Then determine if there is a run of five consecutive Heads or a run of five consecutive Tails. See Fig. 6.8. (**Note:** When you toss a coin 2^r times, you are more likely than not to have a run of r Heads or r Tails.)

```
THTHHTHHTTTTHTHHHHHTTHHHHHHTTHHHTH
There was a run of five consecutive
same outcomes.
```

```
The average number of cards
turned up was 10.61.
```

FIGURE 6.8 Possible outcome of Exercise 21.   **FIGURE 6.9** Possible outcome of Exercise 22.

22. Locate First Ace Suppose you shuffle an ordinary deck of 52 playing cards, and then turn up cards from the top until the first ace appears. On average, how many cards do you think must be turned up until the first ace appears? Estimate the average by writing a program that shuffles a deck of cards 100,000 times and finds the average of the number of cards that must be turned up to obtain an ace for each shuffle. See Fig. 6.9. **Note:** Your average will differ from the one in the figure, but should be close to 10.6.

23. Bridge (HPC) A bridge hand consists of 13 cards. One way to evaluate a hand is to calculate the total high point count (HPC) where an ace is worth four points, a king is worth three points, a queen is worth two points, and a jack is worth one point. Write a program that randomly selects 13 cards from a deck of cards and calculates the HPC for the hand. See Fig. 6.10. **Note:** Use the pickled file **DeckOfCardsList.dat**.

```
7♥, A♦, Q♠, 4♣, 8♠, 8♥, K♠, 2♦, 10♦, 9♦, K♥, Q♦, Q♣
HPC = 16
```

FIGURE 6.10 Possible outcome of Exercise 23.

In Exercise 24, use the file `StatesANC.txt` that contains the name, abbreviation, nickname, and capital of each state in the United States. The states are listed in alphabetical order. The first three lines of the file are

```
Alabama,AL,Cotton State,Montgomery
Alaska,AK,The Last Frontier,Juneau
Arizona,AZ,Grand Canyon State,Phoenix
```

24. State Capital Quiz   Write a program that asks the user to name the capitals of five randomly chosen states. The program should then report the number of incorrect answers and display the answers to the missed questions. See Fig. 6.11.

```
What is the capital of Minnesota? Saint Paul
What is the capital of California? Sacramento
What is the capital of Illinois? Chicago
What is the capital of Alabama? Montgomery
What is the capital of Massachusetts? Boston

You missed 1 question.
Springfield is the capital of Illinois.
```

FIGURE 6.11   Possible outcome of Exercise 24.

Solutions to Practice Problems 6.2

1.
```
import random
random.shuffle(list1)
print(list1[:2])
```

or

```
import random
m = random.choice(list1)
list1.remove(m)
n = random.choice(list1)
print([m, n])
```

2.
```
import random
n = random.randint(0, len(list1) - 1)
print(list1[n])
```

or

```
import random
random.shuffle(list1)
print(list1[0])
```

6.3   Turtle Graphics

Turtle graphics uses objects and methods from the *turtle* module.

VideoNote
Turtle
Graphics

■ Coordinates

After the statements

```
import turtle
t = turtle.Turtle()
```

are executed, the window in Fig. 6.12 appears. The white region inside the border is called the **canvas** and the small chevron in the center of the canvas is called a **turtle**. The canvas contains around 360,000 points called **pixels** that are identified by ordered pairs of numbers determined by the coordinate system in Fig. 6.13. The pixel in the center of the canvas has coordinates (0, 0). The variable t is said to refer to a turtle object, and for simplicity is called a **turtle**.

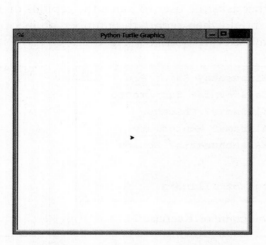

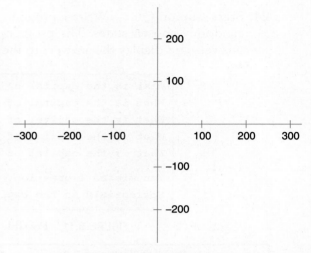

FIGURE 6.12 **Turtle graphics window.**   FIGURE 6.13 **Coordinate system for canvas.**

Think of the chevron as a small turtle with a pen attached to its tail. Python statements can move the tail up or down (thereby raising or lowering the pen), select a color for the pen, change the direction the turtle is facing, move the turtle in a straight line, and draw a dot of any diameter centered at the current position of the pen. Initially the turtle's tail is located at the origin of the coordinate system, the turtle is facing East, and its tail is down.

Intricate shapes can be drawn by repeating simple moves. The figure on the right was drawn by repeatedly having the turtle move 200 pixels in a straight line and rotate 170° counterclockwise. The program that draws the figure is given in Comment 4.

■ Methods from the *turtle* Module

The statements

`t.up()`   and   `t.down()`

raise and lower the pen. At any time, the turtle has a position (given by its coordinates), heading (the counterclockwise angle it makes with a horizontal line through it), pen status (up or down), and color. Turtles facing East, North, West, and South have headings of 0°, 90°, 180°, and 270°, respectively. All of the standard colors (such as, red, blue, green, white, and black) are available as pen colors. The colorful insert page shows 32 available colors.

The statement

`t.hideturtle()`

makes the chevron invisible. The statement

`t.forward(dist)`

moves the turtle *dist* pixels in the direction it is headed, the statement

`t.backward(dist)`

moves the turtle *dist* pixels in the opposite direction in which it is headed, and the statement

`t.goto(x, y)`

moves the turtle to the pixel having coordinates (x, y).

The color of the pen is initially black, but can be changed with a statement of the form

`t.pencolor(colorName)`

When the pen is down, each of the three statements above that move the turtle draw a line in the current color.

The statement

`t.setheading(deg)`

sets the heading of the turtle to *deg* degrees. The statements

`t.left(deg)`   and   `t.right(deg)`

rotate the turtle *deg* degrees counterclockwise or clockwise, respectively, from the direction it was headed.

The statement

`t.dot(diameter, colorName)`

draws a dot with the specified diameter and color centered at the current position of the pen. If the *colorName* argument is omitted, the current pen color is used. If both arguments are omitted, the statement uses a diameter of five pixels and the current pen color.

■ Rectangles

Figure 6.14 shows a rectangle of width w, height h, and lower-left corner at (x, y). After the statements **import turtle**, **t = turtle.Turtle()**, and **t.hideturtle()** have been executed, either of the following two functions can be used to draw a rectangle of any size, in any color, and any location specified by a calling statement. The first function uses the coordinates of the corners of the rectangle, and the second function uses the width and height of the rectangle.

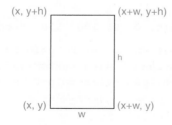

FIGURE 6.14   **A general rectangle.**

```
import turtle
def drawRectangle(t, x, y, w, h, colorP="black"):
    ## Draw a rectangle with bottom-left corner (x, y),
    ## width w, height h, and pencolor colorP.
```

```
        t.pencolor(colorP)
        t.up()
        t.goto(x, y)            # start at bottom-left corner of rectangle
        t.down()
        t.goto(x + w, y)        # draw line to bottom-right corner
        t.goto(x + w, y + h)    # draw line to top-right corner
        t.goto(x, y + h)        # draw line to top-left corner
        t.goto(x, y)            # draw line to bottom-left corner

def drawRectangle2(t, x, y, w, h, colorP="black"):
    ## Draw a rectangle with bottom-left corner (x, y),
    ## width w, height h, and pencolor colorP.
    t.pencolor(colorP)
    t.up()
    t.goto(x, y)            # start at bottom-left corner of rectangle
    t.down()
    for i in range(2):
        t.forward(w)        # draw horizontal side of rectangle
        t.left(90)          # rotate 90 degrees counterclockwise
        t.forward(h)        # draw vertical side of rectangle
        t.left(90)          # rotate 90 degrees counterclockwise
```

Enclosed regions, such as rectangles, can be filled with any color. The statement

```
t.fillcolor(colorName)
```

is used to specify the color for the interior of the region. Then the statements

```
t.begin_fill()  and  t.end_fill()
```

must be placed before and after the statements that actually draw the region.

✓   **Example 1**   Draw a Filled Rectangle   The following program draws a rectangle having a red border and a yellow interior.

```
import turtle

def main():
    t = turtle.Turtle()
    t.hideturtle()
    drawFilledRectangle(t, 0, 0, 100, 150, "red", "yellow")

def drawFilledRectangle(t, x, y, w, h, colorP="black", colorF="white"):
    ## Draw a filled rectangle with bottom-left corner (x, y),
    ## width w, height h, pen color colorP, and fill color colorF.
    t.pencolor(colorP)
    t.fillcolor(colorF)
    t.up()
    t.goto(x, y)            # start at bottom-left corner of rectangle
    t.down()
    t.begin_fill()
    t.goto(x + w, y)        # draw line to bottom-right corner
    t.goto(x + w, y + h)    # draw line to top-right corner
```

```
    t.goto(x, y + h)       # draw line to top-left corner
    t.goto(x, y)           # draw line to bottom-left corner
    t.end_fill()

main()
```

■ Flags

Many types of flags can easily be drawn with turtle graphics.

Example 2   Flag   The following program draws the flag shown on the right. The width of the flag is 1.5 times the height, the center blue strip is twice the height of each of the light blue strips, and the diameter of the circle is .8 times the height of the center blue strip. We have made the height of each light blue strip 25 pixels. Therefore, the center blue strip will have height 50 pixels and flag itself will have height 100 pixels. The width of the flag will be 1.5 · 100 = 150 pixels. We have placed the bottom-left corner of the flag at (0, 0), the center of the canvas.

```
import turtle

def main():
    t = turtle.Turtle()
    t.hideturtle()
    # Draw the three stripes.
    drawFilledRectangle(t, 0, 0, 150, 25, "light blue", "light blue")
    drawFilledRectangle(t, 0, 25, 150 , 50, "blue", "blue")
    drawFilledRectangle(t, 0, 75, 150, 25, "light blue", "light blue")
    # Draw white dot. Center of flag is (75, 50). 40 = .8 * 50.
    drawDot(t, 75, 50, 40, "white")

def drawFilledRectangle(t, x, y, w, h, colorP="black", colorF="white"):
    ## Draw a filled rectangle with bottom-left corner (x, y),
    ## width w, height h, pen color colorP, and fill color colorF.
    t.pencolor(colorP)
    t.fillcolor(colorF)
    t.up()
    t.goto(x, y)           # bottom-left corner of rectangle
    t.down()
    t.begin_fill()
    t.goto(x + w, y)       # bottom-right corner of rectangle
    t.goto(x + w, y + h)   # top-right corner of rectangle
    t.goto(x, y + h)       # top-left corner of rectangle
    t.goto(x, y)           # bottom-left corner of rectangle
    t.end_fill()

def drawDot(t, x, y, diameter, colorP):
    ## Draw a dot with center (x, y) and color colorP.
    t.up()
    t.goto(x, y)
    t.pencolor(colorP)
    t.dot(diameter)

main()
```

Example 3   Five-Pointed Star Figure 6.15(a) shows the star that appears on the American flag. In Fig. 6.15(b), L is the length of each side of the star, and the lower-left point of the star is at (0, 0). The coordinates of the center of the star are given, but are not needed in order to draw the star. However, the coordinates are useful if you want to draw a five-pointed star having a specified center rather than a specified lower-left point. The following program draws the five-pointed star in Fig. 6.15(b). The drawing of the entire American flag is given as a programming project.

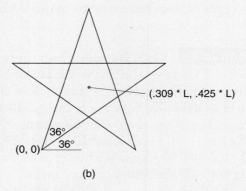

(a)   (b)

FIGURE 6.15   **Five-pointed star.**

```
import turtle

def main():
    t = turtle.Turtle()
    t.hideturtle()
    lengthOfSide = 200
    drawFivePointStar(t, 0, 0, lengthOfSide)

def drawFivePointStar(t, x, y, lengthOfSide):
    # Drawing begins at (x, y) and moves in a north-east direction.
    t.up()
    t.goto(x, y)
    t.left(36)
    t.down()
    for i in range(5):
        t.forward(lengthOfSide)
        t.left(144)     # 144 = 180 - 36

main()
```

■ **The *write* Method**

If *s* is a string, then the statements

```
t.write(s)
```

displays the string *s* with the bottom-left corner of the string approximately[1] at the current position of the pen. The statements

-----

[1]The exact positioning of the string is tricky to describe and depends in part on whether the string contains descending letters (that is, *g*, *j*, *p*, *q*, and *y*). Often slight trial-and-error modifications must be made in order to place strings exactly where we want them.

`t.write(s, align="right")` and `t.write(s, align="center")`

display the string *s* with the bottom-right corner and bottom center of the string approximately at the current position of the pen, respectively. The write method displays its string whether the pen is up or down. (*Note:* The statement `t.write(s, align="left")` has the same effect as the statement `t.write(s)`.)

✓ **Example 4** Demonstration of the *write* Method The following program displays the word Python with different alignments.

```
import turtle

t = turtle.Turtle()
t.hideturtle()
t.up()
t.goto(0, 60)
t.dot()
t.write("Python")
t.goto(0, 30)
t.dot()
t.write("Python", align="right")
t.goto(0, 0)
t.dot()
t.write("Python", align="center")
```

[Run]

Python
.

Python
.

Python
.

The font used to display the string can be specified by assigning a three-tuple of the form (*fontName*, *fontSize*, *styleName*) to the **font** argument of the **write** method. The value of *styleName* can be *italic*, *bold*, *underline*, or *normal*. For instance, the statement

`t.write("Python", font=("Courier New", 12, "bold"))`

displays the word Python in a boldface, 12-point, Courier New font. A write method can contain one, both, or neither of the **align** and **font** arguments.

■ Bar Charts

Certain types of data is visually enhanced when placed in a bar chart.

Example 5 Languages The following program creates the bar chart on the next page. The *x*-coordinates of the bottom-left corners of the rectangles begin at -200 and successively increase by 76 pixels. The *y*-coordinates of the points are given by the list *heights*, with each value divided by 4. (The divisor is needed in order for the bar chart to fit in the canvas.) In the *displayText* function, the numbers −162, −10, −25, and −45 were obtained by trial-and-error.

Principal Languages of the World
(in millions of "first language" speakers)

```python
import turtle

heights = [856, 420, 360, 260, 205]  # number of speakers for each language

def main():
    t = turtle.Turtle()
    t.hideturtle()
    for i in range(5):
        drawFilledRectangle(t, -200 + (76 * i), 0, 76, heights[i] / 4,
                            "black", "light blue")
    displayText(t)

def drawFilledRectangle(t, x, y, w, h, colorP="black", colorF="white"):
    ## Draw a filled rectangle with bottom-left corner (x, y), width w,
    ## height h, pen color colorP, and fill color colorF.
    t.pencolor(colorP)
    t.fillcolor(colorF)
    t.up()
    t.goto(x, y)            # bottom-left corner of rectangle
    t.down()
    t.begin_fill()
    t.goto(x + w, y)       # bottom-right corner of rectangle
    t.goto(x + w, y + h)   # top-right corner of rectangle
    t.goto(x, y + h)       # top-left corner of rectangle
    t.goto(x, y)           # bottom-left corner of rectangle
    t.end_fill()

def displayText(t):
    languages = ["Mandarin", "Spanish", "English",
                 "Hindi", "Bengali"]
    t.pencolor("blue")
    t.up()
    for i in range(5):
        # Display number at top of rectangle.
        t.goto(-162 + (76 * i), heights[i] / 4)
        t.write(str(heights[i]), align="center",
                font=("Arial", 10, "normal"))
        # Display language.
        t.goto(-162 + (76 * i), 10)
        t.write(languages[i], align="center",
                font=("Arial", 10, "normal"))
    # Display title of bar chart.
    t.goto(-200, -25)
```

```
      t.write("Principal Languages of the World",
              font=("Arial", 10, "normal"))
      t.goto(-200, -45)
      t.write('(in millions of "first language" speakers)',
              font=("Arial", 10, "normal"))

main()
```

■ Line Charts

Simple tabular data, such as that in Table 6.3, can be visually displayed in a line chart.

TABLE 6.3	Percentage of college freshmen who smoke.						
	2000	2002	2004	2006	2008	2010	2012
Percent	10.0	7.4	6.4	5.3	4.4	3.7	2.6

Source: Higher Education Research Institute.

 Example 6 Smokers The following program uses the data in Table 6.3 to create the line chart on the right. The *x*-coordinates of the points begin at 40 and successively increase by 40. The *y*-coordinates of the points are given by the list *yValues*, with each value multiplied by 15. (The multiplier improves the readability of the graph.)

In the *displayText* function, the numbers −3, −10, −20, and −50 were obtained by trial-and-error.

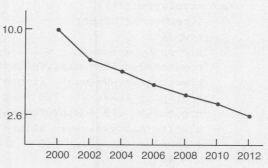

Percentage of College Freshmen Who Smoke

```
import turtle

yValues = [10.0, 7.4, 6.4, 5.3, 4.4, 3.7, 2.6]   # percent for each year

def main():
    t = turtle.Turtle()
    t.hideturtle()
    drawLine(t, 0, 0, 300, 0)          # Draw x-axis.
    drawLine(t, 0, 0, 0, 175)          # Draw y-axis.
    for i in range(6):
        drawLineWithDots(t, 40 + (40 * i), 15 * yValues[i],
                         40 + (40 * (i + 1)), 15 * yValues[i + 1], "blue")
    drawTickMarks(t)
    displayText(t)

def drawLine(t, x1, y1, x2, y2, colorP="black"):
    ## Draw line segment from (x1, y1) to (x2, y2) having color colorP.
    t.up()
    t.goto(x1, y1)
    t.down()
    t.pencolor(colorP)
    t.goto(x2, y2)
```

```python
def drawLineWithDots(t, x1, y1, x2, y2, colorP="black"):
    ## Draw line segment from (x1, y1) to (x2, y2) having color
    ## colorP and insert dots at both ends of the line segment.
    t.pencolor(colorP)
    t.up()
    t.goto(x1, y1)  # beginning of line segment
    t.dot(5)
    t.down()
    t.goto(x2, y2)  # end of line segment
    t.dot(5)

def drawTickMarks(t):
    ## Draw tick marks along x-axis.
    for i in range(1, 8):
        drawLine(t, 40 * i, 0, 40 * i , 10)
    # Draw tick mark on y-axis to indicate greatest value.
    drawLine(t, 0, 15 * max(yValues), 10, 15 * max(yValues))
    # Draw tick mark on y-axis to indicate least value.
    drawLine(t, 0, 15 * min(yValues), 10, 15 * min(yValues))

def displayText(t):
    t.pencolor("blue")
    t.up()
    # Display greatest y-value next to upper tick mark on y-axis.
    t.goto(-3, (15 * max(yValues)) - 10)
    t.write(max(yValues), align="right")
    # Display least y-value next to lower tick mark on y-axis.
    t.goto(-3, (15 * min(yValues)) - 10)
    t.write(min(yValues), align="right")
    # Display the years below the tick marks on x-axis.
    x = 40
    for i in range(2000, 2013, 2):
        t.goto(x, -20)
        t.write(str(i), align="center")
        x += 40
    # Display title of graph.
    t.goto(0, -50)
    t.write("Percentage of College Freshmen Who Smoke")

main()
```

■ Comments

1. The pair of statements

```python
t.pencolor(colorP)
t.fillcolor(colorF)
```

can be condensed into the single statement

```python
t.color(colorP, colorF)
```

2. An optional statement of the form **t.speed(n)**, where *n* is an integer from 0 through 10, determines the quickness that the turtle moves. The value $n = 1$ produces the slowest

speed and $n = 10$ produces the fastest speed. If the argument is omitted, the speed will be 3. An argument of 0 causes the turtle to move instantly.

3. Some drawings are easier to program if you first sketch them on a piece of paper. Graph paper can be especially useful.

4. The following program generates the 36-leaved flower shown at the beginning of this section (p. 258):

```python
import turtle

t = turtle.Turtle()
t.hideturtle()
t.color("blue", "light blue")
t.begin_fill()
for i in range(36):
    t.forward(200)
    t.left(170)
t.end_fill()
```

Practice Problems 6.3

1. Change the function *drawFivePointStar* in Example 3, so that the star has its center, rather than its lower-left point, at (x, y)?

2. The *drawFilledRectangle* function appearing in Example 1 is a useful function that could be reused in other programs. However, after it executes, the current pen colors might be altered. Modify the function definition so that it does not alter the current colors.

EXERCISES 6.3

In Exercises 1 through 8, write a few lines of code to draw the requested figure without using the *drawLine*, *drawRectangle*, *drawFilledRectangle*, or *drawDot* function.

1. A blue line segment from (20, 30) to (80, 90) with small dots at each end.

2. A blue horizontal line tangent to a red dot of diameter 100 pixels.

3. Two blue dots of different sizes with one sitting on top of the other.

4. A purple line segment from (25, 55) to (80, 40) with small dots at each end.

5. A solid rectangle with lower-left corner at $(-30, -40)$ and upper-right corner at (50, 60).

6. An orange square with a red border having sides of length 80 pixels and centered in the turtle window.

7. A right triangle having sides of length 60 and 80 pixels.

8. An equilateral triangle with each side having length 100 pixels. (**Note:** The interior angles will each have measure 60°.)

Exercises 9 through 26 can be found on the colorful insert pages.

27. College Majors   Write a program to create the bar chart in Fig. 6.16.

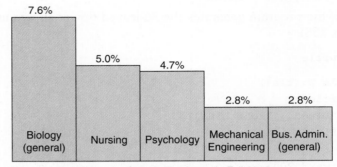

FIGURE 6.16   Bar chart for Exercise 27.

28. High Schools   Write a program to create the bar chart in Fig. 6.17.

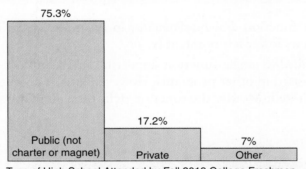

FIGURE 6.17   Bar chart for Exercise 28.

29. College Enrollments   Write a program to create the line chart in Fig. 6.18. Use the data in Table 6.4.

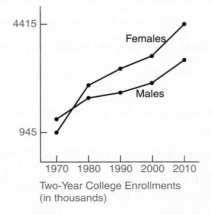

FIGURE 6.18   Line chart for Exercise 29.

TABLE 6.4	Two-year college enrollments (in thousands).				
	1970	1980	1990	2000	2010
Male	1,375	2,047	2,233	2,559	3,265
Female	945	2,479	3,007	3,398	4,415

30. Life Goals Write a program to create the line chart in Fig. 6.19. Use the data in Table 6.5.

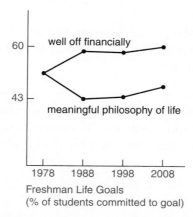

FIGURE 6.19 Line chart for Exercise 30.

TABLE 6.5	Freshman life goals (% of students committed to goal).			
	1978	1988	1998	2008
Be very well off financially	59	74	73	77
Develop a meaningful philosophy of life	60	43	44	51

Solutions to Practice Problems 6.3

1. Replace the statement `t.goto(x, y)` with

   ```
   t.goto(x - .309 * lengthOfSide, y - .425 * lengthOfSide)
   ```

2. Insert the first two lines below at the beginning of the function definition, and the last two lines at the end of the function definition.

   ```
   originalPenColor = t.pencolor()
   originalFillColor = t.fillcolor()

   t.pencolor(originalPenColor)
   t.fillcolor(originalFillColor)
   ```

6.4 Recursion

A **recursive function** is a function that calls itself, where successive calls reduce a computation to smaller computations of the same type until a **base case** with a trivial solution is reached.

VideoNote
Recursion

■ A Recursive Power Function

The nth power of a number can be defined iteratively as

$$r^n = \underbrace{r \cdot r \cdot \ \ldots \ \cdot r}_{n \text{ terms}}$$

or recursively as

$$r^1 = r$$
$$r^n = r \cdot r^{n-1}$$

In the recursive definition, the power function is defined in terms of a simpler version of itself. For instance, the computation of r^4 is successively reduced to the computation of r^3, r^2, and finally r^1, a trivial case.

 Example 1   Power Function The following program uses the iterative definition of a *power* function. The function definition requires two temporary variables (*value* and *i*). Also, the function definition does not resemble the iterative definition above.

```python
def power(r, n):
    ## iterative definition of power function
    value = 1
    for i in range(1, n + 1):
        value = r * value
    return value

print(power(2, 3))
```

[Run]

8

 Example 2   Power Function The following program uses the recursive definition of a *power* function. The function definition resembles the recursive definition above.

```python
def power(r, n):
    ## recursive definition of power function
    if n == 1:
        return r
    else:
        return r * power(r, n - 1)
print(power(2, 3))
```

[Run]

8

Recursive algorithms have two traits.

1. There are one or more base cases with trivial solutions.
2. There is an "inductive step" that successively reduces the problem to smaller versions of the same problem, with the reduction eventually culminating in a base case. This inductive step is called the **reducing step**.

The pseudocode for a recursive solution to a problem has the general form

if a base case is reached
    Solve the base case directly.
else
    Repeatedly reduce the problem to a version increasingly closer to a base case until it
    becomes a base case.

Suppose the recursive function *power* is called upon to compute **power(r, n)**, with $r = 2$ and $n = 3$. Figure 6.20 traces the process of evaluation. The value in (a) cannot be calculated right away since $n \neq 1$. Therefore, the recursive step replaces **power(2, 3)** with the expression in (b). (That is, the return statement does not immediately return a value.) Similarly, **power(2, 2)** in (b) is replaced by the expression in (c). Since $n = 1$ in (c), the base case has been reached. **power(2,1)** is evaluated directly as 2. Now the recursion process traces backward through (c), (b), and (a), denoted as (c'), (b'), and (a') for the return trip.

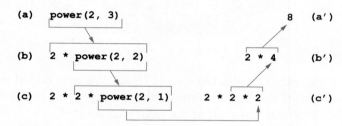

FIGURE 6.20 **The recursive computation of power(2, 3).**

■ A Recursive Palindrome Function

Any function definition using recursion can be rewritten using iteration, but sometimes the recursive solution is easier to understand and code. The Boolean-valued function *isPalindrome*, which determines whether or not a word is a palindrome, is one such function. (A word is a **palindrome** if it reads the same forward and backward. Some examples are *racecar*, *kayak*, and *pullup*.) When designing the recursive function we use the fact that a word is a palindrome if the beginning and ending letters are the same and the remaining letters form a palindrome. Therefore, we initially look at the first and last letters of the word. If they are different, we end the examination and return False. Otherwise, we delete the first and last letters, and continue the process with the shorter remaining word. We continue this process until we find a mismatch or the reduced word has 0 or 1 letter. We have solved the problem by breaking it into smaller problems of the same type.

> **Example 3**   Palindrome   The following function uses recursion to determine whether or not a word containing no punctuation is a palindrome.

```
def isPalindrome(word):
    word = word.lower()         # Convert all letters to lowercase.
    if len(word) <= 1:          # Words of zero or one letters are palindromes.
        return True
    elif word[0] == word[-1]:   # First and last letters match.
        word = word[1:-1]       # Remove first and last letters.
        return isPalindrome(word)
    else:
        return False
```

■ A Recursive Fractal Function

  Example 4   Draw a Fractal   The program in this example uses recursion to create Fig. 6.21, a drawing known as a *fractal*.

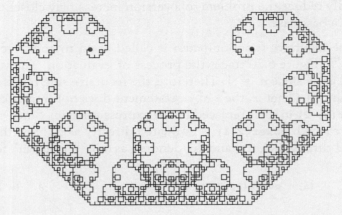

FIGURE 6.21   A fractal.

A four-step algorithm creates the fractal. (**Note:** We have added two blue dots to the figure that are not part of the fractal to show where the drawing begins and ends. The drawing begins at the left blue dot and ends at the right blue dot.)

a. Specify an intricacy level, a nonnegative integer, for the fractal.

b. Start with a straight line. The line, shown in Figure 6.22(a), is called the level 0 fractal.

c. To obtain the fractal for the next level, replace each line in the drawing with the sides of an isosceles right triangle having the line as hypotenuse. Figures 6.22(b), (c), and (d) show the level 1, 2, and 3 fractals.

d. Repeat step (c) until the desired level of recursion is reached. The fractal in Fig. 6.21 has intricacy level 12.

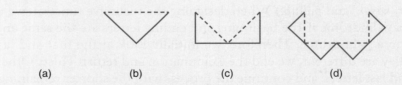

| (a) | (b) | (c) | (d) |

FIGURE 6.22   Fractals of levels 0, 1, 2, and 3.

The following program creates the level 12 fractal in Fig. 6.21:

```python
import turtle

def main():
    t = turtle.Turtle()
    t.hideturtle()
    t.speed(10)
    level = 12
    fract(t, -80, 60, 80, 60, level)

def fract(t, x1, y1, x2, y2, level):
    # Drawing begins at (x1, y1) and ends at (x2, y2).
    newX = 0
    newY = 0
```

```
        if level == 0:
            drawLine(t, x1, y1, x2, y2)
        else:
            newX = (x1 + x2)/2 + (y2 - y1)/2
            newY = (y1 + y2)/2 - (x2 - x1)/2
            fract(t, x1, y1, newX, newY, level - 1)
            fract(t, newX, newY, x2, y2, level - 1)
def drawLine(t, x1, y1, x2, y2):
    # Draw line from (x1, y1) to (x2, y2).
    t.up()
    t.goto(x1, y1)
    t.down()
    t.goto(x2, y2)
main()
```

■ Comments

1. The base case of the recursive solution of a problem is also called the *terminating case* or *stopping condition*.

2. Any problem that can be solved with recursion can also be solved with iteration. Iterative methods usually execute faster and make less of a demand on memory. However, recursive solutions often generate less code, and are more elegant and easier to read.

3. If a recursive algorithm is coded incorrectly and the terminating case is never reached, the program probably will end with the error message "RuntimeError: maximum recursion depth exceeded."

4. Another kind of recursion, called *indirect recursion*, results when two procedures call each other. In the following program, the variable *counter* is used to terminate repetition:

```
counter = 0

def main():
    one()

def one():
    global counter
    counter += 1
    if counter < 5:
        print("1 ", end="")
        two()

def two():
    print("2 ", end="")
    one()

main()
```

[Run]

```
1 2 1 2 1 2 1 2
```

Practice Problems 6.4

1. If n is a positive integer, then n factorial (written $n!$) is the product of the numbers from 1 through n. Write a recursive function to calculate n factorial.

2. What is the output of the following program? (**Note:** chr(ord(letter) − 1) is the letter of the alphabet that precedes *letter*.)

```
def main():
    print(alpha('H'))

def alpha(letter):
    if letter == 'A':
        return 'A'
    else:
        return letter + alpha(chr(ord(letter) - 1))

main()
```

EXERCISES 6.4

In Exercises 1 through 5, determine the output of the program.

1.
```
def main():
    print(factorial(5))

def factorial(n):
    if n == 1:
        return 1
    else:
        return n * factorial(n - 1)

main()
```

2.
```
def main():
    digitSum(12345)

def digitSum(n):
    total = 0
    while n:
        total += n % 10
        n = n / 10
    print total

main()
```

3.
```
def main():
    stars(6)

def stars(n):
    if n==0:
        return
    else:
        print ("*"*n )
        stars(n - 1)

main()
```

4.
```
def main():
    print(power(5, 4))

def power(m, n):
    if n == 1:
        return m
    else:
        return m * power(m, n-1)

main()
```

5.
```
def main():
    print(repeatLastLetter("oprah"))

def repeatLastLetter(w):
    if len(w) == 1:
        return w
    else:
        return repeatLastLetter(w[1:]) + repeatLastLetter(w[1:])

main()
```

6. **Prime Factors**   The following recursive function returns the prime factors of the number n. Explain how the function works.

```
def factor(n):
    ## Return a list containing the prime factors of n.
    if n==1:
        return []
    b = 2
    while b <= n:
        while not n % b:
            return [b] + factor(n // b)
        b += 1
```

7. **Alphabetical Order**   The following iterative function determines whether a list of lowercase words is in alphabetical order. Write the equivalent recursive function.

```
def isAlpha(L):
    ## Determine whether list of lowercase words is in alphabetical order.
    for i in range(len(L) - 1):
        if L[i] > L[i + 1]:
            return False
    return True
```

8. **Sequence of Numbers**   The following iterative function displays a sequence of numbers. Write the equivalent recursive function.

```
def displaySequenceOfNumbers(m, n):
    ## Display the numbers from m to n, where m <= n.
    while m <= n:
        print(m)
        m = m + 1
```

9. **Subsets**   The number of subsets of r elements that can be selected from a set of n elements is written as $C(n, r)$. The value of $C(n, r)$ is also the coefficient of x^r in the binomial expansion of $(x + 1)^n$. If $r = 0$ or $r = n$, then the value of $C(n, r)$ is 1. Otherwise, $C(n, r) = C(n - 1, r - 1) + C(n - 1, r)$. Write a program using a recursive function

that allows n to be input by the user and displays the coefficients in the expansion of $(x + 1)^n$. See Fig. 6.23.

```
Enter a positive integer: 5
1 5 10 10 5 1
```

```
Enter a positive integer: 7
Fibonacci number: 13
```

FIGURE 6.23   Possible outcome of Exercise 9.   **FIGURE 6.24   Possible outcome of Exercise 10.**

10. Fibonacci Sequence   The famous Fibonacci sequence, 1, 1, 2, 3, 5, 8, 13, ..., begins with two 1s. After that, each number is the sum of the preceding two numbers. Write a program using a recursive function that requests an integer n as input and then displays the nth number of the Fibonacci sequence. See Fig. 6.24.

11. Greatest Common Divisor   The *greatest common divisor (GCD)* of two nonnegative integers is the largest integer that divides both numbers. For instance, GCD(6, 15) = 3 and GCD(9, 0) = 9. The standard algorithm for calculating the GCD of two numbers depends on the fact that GCD(m, n) = GCD(n, m % n), where % is the modulus operator. Write a program that requests two positive integers as input and displays their GCD. Use a recursive function (with $n = 0$ as the terminating case) to calculate the GCD. See Fig. 6.25.

```
Enter the first integer: 35
Enter the second integer: 14
GCD = 7
```

FIGURE 6.25   Possible outcome of Exercise 11.

12. Mortgage   The mortgage on a house is paid off in equal monthly payments for a period of years. If p is the initial amount of the mortgage, pmt is the monthly payment, and r is the annual rate of interest, then the amount owed after n months can be computed as

$$\text{balance}(p, pmt, r, n) = \left(1 + \frac{r}{1200}\right) * \text{balance}(p, pmt, r, n - 1) - pmt$$

Write a program that requests the amount of the mortgage, the monthly payment, the annual rate of interest, and the number of months elapsed as input, and displays the amount owed. See Fig. 6.26. **Note:** balance(p, pmt, r, 0) = p.

```
Enter the principal: 204700
Enter the annual rate of interest: 4.8
Enter the monthly payment: 1073.99
Enter the number of monthly payments
made: 300
The amount still owed is $57,188.74.
```

FIGURE 6.26   Possible outcome of Exercise 12.

```
Enter a state: Ohio
Enter a state: Texas
Enter a state: Oregon
Enter a state: End
Oregon
Texas
Ohio
```

FIGURE 6.27   Possible outcome of Exercise 13.

13. Reverse Order   Write a program that asks the user to input an arbitrary number of names of states, and then displays the names in the reverse order they were entered. Do not use lists or files to store the names. See Fig. 6.27.

14. Sum Function   Suppose that the **sum** function for lists did not exist. Write a recursive function that totals the numbers in a list of numbers.

Solutions to Practice Problems 6.4

1. $n! = n \cdot (n - 1) \cdot (n - 2) \cdot \cdots \cdot 3 \cdot 2 \cdot 1$

   As written, $n!$ can be calculated iteratively with a for loop—however, when rewritten as

   $$n! = n \cdot ((n - 1) \cdot (n - 2) \cdot \cdots \cdot 3 \cdot 2 \cdot 1) = n \cdot (n - 1)!$$

   $n!$ is expressed in terms of $(n - 1)!$ and can be calculated recursively with $n = 1$ as the base case.

   ```python
   def factorial(n):
       if n == 1:
           return 1
       else:
           return n * factorial(n - 1)
   ```

2. **HGFEDCBA**

   Recursive functions needn't have numeric parameters.

CHAPTER 6 KEY TERMS AND CONCEPTS

EXAMPLES

6.1 Exception Handling

Table 6.1 contains a list of several common exceptions. **Exception handling** allows the programmer to deal with runtime errors that otherwise might crash the program. If an exception occurs while the code in the **try** block is executing, execution branches to the code in an **except clause** that hopefully provides a workaround. An **else clause** contains code that runs if no exceptions have occurred. Except clauses can be either exception specific or activated by any exception. The block of a **finally clause** is always executed, even when no exceptions occur.

```python
while True:
    try:
        s = "Enter a number: "
        num = float(input(s))
    except ValueError:
        print("You didn't",end="")
        print(" enter a number.")
    else:
        print("You entered", num)
        break
    finally:
        print("This prints ",end="")
        print("even when we break.")
```

6.2 Selecting Random Values

Three functions from the *random* module that operate on lists are **choice** (selects an item at random), **sample** (selects a sublist of a specified size at random), and **shuffle** (randomly reorders the items of the list). The **randint** function selects a number at random from a sequence of numbers.

```python
import random
L = ["red", "blue", "tan", "gray"]
print(random.choice(L))
print(random.sample(L, 2))
random.shuffle(L)
print(L)
print(random.randint(1, 6))
```

CHAPTER 6 KEY TERMS AND CONCEPTS	EXAMPLES
	``[Run, possible outcome]
tan
['tan', 'red']
['blue', 'gray', 'red', 'tan']
4```

6.3 Turtle Graphics

Turtle graphics are drawn with a pen that can be thought of as being attached to the tail of a robotic turtle. The turtle responds to commands from the *turtle* module. The turtle can be instructed to raise or lower the pen, use a specified color, rotate in place, move to a designated point, move forward or backward for a specified distance, draw a dot, and display text. When the pen is lowered, the pen draws while the turtle moves. If the set of statements that draw an enclosed region are preceded by **t.begin_fill()** and followed by **t.end_fill()**, the inside of the region will have the color specified by a statement of the form **t.fillcolor(colorName)**.

```
import turtle
t = turtle.Turtle()
t.hideturtle()
t.up()  # raise the pen
# move to (10,20) without drawing
t.goto(10,20)
# draw red dot of diameter 6 with
# center at (10,20)
t.dot(6, "red")
t.down() # lower the pen
t.pencolor("blue")
# draw blue line from (10,20) to
# (30,40)
t.goto(30,40)
# display hi to right of (30,40)
t.write("hi")
```

Section 6.3 defines functions that draw rectangles, lines, dots, stars, and text with specified locations, sizes, and colors. These functions simplify writing programs that draw flags and charts.

Percentage of College Freshmen Who Smoke

6.4 Recursion

A **recursive function** is a function that calls itself, where successive calls reduce a computation to smaller computations of the same type until a **base case** with a trivial solution is reached.

```
def factorial(n):
    if n == 1:  # base case
        return 1
    else:
        return n * factorial(n - 1)
```

CHAPTER 6   PROGRAMMING PROJECTS

1. **Guess My Number**   Write a robust program that randomly selects a number from 1 through 100 and asks the user to guess the number. At each guess the user should be told if the guess is proper, and if so, whether it is too high or too low. The user should be told of the number of guesses when finally guessing the correct number. See Fig. 6.28.

```
I've thought of a number from 1 through 100.
Guess the number: 50
Too low
Try again: 123
Number must be from 1 through 100.
Try again: sixty
You did not enter a number.
Try again: 60
Too high
Try again: 56
Correct. You took 5 guesses.
```

FIGURE 6.28   Possible outcome of Programming Project 1.

2. **Analyze a Poker Hand**   Write a program using the file **DeckOfCardsList.dat** that randomly selects and displays five cards from the deck of cards and determines which of the following seven categories describes the hand: four-of-a-kind, full house (three cards of one rank, two cards of another rank), three-of-a-kind, two pairs, one pair, or ranks-all-different. See Fig. 6.29. (**Hint:** Determine the number of different ranks in the hand and analyze each of the four possible cases.)

```
K♥, K♦, 2♦, K♣, 5♠
three-of-a-kind
```

FIGURE 6.29   Possible outcome of Programming Project 2.

3. **Analyze a Bridge Hand**   Write a program using the file **DeckOfCardsList.dat** that randomly selects and displays 13 cards from the deck of cards and gives the suit distribution. See Fig. 6.30.

```
10♥, 3♥, J♣, 2♣, 10♦, K♣, 2♥, 6♦, 6♣, 4♣, 7♦, 6♠, 4♦
Number of ♣ is 5
Number of ♦ is 4
Number of ♥ is 3
Number of ♠ is 1
```

FIGURE 6.30   Possible outcome of Programming Project 3.

4. **American Flag**   The width (w) of the official American flag is 1.9 times the height (h). The blue rectangular canton (referred to as the "union") has width $\frac{2}{5} w$ and height $\frac{7}{13} h$. Write a program that draws an American flag. See Fig. 6.31. The colorful insert pages contain a picture of the flag with its true colors.

5. **Permutations**   A reordering of the letters of a word is called a *permutation* of the word. A word of n different characters has $n!$ permutations where $n! = n \cdot (n-1) \cdot (n-2) \cdot \ldots \cdot 2 \cdot 1$. For instance, the word *python* has 6! or 720 permutations. Some of its permutations are *pythno*, *ypntoh*, *tonyhp*, and *ontphy*. Write a program that requests a word without repeated characters as input and then displays all the

FIGURE 6.31   **Outcome of Programming Project 4.**

permutations of the word. See Fig. 6.32. (*Hint:* Suppose the word has six characters. Consider the characters of the word one at a time. Then display the words beginning with that character and followed by each of the 5! permutations of the remaining characters of the word.)

```
Enter a word: ear
ear era aer are rea rae
```

FIGURE 6.32   **Possible outcome of Programming Project 5.**

6. Pascal's Triangle   The triangular array of numbers in Fig. 6.33 is called *Pascal's triangle*, in honor of the seventeenth century mathematician Blaise Pascal. The nth row of the triangle gives the coefficients of the terms in the expansion of $(1 + x)^n$. For instance, the 5th row tells us that

$$(1 + x)^5 = 1 + 5x + 10x^2 + 10x^3 + 5x^4 + 1x^5$$

```
                                              Row
                    1                          0
                1       1                      1
            1       2       1                  2
        1       3       3       1              3
    1       4       6       4       1          4
1       5       10      10      5       1      5
```

FIGURE 6.33   **Pascal's Triangle.**

With the coefficients arranged in this way, each number in the triangle is the sum of the two numbers directly above it (one to the left and one to the right). For example, in row four, 1 is the sum of 1 (the only number above it), 4 is the sum of 1 and 3, 6 is the sum of 3 and 3, and so on. Since each row can be calculated from the previous row, recursion can easily be used to generate any row of Pascal's triangle. Write a program that prompts the user for a nonnegative integer n and then displays the numbers in the nth row of the triangle. See Fig. 6.34.

```
Enter a nonnegative integer: 6
Row 6: 1 6 15 20 15 6 1
```

FIGURE 6.34   **Possible outcome of Programming Project 6.**

7

Object-Oriented Programming

7.1   Classes and Objects

Practical experience in the financial, scientific, engineering, and software design industries has revealed some difficulties with traditional program design methodologies. As programs grow in size and become more complex, and as the number of programmers working on the same project increases, the number of dependencies and interrelationships throughout the code increases exponentially. A small change made by one programmer in one place may have unintended effects in other places. The effects of this change may ripple throughout the entire program, requiring the rewriting of a great deal of code along the way. A partial solution to this problem is **data hiding** where, within a program, as much implementation detail as possible is hidden. Data hiding is an important principle underlying object-oriented programming. An object is an encapsulation of data and methods that act on the data. A programmer using an object is concerned only with the tasks that the object can perform and the parameters used by these tasks. The details of the data structures and methods are hidden within the object.

■ Built-in Classes

We have been using the word *object* throughout this book. For instance, we have made the following sorts of statements:

> "Hello World!" is an object of type *str*.
> [1, 2, 3] is an object of type *list*.

 Example 1   Object Types The following program identifies the types of the above two objects. Notice that Python uses the word **class** instead of the word **type** in the output of the program.

```
s = "Hello World!"
L = [1, 2, 3]
print(type(s))
print(type(L))
```

[Run]

```
<class 'str'>
<class 'list'>
```

All strings are instances of the class *str*, and all lists are instances of the class *list*. Although each string holds its own value, all strings have the same methods. Similarly, all lists have the same methods. We will refer to the data types *str*, *int*, *float*, *list*, *tuple*, *dictionary*, and *set* as **built-in Python classes**. We will refer to a specific literal from one of these classes as an **instance** of the class.

■ User-Defined Classes

Python allows us to create our own classes, that is, data types. Like a Python built-in class, each class we define will have a specified set of methods and each object (that is, instance) of the class will have its own value(s). As an analogy, the difference between a class and an object is often compared to the difference between a cookie cutter and a cookie. A cookie cutter is a template that can be used to create cookies. You can't eat a cookie cutter, but you can eat the cookies it creates. A class is used to create objects that appear in programs.

Class definitions have the general form

VideoNote

Defining
a Class

```
class ClassName:
    indented list of methods for the class
```

The class header consists of the reserved word **class**, followed by the name of the class, and a colon. Class names must follow the same naming rules as variables. By convention, class names begin with an uppercase letter and use camel casing.

Methods are defined much like ordinary functions. The main difference is that methods have *self* as their first parameter. When an object (that is, an instance of the class) is created, each method's *self* parameter references the object so that the method knows which object to operate on. Figure 7.1 shows a typical class definition.

```
class Rectangle:
    def __init__(self, width=1, height=1):
        self._width = width          instance
        self._height = height        variables

    def setWidth(self, width):
        self._width = width

    def setHeight(self, height):
        self._height = height

    def getWidth(self):
        return self._width

    def getHeight(self):
        return self._height

    def area(self):
        return self._width * self._height

    def perimeter(self):
        return 2 * (self._width + self._height)

    def __str__(self):
        return ("Width: " + str(self._width)
            + "\nHeight: " + str(self._height))
```

initializer method

mutator methods

accessor methods

other methods

state-representation method

FIGURE 7.1   A typical class definition.

The *Rectangle* class defined in Fig. 7.1 has variables that store the values for the width and height of a rectangle. The first and last methods (__init__ and __str__) are special methods whose names have beginning and ending double underscores. (You should never name a method of your own in such a way.) The __init__ method (also known as the **constructor**) is automatically called when an object is created. It creates and assigns values to the **instance variables** _width and _height that store the values for the object. Instance variables are also called the **properties** of the class, and the collections of values of the instance variables are called the **state** of the object. Unlike variables declared in other definitions, instance variables are visible everywhere in the class. They can be accessed from every method in the class. The __str__ method provides a customized way to represent the state of an object as a string. The **mutator methods** are used to assign new values to the instance variables, and the **accessor methods** are used to retrieve the values of instance variables. The other methods operate on objects just like the methods we have been using in previous chapters of the book.

A class is a template from which objects are created. The class specifies the properties and methods that will be common to all objects that are instances of that class. Classes can be either typed directly into programs or stored in modules and brought into programs with **import** statements. An object, which is an instance of a class, is created in a program with a statement of the form

```
objectName = ClassName(arg1, arg2, . . .)
```

or

```
objectName = moduleName.ClassName(arg1, arg2, . . .)
```

This type of statement declares what type of object the variable will refer to, automatically calls the class' initializer, causes the parameter *self* to reference the object, and passes its arguments to the other parameters of the initializer.

✔ **Example 2**   Rectangle Suppose the class *Rectangle* from Fig. 7.1 has been stored in the file **rectangle.py**. The following program shows the effect of three different constructor statements. The statement **print(r)** calls the special __*str*__ method that displays the state of the object in a form specified by the programmer.

```
import rectangle

# Create a rectangle of width 4 and height 5
r = rectangle.Rectangle(4, 5)
print(r)
print()
# Create a rectangle with the default values for width and height
r = rectangle.Rectangle()
print(r)
print()
# Create a rectangle of width 4 and default height 1
r = rectangle.Rectangle(4)
print(r)
```

[Run]

```
Width: 4
Height: 5

Width: 1
Height: 1

Width: 4
Height: 1
```

In Example 2, we used only two methods. The two special methods whose names began and ended with double underscores were called implicitly. The method __*init*__ set the values of the instance variables and the __*str*__ method (along with the **print** function) reported the values of the instance variables. These same tasks, along with the computation of the area and perimeter of the rectangle, can be carried out with the other methods of the *Rectangle* class. The two mutator methods can be used to assign values to the instance variables, and the two accessor methods can be used to obtain the values of the instance variables. The *area* and *perimeter* methods calculate the values indicated by their names.

Example 3 Rectangle The following program employs the *Rectangle* class methods not used in Example 2 to set and get various measurements of a rectangle.

```
import rectangle

# Create a rectangle with the default values for width and height
r = rectangle.Rectangle()
# Use the mutators to assign values to the instance variables.
r.setWidth(4)
r.setHeight(5)
print("The rectangle has the following measurements:")
# Use the accessor methods to retrieve the values of the instance variables.
print("Width is", r.getWidth())
print("Height is", r.getHeight())
# Use methods to calculate the area and perimeter of the rectangle.
print("Area is", r.area())
print("Perimeter is", r.perimeter())
```

[Run]

```
The rectangle has the following measurements:
Width is 4
Height is 5
Area is 20
Perimeter is 18
```

Note: Instead of using the mutator methods in the fifth and sixth lines of the program in Example 3, we could have replaced the two lines with the lines

```
r._width = 4
r._height = 5
```

Similarly, the accessor methods in the ninth and tenth lines could have been replaced with

```
print("Width is", r._width)
print("Height is", r._height)
```

However, such replacements are considered poor programming style. We have given instance variables names beginning with a single underscore to indicate to users of the class that these variables should not be directly accessed from outside of the class definition. They should only be accessed from outside of the class definition via methods. One reason for only using methods to access instance variables is that validity-checking code can be inserted into the methods to make programs more robust. Also, one objective of object-oriented programming is to hide the implementation of methods from the users of the class.

■ Other Forms of the Initializer Method

The way we defined the initializer of the *Rectangle* class gives the greatest flexibility to the programmer. However, three other ways the initializer could have been defined are as follows:

```
def __init__(self):
    self._width = 1
    self._height = 1
```

```
def __init__(self, width=1):
    self._width = width
    self._height = 1

def __init__(self, width, height):
    self._width = width
    self._height = height
```

With the third form of the initializer method, constructor statements *must* provide two arguments. Also, like the parameters in any other functions, the parameters having default values must come after those without default values.

■ Number of Methods in a Class Definition

Class definitions can contain as many methods as desired. The following valid class definition contains no methods.

```
class Trivial:
    Pass
```

   Example 4   Card The following program uses a class containing no mutator or accessor methods.

```
import random

def main():
    ## Select a card at random.
    c = Card()  # Create an instance of a Card object and call __init__ method.
    c.selectAtRandom()  # Invokes the selectAtRandom method on the object c.
    print(c)    # Calls the __str__ method that displays the returned value.

class Card:
    def __init__(self, rank="", suit=""):
        self._rank = rank
        self._suit = suit

    def selectAtRandom(self):
        ## Randomly select a rank and a suit.
        ranks = ['2', '3', '4', '5', '6', '7', '8', '9',
                 "10", "jack", "queen", "king", "ace"]
        self._rank = random.choice(ranks)
        self._suit = random.choice(["spades", "hearts", "clubs", "diamonds"])

    def __str__(self):
        return (self._rank + " of " + self._suit)

main()
```

[Run. Outcomes will vary.]

```
queen of hearts
```

Example 5   Semester Grade The following program uses a class containing no accessor methods. The program requests a student's name and two grades, and then calculates the letter grade for the semester. The "LG" at the beginning of the class name signifies that the student is registered to receive a letter grade at the end of the semester. In Section 7.2 we will consider a class named *PFstudent* that calculates the grade for a student who is registered on a Pass/Fail basis. The mutator methods increase flexibility. See first Practice Problem.

```python
def main():
    ## Calculate and display a student's semester letter grade.
    # Obtain student's name, grade on midterm exam, and grade on final.
    name = input("Enter student's name: ")
    midterm = float(input("Enter student's grade on midterm exam: "))
    final = float(input("Enter student's grade on final exam: "))
    # Create an instance of an LGstudent object.
    st = LGstudent(name, midterm, final)
    print("\nNAME\tGRADE")
    # Display student's name and semester letter grade.
    print(st)

class LGstudent:
    def __init__(self, name="", midterm=0, final=0):
        self._name = name
        self._midterm = midterm
        self._final = final

    def setName(self, name):
        self._name = name

    def setMidterm(self, midterm):
        self._midterm = midterm

    def setFinal(self, final):
        self._final = final

    def calcSemGrade(self):
        average = (self._midterm + self._final) / 2
        average = round(average)
        if average >= 90:
            return "A"
        elif average >= 80:
            return "B"
        elif average >= 70:
            return "C"
        elif average >= 60:
            return "D"
        else:
            return "F"

    def __str__(self):
        return self._name + "\t" + self.calcSemGrade()

main()
```

[Run]

```
Enter student's name: Fred
Enter student's grade on midterm exam: 87
Enter student's grade on final exam: 92

NAME    GRADE
Fred    A
```

■ Lists of Objects

The items of a list can have any data type—including a user-defined class. The program in Example 6 uses a list where each item is an *LGstudent* object.

Example 6   Semester Grades In the following program, assume that the class *LGstudent* has been stored in the file **lgStudent.py**.

```python
import lgStudent

def main():
    ## Calculate and display several students' semester letter grades.
    listOfStudents = []  # List to hold an object for each student.
    carryOn = 'Y'
    while carryOn == 'Y':
        st = lgStudent.LGstudent()
        # Obtain student's name, grade on midterm exam, and grade on final.
        name = input("Enter student's name: ")
        midterm = float(input("Enter student's grade on midterm exam: "))
        final = float(input("Enter student's grade on final exam: "))
        # Create an instance of an LGstudent object.
        st = lgStudent.LGstudent(name, midterm, final)
        listOfStudents.append(st)    # Insert object into list.
        carryOn = input("Do you want to continue (Y/N)? ")
        carryOn = carryOn.upper()
    print("\nNAME\tGRADE")
    # Display students, names, and semester letter grades.
    for pupil in listOfStudents:
        print(pupil)

main()
```

[Run]

```
Enter student's name:  Alice
Enter student's grade on midterm exam:  88
Enter student's grade on final exam:  94
Do you want to continue (Y/N)?  Y
Enter student's name:  Bob
Enter student's grade on midterm exam:  82
Enter student's grade on final exam:  85
Do you want to continue (Y/N)?  N

NAME     GRADE
Alice    A
Bob      B
```

■ Comments

1. Consider Example 4. If the *Card* class did not contain the _ _str_ _ method, the statement **print(c)** would display something like **<_ _main_ _.Card object at 0x0000000002FE1320>**.

2. The statement **objectName = ClassName(arg1, arg2, . . .)** is said to **instantiate** the object.

3. Additional code can be added to mutator and accessor methods to prevent the object from storing or returning invalid or corrupted data. For example, an if block could be added to allow only grades between 0 and 100 to be processed.

4. The process of bundling together data and methods that operate on the data, while hiding the implementation of the methods, is called **encapsulation**.

5. The parameter *self* is always the first parameter of every method in a class definition. When a method is applied to an object, the object itself is implicitly passed to the *self* parameter of the method definition.

6. We have given the name *self* to the parameter that refers to the object on which the __init__ method was invoked. Any name, such as *this*, could have been used for the parameter. However, *self* is almost universally used by Python programmers.

Practice Problems 7.1

1. Rewrite the *main* function in the *Student Grade* program of Example 5 under the assumption that that initializer method of *LGstudent* was changed to

```
def __init__(self):
    self._name = ""
    self._midterm = 0
    self._final = 0
```

2. Add a line of code to the *main* function of the *Student Grades* program in Example 6 so that the names will always be displayed in alphabetical order in the output.

EXERCISES 7.1

In Exercises 1 through 4, identify the errors.

1.
```
class Triangle:
    def __init__(base, altitude):
        self._base = base
        self._altitude = altitude
```

2.
```
class Triangle:
    def __init__(self, base, altitude)
        self._base = base
        self._altitude = altitude
```

3.
```
class Triangle()
    def __init__(self, base, altitude)
        self._base = base
        self._altitude = altitude
```

4.
```
class Triangle:
    def __init__(self, base=1, altitude):
        self._base = base
        self._altitude = altitude
```

In Exercises 5 through 12, assume that the code shown below is contained in the file `circle.py` and determine the output produced by the lines of code.

```python
class Circle:
    def __init__(self, radius=1):
        self._radius = radius

    def setRadius(self, radius):
        self._radius = radius

    def getRadius(self):
        return self._radius

    def area(self):
        return 3.14 * self._radius * self._radius

    def circumference(self):
        return 2 * 3.14 * self._radius
```

5.
```python
import circle
c = circle.Circle()
print(c.getRadius())
```

6.
```python
import circle
c = circle.Circle()
print(c.area())
```

7.
```python
import circle
c = circle.Circle(4)
print(c.getRadius())
```

8.
```python
import circle
c = circle.Circle()
c.setRadius(5)
print(c.getRadius())
```

9.
```python
import circle
c = circle.Circle(2)
print(c.area())
```

10.
```python
import circle
c = circle.Circle(3)
print(c.circumference())
```

11.
```python
import circle
c = circle.Circle()
c.setRadius(3)
print(c.circumference())
```

12.
```python
import circle
c = circle.Circle()
c.setRadius(2)
print(c.area())
```

In Exercises 13 and 14, assume that the code shown below is contained in the file `point.py`.

```python
class Point:
    def __init__(self, x, y):
        self._x = x
        self._y = y

    def distanceFromOrigin(self):
        return (self._x ** 2 + self._y ** 2) ** .5
```

13. Point in Plane   Write a program that requests the coordinates of a point as input and then displays the distance of the point from the origin. See Fig. 7.2.

```
Enter x-coordinate of point: 8
Enter y-coordinate of point: -15
Distance from origin: 17.00
```

```
Enter x-coordinate of first point: 2
Enter y-coordinate of first point: 3
Enter x-coordinate of second point: 7
Enter y-coordinate of second point: 15
Distance between points: 13.00
```

FIGURE 7.2   Possible outcome of Exercise 13.   **FIGURE 7.3**   Possible outcomes of Exercise 14.

14. **Distance Between Two Points** Write a program that requests the coordinates of two points as input and then displays the distance between the two points. See Fig. 7.3. *Note:* The distance between the points (x_1, y_1) and (x_2, y_2) is the same as the distance of the point $(x_2 - x_1, y_2 - y_1)$ from the origin.

In Exercises 15 through 18, assume that the code shown below is contained in the file `pairOfDice.py`.

```
import random

class PairOfDice:
    def __init__(self):
        self._redDie = 0
        self._blueDie = 0

    def getRedDie(self):
        return self._redDie

    def getBlueDie(self):
        return self._blueDie

    def roll(self):
        self._redDie = random.choice(range(1, 7))
        self._blueDie = random.choice(range(1, 7))

    def sum(self):
        return self._redDie + self._blueDie
```

15. **Dice** Write a program that displays the outcome from rolling a pair of dice (a red die and a blue die). See Fig. 7.4.

```
Red die: 4
Blue die: 2
Total: 6
```

```
Player 1: 8
Player 2: 6
Player 1 wins.
```

```
Player 1: 7
Player 2: 7
TIE
```

FIGURE 7.4 Possible outcome of Exercise 15.   **FIGURE 7.5** Possible outcomes of Exercise 16.

16. **Dice** Write a program for a game in which each of two players rolls a pair of dice. The person with the highest tally wins. See Fig. 7.5. The program should use two instances of the class *PairOfDice*.

17. **Dice** Write a program that rolls a pair of dice 100,000 times, and displays the percentage of times that the sum of the two faces is 7. (*Note:* The outcome should be around 16.67%.)

18. **Dice** One of the earliest probability problems was posed in 1654 by Chevalier de Méré, a French nobleman with an interest in gambling. A casino was betting even odds that the gambler would get at least one double-six in 24 throws of a pair of dice. Chevalier de Méré asked some prominent mathematicians to determine if the game favored the house or the gambler. Write a program that repeats the 24 rolls 10,000 times and determines the percentage of times that at least one double-six appeared. (*Note:* The outcome should be around .4914. Therefore, the game slightly favors the gambler.)

In Exercises 19 through 24, assume that the code shown below is contained in the file `pCard.py` and determine the output produced by the lines of code.

```
import random

class PlayingCard:
    def __init__(self, rank="queen", suit="hearts"):
```

```
        self._rank = rank
        self._suit = suit

    def setRank(self, rank):
        self._rank = rank

    def setSuit(self, suit):
        self._suit = suit

    def getRank(self):
        return self._rank

    def getSuit(self):
        return self._suit

    def selectAtRandom(self):
        ## Randomly select a rank and a suit.
        ranks = ['2', '3', '4', '5', '6', '7', '8', '9',
                 "10", "jack", "queen", "king", "ace"]
        self._rank = random.choice(ranks)
        self._suit = random.choice(["spades", "hearts", "clubs", "diamonds"])

    def __str__(self):
        return(self._rank + " of " + self._suit)
```

19.
```
import pCard
c = pCard.PlayingCard()
print(c)
```

20.
```
import pCard
c = pCard.PlayingCard()
print(c.getRank())
```

21.
```
import pCard
c = pCard.PlayingCard()
c.setRank("10")
c.setSuit("clubs")
print(c)
```

22.
```
import pCard
c = pCard.PlayingCard()
c.setSuit("diamonds")
print(c.getSuit())
```

23.
```
import pCard
c = pCard.PlayingCard('7')
print(c)
```

24.
```
import pCard
c = pCard.PlayingCard('5', "clubs")
print(c)
```

25. Cards   Write a program that displays a face card (*jack*, *queen*, or *king*) selected at random. Use the class *pCard* defined above.

26. Cards   Write a program that displays a card with suit *diamond* selected at random. Use the class *pCard* defined above.

27. Fraction   Create a class named *Fraction* having instance variables for numerator and denominator, and a method that reduces a fraction to lowest terms by dividing the numerator and denominator by their greatest common divisor. (Exercise 17 of Section 3.3 gives an algorithm for calculating the greatest common divisor of two numbers.) Save the class in the file **fraction.py**. *Note:* This class will be used in Exercises 28 through 30.

28. Reduce a Fraction   Write a program that requests a fraction as input and reduces the fraction to lowest terms. See Fig. 7.6. Use the class *Fraction* created in Exercise 27.

```
Enter numerator of fraction: 12
Enter denominator of fraction: 30
Reduction to lowest terms: 2/5
```

FIGURE 7.6   Possible outcome of Exercise 28.

29. Convert a Decimal to a Fraction Write a program that converts a decimal number to an equivalent fraction. See Fig. 7.7. Use the class *Fraction* created in Exercise 27.

```
Enter a positive decimal number less than 1: .375
Converted to fraction: 3/8
```

FIGURE 7.7 Possible outcome of Exercise 29.

30. Add Fractions Write a program to find and display the roots of a quadratic equation if the equation is of the form $ax^2 + bx + c$ and the roots are real.

Note: $x = \dfrac{-b \pm \sqrt{b^2 - 4ac}}{2a}$, x is real if $b^2 - 4ac > 0$

```
Enter numerical coefficient a: 6
Enter numerical coefficient b: 3
Enter numerical coefficient c: -63
The roots are 3.0 and -3.5
```

FIGURE 7.8 Possible outcome of Exercise 30.

31. Earnings Write a program that requests an hourly worker's name, hours worked, and hourly wage, and then calculates his or her week's pay. The program should contain a class named *Wages* with instance variables for a worker's name, hours worked, and hourly wage, and a method named *payForWeek*. See Fig. 7.9. **Note:** Federal law requires that hourly employees be paid "time-and-a-half" for work in excess of 40 hours in a week.

```
Enter person's name: Alice
Enter number of hours worked: 45
Enter hourly wage: 20
Pay for Alice: $950.00
```

```
Enter grade on quiz 1: 9
Enter grade on quiz 2: 10
Enter grade on quiz 3: 5
Enter grade on quiz 4: 8
Enter grade on quiz 5: 10
Enter grade on quiz 6: 10
Quiz average: 9.4
```

FIGURE 7.9 Possible outcome of Exercise 31.   **FIGURE 7.10** Possible outcome of Exercise 32.

32. Quiz Grades An instructor gives six quizzes during a semester with quiz grades 0 through 10, and drops the lowest grade. Write a program to find the average of the remaining five grades. The program should use a class named *Quizzes* that has an instance variable to hold a list of the six grades, a method named *average*, and a __str__ method. See Fig. 7.10.

In Exercises 33 and 34, use the class *PlayingCard* given before Exercise 19 and saved in the file pCard.py. Each program should create a list of 52 playing cards.

33. Poker Hand Write a program to randomly select and display five cards from a deck of cards. Cards having the same rank should appear adjacent to one another. See Fig. 7.11 on the next page.

```
6 of diamonds
6 of clubs
king of spades
king of clubs
king of hearts
```

FIGURE 7.11 Possible outcome of Exercise 33.

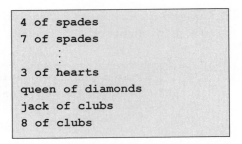

```
4 of spades
7 of spades
    .
    .
3 of hearts
queen of diamonds
jack of clubs
8 of clubs
```

FIGURE 7.12 Partial possible outcome of Exercise 34.

34. Bridge Hand   Write a program to randomly select and display 13 cards from a deck of cards. The cards should be sorted by suits in the order *spades*, *hearts*, *diamonds*, and *clubs*. See Fig. 7.12.

35. Proceed to Checkout   Write a program that checks out the items in the user's cart on a shopping website. The program should use a class named *Purchase* to hold the information about a single item purchased (that is, description, price, and quantity) and a class named *Cart* to hold a list whose items are objects of type *Purchase*. See Fig. 7.13.

```
Enter description of article: shirt
Enter price of article: 35
Enter quantity of article: 3
Do you want to enter more articles (Y/N)? Y
Enter description of article: tie
Enter price of article: 15
Enter quantity of article: 2
Do you want to enter more articles (Y/N)? N

ARTICLE        PRICE     QUANTITY
shirt          $35.00       3
tie            $15.00       2

TOTAL COST: $135.00
```

FIGURE 7.13 Possible outcome of Exercise 35.

36. Toll Booth Register   Write a program to count the number of vehicles and the amount of money collected at a toll booth. The program should use a class named *Register* with instance variables for the number of vehicles processed and the total amount of money collected. One dollar should be collected for each car and two dollars for each truck. See Fig. 7.14.

```
Enter type of vehicle (car/truck): car
Number of vehicles: 1
Money Collected: $1.00
Do you want to enter more vehicles (Y/N)? Y
Enter type of vehicle (car/truck): truck
Number of vehicles: 2
Money Collected: $3.00
Do you want to enter more vehicles (Y/N)? N
Have a good day.
```

FIGURE 7.14 Possible outcome of Exercise 36.

Solutions to Practice Problems 7.1

```
1. def main():
       st = LGstudent()
       # Obtain student's name, grade on midterm exam, and grade on final.
       name = input("Enter student's name: ")
       st.setName(name)
       midterm = float(input("Enter student's grade on midterm exam: "))
       st.setMidterm(midterm)
       final = float(input("Enter student's grade on final exam: "))
       st.setFinal(final)
       # Display student's name and semester letter grade.
       print("\nNAME\tGRADE")
       print(st)
```

The version of the __init__ method in this practice problem is less flexible than the version in Example 5, since it requires the use of mutators, whereas in Example 5 the programmer can assign values to the instance variables with or without mutators.

2. Precede the for statement with the following statement:

```
listOfStudents.sort(key=lambda x: x.getName())
```

7.2   Inheritance

VideoNote
Inheritance

Inheritance is a feature of object-oriented programming that allows us to define a new class (called the **subclass**, **child class**, or **derived class**) that is a modified version of an existing class (called the **superclass**, **parent class**, or **base class**). The subclass inherits properties and methods of the superclass in addition to adding some of its own properties and methods, and overriding some of the superclass' methods.

■ A Semester Grade Class

Consider the class *LGstudent* presented in Example 5 of Section 7.1. *LGstudent* could have been defined as a subclass of a superclass named *Student*.

 Example 1   Create Two Subclasses   In the following class definitions, the statements

```
class LGstudent(Student):
```

and

```
class PFstudent(Student):
```

specify that *LGstudent* and *PFstudent* are subclasses of the superclass *Student* and inherit all the properties and methods of the class *Student*. Students in the class *PFstudent* receive either *Pass* or *Fail* as their semester grades.

```
class Student:
    def __init__(self, name="", midterm=0, final=0):
        self._name = name
        self._midterm = midterm
        self._final = final

    def setName(self, name):
        self._name = name
```

```
        def setMidterm(self, midterm):
            self._midterm = midterm

        def setFinal(self, final):
            self._final = final

        def getName(self):
            return self._name

        def __str__(self):
            return self._name + "\t" + self.calcSemGrade()

class LGstudent(Student):

        def calcSemGrade(self):
            average = round((self._midterm + self._final) / 2)
        if average >= 90:
            return 'A'
        elif average >= 80:
            return 'B'
        elif average >= 70:
            return 'C'
        elif average >= 60:
            return 'D'
        else:
            return 'F'

class PFstudent(Student):

        def calcSemGrade(self):
            average = round((self._midterm + self._final) / 2)
        if average >= 60:
            return "Pass"
        else:
            return "Fail"
```

✔ **Example 2**   **Semester Grades**   The following function creates a list of both types of students and uses the list to display the names of the students and their semester grades, where the names are displayed in alphabetical order. Assume that the class definitions in Example 1 are contained in the file **student.py**.

```
import student

def main():
    listOfStudents = obtainListOfStudents()  # students and grades
    displayResults(listOfStudents)

def obtainListOfStudents():
    listOfStudents = []
    carryOn = 'Y'
    while carryOn == 'Y':
        name = input("Enter student's name: ")
        midterm = float(input("Enter student's grade on midterm exam: "))
        final = float(input("Enter student's grade on final exam: "))
        category = input("Enter category (LG or PF): ")
        if category.upper() == "LG":
            st = student.LGstudent(name, midterm, final)
```

```
        else:
            st = student.PFstudent(name, midterm, final)
        listOfStudents.append(st)
        carryOn = input("Do you want to continue (Y/N)? ")
        carryOn = carryOn.upper()
    return listOfStudents

def displayResults(listOfStudents):
    print("\nNAME\tGRADE")
    listOfStudents.sort(key=lambda x: x.getName())  # Sort students by name.
    for pupil in listOfStudents:
        print(pupil)

main()
```

[Run]

```
Enter student's name:  Bob
Enter student's grade on midterm exam:  79
Enter student's grade on final exam:  85
Enter category (LG or PF):  LG
Do you want to continue (Y/N)?  Y
Enter student's name:  Alice
Enter student's grade on midterm exam:  92
Enter student's grade on final exam:  96
Enter category (LG or PF):  PF
Do you want to continue (Y/N)?  Y
Enter student's name:  Carol
Enter student's grade on midterm exam:  75
Enter student's grade on final exam:  76
Enter category (LG or PF):  LG
Do you want to continue (Y/N)?  N

NAME      GRADE
Alice     Pass
Bob       B
Carol     C
```

■ The "is-a" Relationship

Child classes are specializations of their parent's class. They normally have all the characteristics of their parents, but more functionality. Such child classes have a so-called "is-a" relationship with their parent class. For instance, consider Example 2. Each letter-grade student *is a* student. Similarly, each pass-fail student *is a* student.

Some parent–child pairs appearing in the exercises are shown in Table 7.1. In each pair, the child is a specialized version of the parent and each child satisfies the "is-a" relationship with the parent.

TABLE 7.1 **Some parent–child pairs.**

Parent	Children
employee	hourly employee, salaried employee
mortgage	mortgage with points, interest-only mortgage
regular polygon	equilateral triangle, square

■ The *isinstance* Function

A statement of the form

```
isinstance(object, className)
```

returns True if *object* is an instance of the named class or any of its subclasses, and otherwise returns False. The *isinstance* function can be applied to both built-in and user-defined classes. Table 7.2 shows the values of some expressions involving the *isinstance* function.

TABLE 7.2   **Some expressions involving the *isinstance* function.**

Expression	Value	Expression	Value
`isinstance("Hello", str)`	True	`isinstance((), tuple)`	True
`isinstance(3.4, int)`	False	`isinstance({'b':"be"}, dict)`	True
`isinstance(3.4, float)`	True	`isinstance({}, dict)`	True
`isinstance([1, 2, 3], list)`	True	`isinstance({1, 2, 3}, set)`	True
`isinstance([], list)`	True	`isinstance({}, set)`	False
`isinstance((1, 2, 3), tuple)`	True	`isinstance(set(), set)`	True

✓ **Example 3**   Semester Grades The following function displays semester grades as in Example 2. However, the addition of a few lines of code to the *displayResults* function results in the program counting the number of letter-grade and the number of pass-fail students. As each student is displayed, the isinstance function is used to count the number of letter-grade students. The expanded *displayResults* function is as follows:

```python
def displayResults(listOfStudents):
    print("\nNAME\tGRADE")
    numberOfLGstudents = 0    # Counter for number of letter-grade students.
    listOfStudents.sort(key=lambda x: x.getName())
    for pupil in listOfStudents:
        print(pupil)
        # Keep track of number of letter-grade students.
        if isinstance(pupil, student.LGstudent):
            numberOfLGstudents += 1
    # Display number of students in each category.
    print("Number of letter-grade students:", numberOfLGstudents)
    print("Number of pass-fail students:",
          len(listOfStudents) - numberOfLGstudents)
```

The following output results when the program from Example 2 is run with the revised *displayResults* function.

```
NAME    GRADE
Alice   Pass
Bob     B
Carol   C
Number of letter-grade students: 2
Number of pass-fail students: 1
```

■ Adding New Instance Variables to a Subclass

So far, the child classes in our examples have only added functions to their parent classes. However, they can also add properties, that is, instance variables. In that situation, the child class must contain an initializer method which draws in the parent's properties and then adds its own new properties. The parameter list in the header of the child's initializer method should begin with self, list the parent's parameters, and add on the new child's parameters. The first line of the block should have the form

```
super().__init__(parentParameter1, . . . , parentParameterN)
```

This line should be followed by standard declaration statements for the new parameters of the child.

Example 4   PFstudent The following class definition adds a new parameter to the class *PFstudent*. We will assume that pass–fail students can be registered as either *full-time* or *part-time*. The new Boolean-valued parameter (named *_fullTime*) has the value **True** for full-time students and the value **False** for part-time students.

```python
class PFstudent(Student):
    def __init__(self, name="", midterm=0, final=0, fullTime=True):
        super().__init__(name, midterm, final)  # Import base's parameters.
        self._fullTime = fullTime

    def setFullTime(self, fullTime):
        self._fullTime = fullTime

    def getFullTime(self):
        return self._fullTime

    def calcSemGrade(self):
        average = round((self._midterm + self._final) / 2)
        if average >= 60:
            return "Pass"
        else:
            return "Fail"

    def __str__(self):
        if self._fullTime:
            status = "Full-time student"
        else:
            status = "Part-time student"
        return (self._name + "\t" + self.calcSemGrade() +
                "\t" + status)
```

Example 5   Semester Grade and Status Assume that the file **studentWithStatus.py** is a modified version of the file **student.py**, where the definition of the class *PFstudent* has been replaced with the altered version shown in Example 4.

```python
import studentWithStatus

def main():
    ## Calculate and display a student's semester letter grade and status.
    # Obtain student's name, grade on midterm exam, and grade on final.
```

```
      name = input("Enter student's name: ")
      midterm = float(input("Enter student's grade on midterm exam: "))
      final = float(input("Enter student's grade on final exam: "))
      category = input("Enter category (LG or PF): ")
      if category.upper() == "LG":
          st = studentWithStatus.LGstudent(name, midterm, final)
      else:
          question = input("Is" + name + "a full time student (Y/N)? ")
          if question.upper() == 'Y':
              fullTime = True
          else:
              fullTime = False
          st = studentWithStatus.PFstudent(name, midterm, final, fullTime)
      # Display student's name, semester letter grade, and status.
      semesterGrade = st.calcSemGrade()
      print("\nNAME\tGRADE\tSTATUS")
      print(st)

main()
```

[Run]

```
Enter student's name: Alice
Enter student's grade on midterm exam: 92
Enter student's grade on final exam: 96
Enter category (LG or PF): PF
Is Alice a full-time student (Y/N)? N

NAME    GRADE    STATUS
Alice   Pass     Part-time student
```

■ Overriding a Method

A subclass can change the behavior of an inherited method. If a method defined in the subclass has the same name as a method in its superclass, the child's method will override the parent's method.

Example 6 **Semester Grade** The following program is an alternate version of Example 2, where *PFstudent* is defined as a subclass of *LGstudent*. Although the two classes do not have an "is-a" relationship, this new class definition is shorter and easier to read than the original definition.

```
def main():
    listOfStudents = obtainListOfStudents()   # students and grades
    displayResults(listOfStudents)

def obtainListOfStudents():
    listOfStudents = []
    carryOn = 'Y'
    while carryOn == 'Y':
        name = input("Enter student's name: ")
        midterm = float(input("Enter student's grade on midterm exam: "))
        final = float(input("Enter student's grade on final exam: "))
```

```
            category = input("Enter category (LG or PF): ")
            if category.upper() == "LG":
                st = LGstudent(name, midterm, final)
            else:
                st = PFstudent(name, midterm, final)
            listOfStudents.append(st)
            carryOn = input("Do you want to continue (Y/N)? ")
            carryOn = carryOn.upper()
        return listOfStudents

    def displayResults(listOfStudents):
        print("\nNAME\tGRADE")
        listOfStudents.sort(key=lambda x: x.getName())
        for pupil in listOfStudents:
            print(pupil)

class LGstudent:
    def __init__(self, name="", midterm=0, final=0):
        self._name = name
        self._midterm = midterm
        self._final = final

    def setName(self, name):
        self._name = name

    def setMidterm(self, midterm):
        self._midterm = midterm

    def setFinal(self, final):
        self._final = final

    def getName(self):
        return self._name

    def calcSemGrade(self):
        average = round((self._midterm + self._final) / 2)
        if average >= 90:
            return "A"
        elif average >= 80:
            return "B"
        elif average >= 70:
            return "C"
        elif average >= 60:
            return "D"
        else:
            return "F"

    def __str__(self):
        return self._name + "\t" + self.calcSemGrade()

class PFstudent(LGstudent):
    def calcSemGrade(self):
        average = round((self._midterm + self._final) / 2)
        if average >= 60:
            return "Pass"
        else:
            return "Fail"

main()
```

■ Polymorphism

In Example 1, the child classes *LGstudent* and *PFstudent* have *calcSemGrade* methods with the same header but with different definitions. The feature of Python (and every object-oriented programming language) that allows two classes to use the same method name (but with different implementations) is called **polymorphism**. The program in Example 2 adjusts the implementation of the *calcSemGrade* method depending on the type of object that calls it. The word *polymorphism* is derived from a Greek word meaning "many forms."

Practice Problems 7.2

1. What is the output of the following program?

```python
def main():
    creature = Vertebrate()
    print(creature.msg())
    print(isinstance(creature, Animal))

class Animal:
    def msg(self):
    return("Can Move.")

class Vertebrate:
    def msg(self):
    return("Has a backbone.")

main()
```

2. If the line

```python
class Vertebrate:
```

in Problem 1 is changed to

```python
class Vertebrate(Animal):
```

how will the output of the program be affected?

EXERCISES 7.2

In Exercises 1 through 4, determine the output of the code where the code uses the following classes:

```python
class RegularPolygon:
    def __init__(self, side=1):
        self._side = side

class Square(RegularPolygon):
    def area(self, side):
        return side * side

class EquilateralTriangle(RegularPolygon):
    def area(self, side):
        return side * side * 0.433
```

1.
```
sq = Square()
print(sq.area(2))
```

2.
```
et = EquilateralTriangle()
print(et.area(1))
```

3.
```
sq = Square()
et = EquilateralTriangle()
print(et.area(sq.area(2)))
```

4.
```
sq = Square()
et = EquilateralTriangle()
print(sq.area(et.area(2)))
```

5. What is the output of the following program?

```
def main():
    r = Rectangle(2, 3)
    print("The {0} has area {1:,.2f}.".format(r.name(), r.area()))

class Shape:
    def __init__(self, width=1, height=1):
        self._width = width
        self._height = height

    def setWidth(self, width):
        self._width =  width

    def setHeight(self, height):
        self._height =  height

class Rectangle(Shape):
    def name(self):
        return "rectangle"

    def area(self):
        return (self._width * self._height)

main()
```

6. What is the output of the program in Exercise 5 if the second line of code is replaced with the following two lines of code?

```
r = Rectangle(5)
r.setHeight(6)
```

The programs in Exercises 7 and 8 illustrate the concept of polymorphism. Determine the output of these programs.

7.
```
def main():

class Shape:
    def __init__(self, l, h):
        self._length = l
        self._height = h

class Rectangle(Shape):
    def area(self):
        return self._length * self._height
```

```
class Triangle(Shape):
    def area(self):
        return (self._length * self._height) / 2

    calculateArea = Rectangle(5,10)

    print("Area of Rectangle is: " + str(calculateArea.area()))

    calculateArea = Triangle(5,10)

    print("Area of Triangle is: " + str(calculateArea.area()))

main()
```

8.
```
def main():

    class TempratureConversion:
        def __init__(self, temp = 1 ):
            self._temp = temp

    class CelsiusToFahrenheit(TempratureConversion):
        def conversion(self):
            return (self._temp * 9) / 5 + 32

    class CelsiusToKelvin(TempratureConversion):
        def conversion(self):
            return self._temp + 273.15

    tempInCelsius = float(input("Enter the temprature in Celsius: "));

    convert = CelsiusToKelvin(tempInCelsius)

    print(str(convert.conversion()) + " Kelvin")

    convert = CelsiusToFahrenheit(tempInCelsius)

    print(str(convert.conversion()) + " Fahrenheit")

main()
```

9. **Semester Grades**   Modify the program in Example 2 so that only the names of the letter-grade students with the grade A are displayed.

10. **Semester Grades**   Modify the program in Example 2 so that only the names of the pass–fail students who pass are displayed.

11. **Rock, Paper, Scissors**   Write a program to play a three-game match of "rock, paper, scissors" between a person and a computer. See Fig. 7.15. The program should use a class named *Contestant* having two subclasses named *Human* and *Computer*. After the person makes his or her choice, the computer should make its choice at random. The *Contestant* class should have instance variables for *name* and *score*. (**Note:** *Rock* beats *scissors, scissors* beats *paper*, and *paper* beats *rock*.)

```
Enter name of human: Garry
Enter name of computer: Big Blue

Garry, enter your choice: rock
Big Blue chooses paper
Garry: 0  Big Blue: 1

Garry, enter your choice: scissors
Big Blue chooses paper
Garry: 1  Big Blue: 1

Garry, enter your choice: rock
Big Blue chooses scissors
Garry: 2  Big Blue: 1

GARRY WINS
```

FIGURE 7.15   Possible outcome of Exercise 11.

12. **Semester Grades**   Redo Example 2 so that each subclass has its own __str__ method, and therefore the program will illustrate polymorphism with the __str__ methods. Assume that all letter-grade students are full-time students, but that pass–fail students might be either full-time or part-time. The output of the program should give each student's name, grade, and status. See Fig. 7.16.

```
Enter student's name: Bob
Enter student's grade on midterm exam: 79
Enter student's grade on final exam: 85
Enter category (LG or PF): LG
Do you want to continue (Y/N)? Y
Enter student's name: Alice
Enter student's grade on midterm exam: 92
Enter student's grade on final exam: 96
Enter category (LG or PF): PF
Are you a full-time student (Y/N)? N
Do you want to continue (Y/N)? N

NAME     GRADE     STATUS
Alice    Pass      Part-time student
Bob      B         Full-time student
```

FIGURE 7.16   Possible outcome of Exercise 12.

Exercises 13 through 16 involve mortgages. A mortgage is a long-term loan used to purchase a house. The house is used as collateral to guarantee the loan. The amount borrowed, called the *principal*, is paid off in monthly payments over a stated number of years called the *term* (usually 25 or 30 years). The amount of the monthly payment depends on the principal, the interest rate, and the term of the mortgage.

13. **Mortgage**   If A dollars are borrowed at $r\%$ interest compounded monthly to purchase a house with monthly payments for n years, then the monthly payment is given by the formula

$$\text{monthly payment} = \frac{i}{1 - (1 + i)^{-12n}} \cdot A,$$

where $i = \dfrac{r}{1200}$.

Create a class named *Mortgage* with instance variables for *principal*, *interest rate*, and *term*, and a method named *calculateMonthlyPayment*.

14. **Mortgage** Write a program that uses the class *Mortgage* from Exercise 13 to calculate the monthly payment where the principal, interest rate, and term are input by the user. See Fig. 7.17.

```
Enter principal of mortgage: 350000
Enter percent interest rate: 5.25
Enter duration of mortgage in years: 30
Monthly payment: $1,932.71
```

FIGURE 7.17 Possible outcome of Exercise 14.

15. **Interest-Only Mortgage** With an **interest-only mortgage**, the monthly payment for a certain number of years (usually, five or ten years) consists only of interest payments. At the end of the interest-only period, the amount owed is the original principal and the monthly payment is determined by the number of years remaining. We will assume that the interest rate for the second period is the same as the interest rate for the first period. With some interest-only mortgages, the interest rate is reset to conform to prevailing interest rates at that time.

Create a class named *InterestOnlyMortgage* that is a subclass of the class *Mortgage* from Exercise 13. The class should inherit the instance variables from its parent class and have an additional instance variable named *numberOfInterestOnlyYears*, a method to calculate the monthly payment for the interest-only years, a mutator method named *setTerm*, and an accessor method named *getTerm*. Write a program that uses the class *InterestOnlyMortgage* to calculate the monthly payment where the principal, interest rate, term, and number of interest-only years are input by the user. The program should calculate the monthly payments for the early years and for the later years. See Fig. 7.18.

```
Enter principal of mortgage: 350000
Enter percent interest rate: 5.25
Enter duration of mortgage in years: 30
Enter number of interest-only years: 10
Monthly payment for first 10 years: $1,531.25
Monthly payment for last 20 years: $2,358.45
```

FIGURE 7.18 Possible outcome of Exercise 15.

16. **Mortgage with Points** Some loans carry **discount points**. Each discount point requires the borrower to pay up-front an additional amount of money equal to 1% of the stated loan amount. For instance, for a $200,000 mortgage with 3 discount points, the purchaser must pay $6,000 immediately. Even though this payment has the effect of reducing the loan to $194,000, the monthly payment is calculated using a principal

of \$200,000. The up-front interest payment is tax deductible and the interest rate on a mortgage with points is slightly lower than the interest rate on a standard mortgage without points. Mortgages with discount points usually are advantageous to people who intend to keep their house for more than seven years.

Create a class named *MortgageWithPoints* that is a subclass of the class *Mortgage* from Exercise 13. The class should inherit the instance variables from its parent class, have an additional instance variable named *numberOfPoints*, and have an additional method to calculate the cost of the points. Write a program that uses the class *MortgageWithPoints* to calculate the monthly payment where the principal, interest rate, term, and number of discount points are input by the user. See Fig. 7.19.

```
Enter principal of mortgage: 350000
Enter percent interest rate: 5
Enter duration of mortgage in years: 30
Enter number of discount points: 2
Cost of discount points: $7,000.00
Monthly payment: $1,878.88
```

FIGURE 7.19   Possible outcome of Exercise 16.

Solutions to Practice Problems 7.2

1. `Has a backbone.`
   `False`

2. Since every instance of a subclass is also an instance of its superclass, the output will change to

   `Has a backbone.`
   `True`

CHAPTER 7 KEY TERMS AND CONCEPTS

EXAMPLES

7.1 Classes and Objects

Python has many built-in classes such as int, float, str, list, tuple, bool, dict, and set.

```
print(type(2), type({1:"one"}))
[Run]
<class 'int'> <class 'dict'>

class Rectangle:
    def __init__(self, width=1,
                     height=1):
        self._width = width
        self._height = height
```

An **object** is an entity that stores data (in instance variables), and has **methods** that manipulate the data. A **class** is a template from which objects are created. The header of a class definition has the form `class ClassName:`. The first method is usually an **initializer** named `__init__` that is called automatically when an object is created. The first parameter of the initializer is named **self**. The parameter *self* is a variable that refers to the object itself.

CHAPTER 7 KEY TERMS AND CONCEPTS	EXAMPLES
An object is created with a statement of the form `objectName = ClassName(arg1, arg2, ...)`	`r = Rectangle(4, 5)`

Data are stored in instance variables and accessed by methods called **mutators** (change values of instance variables) and **accessors** (retrieve values of instance variables).	`def setWidth(self, width):`
	`    self._width = width`
	`def getWidth(self):`
	`    return self._width`

The `__str__` method returns a customized string representation of an object.	`def __str__(self):`
	`    return ("Width: " +`
	`            str(self._width))`

7.2 Inheritance

Inheritance allows a new class (called the **subclass**, **child class**, or **derived class**) to be created from an existing class (called the **superclass**, **parent class**, or **base class**) and to inherit its instance variables and methods.

parent

`class LGstudent(Student)`

child

Usually a child object has an "is-a" relationship with its parent.

Every *letter-grade student* is a *student*.

The **isinstance** function is used to identify the type of an object.

`st = LGstudent()`
`print(isinstance(st, LGstudent))`
`[Run]`
`True`

When a child class creates a new instance variable, it must include a **super** function in its initializer block to pull in its parent's instance variables.

`super().__init__(name, midterm,`
`                 final)`

A method defined in a child class with the same name as a method in its parent class **overrides** the parent's method.

Polymorphism is the ability to use the same syntax for objects of different types.

CHAPTER 7   PROGRAMMING PROJECTS

1. United Nations   The file **UN.txt** gives data about the 193 members of the United Nations. Each line of the file contains four pieces of data about a country—*name*, *continent*, *population* (in millions), and *land area* (in square miles). Some lines of the file are

```
Canada,North America,34.8,3855000
France,Europe,66.3,211209
New Zealand,Australia/Oceania,4.4,103738
Nigeria,Africa,177.2,356669
```

```
Pakistan,Asia,196.2,310403
Peru,South America,30.1,496226
```

(a) Create a class named *Nation* with four instance variables to hold the data for a country and a method named *popDensity* that calculates the population density of the country. Write a program that uses the class to create a dictionary of 193 items, where each item of the dictionary has the form

name of a country: Nation object for that country

Use the file **UN.txt** to create the dictionary, and save the dictionary in a pickled binary file named **nationsDict.dat**. Also, save the class *Nation* in a file named **nation.py**.

(b) Write a program that requests the name of a U.N. member country as input, and then displays information about the country as shown in Fig. 7.20. Use the pickled binary file **nationsDict.dat** and the file **nation.py** created in part (a).

```
Enter a country: Canada
Continent: North America
Population: 34,800,000
Area: 3,855,000.00 square miles
```

FIGURE 7.20   Possible outcome of Prog.
Project 1(b).

```
Enter a continent: South America
    Ecuador
    Colombia
    Venezuela
    Brazil
    Peru
```

FIGURE 7.21   Outcome of Prog.
Project 1(c).

(c) Write a program that requests the name of a continent as input, and then displays the names (in descending order) of the five most densely populated U.N. member countries in that continent. See Fig. 7.21. Use the pickled binary file **nationsDict.dat** and the file **nation.py** created in part (a).

2. Savings Account   Write a program to maintain a savings account. The program should use a class named *SavingsAccount* with instance variables for the customer's name and the account balance, and two methods named *makeDeposit* and *makeWithdrawal*. The *makeWithdrawal* method should deny withdrawals that exceed the balance in the account. See Fig. 7.22.

```
Enter person's name: Fred
D = Deposit, W = Withdrawal, Q = Quit
Enter D, W, or Q: D
Enter amount to deposit: 1000
Balance: $1,000.00
Enter D, W, or Q: W
Enter amount to withdraw: 4000
Insufficient funds, transaction denied.
Balance: $1,000.00
Enter D, W, or Q: W
Enter amount to withdraw: 400
Balance: $600.00
Enter D, W, or Q: Q
End of transactions. Have a good day Fred.
```

FIGURE 7.22   Possible outcome of Programming Project 2.

3. Cab Fare Management   Write a program for a cab owner to display the complete list of rides for his cabs. He has both sedans and hatchbacks. The program should contain a class named Cab having two subclasses named Sedan and Hatchback. The Cab class should have instance variables for type of cab and number of kilometers driven. Each subclass should have a caculateFare method. The fare for sedans should be $2 per kilometer and the fare for hatchbacks should be $1.5 per kilometer.

After the data for all cabs has been entered, the program should display the total kilometers driven for both types of cabs. The program should also display the total kilometers driven for all cabs, and the total fare earned from all cabs. See Fig 7.23. The program should use a list of objects.

```
Enter cab type(Hatchback/Sedan): hatchback
Enter the number of kilometers travelled: 10
Do you want to continue (Y/N)? Y
Enter cab type(Hatchback/Sedan): Sedan
Enter the number of kilometers travelled: 12
Do you want to continue (Y/N)? N

-----Kilometers driven for each cab-----
Hatchback: 10 kilometers
Sedan: 12 kilometers
------------------------

Total number of kilometers driven by all Cabs: 22.0
Total fare earned from all cabs (in dollars): 39.0
```

FIGURE 7.23   Possible outcome of Programming Project 3.

8

Graphical User Interface

8.1　Widgets

Widgets are the components of a graphical user interface. In this section we discuss the capabilities of five widgets. In the next two sections we show how to position widgets in a window and how to write programs that manipulate the widgets. Widgets are objects, and their classes are defined in a module named **tkinter** (pronounced t-k-inter; stands for TK interface). The screen captures appearing in this chapter were generated with a PC computer running Windows. They will appear slightly different when the programs are executed with other operating systems.

VideoNote

Introduction to GUI

■ What Is a Graphical User Interface?

The programs in previous chapters are said to have a **text-based user interface (TUI)**. A **graphical user interface**, or GUI (pronounced "gooie"), presents the user with a window containing visual objects such as boxes where the user can type in data, and buttons that initiate actions. These visual objects (called **widgets**) respond to events such as mouse clicks. Since events are so central to GUI programs, GUI programs are said to be **event driven**.

Figure 8.1 shows the output of Python programs that calculate the monthly payment for a mortgage. Each program requests three pieces of data and then displays the amount of the monthly payment.

```
Enter principal: 300000
Enter interest rate (as percent): 4.9
Enter number of years: 30
Monthly payment: $1,592.18
```

(a) Output of TUI program.　　　　(b) Output of GUI program.

FIGURE 8.1　Mortgage Program.

In Fig. 8.1(b) the three white boxes above the button may be filled in any order. When the user clicks on a white box with the mouse, the cursor moves to that box. The user can either type in new information or edit the existing information. When satisfied that all the information is as intended, the user clicks on the *Calculate Monthly Payment* button to display the amount of the monthly payment in the box below the button. The user can experiment with different input values. For instance, the user can replace the number 30 with the number 25 and then click on the button to see how much the monthly payment would be for a 25-year mortgage. There is no need for the user to reenter the other two pieces of input.

The boxes appearing in the GUI window are called Entry widgets, the text displayed to the left of the boxes is contained in Label widgets, and the button is called a Button widget. Each widget is an object with properties and each widget can respond to events such as mouse movements, key presses, and mouse clicks. For example, each Entry widget has a **width** property and each Label widget has a **text** property. In Fig. 8.1(b), the button responds to a **mouse click** event. When the user clicks on the button, the event calls a function that calculates the monthly payment and displays it in the tinted Entry widget in the bottom right corner of the window. The employment of widgets and events allows the user to decide the order in which things happen by triggering events.

In this section we will discuss buttons, labels, entry boxes, list boxes, and scroll bars one at a time, and will write short programs that illustrate some of their properties and events. Each program will begin with the two statements

```
from tkinter import *
window = Tk()
```

and end with the statement

```
window.mainloop()
```

The first statement imports the *tkinter* module and the second statement creates an instance of the Tk class and gives it the name *window*. Most GUI programs contain events. The **mainloop** function acts like an infinite loop that keeps looking for events until you close the window by clicking on its Close button (, or) at the top of the window.

Depending on the operating system and the way the program is invoked, the **mainloop** function may or may not be needed. However, in order to cover all bases, we will always include the function.

Each window has a **title** property that places text in its title bar. For instance, in Fig. 8.1(b) the word "Mortgage" is placed in the title bar with the statement

```
window.title("Mortgage")
```

■ The Button Widget

The code in Fig. 8.2(a) produces the output in Fig. 8.2(b), where the color of the button is light blue.

```
from tkinter import *

window = Tk()
window.title("Button")
btnCalculate = Button(window,
        text="Calculate", bg="light blue")
btnCalculate.grid(padx=75, pady=15)
window.mainloop()
```

(a) Code.

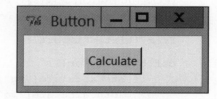

(b) Output.

FIGURE 8.2 Button Demo.

The fourth statement in Fig. 8.2(a) creates an instance of a Button widget and the fifth statement displays the widget in the window. [The **grid** method controls the placement of widgets on the window, and plays such an essential role in GUI programming that the entire second section of this chapter is devoted to it. For now, we just need to know that the **grid** method makes the button visible and puts blank space around it. The setting for **padx** specifies how much blank space (in pixels) should be placed to the left and right of the widget and **pady** does the same for blank space above and below the widget.] The left side of the fourth statement is the name chosen for the widget. We like to begin each name with three letters that indicate the type of widget being instantiated. The right side of the statement (called the **constructor**) contains the type of widget followed by several arguments inside a pair of parentheses. The first argument is always the name of the widget's container. (In this book, the container will always be named *window*.) The terms **text** and **bg** In the arguments **text="Calculate"** and **bg="light blue"** are called **attributes**. The **text** attribute specifies the caption to be displayed on the button. The optional **bg** (background) attribute specifies the color of the button. If this attribute is omitted, the button will have the color gray. By default the button will be just wide enough to accommodate its caption. However, an argument of the form **width=n** can be inserted to set the width of the button to *n* characters. By default, the caption is centered in its button. There are several other arguments that can be inserted into the constructor to make additional alterations to the appearance of the button and its caption.

Run the program in Fig. 8.2(a) and then left-click on the button with the mouse. The button appears to be pushed in and then to pop out. The left-click triggered an event that pushed the button. However, the event can do much more than just push the button; it can call a function. *Note:* To end the program, click on the Close button at the top of the window.

The program in Example 1 extends the program in Fig. 8.2(a) by inserting a function named *changeColor* and adding an additional argument (**command=changeColor**) into the constructor. The argument **command=changeColor** causes the left-click event to call the *changeColor* function. (This function is referred to as the **callback function** associated with the event, or the **event handler**, and the argument is said to **bind** the function to the button.) The value of the expression **btnCalculate["fg"]** is the color of the caption. In general, the value of an expression of the form

widgetName["attribute"]

gives the value assigned to the attribute. For instance, the value of **btnCalculate["text"]** is the string "Calculate".

✓ **Example 1** Toggle Colors Buttons have two colors—a foreground color (the color of the caption) and a background color (the color of the button itself). By default, the foreground color is black and the background color is gray. However, these colors can be altered by **fg** and **bg** arguments. The following program extends the program in Fig. 8.2(a) by using an event to toggle the foreground color of the Button widget. Run the program and then press the button several times. Each press triggers an event that calls the *changeColor* function that toggles the color of the button's caption between blue and red.

```
from tkinter import *

def changeColor():
    if btnCalculate["fg"] == "blue":   # if caption is blue
        btnCalculate["fg"] = "red"     # change color to red
    else:
        btnCalculate["fg"] = "blue"    # change color to blue

window = Tk()
window.title("Button")
btnCalculate = Button(window, text="Calculate",
                    fg="blue", command=changeColor)
btnCalculate.grid(padx=100, pady=15)
window.mainloop()
```

■ The Label Widget

The Label widget is one of the simplest widgets. In Fig. 8.1(b), Label widgets were placed to the left of each Entry widget to identify the contents of the boxes. In this book, that is the only use we will make of labels. The code in Fig. 8.3(a) produces the output in Fig. 8.3(b). *Note:* By default, all text placed into widgets has the color black. However, the process that converted the multi-colored screen captures to the figures for this book, changed all the black text to blue. Therefore, unless an example or exercise specifically calls for blue text, treat all text in the figures as if it were colored black. The Student Solution Manual for the book, which can be downloaded from the Pearson website, contains all the screen captures in their true colors.

```
from tkinter import *

window = Tk()
window.title("Label")
lblPrincipal = Label(window, text="Principal:")
lblPrincipal.grid(padx=100, pady=15)
window.mainloop()
```

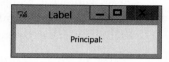

(a) **Code.**   (b) **Output.**

FIGURE 8.3   Label Demo.

By default the Label widget has the same background color as the window itself. Actually, the label is just wide enough to accommodate its caption. If we insert the argument **bg="light blue"** into the constructor, the actual width of the label will be revealed. See Fig. 8.4. Although Labels have a width attribute, it is never needed in the programs we will write.

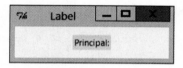

FIGURE 8.4   Label with light blue background color.

■ The Entry Widget

The Entry widget is used both to obtain input from the user and to display output. The code in Fig. 8.5(a) produces the output in Fig. 8.5(b).

```
from tkinter import *

window = Tk()
window.title("Entry Widget")
entName = Entry(window, width=20)
entName.grid(padx=100, pady=15)
window.mainloop()
```

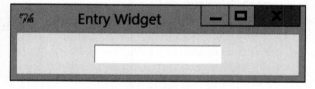

(a) **Code.**   (b) **Output.**

FIGURE 8.5   Entry Demo.

Run the program in Fig. 8.5(a) and then left-click on the Entry widget to place the cursor inside the widget. You can now type any characters into the Entry box. Since the width was set to 20 characters in the constructor, if you type more than 20 characters your text will scroll to the left. You can use many features that are common to word processors. For instance, you can double-click on a word to select it and then use the Delete key to remove it, or use Ctrl+C to place the word in the clipboard. You can also use the Home, End, Insert, and Backspace keys as you would with any word processor. However, you cannot use Ctrl+B to bold text or Ctrl+I to italicize text.

Unlike Button widgets, Entry widgets do not have a **command** argument that binds it to a callback function that is called when a certain event is triggered. However, the **bind** method can be used with Entry widgets to play that role. For instance, a line of code of the form

nameOfEntryWidget.bind("<Button-3>", *functionName*)

calls the named function when the Entry widget is clicked on with the right mouse button. *Note:* In this situation, the named function must contain a parameter. We will give the parameter the name *event*.

 Example 2 Toggle Colors The following program is similar to the program in Example 1. Run the program, left-click on the Entry widget with the mouse, and type some words into the widget. The words will appear in the color blue. However, right-clicks on the widget with the mouse toggle the color of the text between blue and red. At any time you can change the contents of the widget from the keyboard.

```
from tkinter import *

def changeColor(event):
    if entName["fg"] == "blue":  # if Entry widget text is colored blue
        entName["fg"] = "red"    # change color of text to red
    else:
        entName["fg"] = "blue"   # change color of text to blue

window = Tk()
window.title("Entry widget")
entName = Entry(window, fg="blue")
entName.grid(padx=100, pady=15)
entName.bind("<Button-3>", changeColor)  # specify right-click as an event
window.mainloop()
```

The standard way of retrieving data from an Entry widget is to first create a string variable with a statement of the form

variableName = **StringVar()**

and insert the argument **textvariable=*variableName*** into the Entry's constructor. After that, the value of

variableName.**get()**

will be a string consisting of the data in the Entry widget, and a statement of the form

variableName.**set(*aValue*)**

will place the specified string or numeric value into the Entry widget. In our examples, *variableName* will have the form *conOFentEntryName*, an abbreviation of *contents of the named Entry widget*.

 Example 3 Convert to Uppercase The following program uses both the get and set methods. Run the program, type some lowercase letters into the Entry widget, and then right-click on the widget with the mouse. The letters in the Entry widget will be converted to uppercase.

```
from tkinter import *

def convertToUpperCase(event):
    conOFentName.set(conOFentName.get().upper())

window = Tk()
window.title("Entry widget")
```

```
conOFentName = StringVar()    # contents of the Entry widget
entName = Entry(window, textvariable=conOFentName )
entName.grid(padx=100, pady=15)
entName.bind("<Button-3>", convertToUpperCase)
window.mainloop()
```

■ The ReadOnly Entry Widget

The ReadOnly Entry widget is a special type of Entry widget that is used only to display output. The code in Fig. 8.6(a) produces the output in Fig. 8.6(b). A ReadOnly Entry widget is specified by adding the argument **state="readonly"** to the constructor of an ordinary Entry widget.

```
from tkinter import *

window = Tk()
window.title("ReadOnly Entry Widget")
entOutput = Entry(window, width=20,
               state="readonly")
entOutput.grid(padx=100, pady=15)
window.mainloop()
```

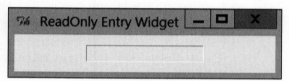

(a) **Code.**   (b) **Output.**

FIGURE 8.6   **ReadOnly Entry Demo.**

Run the program in Fig. 8.6(a) and notice that the box is not white. Left-click on the Entry widget. Nothing happens; the cursor does not appear in the widget, and therefore you cannot type any text into the widget. The only way to display text in a ReadOnly widget is to insert a textvariable attribute into the constructor and modify the attribute's contents using the set method.

Example 4   Hello World The following program uses the textvariable attribute and the set method to display text into a ReadOnly Entry widget.

```
from tkinter import *

window = Tk()
window.title("ReadOnly Entry Widget")
conOFentOutput = StringVar()    # contents of widget
entOutput = Entry(window, state="readonly", textvariable=conOFentOutput)
entOutput.grid(padx=100, pady=15)
conOFentOutput.set("Hello World!")
window.mainloop()
```

[Run]

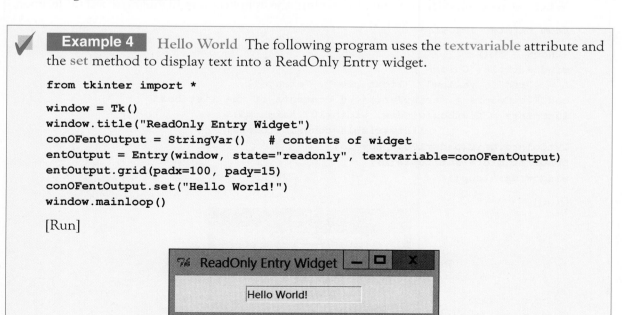

■ The Listbox Widget

The Listbox widget is primarily used to select from a list of items displayed in a vertical rectangular box. However, it also can be used to display data generated by the program. The code in Fig. 8.7(a) produces the output in Fig. 8.7(b). The height attribute specifies the number of lines that can appear in the list box at one time, and the width attribute specifies the number of characters that can appear in each line. The default values of height and width are 10 and 20, respectively.

```
from tkinter import *

window = Tk()
window.title("Listbox")
lstName = Listbox(window, width=10,
                  height=5)
lstName.grid(padx=100, pady=15)
window.mainloop()
```

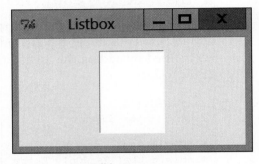

| (a) Code. | (b) Output. |

FIGURE 8.7 Listbox Demo.

Code places data into and retrieves data from a Listbox widget in a way similar to that of an Entry widget. The statement that instantiates the Listbox widget is proceeded with a statement of the form **variableName = StringVar()**. However, the Entry attribute textvariable in the constructor is replaced with the Listbox attribute listvariable.

To place items into a list box, first create a list (call it *L*) containing the items and then execute a statement of the form

variableName.set(tuple(L))

✔ **Example 5** List of Colors The following program places four items into a list box. When the user left-clicks on one of the items, the item becomes highlighted and underlined.

```
from tkinter import *

window = Tk()
window.title("Colors")
L = ["red", "yellow", "light blue", "orange"]
conOFlstColors = StringVar()    # contents of the list box
lstColors = Listbox(window, width=10, height=5,
                    listvariable=conOFlstColors)
lstColors.grid(padx=100, pady=15)
conOFlstColors.set(tuple(L))
window.mainloop()
```

[Run]

[Left-click on one of the items in the list box.]

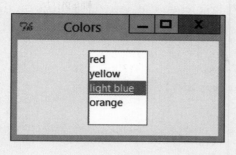

When the user left-clicks on an item in a list box, the event **<<ListboxSelect>>** is triggered and the value of the item (a string) is returned by an expression of the form

listboxName.**get(***listboxName*.**curselection())**

where the *curselection* method identifies the selected item.

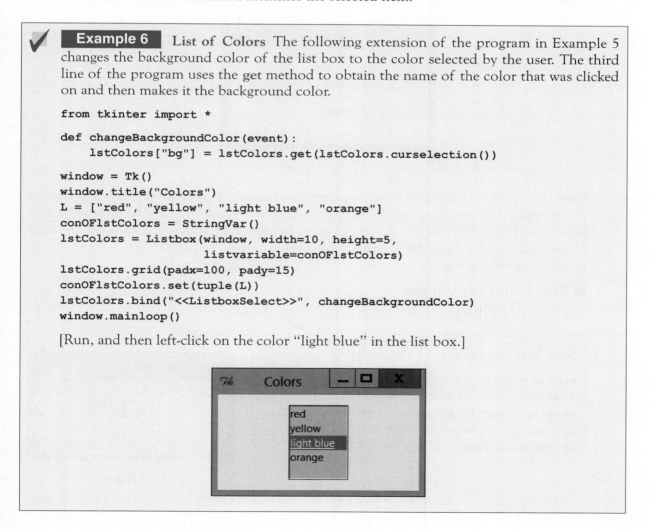

Example 6   List of Colors The following extension of the program in Example 5 changes the background color of the list box to the color selected by the user. The third line of the program uses the get method to obtain the name of the color that was clicked on and then makes it the background color.

```
from tkinter import *

def changeBackgroundColor(event):
    lstColors["bg"] = lstColors.get(lstColors.curselection())

window = Tk()
window.title("Colors")
L = ["red", "yellow", "light blue", "orange"]
conOFlstColors = StringVar()
lstColors = Listbox(window, width=10, height=5,
                    listvariable=conOFlstColors)
lstColors.grid(padx=100, pady=15)
conOFlstColors.set(tuple(L))
lstColors.bind("<<ListboxSelect>>", changeBackgroundColor)
window.mainloop()
```

[Run, and then left-click on the color "light blue" in the list box.]

To change the contents of a list box, use list methods to change the list *L* and then execute the **set** method. For instance, you can use the **sort** method to order the items in the list box.

Example 7 **List of Colors** The following extension of the program in Example 5 sorts the colors in the list box when the user right-clicks on the list box.

```
from tkinter import *

def sortItems(event):
    L.sort()
    conOFlstColors.set(tuple(L))

window = Tk()
window.title("Colors")
L = ["red", "yellow", "light blue", "orange"]
conOFlstColors = StringVar()
lstColors = Listbox(window, width=10, height=5, listvariable=conOFlstColors)
lstColors.grid(padx=100, pady=15)
conOFlstColors.set(tuple(L))
lstColors.bind("<Button-3>", sortItems)
window.mainloop()
```

[Run, and then right-click on the list box.]

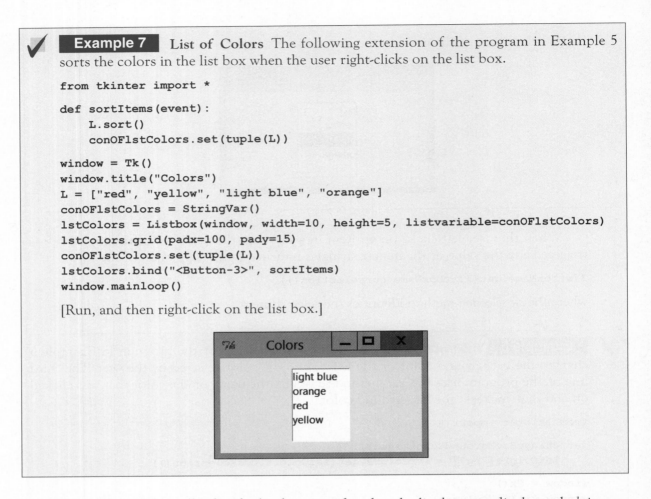

Note: The height, call it h, of a list box specifies that the list box can display only h items at a time. If you use a list containing more than h items to fill the list box, only the first h items will be visible initially. However, you can press the Tab key and then use the Page Down and Page Up keys, the DownArrow and UpArrow keys, or the scroll wheel on the mouse to scroll through the list box.

■ The Scroll bar Widget

The code in Fig. 8.8(a) produces the output in Fig. 8.8(b).

```
from tkinter import *

window = Tk()
window.title("Scrollbar")
yscroll = Scrollbar(window, orient=VERTICAL)
yscroll.grid(padx=110, pady=15)
window.mainloop()
```

(a) Code.   (b) Output.

FIGURE 8.8 Vertical Scroll bar Demo.

Vertical scroll bars can be connected to list boxes containing long lists to allow the user to move up and down through the items. Scrolling takes place when the user clicks on one of the arrows or drags the small raised-looking rectangle located between the two arrows.

The process of connecting a vertical scroll bar to a list is covered in Section 8.2 since it requires an understanding of the intricacies of the grid geometry manager.

■ Comments

1. The event triggered by <Button-1> is the left-button equivalent of the right-button event triggered by <Button-3>.

2. In Example 6, the horizontal blue bar that extends from the selected item will be eliminated if the statement **lstColors.selection_clear(0, END)** is added to the end of the *changeBackgroundColor* function.

3. The Label, Entry, and Listbox widgets each have both a **fg** (foreground) and **bg** (background) attribute. However, a ReadOnly Listbox widget ignores the setting of its **bg** attribute.

4. The third and fourth lines in Fig. 8.3(a) can be combined to the single line shown below. If so, the widget will appear in the window, but will not have a name. The name is not needed since in most programs, labels just sit there and do not have any of their properties accessed while the program is executing.

```
Label(window, text="Principal:").grid(padx=100, pady=15)
```

5. The text in a Label or Button widget can consist of more than one line. For instance, the code in Fig. 8.9(a) produces the output in Fig. 8.9(b).

```
from tkinter import *

window = Tk()
btn = Button(window, text="Push\nMe")
btn.grid(padx=75)
window.mainloop()
```

(a) Code.   (b) Output.

FIGURE 8.9   **Button Program.**

Practice Problems 8.1

1. The code in Fig. 8.10(a) produces the output in Fig. 8.10(b). Alter the code so that the caption in the title bar will not be cut off.

```
from tkinter import *

window = Tk()
window.title("Python")
btnTest = Button(window, text="PYTHON")
btnTest.grid(padx=70, pady=15)
window.mainloop()
```

(a) Code.   (b) Output.

FIGURE 8.10   **Flawed Button Program.**

2. Buttons and labels automatically adjust their widths to accommodate the text placed in them. Do Listbox and Entry widgets do the same?

3. Consider the program in Example 6. Change the event so that the clicked-on item is removed from the list box.

EXERCISES 8.1

In Exercises 1 through 6, write a program to produce the display.

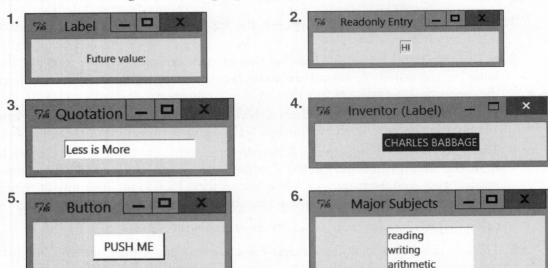

7. **Padding**   Consider the program in Fig. 8.2(a). Assign different values to **padx** and **pady** and observe the effect.

8. **Padding**   Consider the program in Fig. 8.2(a). In the last line of the program add the argument **ipadx=50** and determine its effect. Do the same with **ipady=50**.

In Exercises 9 and 10, use the file **USpres.txt** that contains the names of the U.S. presidents in the order they served.

9. **U.S. Presidents**   Write a program that places the names of the presidents into a list box. See Fig. 8.11. *Hint:* Use list comprehension.

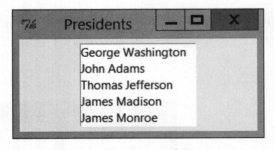

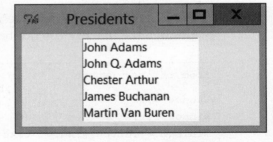

FIGURE 8.11   Outcome of Exercise 9.   FIGURE 8.12   Outcome of Exercise 10.

10. **U.S. Presidents**   Write a program that places the names of the presidents into a list box ordered by their last names. See Fig. 8.12. *Hint:* Use list comprehension.

In Exercises 11 through 14, use the file **StatesANC.txt** containing the name, abbreviation, nickname, and capital of each state in the United States. The states are listed in alphabetical order. The first three lines of the file are

```
Alabama,AL,Cotton State,Montgomery
Alaska,AK,The Last Frontier,Juneau
Arizona,AZ,Grand Canyon State,Phoenix
```

11. U.S. States   Write a program that places the names of the states into a list box. See Fig. 8.13. *Hint:* Use list comprehension.

FIGURE 8.13   Outcome of Exercise 11.

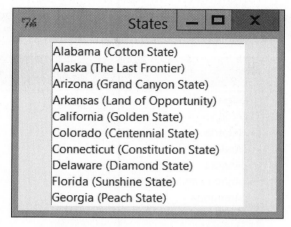

FIGURE 8.14   Outcome of Exercise 12.

12. U.S. States   Modify the program in Exercise 11 so that both the name of the state and its nickname are displayed in the list box. See Fig. 8.14.

13. U.S. States   Extend the program in Exercise 11 so that when you click on the name of a state, the name is converted to all uppercase letters. See Fig. 8.15.

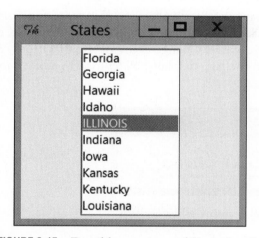

FIGURE 8.15   Possible outcome of Exercise 13.

FIGURE 8.16   Possible outcome of Exercise 14.

14. U.S. States   Extend the program in Exercise 11 so that when you click on the name of a state, the state's abbreviation is written alongside the name. See Fig. 8.16.

In Exercises 15 and 16, use the file UN.txt that gives data about the 193 members of the United Nations with the countries listed in alphabetical order. Each line of the file gives the name, continent, population (in millions), and area (in square miles) of a U.N. member. Some lines of the file are

```
Canada,North America,34.8,3855000
France,Europe,66.3,211209
New Zealand,Australia/Oceania,4.4,103738
Nigeria,Africa,177.2,356669
```

```
Pakistan,Asia,196.2,310403
Peru,South America,30.1,496226
```

15. United Nations   Write a program that uses the file **UN.txt** to place the names of the U.N. member nations in a list box of width=38 and height=10. See Fig. 8.17. *Hint:* Use list comprehension.

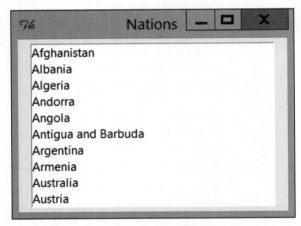

FIGURE 8.17   Outcome of Exercise 15.

FIGURE 8.18   Outcome of Exercise 16.

16. Continents Having Countries   Write a program that uses the file **UN.txt** to determine the names of the continents that contain countries, and places the continents in alphabetical order in a list box. See Fig. 8.18. *Hint:* Use set comprehension.

17. Change Colors   Write a program that initially displays the button in Fig. 8.19 with blue text. When the button is left-clicked with the mouse, the button should appear with black text and the caption replaced with "Change color of Text to Blue". Subsequent left-clicks should toggle between the two displays. *Note:* Insert **padx=50** into the grid statement.

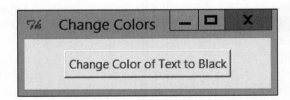

FIGURE 8.19   Original window of Exercise 17.

18. Change Colors   Redo Exercise 17 with a label instead of a button.

19. Change Salutation   Write a program that initially displays the button in Fig. 8.20(a). When the button is left-clicked with the mouse, the caption should change to GOODBYE as in Fig. 8.20(b). Subsequent left-clicks should toggle between the two salutations.

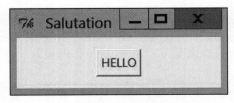
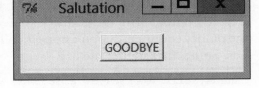

(a) Original display.   (b) Display after first left-click.

FIGURE 8.20   Outputs of Exercise 19.

20. Change Salutation Consider the program in Exercise 19. Each time the button was pressed, the width of the button changed. Modify the program so that the width always stays the same.

Solutions to Practice Problems 8.1

1. Either increase the value assigned to the padx attribute in the fifth statement or insert an argument such as **width=10** into the constructor for the button.

2. No. For instance, consider the program in Fig. 8.21.

```
from tkinter import *

window = Tk()
window.title("Monty Python")
conOFentSong = StringVar()
entSong = Entry(window, state="readonly",
            textvariable=conOFentSong)
entSong.grid(padx=60, pady=15)
song = "Always look on the bright" + \
      "side of life."
conOFentSong.set(song)
window.mainloop()
```

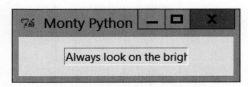

(a) Code.   (b) Output.

FIGURE 8.21   Filling an Entry widget.

3. The new program is as follows:

```
from tkinter import *

def deleteItem(event):
    L.remove(lstColors.get(lstColors.curselection()))
    conOFlstColors.set(tuple(L))
    lstColors.selection_clear(0, END)

window = Tk()
window.title("Listbox")
L = ["red", "yellow", "green", "orange"]
conOFlstColors = StringVar()
lstColors = Listbox(window, width=25, height=5,
                    listvariable=conOFlstColors)
lstColors.grid(padx=100, pady=15)
conOFlstColors.set(tuple(L))
lstColors.bind("<<ListboxSelect>>", deleteItem)
window.mainloop()
```

8.2   The Grid Geometry Manager

Geometry managers are tools used to place widgets on the screen. There are three geometry managers available in tkinter—*grid*, *pack*, and *place*. In this book we will use the grid geometry manager since it is the easiest to learn and produces the nicest layouts. The pack manager is also easy to use, but is limited in its possibilities compared to the grid manager.

The place manager provides complete control in the positioning of widgets, but is complicated to program.

In this section we learn how to use the grid geometry manager. In the next section we will combine the knowledge gained from the first two sections of this chapter to write complete GUI programs.

■ Grids

A **grid** is an imaginary rectangle containing horizontal and vertical lines that subdivide it into rectangles called **cells**. The first row of cells is referred to as row 0, the second row is referred to as row1, and so on. Similarly, the first column of cells is referred to as column 0, the second column of cells is referred to as column 1, and so on. Each cell is identified by its row and column numbers. Figure 8.22 shows a grid having three rows and four columns, with each cell identified by its row and column number.

row 0 , column 0	row 0 , column 1	row 0 , column 2	row 0 , column 3
row 1 , column 0	row 1 , column 1	row 1 , column 2	row 1 , column 3
row 2 , column 0	row 2 , column 1	row 2 , column 2	row 2 , column 3

FIGURE 8.22   A grid of three rows and four columns.

In Fig. 8.22 the horizontal and vertical lines are uniformly spaced. However, such is not the case for grids used in GUI programs. Figure 8.23 shows grids typical of those used in GUI programs.

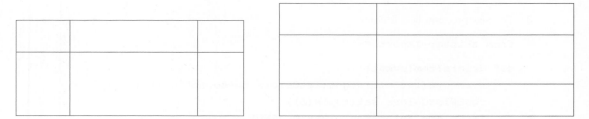

FIGURE 8.23   Typical grids used in GUI programs.

A graphical interface is created by placing widgets into a grid. A widget can be inserted into an individual cell or can span a consecutive sequence of rows or columns. Each row and column expands to fit the largest widget in that row and column. Padx and pady can be used to specify how much blank space should be put around a widget within its cell. By default, widgets are centered within a cell. However, an attribute named **sticky** can be used to change the placement inside a cell and also to enlarge the widget so that it fills an entire cell.

Figure 8.24 shows the visual interface from Fig. 8.1 in the previous section. The grid consists of five rows (row 0 through row 4) and two columns (column 0 and column 1). Each Label and Entry widget is placed in a single cell. For instance, the Entry widget containing the number 30 has been placed in the cell in row 2, column 1. The button begins at the cell in row 3, column 0 and spans two columns. Those two widgets are declared and placed in the window with the lines of code below. The argument **padx=5** places five pixels of space both to the left and to the right of the widget. The argument **pady=5** places five pixels of space both above and below the widget. The argument **sticky=W** moves the Entry widget to the left side (that is, the West side) of its cell. The argument **columnspan=2** specifies that the button should span two columns.

```
entNumberOfYears = Entry(window, width=2)
entNumberOfYears.grid(row=2, column=1, padx=5, pady=5, sticky=W)

btnCalculate = Button(window, text="Calculate Monthly Payment")
btnCalculate.grid(row=3, column=0, columnspan=2, pady=5)
```

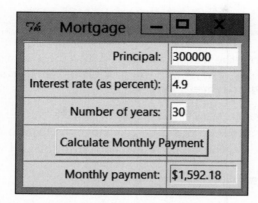

FIGURE 8.24 Grid for the mortgage program.

In general, a statement of the form

widgetName.grid(row=m, column=n)

places the widget in the cell located at row m and column n. Additional attributes, such as padx, pady, and sticky, can be placed into the grid method.

A statement of the form

widgetName.grid(row=m, column=n, columnspan=c)

places the widget beginning in the cell located at row m and column n, and spanning c columns. (If **columnspan** is replaced with **rowspan**, the widget will span c rows.)

The arguments in Table 8.1 improve layouts by adding space to the sides of widgets.

TABLE 8.1	Padding arguments.
Argument	**Effect**
padx=r	puts r pixels of space to the left and to the right of the widget
pady=r	puts r pixels of space above and below the widget
padx=(r,s)	puts r pixels of space to the left and s pixels of space to the right of the widget
pady=(r,s)	puts r pixels of space above and s pixels of space below the widget

Note: You don't have to specify the number of rows and columns in the grid; the grid manager automatically determines them from the locations of the widgets that have been placed into the grid. Also, the width of each column and the height of each row are automatically adjusted to accommodate the widths, heights and paddings of the widgets they contain.

■ The *sticky* Attribute

A statement of the form

widgetName.grid(row=m, column=n, sticky=letter)

where *letter* is N, S, E, or W, causes the widget (along with its padding) to attach to the North (that is: top) side of the cell, South (that is: bottom) side of the cell, East (that is: right) side of the cell, or West (that is: left) side of its cell, respectively.

The contents of the windows in Fig. 8.25 are similar to the contents of the third and fourth rows of Fig. 8.24. The Entry widget containing the number 30 was declared with the statement

```
entNumberOfYears = Entry(window, width=2)
```

In the top-left window, the widget was placed into the grid with the statement

```
entNumberOfYears.grid(row=0, column=1)
```

Notice that the widget appears in the center of its cell—its default location. In the remaining windows, the sticky attribute was used to change the location of the widget within its cell. In the top-right window, the widget was placed into the grid with the statement

```
entNumberOfYears.grid(row=0, column=1, sticky=N)
```

The remaining three windows were created by setting the value of **sticky** to S, W, and E, respectively.

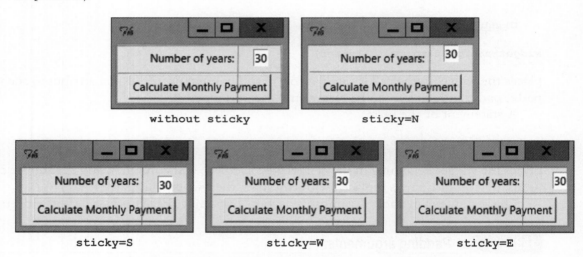

FIGURE 8.25 **Some interfaces produced by the sticky attribute.**

The value assigned to the **sticky** attribute also can consist of two letters chosen from N, S, E, and W or can even consist of all four of the letters. The argument **sticky=NS** causes the widget to attach to both the North and South sides of its cell. This can only happen if the widget is stretched vertically. Similarly, the argument **sticky=EW** stretches the widget horizontally, and the argument **sticky=NSEW** stretches the widget both vertically and horizontally so that it fills the entire cell. See Fig. 8.26.

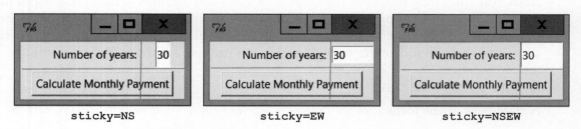

FIGURE 8.26 **Sticky attributes that resize the widget.**

■ Attaching a Vertical Scroll Bar to a List Box

Figure 8.27 shows a list box with a vertical scroll bar attached to its right side. The items in the list box scroll when the user clicks on one of the scroll bar's arrows or drags the small raised-looking rectangle located between the two arrows.

FIGURE 8.27 List box with scroll bar attached.

The following code produces Fig. 8.27, where the names of the two widgets are *lstNE* and *yscroll*.

```
from tkinter import *

window = Tk()
window.title("New England")
yscroll = Scrollbar(window, orient=VERTICAL)
yscroll.grid(row=0, column=2, rowspan=4, padx=(0,100), pady=5, sticky=NS)
statesList = ["Connecticut", "Maine", "Massachusetts",
              "New Hampshire","Rhode Island", "Vermont"]
conOFlstNE = StringVar()
lstNE = Listbox(window, width=14, height=4, listvariable=conOFlstNE,
                yscrollcommand=yscroll.set)
lstNE.grid(row=0, column=1, rowspan=4, padx=(100,0), pady=5, sticky=E)
conOFlstNE.set(tuple(statesList))
yscroll["command"] = lstNE.yview
window.mainloop()
```

Notes:

1. The scroll bar must be declared before the list box.

2. The argument `yscrollcommand=yscroll.set` must be inserted into the list box's constructor.

3. The statement `yscroll["command"] = lstNE.yview` must be added to the program.

The last two steps attach the scroll bar to the list box.

To create the interface shown in Fig. 8.27, the list box and the scroll bar were placed in adjacent cells and given the same *rowspan* values. In addition, **sticky** was used to guarantee they are touching and that the scroll bar fills its cells vertically. The arguments **padx=(100,0)** and **padx=(0,100)** put some space to the left of the list box and to the right of the scroll bar without separating them.

■ Designing the Screen Layout

The following guidelines are useful in creating the layout for a GUI program:

1. Input from the user can be obtained by having the user type the information into an Entry widget or click on an item in a list box. A label should be placed to the left of each

Entry widget to specify the type of information that should be typed into the Entry widget. Often labels are placed above list boxes to describe their contents.

2. The output of a program is usually displayed either in a ReadOnly Entry widget or in a list box. If the output consists of a large number of items displayed in a list box, a vertical scroll bar should be connected to the list box.

3. Often, but not necessarily, buttons span more than one column.

4. By default, list boxes hold 10 items.

5. Some programmers make a rough sketch of the screen layout on a piece of paper and then draw grid lines to guide them in deciding where to place each of the widgets. If the grid lines look awkward, the programmers make adjustments to the layout.

6. After the first draft of the program is run, the programmer usually will want to tweak the layout by adding padding and **sticky** arguments into the grid methods of the widgets. This process is typically repeated many times.

■ Comments

1. Empty rows are discarded—that is, they do not make blank space. For instance, the pair of lines

```
Label(window, text="Hello").grid(row=0, column=0, padx=25)
Label(window, text="World").grid(row=0, column=5, padx=25)
```

produce the same effect as the pair of lines

```
Label(window, text="Hello", bg="beige").grid(row=0, column=0, padx=25)
Label(window, text="World", bg="tan").grid(row=0, column=1, padx=25)
```

2. Some other settings for the **sticky** attribute are *NW*, *NE*, *SE*, and *SW* that place the associated widget in one of the corners of its cell.

Practice Problems 8.2

1. Write a program to produce the interface in Fig. 8.28.

FIGURE 8.28 **Interface for Practice Problem 1.**

2. Consider the interface in Fig. 8.29.

   (a) What argument was inserted into the Workplace list box's grid statement to cause the list box to be attached to the top of its cell?
   (b) Which three widgets most likely had the argument **padx=10** in their **grid** methods?
   (c) Which widget had the argument **pady=5** in its **grid** method?
   (d) Which widget had the argument **pady=(0,5)** in its **grid** method?

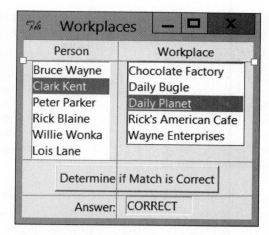

FIGURE 8.29   Interface for Practice Problem 2.

EXERCISES 8.2

Consider the six lines of code below and the interfaces labeled *A* through *F* in Fig. 8.30. In Exercises 1 through 6 determine the interface from Fig. 8.30 generated by adding the line of code as a seventh line of code.

```
from tkinter import *
window = Tk()
window.title("Button")
Label(window, text="Column 0").grid(row=0, column=0, padx=25, pady=5)
Label(window, text="Column 1").grid(row=0, column=1, padx=25, pady=5)
btnButton = Button(window, text="I'm a Button")
```

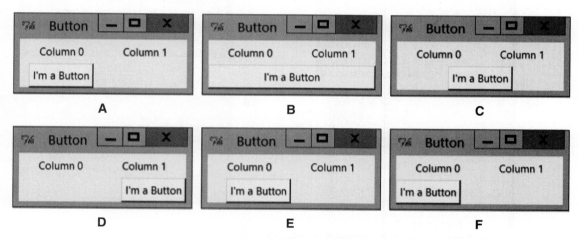

FIGURE 8.30   Six interfaces.

1. `btnButton.grid(row=1, column=0, columnspan=2, sticky=E)`

2. `btnButton.grid(row=1, column=0, columnspan=2, sticky=W)`

3. `btnButton.grid(row=1, column=0, columnspan=2, sticky=EW)`

4. `btnButton.grid(row=1, column=0, columnspan=2)`

5. `btnButton.grid(row=1, column=0)`

6. `btnButton.grid(row=1, column=0, sticky=E)`

In Exercises 7 and 8, write a program to produce the output shown. (*Note:* In Exercise 7, the first reindeer is *Cupid* and the last is *Vixen.* In Exercise 8, the last ocean is *Antarctic.*)

7.

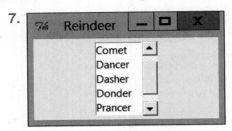

8.

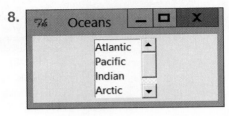

Each screen capture below shows the output of a complete program. In Exercises 9 through 22, write just the part of the program that displays the interface. When the half-finished program is run, all widgets should appear as shown, but no text should appear inside the Entry widgets or list boxes.

9.

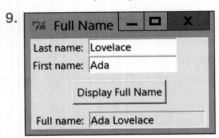

10.

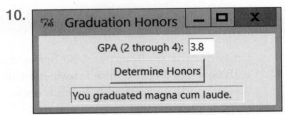

11.

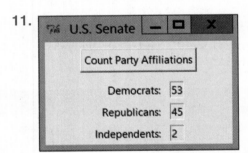

12.

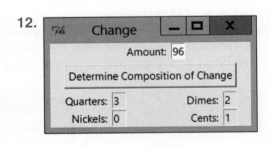

13.

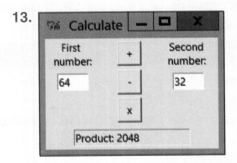

14.

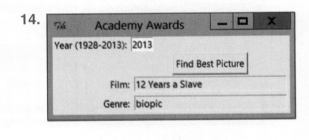

15.

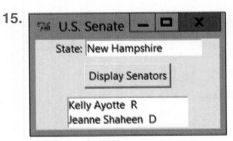

16.

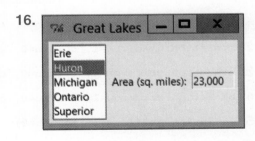

17.

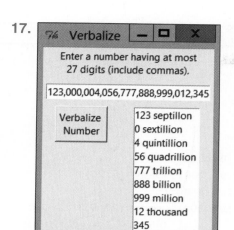

18.

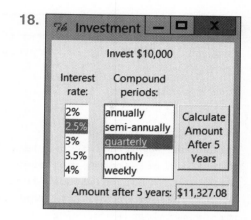

19.

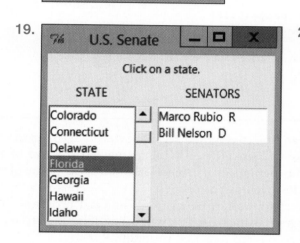

20.

21.

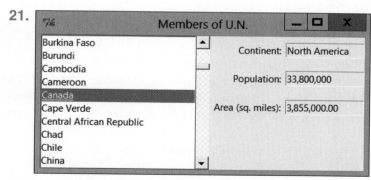

22.

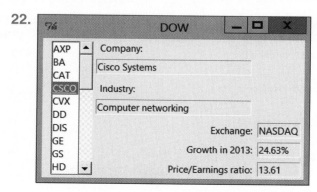

Solutions to Practice Problems 8.2

1. Arguments of the form **pady=(m, n)** can be used to place the buttons at the top and bottom of the window with a large space between them.

```
from tkinter import *

window = Tk()
window.title("Buttons")
btnButton1 = Button(window, text="I'm a Button")
btnButton1.grid(row=0, column=0, padx=(100,100), pady=(0,20))
btnButton2 = Button(window, text="I'm also a Button")
btnButton2.grid(row=1, column=0, padx=(100,100), pady=(20,0))
window.mainloop()
```

2. **(a)** The argument **sticky=N**. The argument **pady=(0,18)** also would have worked, but repeated trial and error would have been required to determine the number 18.
   (b) The two list boxes and the Entry widget.
   (c) The button, since it is the only widget having space both above and below it in its cell.
   (d) The ReadOnly Entry widget.

8.3 Writing GUI Programs

GUI programs are normally written in an object-oriented style. However, in order to simplify the coding as much as possible, we will use a direct coding style. At the end of the section, we will show how to write GUI programs in an object-oriented style. Some of the programs in the Solutions Manual will be given in both styles.

Every program from the preceding chapters can be written as a GUI program—but not conversely. For instance, a GUI program using a list box with a scroll bar tied to it and containing a long list usually cannot be converted to a TUI program.

■ Converting TUI Programs to GUI Programs

In general, programs consist of three components—input, processing, and output. In TUI programs, input is usually obtained from an input statement or by importing data from a file. Output is usually given by a **print** statement or stored in a file. When we convert a TUI program to a GUI program, we replace **input** and **print** statements with Label/Entry pairs. Processing data and inputting and outputting data to files works much the same in both types of programs. The primary difference is that the processing in GUI programs is usually triggered by an event

Figure 8.31 shows a TUI program and a possible output.

```
def main():
    ## Find the largest of three numbers.
    L = []
    num1 = eval(input("Enter the first number: "))
    L.append(num1)
    num2 = eval(input("Enter the second number: "))
    L.append(num2)
    num3 = eval(input("Enter the third number: "))
    L.append(num3)
    print("The largest number is", str(max(L)) + '.')

main()
```

```
Enter the first number: 2345
Enter the second number: 5678
Enter the third number: 1234
The largest number is 5678.
```

FIGURE 8.31 A TUI program and a possible output.

✓ **Example 1** **Conversion to a GUI Program** The following program is a conversion of the TUI program in Fig. 8.31 to a GUI program. The grid consists of five rows and two columns.

```
from tkinter import *

def findLargest():
    L = []
    L.append(eval(conOFentNum1.get()))
    L.append(eval(conOFentNum2.get()))
    L.append(eval(conOFentNum3.get()))
    conOFentLargest.set(max(L))

window = Tk()
window.title("Largest Number")
Label(window, text="First number: ").grid(row=0, column=0, pady=5, sticky=E)
conOFentNum1 = StringVar()
ententNum1 = Entry(window, width=8, textvariable=conOFentNum1)
ententNum1.grid(row=0, column=1, sticky=W)
Label(window, text="Second number: ").grid(row=1, column=0, pady=5, sticky=E)
conOFentNum2 = StringVar()
ententNum2 = Entry(window, width=8, textvariable=conOFentNum2)
ententNum2.grid(row=1, column=1, sticky=W)
Label(window, text="Third number: ").grid(row=2, column=0, pady=5, sticky=E)
conOFentNum3 = StringVar()
ententNum3 = Entry(window, width=8, textvariable=conOFentNum3)
ententNum3.grid(row=2, column=1, sticky=W)
btnFind = Button(window, text="Find the Largest Number", command=findLargest)
btnFind.grid(row=3, column=0, columnspan=2, padx=75)
Label(window, text="Largest number: ").grid(row=4, column=0, sticky=E)
conOFentLargest = StringVar()
entLargest = Entry(window, state="readonly", width=8,
                   textvariable=conOFentLargest)
entLargest.grid(row=4, column=1, pady=5, sticky=W)
window.mainloop()
```

[Run, type three numbers into the Entry widgets, and click on the button.]

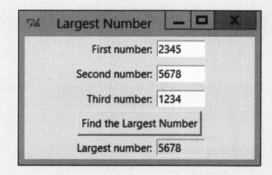

■ Filling List Boxes from a File

List boxes tied to scroll bars are extremely useful in GUI programming. List boxes containing long lists are usually filled from files. The program in Example 2 uses set comprehension to fill a list box in order to avoid the duplication of items in the list box.

Example 2   State Birds   The file **StateBirds.txt** contains the name and state bird of each state in the United States, where the states are listed in alphabetical order. (**Note:** Often two of more states have the same state bird. For instance, seven states have the cardinal as their state bird.) The first three lines of the file are

```
Alabama,Yellowhammer
Alaska,Willow ptarmigan
Arizona,Cactus wren
```

The following program uses the file **StateBirds.txt** to display the state birds in a list box, and gives the number of different state birds. Each bird appears once in the list box and the birds are in alphabetical order.

```python
from tkinter import *

def displayBirds():
    infile = open("StateBirds.txt", 'r')
    birdSet = {line.split(',')[1].rstrip() for line in infile}
    infile.close()
    conOFlstBirds.set(tuple(sorted(birdSet)))   # sorted(birdSet) is a list
    numBirds = len(birdSet)
    conOFentNumBirds.set(numBirds)

window = Tk()
window.title("State Birds")
textForButton = "Display the Different State Birds"
btnDisplay = Button(window, text=textForButton, command=displayBirds)
btnDisplay.grid(row=0, column=0, columnspan=3, pady=5)
yscroll = Scrollbar(window, orient=VERTICAL)
yscroll.grid(row=1, column=1, rowspan=10, pady=(0,5), sticky=NS)
conOFlstBirds = StringVar()
lstBirds = Listbox(window, width=20, height=8, listvariable=conOFlstBirds,
                   yscrollcommand=yscroll.set)
lstBirds.grid(row=1, column=0, padx=(5,0), pady=(0,5), rowspan=10)
yscroll["command"] = lstBirds.yview
textForLabel = "Number of\ndifferent\nstate birds:"
Label(window, text=textForLabel).grid(row=1, column=2, padx=10, pady=5)
conOFentNumBirds = StringVar()
entNumBirds = Entry(window, width=2, state="readonly",
                    textvariable=conOFentNumBirds)
entNumBirds.grid(row=2, column=2)
window.mainloop()
```

[Run, and click on the button.]

■ GUI Programs Written in Object-Oriented Style

| Example 3 | Object-Oriented Style The following program is an object-oriented version of the program in Example 2. |

```
from tkinter import *

class StateBirds:
    def __init__(self):
        window = Tk()
        window.title("State Birds")
        textForButton = "Display the Different State Birds"
        btnDisplay = Button(window, text=textForButton,
                            command=self.displayBirds)
        btnDisplay.grid(row=0, column=0, columnspan=3, pady=5)
        yscroll = Scrollbar(window, orient=VERTICAL)
        yscroll.grid(row=1, column=1, rowspan=10, pady=5, sticky=NS)
        self._conOFlstBirds = StringVar()
        self._lstBirds = Listbox(window, width=20, height=8,
                listvariable=self._conOFlstBirds, yscrollcommand=yscroll.set)
        self._lstBirds.grid(row=1, column=0, padx=(5,0), pady=(0,5),
                            rowspan=10)
        yscroll["command"] = self._lstBirds.yview
        textForLabel = "Number of\ndifferent\nstate birds:"
        Label(window, text=textForLabel).grid(row=1, column=2, padx=10, pady=5)
        self._conOFentNumBirds = StringVar()
        entNumBirds = Entry(window, width=2, state="readonly",
                            textvariable=self._conOFentNumBirds)
        entNumBirds.grid(row=2, column=2)
        window.mainloop()

    def displayBirds(self):
        infile = open("StateBirds.txt", 'r')
        birdSet = {line.split(',')[1].rstrip() for line in infile}
        self._conOFlstBirds.set(tuple(sorted(birdSet)))
        numBirds = len(birdSet)
        self._conOFentNumBirds.set(numBirds)

StateBirds()
```

■ Comments

1. The program in Example 3 ended with the statement **StateBirds()**. That statement could have been replaced with a statement such as **bird = StateBirds()** that creates an instance of the class *StateBirds*. This works since whenever a class is instantiated, the *__init__* function is automatically executed.

2. The class created in Example 3 could have been saved in a file named **stateBirds.py**. Then the following program would produce the same output.

```
from stateBirds import *
bird = StateBirds
```

1. **Full Name**　Write a program that requests a person's last name and first name, and then displays their full name. See Fig. 8.32.

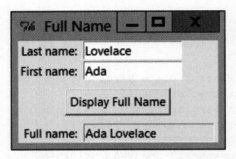

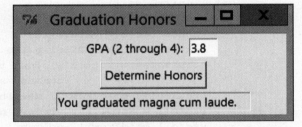

FIGURE 8.32　Possible outcome of Exercise 1.　　FIGURE 8.33　Possible outcome of Exercise 2.

2. **Graduation Honors**　Write a program that assumes that the user will graduate (that is, has a GPA of 2 or more) and determines if the user will graduate with honors. (*Summa cum laude* requires a GPA of 3.9, *magna cum laude* requires a GPA of 3.6, and *cum laude* requires a GPA of 3.3.) See Fig. 8.33.

3. **Buy Two, Get One Free Sale**　A clothing store advertises "BUY 2 ITEMS AND THE 3RD IS FREE." What they mean is that if you buy three items, then the lowest cost item is free. Write a program that accepts the three costs as input and then calculates the total cost after dropping the lowest cost. See Fig. 8.34.

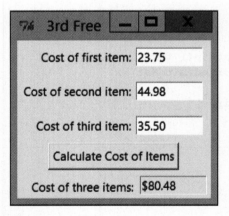

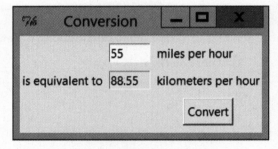

FIGURE 8.34　Possible outcome of Exercise 3.　　FIGURE 8.35　Possible outcome of Exercise 4.

4. **Convert Speeds**　Speedometers in the United States measure speed in *miles per hour*, whereas speedometers in European countries measure speed in *kilometers per hour*. Write a program that converts *miles per hour* to *kilometers per hour*. See Fig. 8.35. **Note:** kph $= 1.61 \cdot$ mph.

5. **Change in Salary**　A common misconception is that if you receive a 10% pay raise and later a 10% pay cut, your salary will be unchanged. Write a program that requests a salary as input and then calculates the salary after receiving a 10% pay raise followed by a 10% pay cut. The program also should display the percentage change in salary. See Fig. 8.36.

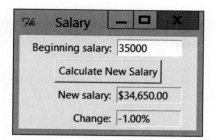

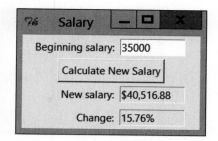

FIGURE 8.36 Possible outcome of Exercise 5.   **FIGURE 8.37** Possible outcome of Exercise 6.

6. **Change in Salary** A common misconception is that if you receive three successive 5% pay raises, then your original salary will have increased by 15%. Write a program that requests a salary as input and then calculates the salary after receiving three successive 5% pay raises. The program also should display the percentage change in salary. See Fig. 8.37.

7. **Car Loan** If A dollars are borrowed at r% interest compounded monthly to purchase a car with monthly payments for n years, then the monthly payment is given by the formula

$$\text{monthly payment} = \frac{i}{1 - (1 + i)^{-12n}} \cdot A$$

where $i = \frac{r}{1200}$. Write a program that calculates the monthly payment after the user gives the amount of the loan, the interest rate, and the number of years. Figure 8.38 shows that monthly payments of $234.23 are required to pay off a five-year car loan of $12,000 at 6.4% interest.

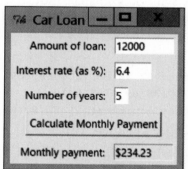

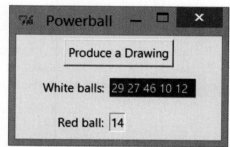

FIGURE 8.38 Possible outcome of Exercise 7.   **FIGURE 8.39** Possible outcome of Exercise 8.

8. **Powerball** Powerball numbers are obtained by drawing 5 balls out of a drum containing 59 white balls (numbered 1 through 59) and then drawing 1 ball (the Powerball) out of a drum containing 35 red balls (numbered 1 through 35). Write a program to produce a Powerball drawing. See Fig. 8.39. **Note:** The attribute bg has no effect on ReadOnly Entry widgets. Therefore, the first Entry widget should not be designated as ReadOnly.

9. **Calculator** Write a program that allows the user to specify two numbers and then adds, subtracts, or multiplies them when the user clicks on the appropriate button. See Fig. 8.40 on the next page.

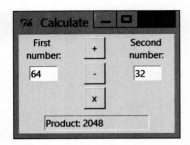

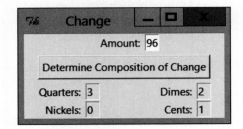

FIGURE 8.40 Possible outcome of Exercise 9.   **FIGURE 8.41** Possible outcome of Exercise 10.

10. **Change**   Write a program to make change for an amount of money from 0 through 99 cents input by the user. The output of the program should show the number of coins from each denomination used to make change. See Fig. 8.41.

11. **Great Lakes**   Table 8.2 contains the names and areas of the five Great Lakes. Write a program that displays the lakes in alphabetical order in a list box and produces the area of the lake selected by the user. See Fig. 8.42. *Hint:* Use the dictionary lakesDict = {"Huron":23000, "Ontario":8000, "Michigan":22000, "Erie":10000, "Superior":32000}.

TABLE 8.2	Great Lakes.
Lake	Area (sq. miles)
Huron	23,000
Ontario	8,000
Michigan	22,000
Erie	10,000
Superior	32,000

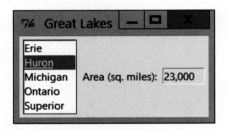

FIGURE 8.42 Possible outcome of Exercise 11.

12. **DOW**   The file **DOW.txt** contains the name, symbol, exchange, industry, price at the end of trading on 12/31/2012, price at the end of trading on 12/31/2013, 2013 earnings per share, and dividend paid in 2013 for each of the 30 stocks in the Dow Jones Industrial Average. The first three lines of the file are

```
American Express,AXP,NYSE,Consumer finance,57.48,90.73,4.88,.89
Boeing,BA,NYSE,Aerospace & defense,75.36,136.49,5.96,2.19
Caterpillar,CAT,NYSE,Construction & mining equipment,89.61,90.81,5.75,2.32
```

Write a program that displays the symbols for the 30 DOW stocks in a list box. When the user clicks on one of the symbols, the information shown in Fig. 8.43 should be displayed. The Price/Earnings ratio should be calculated as the price of a share of stock on 12/31/2013 divided by the 2013 earnings per share.

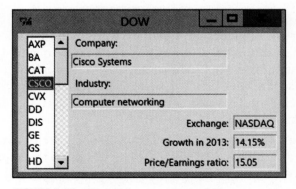

FIGURE 8.43 Possible outcome of Exercise 12.

In Exercises 13 and 14, use the file `Oscars.txt` that contains the names and genres of each film that won an Oscar for best picture. The films are listed in the order they received the award. The first three lines of the file are

```
Wings,silent
The Broadway Melody,musical
All Quiet on the Western Front,war
```

13. Academy Awards   Write a program using the file `Oscars.txt` that fills a list box with genres and then displays the Oscar-winning films of a specific genre when the user clicks on the genre in the list box. See Fig. 8.44.

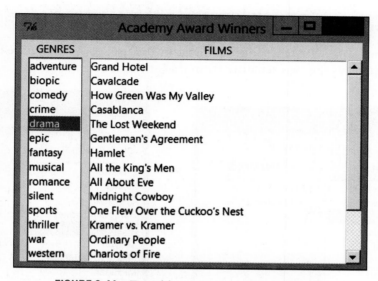

FIGURE 8.44   Possible outcome of Exercise 13.

14. Academy Awards   Write a program using the file `Oscars.txt` that requests a year and then displays the name and genre of that year's best picture winner. See Fig. 8.45.

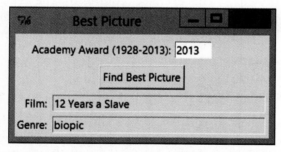

FIGURE 8.45   Possible outcome of Exercise 14.

In Exercises 15 through 17, use the file `Senate114.txt` that contains a record for each member of the 114th U.S. Senate. (The 114th U.S. Senate was installed in 2015.) Each record contains three fields—name, state, and party affiliation. Some records in the files are

```
John McCain,Arizona,R
Bernie Sanders,Vermont,I
Kirsten Gillibrand,New York,D
```

15. U.S. Senate   Write a program that asks the user to type the name of a state into an Entry widget and then displays the two senators from that state. See Fig. 8.46.

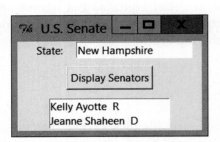

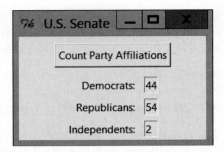

FIGURE 8.46 Possible outcome of Exercise 15. **FIGURE 8.47** Possible outcome of Exercise 16.

16. U.S. Senate   Write a program that determines the number of senators of each affiliation. See Fig. 8.47.

17. U.S. Senate   Write a program that asks the user to select a state from a list box, and then displays the two senators from that state. See Fig. 8.48.

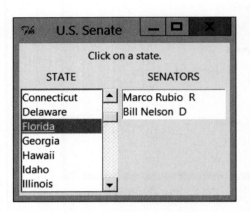

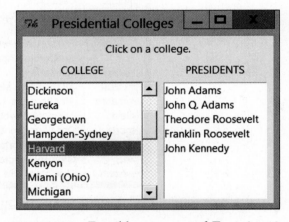

FIGURE 8.48 Possible outcome of Exercise 17. **FIGURE 8.49** Possible outcome of Exercise 18.

18. Presidential Colleges   This exercise requires the file **PresColl.txt** that contains the names of U.S. presidents and the undergraduate college attended by each of them. The presidents are listed in the order they served. The first three lines of the file are

```
George Washington,No college
John Adams,Harvard
Thomas Jefferson,William and Mary
```

Write a program that fills a list box with the colleges (in alphabetical order) attended by U.S. presidents and then displays the presidents who attended that college when the user clicks on a college in the list box. See Fig. 8.49.

19. Workplaces   Table 8.3 holds the names of five people and their places of employment. Write a program that displays the people in one list box and the workplaces in another list box, with the items in each list box in alphabetical order. The user should try to match a person with their workplace by selecting an item from each list. When they click on the button, they should be told whether or not they made a correct match. See Fig. 8.50. **Note:** Normally, if there are two list boxes in the window, when you select a value in one, it deselects whatever you selected in the other. However, this behavior will not occur if you insert the argument **exportselection=0** into each list box's constructor.

TABLE 8.3 **Place of employment.**

Person	Workplace
Bruce Wayne	Wayne Enterprises
Clark Kent	Daily Planet
Peter Parker	Daily Bugle
Rick Blaine	Rick's American Cafe
Willie Wonka	Chocolate Factory

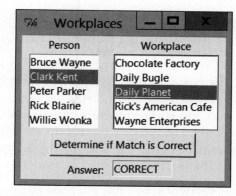

FIGURE 8.50 Possible outcome of Exercise 19.

CHAPTER 8 KEY TERMS AND CONCEPTS

EXAMPLES

8.1 Widgets

Some **widgets** (short for "window gadgets") are:

Button: triggers an event when clicked on with the mouse

Label: provides an identity for another widget

Entry: accepts input from the user and displays output

Listbox: allows user to select from a list of options or to display output

Scrollbar: adds scrolling capability to list boxes

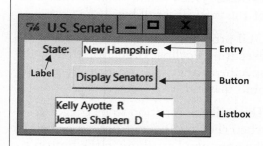

The captions for Button and Label widgets are specified by **text** attributes in their constructors.

```
lblName=Label(window,text="Name:")
```

Code can be used to retrieve text from and put text into an Entry widget. First an object (call it *x*) of type **StringVar** is declared and assigned to the Entry widget's **textvariable** attribute. Then *x*'s **get** and **set** methods can be used to retrieve text from and put text into the Entry widget.

```
# Display "Hello World!" in Entry
x = StringVar()
entHW = Entry(window, textvariable=x)
entHW.grid()
x.set("Hello")
y = x.get()
x.set(y + " World!")
```

Although text can be typed into ordinary Entry widgets, text only can be placed into ReadOnly Entry widgets via the **set** method. An Entry widget is specified as ReadOnly by inserting **state="readonly"** into its constructor.

```
entOutput = Entry(window,
    state="readonly", textvariable=x)
```

CHAPTER 8 KEY TERMS AND CONCEPTS	EXAMPLES
The best way to put items into a list box is to create a list and a StringVar object (call it x), insert the argument **listvariable=x** into the list box's constructor, and then evaluate x's set method at a tupled version of the list.	```L = ["red", "blue", "tan"]\nx = StringVar()\nlstC = Listbox(window, listvariable=x)\nlstC.grid()\nx.set(tuple(L))```
A **vertical scroll bar** attached to a list box must contain the argument **orient=VERTICAL** in its constructor and its grid method must contain the argument **sticky=NS**. The constructor of the attached list box must contain the argument **yscrollcommand=yscroll. set** and the program must contain the statement **yscroll["command"] = lstName.yview** where yscroll is the name of the vertical scroll bar.	```yscroll = Scrollbar(window,\n orient=VERTICAL)\nyscroll.grid(row=0,column=1,sticky=NS)\nlstNE = Listbox(window,\n yscrollcommand=yscroll.set)\nlstNE.grid(row=0, column=0, sticky=E)\nyscroll["command"] = lstNE.yview```
GUI programs can react to **events** by executing a callback function that is specified either in a constructor or in a bind method.	
The callback function to be triggered when clicking on a button is specified by the **command** attribute in the button's constructor.	```btnGo = Button(window, text="Go",\n command=doSomething)```
The callback function triggered by clicking on an item in a list box is specified with the list box's bind method having "<<ListboxSelect>>" as its first argument and the callback function as its second argument. The item clicked on is returned by the list box's curselection method.	```lstC.bind("<<ListboxSelect>>",\n changeBackgroundColor)\nlstC["bg"] =\n lstC.get(lstC.curselection())```

8.2 The Grid Geometry Manager

The **grid manager** controls the arrangement of widgets into a table-like structure.	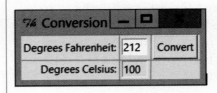
The layout of a widget within a cell is determined by the following attributes specified in the widget's grid method: **row:** row to place the widget in **column:** column to place the widget in	```lstBox.grid(row=1, column=2,\n rowspan=5, padx=(5,0))```

CHAPTER 8 KEY TERMS AND CONCEPTS	EXAMPLES

rowspan: number of rows occupied by the widget
columnspan: number of columns occupied by the widget
padx and **pady:** number of pixels to pad sides of the widget
sticky: used to attach a widget to a particular side of a cell or to enlarge a widget to fill a cell horizontally, vertically, or both.
	```btn.grid(row=2, column=1,```
	``` columnspan=2, pady=5)```
	
	```yscroll.grid(row=1, column=1,```
	``` rowspan=10, sticky=NS)```

8.3 Writing GUI Programs TUI programs can be written as **graphical user interface** programs after importing the **tkinter** module. GUI programs are event driven, visually appealing, and give the user more control than TUI programs.	

CHAPTER 8 PROGRAMMING PROJECTS

1. **Investment** If $10,000 is invested at an annual interest rate r compounded n times per year, then the amount of the investment after five years will be $10,000(1 + \frac{r}{n})^{5 \cdot n}$ Some possible values for r are .02, .025, .03, .035, and .04. Some possible values for n are 1, 2, 4, 12, and 52. Write a program that allows the user to select interest rates and compounding periods from list boxes and calculate the amount after five years. See Fig. 8.51. *Note:* Normally, if there are two list boxes in the window, when you select a value in one, it deselects whatever you selected in the other. However, this behavior will not occur if the argument **exportselection=0** is inserted into each list box's constructor.

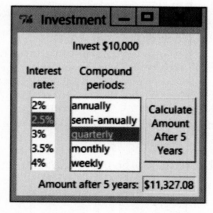

FIGURE 8.51   Possible outcome of Programming Project 1.

2. United Nations Each line of the file **UN.txt** gives the name, continent, population (in millions), and area (in square miles) of a member of the United Nations. Some lines of the file are

```
Canada,North America,34.8,3855000
France,Europe,66.3,211209
New Zealand,Australia/Oceania,4.4,103738
Nigeria,Africa,177.2,356669
Pakistan,Asia,192.2,310403
Peru,South America,30.0,496226
```

This data has been placed into the following dictionary-valued dictionary, and then pickled into the binary file **UNdict.dat**.

```
nations = {"Canada":{"cont":"North America", "popl":34.8, "area":3855000},
           "France":{"cont":"Europe", "popl":66.3}, "area":211209} ...}
```

Write a program using the file **UNdict.dat** that allows the user to display the continent, population, and area of a country by clicking on the name of the country in a list box. See Fig. 8.52.

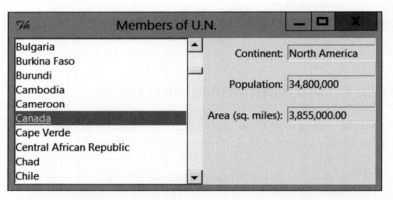

FIGURE 8.52 Possible outcome of Programming Project 2.

3. Pensions A person in the Civil Service Retirement System can retire at age 55 with at least 20 years of service. A simplified variation for the computation of the amount of their pension is as follows:

(a) Calculate the average annual salary for the person's best three years; call it *ave*.

(b) Calculate $\left(\text{number of years} + \dfrac{\text{number of months}}{12}\right)$; call it *yrs*.

(c) Calculate percentage rate: 1.5% for first five years, 1.75% for next five years, and 2% for each additional year. Call it *perRate*.

(d) Take the minimum of *perRate* and 80%; call it *p*.

(e) The amount of the pension is *p*ave*.

Write a program that requests the input shown in Fig. 8.53 and calculates the amount of the pension.

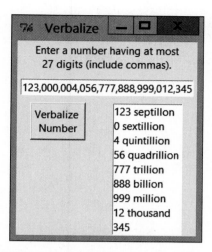

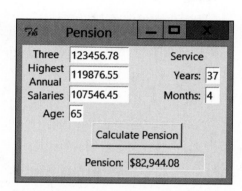

FIGURE 8.53   **Possible outcome of**
Programming Project 3.

FIGURE 8.54   **Possible outcome of**
Programming Project 4.

4. Verbalize a Number   Write a program that allows the user to enter a positive whole number having no more than 27 digits (with commas included) and then verbalizes the number. See Fig. 8.54.

APPENDIX A

ASCII Values

ASCII Value	Character	ASCII Value	Character	ASCII Value	Character
000	(null)	039	'	078	N
001	☐	040	(	079	O
002	☐	041	)	080	P
003	☐	042	*	081	Q
004	☐	043	+	082	R
005	☐	044	,	083	S
006	☐	045	−	084	T
007	☐	046	.	085	U
008	☐	047	/	086	V
009	(tab)	048	0	087	W
010	(line feed)	049	1	088	X
011	☐	050	2	089	Y
012	☐	051	3	090	Z
013	(carriage return)	052	4	091	[
014	☐	053	5	092	\
015	☐	054	6	093	]
016	☐	055	7	094	^
017	☐	056	8	095	_
018	☐	057	9	096	`
019	☐	058	:	097	a
020	☐	059	;	098	b
021	☐	060	<	099	c
022	☐	061	=	100	d
023	☐	062	>	101	e
024	☐	063	?	102	f
025	☐	064	@	103	g
026	☐	065	A	104	h
027	☐	066	B	105	i
028	☐	067	C	106	j
029	☐	068	D	107	k
030	☐	069	E	108	l
031	☐	070	F	109	m
032	(space)	071	G	110	n
033	!	072	H	111	o
034	"	073	I	112	p
035	#	074	J	113	q
036	$	075	K	114	r
037	%	076	L	115	s
038	&	077	M	116	t

ASCII Value	Character	ASCII Value	Character	ASCII Value	Character
117	u	164	¤	211	Ó
118	v	165	¥	212	Ô
119	w	166	¦	213	Õ
120	x	167	§	214	Ö
121	y	168	¨	215	×
122	z	169	©	216	Ø
123	{	170	ª	217	Ù
124			171	«	218	Ú
125	}	172	¬	219	Û
126	,	173	-	220	Ü
127	□	174	®	221	ý
128	□	175	¯	222	þ
129	□	176	°	223	ß
130	,	177	±	224	à
131	ƒ	178	²	225	á
132	”	179	³	226	â
133	…	180	´	227	ã
134	†	181	µ	228	ä
135	‡	182	¶	229	å
136	ˆ	183	·	230	æ
137	‰	184	¸	231	ç
138	Š	185	¹	232	è
139	‹	186	º	233	é
140	Œ	187	»	234	ê
141	□	188	¼	235	ë
142	Ž	189	½	236	ì
143	□	190	¾	237	í
144	□	191	¿	238	î
145	‘	192	À	239	ï
146	’	193	Á	240	ð
147	“	194	Â	241	ñ
148	”	195	Ã	242	ò
149	•	196	Ä	243	ó
150	–	197	Å	244	ô
151	—	198	Æ	245	õ
152	˜	199	Ç	246	ö
153	™	200	È	247	÷
154	š	201	É	248	ø
155	›	202	Ê	249	ù
156	œ	203	Ë	250	ú
157	□	204	Ì	251	û
158	ž	205	Í	252	ü
159	Ÿ	206	Î	253	‡
160	(no-break space)	207	Ï	254	þ
161	¡	208	Đ	255	ÿ
162	¢	209	Ñ		
163	£	210	Ò		

APPENDIX B

Reserved Words

The 33 reserved words (or keywords) in Python are as follows:

and	as	assert	break	class
continue	def	del	elif	else
except	False	finally	for	from
global	if	import	in	is
lambda	None	nonlocal	not	or
pass	raise	return	True	try
while	with	yield		

APPENDIX C

Installing Python and IDLE

Note: IDLE, short for Integrated DeveLopment Environment, is a graphical interface for writing and running Python programs. Integrated development environments (IDEs) integrate the interpreter, text editor, and more to help program more efficiently. IDLE works in Windows, Mac OS, and Linux.

Windows

1. Go to the website http://python.org/downloads. The top part of the display will be similar to the picture in Fig. C.1.
2. To download the installer for the latest version of Python 3, click on the button with a caption of the form "Download Python 3.x.x," and then click on the *Save File* button in the small window that appears. (Python 3.4.2 was the latest version of Python when this book was written.) The name of the installer will be similar to `python-3.4.2.msi`.
3. Run the installer by double-clicking on it and then follow all the prompts. If Windows asks, give the installer permission to continue.
4. With Windows 8, Python can be invoked from the Start screen by typing IDLE. With earlier versions of Windows, IDLE can be invoked from the Start menu.

FIGURE C.1 **Python download screen for Windows.**

Mac OS X

1. Python is usually preinstalled on Mac computers. To see if Python 3 has been installed on your computer, open Finder, select Applications, and check that there is a folder labeled "Python 3.x" in the Applications directory. You likely have Python 2 already, but we will be using Python 3. If you see "Python 3.x," skip to Step 4. Otherwise, download and install Python 3.
2. Visit the website http://python.org/downloads. The top part of the display will be similar to the picture in Fig. C.1, except that "Download the latest version for Windows" will be replaced with

"Download the latest version for Mac OS X." Click on the left yellow button to download the installer for the latest version of Python 3. (Python 3.4.2 was the latest version when this book was written.) The file name will be similar to **python-3.4.2-macosx10.6.pkg**.

3. Run the installation package (with Installer), and follow all the prompts. If OSX asks, give the installer permission to continue.
4. Python 3 and IDLE should appear in the Applications directory, where we looked in Step 1. Run IDLE from there to start programming.

Linux or Unix

Note: The directions below will refer to opening a terminal. The exact process depends on which distribution you are using, so if it is not easy to figure out using your desktop manager, try an Internet search.

Note: If you have a version of Python 3 earlier than 3.3, everything in this book should work except small portions like those involving the *FileNotFoundError*. The installation process below will install the latest stable release your package manager can access, which may be earlier than Python 3.3.

1. Python is usually already installed on computers running the Linux or Unix operating system. To see if you have the right version of Python, open a terminal and enter:

   python3 --version

   If you get something like "command not found," you need to install Python 3. If you get something like "Python 3.x.x," then Python 3 is already installed on your computer, so skip to Step 3.
2. Python 3 should be available by default on most package managers. We will demonstrate using the common **apt-get** package manager. In a terminal, enter:

   sudo apt-get install python3

   You should be asked for your administrator password. Follow any prompts, and Python 3 will be installed as **python3**.
3. To install IDLE for Python 3, use your package manager like we did above. For example, with **apt-get**, enter:

   sudo apt-get install idle3

   and follow any prompts. IDLE can be run from a terminal by entering **idle3** or by navigating to the **/usr/bin** directory and running **idle3** from there. In a terminal, enter:

   idle3

   or

   /usr/bin/idle3

ANSWERS

This section contains the answers to all odd-numbered exercises from Chapters 2 through 7, with the exception of Section 6.3 (Turtle Graphics). In Exercises 6.3, the answers to every other odd-numbered exercise are given. The Student Solutions Manual, which can be downloaded from the companion website for the book, contains the answer to *every* odd-numbered exercise in the book.

CHAPTER 2

EXERCISES 2.1

1. 13.6   **3.** .125   **5.** 2.8

7. 2   **9.** 0   **11.** 4

13. Valid   **15.** Valid   **17.** Not valid

19. 22   **21.** 28   **23.** 9

25. `print((5 * 3)+(3 * 5))`   **27.** `print(200 +(1 * 100))`   **29.** `print(31 * (2 + 28))`

31.

	x	y
`x = -2`	-2	does not exist
`y = x + 5`	-2	3
`x = x**y`	-8	3
`print((x/y)+2)`	-8	3
`y = y % 2 + 0.6`	-8	1.6

33. 75   **35.** 5   **37.** 3.52

39. The third line should read `c = a + b`.

41. The first line should read `interest = 0.05`.

43. 10   **45.** 7   **47.** 3.128

49. −3   **51.** 1   **53.** 6

55. `cost += 5`   **57.** `cost /= 6`   **59.** `sum %= 2`

61.
```
revenue = 98456
costs = 45000
profit = revenue - costs
print(profit)
```

63.
```
price = 19.95
discountPercent = 30
markdown = (discountPercent / 100) * price
price -= markdown
print(round(price, 2))
```

65.
```
balance = 100
balance += 0.05 * balance
balance += 0.05 * balance
balance += 0.05 * balance
print(round(balance, 2))
```

67.
```
balance = 100
balance *= 1.05 ** 10
print(round(balance, 2))
```

69.
```
tonsPerAcre = 18
acres = 30
totalTonsProduced = tonsPerAcre * acres
print(totalTonsProduced)
```

71.
```
averageSpeed = 81.34
elapsedTime = 9 - 5
distance = averageSpeed * elapsedTime
print(distance)
```

73.
```
wattsPerMonth = 750000000
numberOfPeople = 5000000
numberOfDays = 30
wattsPerPersonDaily = wattsPerMonth/ (numberOfPeople * numberOfDays)
print(wattsPerMonth)
```

75.
```
initialMoney = 1000
interestRate = .087
numberOfYears = 2
totalMoney = initialMoney * (1+ (interestRate**numberOfYears))
print(round(totalMoney))
```

77.
```
initialAmt = 2.59e+14
finalAmt = 4.68e+14
percentGrowth = (finalAmt - initialAmt) * 100 / initialAmt
print(round(percentGrowth))
```

EXERCISES 2.2

1. `Python`

3. `Ernie`

5. `o`

7. `o`

9. `Pyt`

11. `Py`

13. `h`

15. `th`

17. `Python`

19. `2`

21. `-1`

23. `7`

25. `python`

27. `Smallelements`

29. `pYtHoN`

31. `8 Ball`

33. `8 BALL`

35. `Pyt`

37. `The Artist`

39. `5`

41. `7`

43. `2`

45. `John's school`

47. `12`
`MUNICIPALITY`
`city`
`6`

49. `flute`

51. `Your age is 21.`

53. `A ROSE IS A ROSE IS A ROSE`

55. `WALLAWALLAWALLA`

57. `goodbye` **59.** Mmmmmmm. **61.** `a    b` **63.** `76 trombones`

65. `8.0` **67.** `8` **69.** `The Great 9` **71.** `s[:-1]`

73. `-8` **75.** True **77.** True

79. `234-5678` should be surrounded with quotation marks.

81. *for* is a reserved word and cannot be used as a variable name.

83. The string should be replaced with `"Say it ain't so."`

85. `UPPER` should be changed to `upper`.

87. A string cannot be concatenated with a number. The second line should be written `print("Age: " + str(age))` or `print("Age:", age)`.

89. *find* accepts a character as an argument, not a number.

91. The *str* object does not support item assignment.

93.
```
## Display an inventor's name and year of birth.
firstName = "Thomas"
middleName = "Alva"
lastName = "Edison"
yearOfBirth = 1847
print("The year of birth of "+firstName, middleName, lastName+" is "+yearOfBirth)
```

95.
```
## Display a copyright statement.
publisher = "Pearson"
print("(c)", publisher)
```

97.
```
## Calculate the distance from a storm.
prompt = "Enter number of seconds between lightning and thunder: "
numberOfSeconds = float(input(prompt))
distance = numberOfSeconds / 5
distance = round(distance, 2)
print("Distance from storm:", distance, "miles.")
```

99.
```
## Calculate weight loss during a triathlon.
cycling = float(input("Enter number of hours cycling: "))
running = float(input("Enter number of hours running: "))
swimming = float(input("Enter number of hours swimming: "))
pounds = (200 * cycling + 475 * running + 275 * swimming) / 3500
pounds = round(pounds, 1)
print("Weight loss:", pounds, "pounds")
```

101.
```
## Calculate percentage of games won by a baseball team.
name = input("Enter name of team: ")
gamesWon = int(input("Enter number of games won: "))
gamesLost = int(input("Enter number of games lost: "))
percentageWon = round(100 * (gamesWon) / (gamesWon + gamesLost), 1)
print(name, "won", str(percentageWon) + '%', "of their games.")
```

103.
```
## Determine the speed of a skidding car.
distance = float(input("Enter distance skidded (in feet): "))
speed = (24 * distance) ** .5
```

```
speed = round(speed, 2)
print("Estimated speed:", speed, "miles per hour")
```

105. ```
Convert speed from kph to mph.
speedInKPH = float(input("Enter speed in KPH: "))
speedInMPH = speedInKPH * .6214
print("Speed in MPH:", round(speedInMPH, 2))
```

107. ```
## Calculate equivalent CD interest rate for municipal bond rate.
taxBracket = float(input("Enter tax bracket (as decimal): "))
bondRate = float(input("Enter municipal bond interest rate (as %): "))
equivCDrate = bondRate / (1 - taxBracket)
print("Equivalent CD interest rate:", str(round(equivCDrate, 3)) + '%')
```

109. ```
Analyze a number.
number = input("Enter number: ")   # Note: number is a string
decimalPoint = number.find('.')
print(decimalPoint, "digits to left of decimal point")
print(len(number) - decimalPoint - 1, "digits to right of decimal point")
```

111. ```
## Convert a number of months to years and months.
numberOfMonths = int(input("Enter number of months: "))
years = numberOfMonths // 12
months = numberOfMonths % 12
print(numberOfMonths, "months is", years, "years and", months, "months.")
```

EXERCISES 2.3

1. merry christmas!

3. Portion: 90%

5. 1 x 2 x 3

7. father-in-law

9. What is your name? John

11. Python

13. Hello
    World!

15. One   Two
       Three Four

17.
```
NUMBER   SQUARE   CUBE
2        4        8
3        9        27
```

19. Hello   World!
    Hello   World!

21. ```
01234567890
 A | B | C
```

23. ```
01234567890123456
   one   two   three
```

25. ```
0123456789
  12.30%
 123.0%
1,230.00%
```

27. $1,234.6

29. 1.2

31.
```
Team   Fifa points   % fans of World Pop.
Germany   1,725   34.12%
Argentina   1,538   25.85%
Columbia   1,450   25.52%
```

33. Be yourself - everyone else is taken.

35. you are the creator of your own destiny.

37. The matrix of 3 and 4 has 12 elements.

39. The square root of 2 is about 1.4142.

41. In a randomly selected group of 23 people, the probability is 0.51 that 2 people have the same birthday.
```

43. You miss 100% of the shots you never take. - Wayne Gretsky

45. 22.28% of the UN nations are in Europe.

47. abracadabra

49. Be kind whenever possible. It is always possible. - Dalai Lama

51. Yes

53.
```
## Calculate a server's tip.
bill = float(input("Enter amount of bill: "))
percentage = float(input("Enter percentage tip: "))
tip = (bill * percentage) / 100
print("Tip: ${0:.2f}".format(tip))
```

55.
```
## Calculate a new salary.
beginningSalary = float(input("Enter beginning salary: "))
raisedSalary = 1.1 * beginningSalary
cutSalary = .9 * raisedSalary
percentChange = (cutSalary - beginningSalary) / beginningSalary
print("New salary: ${0:,.2f}".format(cutSalary))
print("Change: {0:.2%}".format(percentChange))
```

57.
```
## Calculate a future value.
p = float(input("Enter principal: "))
r = float(input("Enter interest rate (as %): "))
n = int(input("Enter number of years: "))
futureValue = p * (1 + (r / 100)) ** n
print("Future value: ${0:,.2f}".format(futureValue))
```

EXERCISES 2.4

1. Algeria Denmark

3. Canada Bosnia

5. Denmark Denmark

7. 12

9. Denmark Denmark

11. japan

13. Denmark

15. Germany

17. ['Algeria', 'Germany', 'England']

19. ['Bosnia', 'Cameroon', 'Canada']

21. ['japan', 'India', 'Algeria', 'Germany', 'England', 'Argentina', 'Portugal', 'China', 'Australia', 'Austria']

23. ['Canada', 'Denmark', 'Nigeria']

25. []   27. Germany   29. Germany

31. 10   33. 0   35. 19   37. ['Nigeria', 'Algeria', 'Cuba']

39. ['Algeria', 'Mongolia', ['New Zealand', 'Norway']]

41. ['japan', 'Russia', 'Algeria']

43. ['Nigeria']

45. Belgium-Bhutan-Bosnia-Cameroon-Canada

47. Cameroon*Canada*Denmark

49. 8   **51.** 100   **53.** 0

55. `Largest Number: 8`   **57.** `Total: 16`

59. `This sentence contains five words.`
`This sentence contains six different words.`

61. `Babbage, Charles`   **63.** `Middle Name: van`

65. `When in the course of human events`   **67.** `editor-in-chief`

69. `e**pluribus**unum`

71. `['New York', 'NY', 'Empire State', 'Albany']`

73. `['France', 'England', 'Spain']`

75. `programmer`   **77.** `Follow your own star.`

79. `987-654-3219`   **81.** `[3, 9, 6]`

83. `each`   **85.** `['soprano', 'tenor', 'alto', 'bass']`

87. `['gold', 'silver', 'bronze']`   **89.** `murmur`

91. `('Happy', 'Sneezy', 'Bashful')`   **93.** `1`

95. Index out of range. The list does not have an item of index 3.

97. The join method only can be applied to a list consisting entirely of strings.

99. The second line is not valid. Items in a tuple cannot be reassigned values directly.

101.
```
## Count the number of words in a sentence.
sentence = input("Enter a sentence: ")
L = sentence.split(" ")
print("Number of words:", len(L))
```

103.
```
## Display a name.
name = input("Enter a 2-part name: ")
L = name.split()
print("{0:s}, {1:s}".format(L[1], L[0]))
```

CHAPTER 3

EXERCISES 3.1

1. `*****`

3. `The upper case of letter g is G.`

5. `Minimum: 3`
`Maximum: 17`

7. `D is 4 positions before H`
`alphabetically.`

9. `True`   **11.** `True`   **13.** `False`   **15.** `True`   **17.** `False`   **19.** `False`

21. `True`   **23.** `False`   **25.** `False`   **27.** `False`   **29.** `False`   **31.** `False`

33. `False`   **35.** `True`   **37.** `False`   **39.** `False`   **41.** `True`   **43.** `False`

45. Equivalent   **47.** Not equivalent   **49.** Equivalent

51. Equivalent   **53.** Equivalent   **55.** `a <= b`

57. (a >= b) or (c == d)

59. a > b

61. ans in ['Y', 'y', "Yes", "yes"]

63. 2010 <= year <= 2013

65. 3 <= n < 9

67. -20 < n <= 10

69. True   **71.** True   **73.** True   **75.** True

77. True   **79.** False   **81.** False   **83.** False

85. print("He said " + chr(34) + "How ya doin?" + chr(34) + " to me.")

EXERCISES 3.2

1. Less than ten.

3. True

5. Remember, tomorrow is New Year's day.

7. 2 2 7

9. To be, or not to be.

11. Hi

13. A nonempty string is true.

15. Syntax error and logic error. Second line should be `if n%2==0`. n should not be a string. Third line should be `print("The square is", n ** 2)`.

17. Syntax error. Second line is full of errors. It should be as follows:

```
if (major == "Business") or (major == "Computer Science"):
```

19. a = 5

21.
```
if (j == 7):
    b = 1
else:
    b = 2
```

23.
```
answer = input("Is the Indian Ocean bigger than the Pacific Ocean?")
if answer[0].upper() == 'Y':
    print("Correct")
else:
    print("Wrong")
```

25.
```
## Calculate a tip.
bill = float(input("Enter amount of bill: "))
tip = bill * 0.15
if (tip < 2):
    tip = 2
print("Tip is ${0:,.2f}".format(tip))
```

27.
```
## Calculate the cost of widgets.
num = int(input("Enter number of widgets: "))
if num < 100:
    cost = num * 0.25
else:
    cost = num * 0.20
print("Cost is ${0:,.2f}".format(cost))
```

29.
```
## A quiz
response = input("Who was the first Ronald McDonald? ")
if response == "Willard Scott":
    print("You are correct.")
```

```
else:
    print("Nice try.")
```

31.
```
## Calculate an average after dropping the lowest score.
scores = []
scores.append(eval(input("Enter first score: ")))
scores.append(eval(input("Enter second score: ")))
scores.append(eval(input("Enter third score: ")))
scores.remove(min(scores))
average = sum(scores) / 2
print("Average of the two highest scores is {0:.2f}".format(average))
```

33.
```
## Make change for a purchase of apples.
weight = float(input("Enter weight in pounds: "))
payment = float(input("Enter payment in dollars: "))
cost = (2.5 * weight)
if payment >= cost:
    change = payment - cost
    print("Your change is ${0:,.2f}.".format(change))
else:
    amountOwed = cost - payment
    print("You owe ${0:,.2f} more.".format(amountOwed))
```

35.
```
## Validate input.
letter = input("Enter a single uppercase letter: ")
if (len(letter) != 1) or (letter != letter.upper()):
    print("You did not comply with the request.")
```

37.
```
## Convert military time to regular time.
militaryTime = input("Enter a military time (0000 to 2359): ")
hours = int(militaryTime[0:2])
minutes = int(militaryTime[2:4])
if hours >= 12:
    cycle = "pm"
    hours %= 12
else:
    cycle = "am"
    if hours == 0:
        hours = 12
print("The regular time is {0}:{1} {2}.".format(hours, minutes, cycle))
```

39.
```
## Use APYs to compare interest rates offered by two banks.
r1 = float(input("Enter annual rate of interest for Bank 1: "))
m1 = float(input("Enter number of compounding periods for Bank 1: "))
r2 = float(input("Enter annual rate of interest for Bank 2: "))
m2 = float(input("Enter number of compounding periods for Bank 2: "))
ipp1 = r1 / (100 * m1)    # interest rate per period
ipp2 = r2 / (100 * m2)
apy1 = ((1 + ipp1) ** m1) - 1
apy2 = ((1 + ipp2) ** m2) - 1
print("APY for Bank 1 is {0:,.3%}".format(apy1))
print("APY for Bank 2 is {0:,.3%}".format(apy2))
if (apy1 == apy2):
    print("Bank 1 and Bank 2 are equally good.")
```

```
    else:
        if(apy1 > apy2):
            betterBank = 1
        else:
            betterBank = 2
        print("Bank", betterBank, "is the better bank.")
```

41.
```
## Bestow graduation honors.
# Request grade point average.
gpa = eval(input("Enter your grade point average (2 through 4): "))
# Validate that GPA is between 2 and 4
if not (2 <= gpa <=4):
    print("Invalid grade point average. GPA must be between 2 and 4.")
else:
    # Determine if honors are warranted and display conclusion.
    if gpa >= 3.9:
        honors = " summa cum laude."
    elif gpa >= 3.6:
        honors = " magna cum laude."
    elif gpa >= 3.3:
        honors = " cum laude."
    else:
        honors = "."
    print("You graduated" + honors)
```

43.
```
## Calculate a person's state income tax.
income = float(input("Enter your taxable income: "))
if income <= 20000:
    tax =.02 * income
else:
    if income <= 50000:
        tax = 400 + .025 * (income - 20000)
    else:
        tax = 1150 + .035 * (income - 50000)
print("Your tax is ${0:,.0f}.".format(tax))
```

EXERCISES 3.3

1. 20   3. 2   5. 20   7.
```
                                                 b
                                                 cc
                                                 ddd
```

9. Infinite loop

11. **while** condition should be **i >0**

13.
```
sum = int(input("Enter a number: "))
for i in range(2):
    sum = sum + int (input("Enter a number: "))
    print(sum)
```

15.
```
## Display a Celsius-to-Fahrenheit conversion table.
print("Celsius\t\tFahrenheit")
for celsius in range(10, 31, 5):
```

```
                fahrenheit = (celsius * (9 / 5)) + 32
                print("{0}\t\t{1:.0f}".format(celsius, fahrenheit))
```

17. ## Find the GCD of two numbers.
```
    m = int(input("Enter value of M: "))
    n = int(input("Enter value of N: "))
    while n != 0:
        t = n
        n = m % n     # remainder after m is divided by n
        m = t
    print("Greatest common divisor:", m)
```

19. ## Find special age.
```
    age = 1
    while (1980 + age) != (age * age):
        age += 1
    print("Person will be {0} \nin the year {1}.".format(age, age * age))
```

21. ## Radioactive decay
```
    mass = 100     # weight in grams
    year = 0
    while(mass > 1):
        mass /= 2
        year += 28
    print("The decay time is")
    print(year, "years.")
```

23. ## Determine when a car loan will be half paid off.
```
    principal = 15000
    balance = principal    # initial balance
    monthlyPayment = 290
    monthlyFactor = 1.005   # multiplier due to interest
    month = 0
    while(balance >= principal / 2):
        balance =  (monthlyFactor * balance) - monthlyPayment
        month += 1
    print("Loan will be half paid \noff after", month, "months.")
```

25. ## Annuity with withdrawals
```
    balance = 10000
    interestMultiplier = 1.003    # multiplier due to interest
    monthlyWithdrawal = 600
    month = 0
    while balance > 600:
        balance = (interestMultiplier * balance) - monthlyWithdrawal
        month += 1
    print("Balance will be ${0:,.2f} \nafter {1} months.".
            format(balance, month))
```

27. ## Determine class size for which the probability is greater
    ## than 50% that someone has the same birthday as you.
```
    num  = 1
    while (364 / 365) ** num > 0.5:
```

```
    num += 1
print("With", num, "students, the probability")
print("is greater than 50% that someone")
print("has the same birthday as you.")
```

29.
```
## Determine when India's population will surpass China's population.
chinaPop = 1.37
indiaPop = 1.26
year = 2014
while indiaPop < chinaPop:
    year += 1
    chinaPop *= 1.0051
    indiaPop *= 1.0135
print("India's population will exceed China's")
print("population in the year", str(year) + '.')
```

31.
```
## Maintain a savings account.
print("Options:")
print("1. Make a Deposit")
print("2. Make a Withdrawal")
print("3. Obtain Balance")
print("4. Quit")
balance = 1000
while True:
    num = int(input("Make a selection from the options menu: "))
    if num == 1:
        deposit = float(input("Enter amount of deposit: "))
        balance += deposit
        print("Deposit Processed.")
    elif num == 2:
        withdrawal = float(input("Enter amount of withdrawal: "))
        while (withdrawal > balance):
            print("Denied. Maximum withdrawal is ${0:,.2f}"
                    .format(balance))
            withdrawal = float(input("Enter amount of withdrawal: "))
        balance -= withdrawal
        print("Withdrawal Processed.")
    elif num == 3:
        print("Balance: ${0:,.2f}".format(balance))
    elif num == 4:
        break
    else:
        print("You did not enter a proper number.")
```

EXERCISES 3.4

1. 1,2,3,4,5,6,7,8,9

3. 10, 9, 8, 7, 6, 5, 4, 3, 2

5.

7. -1

9. range(4, 20, 5)

11. range(-21, -17)

13. range(20, 13, -3)

15. range(5, -1, -1)

17. Pass #1
Pass #2
Pass #3
Pass #4

19. 5
6
7

21. ¢¢¢¢¢¢¢¢¢

23. 2
4
6
8
Who do we appreciate?

25. 3   **27.** 15   **29.** n   **31.** 3 20

33. The shortest word has length 5

35. three   **37.** 18   **39.** North Carolina
North Dakota

41. The range generates no elements because the step argument's direction is opposite the direction from start to stop.

43. The print function call is missing parentheses.

45. The range constructor should read `range(0, 20)` or `range(20)` because `range(20,0)` will not generate any values. Also, the print statement must be indented twice so it belongs to the *if* block.

47.
```
for num in range(1, 10, 2):
    print(num)
```

49.
```
lakes = ["Erie", "Huron", "Michigan", "Ontario", "Superior"]
print(", ".join(lakes))
```

51.
```
## Determine amount of radioactive material remaining after five years.
amount = 10
for i in range(5):
    amount *= .88
print("The amount of cobalt-60 remaining")
print("after five years is {0:.2f} grams.".format(amount))
```

53.
```
## Count the number of vowels in a phrase.
total = 0
phrase = input("Enter a phrase: ")
phrase.lower()
for ch in phrase:
    if ch in "aeiou":
        total += 1
print("The phrase contains", total, "vowels.")
```

55.
```
## Total the fractions 1/n for n = 1 through 100.
sum = 0
for i in range(1, 101):
    sum += 1 / i
print("The sum of 1 + 1/2 + 1/3 + . . .  + 1/100")
print("is {0:.5f} to five decimal places.".format(sum))
```

57.
```python
## Determine if the letters of a word are in alphabetical order.
word = input("Enter a word: ")
firstLetter = ""
secondLetter = ""
flag = True
for i in range(0, len(word) - 1):
    firstLetter = word[i]
    secondLetter = word[i + 1]
    if firstLetter > secondLetter:
        flag = False
        break
if flag:
    print("Letters are in alphabetical order.")
else:
    print("Letters are not in alphabetical order.")
```

59.
```python
## Calculate a person's lifetime earnings.
name = input("Enter name: ")
age = int(input("Enter age: "))
salary = float(input("Enter starting salary: "))
earnings = 0
for i in range(age, 65):
    earnings += salary
    salary += .05 * salary
print("{0} will earn about ${1:,.0f}.".format(name, earnings))
```

61.
```python
## Display the balances on a car loan.
print("          AMOUNT OWED AT")
print("YEAR     ", "END OF YEAR")
balance = 15000
year = 2012
for i in range(1, 49):
    balance = (1.005 * balance) - 290
    if i % 12 == 0:
        year += 1
        print(year, "     ${0:,.2f}".format(balance))
print(year + 1, "     $0.00")
```

63.
```python
## Calculate the average of the best two of three grades.
grades = []
for i in range(3):
    grade = int(input("Enter a grade: "))
    grades.append(grade)
grades.sort()
average = (grades[1] + grades[2]) / 2
print("Average: {0:n}".format(average))
```

65.
```python
## Display the effects of supply and demand.
print("YEAR   QUANTITY    PRICE")
quantity = 80
price = 20 - (.1 * quantity)
print("{0:d}      {1:.2f}      ${2:.2f}".format(2014, quantity, price))
```

```
    for i in range(4):
        quantity = (5 * price) - 10
        price = 20 - (.1 * quantity)
        print("{0:d}     {1:.2f}     ${2:.2f}".format(i + 2015, quantity, price))
```

67.
```
## Compare two salary options.
# Calculate amount earned in ten years with Option 1.
salary = 20000
option1 = 0
for i in range(10):
    option1 += salary
    salary += 1000
print("Option 1 earns ${0:,d}.".format(option1))
# Calculate amount earned in ten years with Option 2.
salary = 10000
option2 = 0
for i in range(20):
    option2 += salary
    salary += 250
print("Option 2 earns ${0:,d}.".format(option2))
```

69.
```
## Determine the number of Super Bowl wins for the Pittsburg Steelers.
teams = open("SBWinners.txt", 'r')
numberOfWins = 0
for team in teams:
    if team.rstrip() == "Steelers":
        numberOfWins += 1
print("The Steelers won")
print(numberOfWins, "Super Bowl games.")
```

71.
```
## Analyze grades on a final exam.
infile = open("Final.txt", 'r')
grades = [line.rstrip() for line in infile]
infile.close()
for i in range(len(grades)):
    grades[i] = int(grades[i])
average = sum(grades) / len(grades)
num = 0     # number of grades above average
for grade in grades:
    if grade > average:
        num += 1
print("Number of grades:", len(grades))
print("Average grade:", average)
print("Percentage of grades above average: {0:.2f}%"
                .format(100 * num / len(grades)))
```

73.
```
## Count the number of different vowels in a word.
word = input("Enter a word: ")
word = word.upper()
vowels = "AEIOU"
vowelsFound = []
numVowels = 0
```

```
    for letter in word:
        if (letter in vowels) and (letter not in vowelsFound):
            numVowels += 1
            vowelsFound.append(letter)
print("Number of vowels:", numVowels)
```

75.
```
## Calculate probabilities that at least two
## people in a group have the same birthday.
print("{0:17} {1}".format("NUMBER OF People", "PROBABILITY"))
# r = size of group
for r in range(21, 26):
    product = 1
    for t in range(1, r):
        product *= ((365 - t) / 365)
    print("{0:<17} {1:.3f}".format(r, 1 - product))
```

77.
```
## Display sentence with Boston accent.
sentence = input("Enter a sentence: ")
newSentence = ""
for ch in sentence:
    if ch.upper() != 'R':
        newSentence += ch
print(newSentence)
```

79.
```
## Identify ICC winner by number.
infile = open("ICCWinners.txt", 'r')
for i in range(5):
    infile.readline()
print("The 6th winner was")
print(infile.readline().rstrip() + '.')
```

81.
```
## Calculate number of odometer readings containing the digit 1.
total = 0
for n in range(1000000):
    if '1' in str(n):
        total += 1
print("{0:,d} numbers on the odometer".format(total))
print("contain the digit 1.")
```

83.
```
## Display vegetable and flower.
mixed = ["Broccoli V", "Lily F", "Cucumber V", "Rose F", "Lotus F",
         "Cabbage V", "Onion V", "Anemone F", "Aster F"]
vegetable = []
fruit = []
for mixed in mixed:
    if mixed[-1] == 'V':
        vegetable.append(mixed[:-2])
    else:
        fruit.append(mixed[:-2])
namesV = ", ".join(vegetable))
namesF = ", ".join(fruit)
print("Vegetable:", namesV)
print("Fruit:", namesF)
```

CHAPTER 4

1. H
   w

3. Enter the time in which you want to double your money: 2
   To double your money in 2.0 years, get an interest rate of about 36.00 %.

5. Your income tax is $499.00

7. Why do clocks run clockwise?

   Because they were invented in the northern
   hemisphere where sundials go clockwise.

9. Message 1: 2015-07-14T16:25:26.169705
   Message 2: 2015-07-14T16:25:26.180707

11. Kailash Satyarthi won the Nobel Peace prize.
    Patrick Modiano won the Nobel Literature prize.

13. 7   15. Fredrick
    5

17. Total cost: $260.00   19. 5

21. When in the course of human events

23. Enter grade on midterm exam: 85
    Enter grade on final exam: 94
    Enter type of student (Pass/Fail) or (Letter Grade): Letter Grade
    Semester grade: A

    Enter grade on midterm exam: 50
    Enter grade on final exam: 62
    Enter type of student (Pass/Fail) or (Letter Grade): Pass/Fail
    Semester grade: Fail

    Enter grade on midterm exam: 56
    Enter grade on final exam: 67
    Enter type of student (Pass/Fail) or (Letter Grade): Letter Grade
    Semester grade: D

25. ```
    def maximum(list1):
        largestNumber = list1[0]
        for number in list1:
            if number > largestNumber:
                largestNumber = number
        return largestNumber
    ```

27. ```
    def main():
        word = input("Enter a word: ")
        if isQwerty(word):
            print(word, "is a Qwerty word.")
        else:
            print(word, "is not a Qwerty word.")
    ```

```python
def isQwerty(word):
    word = word.upper()
    for ch in word:
        if ch not in "QWERTYUIOP":
            return False
    return True

main()
```

29.
```python
def main():
    ## Compare salary options
    opt1 = option1()
    opt2 = option2()
    print("Option 1 = ${0:,.2f}.".format(opt1))
    print("Option 2 = ${0:,.2f}.".format(opt2))
    if opt1 > opt2:
        print("Option 1 pays better.")
    elif opt1 == opt2:
        print("Options pay the same.")
    else:
        print("Option 2 is better.")

def option1():
    ## Compute the total salary for 10 days,
    ## with a flat salary of $100/day.
    sum = 0
    for i in range(10):
        sum += 100
    return sum

def option2():
    ## Compute the total salary for 10 days,
    ## starting at $1 and doubling each day.
    sum = 0
    daySalary = 1
    for i in range(10):
        sum += daySalary
        daySalary *= 2
    return sum

main()
```

31.
```python
# Named constants.
WAGE_BASE = 117000 # There is no social security benefits
                   # tax on income above this level.
SOCIAL_SECURITY_TAX_RATE = 0.062       # 6.2%
MEDICARE_TAX_RATE = 0.0145             # 1.45%
ADDITIONAL_MEDICARE_TAX_RATE = .009    # 0.9%

def main():
    ## Calculate FICA tax for a single employee.
    ytdEarnings, curEarnings, totalEarnings = obtainEarnings()
    socialSecurityBenTax = calculateBenTax(ytdEarnings, curEarnings,
                                           totalEarnings)
```

```
        calculateFICAtax(ytdEarnings, curEarnings, totalEarnings,
                         socialSecurityBenTax)

def obtainEarnings():
    str1 = "Enter total earnings for this year prior to current pay period: "
    ytdEarnings = eval(input(str1))       # year-to-date earnings
    curEarnings = eval(input("Enter earnings for the current pay period: "))
    totalEarnings = ytdEarnings + curEarnings
    return(ytdEarnings, curEarnings, totalEarnings)

def calculateBenTax(ytdEarnings, curEarnings, totalEarnings):
    ## Calculate the Social Security Benefits tax.
    socialSecurityBenTax = 0
    if totalEarnings <= WAGE_BASE:
        socialSecurityBenTax = SOCIAL_SECURITY_TAX_RATE * curEarnings
    elif ytdEarnings < WAGE_BASE:
        socialSecurityBenTax = SOCIAL_SECURITY_TAX_RATE * (WAGE_BASE -
                                        ytdEarnings)
    return socialSecurityBenTax

def calculateFICAtax(ytdEarnings, curEarnings, totalEarnings,
                     socialSecurityBenTax):
    ## Calculate and display the FICA tax.
    medicareTax = MEDICARE_TAX_RATE * curEarnings
    if ytdEarnings >= 200000:
        medicareTax += ADDITIONAL_MEDICARE_TAX_RATE * curEarnings
    elif totalEarnings > 200000:
        medicareTax += ADDITIONAL_MEDICARE_TAX_RATE * (totalEarnings - 200000)
    ficaTax = socialSecurityBenTax + medicareTax
    print("FICA tax for the current pay period: ${0:,.2f}".format(ficaTax))

main()
```

33.
```
colors = []

def main():
    ## Display colors beginning with a specified letter.
    letter = requestLetter()
    fillListWithColors(letter)
    displayColors()

def requestLetter():
    letter = input("Enter a letter: ")
    return letter.upper()

def fillListWithColors(letter):
    global colors
    for color in open("Colors.txt", 'r'):
        if color.startswith(letter):
            colors.append(color.rstrip())

def displayColors():
    for color in colors:
        print(color)

main()
```

EXERCISES 4.2

1. ```
24 blackbirds baked in a pie.
```

3. ```
Cost: $250.00
Shipping cost: $15.00
Total cost: $265.00
```

5. ```
Enter first grade: 88
Enter second grade: 99
Enter third grade: 92
[88, 92, 99]
```

7. ```
['Banana', 'apple', 'pear']
['apple', 'Banana', 'pear']
```

9. ```
nudge nudge
nudge nudge nudge nudge
```

11. ```
spam        and       eggs
spam and eggs
```

13. ```
George Washington
John Adams
```

15. ```
Amadeus
Joseph
Sebastian
Vaughan
```

17. ```
['M', 'S', 'a', 'l', 'o', 't']
['a', 'l', 'M', 'o', 'S', 't']
```

19. ```
VB  Ruby  Python  PHP  Java  C++  C
```

21. ```
Python Java Ruby C++ PHP VB C
```

23. ```
-3  -2  4  5  6
```

25. ```
[10, 7, 6, 4, 5, 3]
```

27. ```
['BRRR', 'TWO']
```

29. ```
['c', 'a']
```

31. ```
names = ["George Boole", "Charles Babbage", "Grace Hopper"]
lastNames = [name.split()[-1] for name in names]
```

33. A list consisting of the 20 countries in uppercase characters.

35. A list consisting of the 20 countries ordered by the lengths of the names in ascending order.

37. Valid   39. Valid   41. Not valid

43. Valid   45. Not valid   47. `almost`

49. ```
def main():
    ## Calculate the original cost of mailing a letter.
    weight = float(input("Enter the number of ounces: "))
    print("Cost: ${0:0,.2f}".format(cost(weight)))
```
```

```python
    def cost(weight):
        return 0.05 + 0.1 * ceil(weight - 1)

    def ceil(x):
        if int(x) != x:
            return int(x + 1)
        else:
            return x

    main()
```

51.
```python
    def main():
        ## Determine whether two words are anagrams.
        string1 = input("Enter the first word or phrase: ")
        string2 = input("Enter the second word or phrase: ")
        if areAnagrams(string1, string2):
            print("Are anagrams.")
        else:
            print("Are not anagrams.")

    def areAnagrams(string1, string2):
        firstString = string1.lower()
        secondString = string2.lower()
        # In the next two lines, the if clauses remove all
        # punctuation and spaces.
        letters1 = [ch for ch in firstString if 'a' <= ch <= 'z']
        letters2 = [ch for ch in secondString if 'a' <= ch <= 'z']
        letters1.sort()
        letters2.sort()
        return (letters1 == letters2)

    main()
```

53.
```python
    def main():
        ## Sort three names.
        programming_language=[("Guido van Rossum", "Python"), ("Dennis
    Ritchie", "C"), ("Bjarne Stroustrup", "C++")]
        programming_language.sort(key=lambda pl: pl[0]) # sort by first name
        programming_language.sort(key=lambda pl: pl[1]) # sort by last name
        for pl in programming_language:
            print(pl[1] + ',', pl[0])

    main()
```

55.
```python
    def main():
        ## Sort planets by surface area.
        Planets = [("Mercury", 75, 1), ("Venus", 460, 2), ("Mars", 140, 4),
                ("Earth",  510, 3), ("Jupiter", 62000, 5), ("Neptune", 7640, 8),
                ("Saturn", 42700, 6), ("Uranus", 8100, 7)]
        Planets.sort(key=lambda planet: planet[2], reverse=True)
        print("Sorted by position from Sun in descending order:")
        for planet in Planets:
            print(planet[0])

    main()
```

57.
```python
def main():
    ## Sort by numbers of vowels in planet name.
    Planets = [("Mercury", 75, 1), ("Venus", 460, 2), ("Mars", 140, 4),
            ("Earth",  510, 3), ("Jupiter", 62000, 5), ("Neptune", 7640, 8),
            ("Saturn", 42700, 6), ("Uranus", 8100, 7)]
    Planets.sort(key=numberOfVowels)
    print("Sort by numbers of vowels in planet name:")
    for planet in Planets:
        print(planet[0])

def numberOfVowels(planet)
    vowels = ('a', 'e', 'i', 'o', 'u',)
    total = 0
    for vowel in vowels:
        total += planet[0].lower().count(vowel)
        return total

main()
```

59.
```python
def main():
    ## Sort numbers by largest prime factor.
    numbers = [865, 1169, 1208, 1243, 290]
    numbers.sort(key=largestPrimeFactor)
    print("Sorted by largest prime factor:")
    print(numbers)

def largestPrimeFactor(num):
    n = num
    f = 2
    max = 1
    while n > 1:
        if n % f == 0:
            n = int(n / f)
            if f > max:
                max = f
        else:
            f += 1
    return max

main()
```

61.
```python
def main():
    ## Sort numbers by the sum of their odd digits.
    numbers = [865, 1169, 1208, 1243, 290]
    numbers.sort(key=sumOfOddDigits, reverse=True)
    print("Sorted by sum of odd digits:")
    print(numbers)

def sumOfOddDigits(num):
    listNums = list(str(num))
    total = 0
    for i in range(len(listNums)):
        if int(listNums[i]) % 2 == 1:
            total += int(listNums[i])
    return total

main()
```

63.
```
def main():
    infile = open("countries.txt", 'r')
    listCountries = [country.rstrip() for country in infile]
    infile.close()
    listCountries.sort(key=sortByLengthOfFirstName, reverse=True)
    for i in range(6):
        print(listCountries[i])

def sortByLengthOfFirstName(country):
    return len(country)

main()
```

65.
```
def main():
    infile = open("countries.txt", 'r')
    listCountries = [country.rstrip() for country in infile]
    infile.close()
    listCountries.sort(key=numberOfVowels, reverse=True)
    for i in range(6):
        print(listCountries[i])

def numberOfVowels(country):
    vowels = ('a', 'e', 'i', 'o', 'u')
    total = 0
    for vowel in vowels:
        total += country.lower().count(vowel)
    return total

main()
```

67.
```
def main():
    ## Calculate new balance and minimum payment for a credit card.
    (oldBalance, charges, credits) = inputData()
    (newBalance, minimumPayment) = calculateNewValues(oldBalance,
                                    charges, credits)
    displayNewData(newBalance, minimumPayment)

def inputData():
    oldBalance = float(input("Enter old balance: "))
    charges = float(input("Enter charges for month: "))
    credits = float(input("Enter credits: "))
    return (oldBalance, charges, credits)

def calculateNewValues(oldBalance, charges, credits):
    newBalance =  (1.015) * oldBalance + charges - credits
    if newBalance <= 20:
        minimumPayment = newBalance
    else:
        minimumPayment = 20 + 0.1 * (newBalance - 20)
    return (newBalance, minimumPayment)

def displayNewData(newBalance, minimumPayment):
    print("New balance: ${0:0,.2f}".format(newBalance))
    print("Minimum payment: ${0:0,.2f}".format(minimumPayment))

main()
```

```
69. def main():
        ## Determine a person's earnings for a week.
        (wage, hours) = getWageAndHours()
        payForWeek = pay(wage, hours)
        displayEarnings(payForWeek)

    def getWageAndHours():
        hoursworked = eval(input("Enter hours worked: "))
        hourlyWage = eval(input("Enter hourly pay: "))
        return(hourlyWage, hoursworked)

    def pay(wage, hours):
        ## Calculate weekly pay with time-and-a-half for overtime.
        if hours <= 40:
            amount = wage * hours
        else:
            amount = (wage * 40) + ((1.5) * wage * (hours - 40))
        return amount

    def displayEarnings(payForWeek):
        print("Week's pay: ${0:,.2f}".format(payForWeek))

    main()
```

CHAPTER 5

EXERCISES 5.1

1. `Aloha`

3. `Hello`
   `Aloha`

5. 6

7. `[4, 1, 0, 1, 4]`

9. `Believe in yourself.`

11. `['a', 'c', 't']`

13. `ABC.txt` should be open for reading, not for writing.

15. `close()` should be called on the file object, *infile*, not on `ABC.txt`. That is, the last line should read `infile.close().`

17. The argument for write() must be a string, not an integer.

19. The code should close the file after writing it. Otherwise, the value of *list1* will still be in the buffer and not on the disk drive when the file is opened for reading.

21. The file cannot be read since it has been closed.

23. The file `ABC.txt` is created. Nothing is displayed on the monitor.

25.
```
def removeDuplicates(list1):
    set1 = set(list1)
    return list(set1)
```

27.
```
def findItemsInEither(list1, list2):
    set1 = set(list1).union(list2)
    return list(set1)
```

29.
```
## Count the words in the Gettysburg Address.
infile = open("Gettysburg.txt")
originalLine = infile.readline()
print(originalLine[:89])
originalLine = originalLine.lower()
# Remove punctuation marks from the original line.
line = ""
for ch in originalLine:
    if ('a' <= ch <= 'z') or (ch == " "):
        line += ch
# Place the words into a list.
listOfWords = line.split()
# Form a set of the words without duplications.
setOfWords = set(listOfWords)
print("The Gettysburg Address contains", len(listOfWords), "words.")
print("The Gettysburg Address contains", len(setOfWords),
        "different words.")
```

31. The new file will contain the names of the people who subscribe to both the *New York Times* and the *Wall Street Journal*.

33.
```
def main():
    ## Update colors.
    setOfNewColors = getSetOfNewColors()
    createFileOfNewColors(setOfNewColors)

def getSetOfNewColors():
    infile = open("Pre1990.txt", 'r')
    colors = {line.rstrip() for line in infile}
    infile.close()
    infile = open("Retired.txt", 'r')
    retiredColors = {line.rstrip() for line in infile}
    infile.close()
    infile = open("Added.txt", 'r')
    addedColors = {line.rstrip() for line in infile}
    infile.close()
    colorSet = colors.difference(retiredColors)
    colorSet = colorSet.union(addedColors)
    return colorSet

def createFileOfNewColors(setOfNewColors):
    orderedListOfColors = sorted(setOfNewColors)
    orderedListOfColorsString =('\n').join(orderedListOfColors)
    outfile = open("NewColors.txt", 'w')
    outfile.write(orderedListOfColorsString)
    outfile.close()

main()
```

35.
```
def main():
    ## Display the largest number in the file Numbers.txt
    max = getMax("Numbers.txt")
    print("The largest number in the \nfile Numbers.txt is",
            str(max) + ".")
```

```python
def getMax(fileName):
    infile = open("Numbers.txt", 'r')
    max = int(infile.readline())
    for line in infile:
        num = int(line)
        if num > max:
            max = num
    infile.close()
    return max

main()
```

37.
```python
def main():
    ## Display the sum of the numbers in the file Numbers.txt.
    sum = getSum("Numbers.txt")
    print("The sum of the numbers in \nthe file Numbers.txt is",
            str(sum) + ".")

def getSum(fileName):
    infile = open("Numbers.txt", 'r')
    sum = 0
    for line in infile:
        sum += int(line)
    infile.close()
    return sum

main()
```

39.
```python
def main():
    ## Display the last number in the file Numbers.txt.
    lastNumber = getLastNumber("Numbers.txt")
    print("The last number in the \nfile Numbers.txt is",
            str(lastNumber) + '.')

def getLastNumber(fileName):
    infile = open("Numbers.txt", 'r')
    for line in infile:
        pass
    lastNumber = eval(line)
    infile.close()
    return lastNumber

main()
```

41.
```python
import os

infile = open("ShortColors.txt", 'r')
outfile = open("Temp.txt", 'w')
for color in infile:
    if len(color.rstrip()) <= 6:
        outfile.write(color)
infile.close()
outfile.close()
os.remove("ShortColors.txt")
os.rename("Temp.txt", "ShortColors.txt")
```

43.
```
def main():
    ## Create alphabetical file of last 13 students who failed.
    failedStudents = getListOfFailedStudents()
    createFileOfFailedStudents(failedStudents)

def getListOfFailedStudents():
    infile = open("Allstudents.txt", 'r')
    students = {student.rstrip() for student in infile.readlines()}
    infile.close()
    infile = open("PassedStudents.txt", 'r')
    passedStudents = {student.rstrip() for student in infile}
    failedStudents = list(students.difference(passedStudents))
    failedStudents.sort()
    return failedStudents

def createFileOfFailedStudents(failedStudents):
    outfile = open("failedStudents.txt", 'w')
    for student in failedStudents:
        outfile.write(student + "\n")
    outfile.close()

main()
```

45.
```
def main():
    ## Display a range of presidents.
    lowerNumber, upperNumber = getRange()
    displayPresidents(lowerNumber, upperNumber)

def getRange():
    lowerNumber = int(input("Enter the lower number for the range: "))
    upperNumber = int(input("Enter the upper number for the range: "))
    return (lowerNumber, upperNumber)

def displayPresidents(lowerNumber, upperNumber):
    infile = open("USpres.txt", 'r')
    count = 0
    for pres in infile:
        count += 1
        if lowerNumber <= count <= upperNumber:
            print(" ", count, pres, end="")

main()
```

EXERCISES 5.2

1. **The area of Afghanistan is 251,772 sq. miles.**
   The area of Albania is 11,100 sq. miles.

3. **Afghanistan,Asia,251772**
   Albania,Europe,11100

5. Each line of the new file contains the name of a European country and its population in millions. The countries are listed in descending order by population. The first two lines of the file contain the data **Russian Federation,142.5** and **Germany,81.0**.

7.
```
def main():
    ## Display information about a DOW stock.
```

```python
    symbols = placeSymbolsIntoList("DOW.txt")
    displaySymbols(symbols)
    print()
    symbol = input("Enter a symbol: ")
    infile = open("DOW.txt", 'r')
    abbrev = ""
    while abbrev != symbol:
        line = infile.readline()
        lineList = line.split(',')
        abbrev = lineList[1]
    print("Company:", lineList[0])
    print("Industry:", lineList[3])
    print("Exchange:", lineList[2])
    increase = ((float(lineList[5]) - float(lineList[4])) /
                float(lineList[4]))
    print("Growth in 2013: {0:0,.2f}%".format(100 * increase))
    priceEarningsRatio = float(lineList[5]) / float(lineList[6])
    print("Price/Earning ratio in 2013: {0:0,.2f}".
                        format(priceEarningsRatio))

def placeSymbolsIntoList(fileName):
    symbolList = [""] * 30
    infile = open(fileName, 'r')
    for i in range(30):
        line = infile.readline()
        lineList = line.split(',')
        symbolList[i] = lineList[1]
    infile.close()
    return symbolList

def displaySymbols(symbols):
    ## Display symbols in alphabetical order
    symbols.sort()
    print("Symbols for the Thirty DOW Stocks")
    for symbol in symbols:
        print("{0:5} \t".format(symbol), end='')

main()
```

9.
```python
def main():
    ## Determine the dogs of the DOW.
    stockList = placeDataIntoList("DOW.txt")
    stockList.sort(key=byDividendToPriceRatio, reverse=True)
    displayDogs(stockList)

def placeDataIntoList(fileName):
    infile = open(fileName, 'r')
    listOfLines = [line.rstrip() for line in infile]
    infile.close()
    for i in range(len(listOfLines)):
        listOfLines[i] = listOfLines[i].split(',')
        listOfLines[i][4] = eval(listOfLines[i][4])
        listOfLines[i][5] = eval(listOfLines[i][5])
        listOfLines[i][6] = eval(listOfLines[i][6])
```

```
                listOfLines[i][7] = eval(listOfLines[i][7])
        return listOfLines

    def byDividendToPriceRatio(stock):
        return stock[7] / stock[5]

    def displayDogs(listOfStocks):
        print("{0:25} {1:11} {2:s}".
                format("Company", "Symbol", "Yield as of 12/31/2013"))
        for i in range(10):
            print("{0:25} {1:11} {2:0.2f}%".format(listOfStocks[i][0],
            listOfStocks[i][1], 100 * listOfStocks[i][7] / listOfStocks[i][5]))

    main()
```

11.
```
    def main():
        ## Display justices appointed by a given president.
        president = input("Enter the name of a president: ")
        justices = getJusticesByPresident(president)
        fixCurrentJustices(justices)
        justices.sort(key=lambda justice: justice[5] - justice[4], reverse=True)
        if len(justices) > 0:
            print("Justices Appointed:")
            for justice in justices:
                print("   " + justice[0] + " " + justice[1])
        else:
            print(president, "did not appoint any justices.")

    def getJusticesByPresident(president):
        infile = open("Justices.txt", 'r')
        listOfRecords = [line for line in infile
                        if line.split(',')[2] == president]
        infile.close()
        for i in range(len(listOfRecords)):
            listOfRecords[i] = listOfRecords[i].split(',')
            listOfRecords[i][4] = int(listOfRecords[i][4])
            listOfRecords[i][5] = int(listOfRecords[i][5])
        return listOfRecords

    def fixCurrentJustices(justices):
        for justice in justices:
            if justice[5] == 0:
                justice[5] = 2015

    main()
```

13.
```
    def main():
        ## Makeup of Supreme Court in 1980.
        infile = open("Justices.txt", 'r')
        justices = [line for line in infile
                    if (int(line.split(',')[4]) < 1980)
                    and (int(line.split(',')[5]) >= 1980)]
        justices.sort(key=lambda x: int(x.split(',')[4]))
        print("{0:20} {1}".format("Justice", "Appointing President"))
```

```
        for justice in justices:
            print("{0:20} {1}".format(justice.split(',')[0] + " " +
                justice.split(',')[1], justice.split(',')[2]))

    main()
```

15.
```
def main():
    ## Twelve Days of Christmas
    listOfDaysCosts = createListOfDaysCosts()
    day = int(input("Enter a number from 1 through 12: "))
    displayOutput(day, listOfDaysCosts)

def createListOfDaysCosts():
    infile = open("Gifts.txt", 'r')
    costs = [float(line.split(',')[2]) for line in infile]
    infile.close()
    listOfDaysCosts = [0] * 12
    for i in range(12):
        listOfDaysCosts[i] = (i + 1) * costs[i]
    return listOfDaysCosts

def displayOutput(day, listOfDaysCosts):
    print("The gifts for day 3 are")
    infile = open("Gifts.txt", 'r')
    for i in range(day):
        data = infile.readline().split(',')
        print(int(data[0]), data[1])
    print()
    print("Cost for day {0}: ${1:,.2f}".
            format(day, sum(listOfDaysCosts[:day])))
    totalCosts = 0
    for i in range(day):
        totalCosts += sum(listOfDaysCosts[:i + 1])
    print("Total cost for the first {0} days: ${1:,.2f}"
            .format(day, totalCosts))

main()
```

17.
```
def main():
    ## Display colleges from requested state.
    colleges = getOrderedListOfColleges()
    displayListOfColleges(colleges)

def getOrderedListOfColleges():
    infile = open("Colleges.txt", 'r')
    colleges = [line.rstrip() for line in infile]
    infile.close()
    colleges.sort()
    return colleges

def displayListOfColleges(colleges):
    found = False
    abbrev = input("Enter a state abbreviation: ")
    for college in colleges:
        college = college.split(",")
```

```
            if college[1] == abbrev:
                print(college[0], college[2])
                found = True
        if not found:
            print("There are no early colleges from", abbrev + '.')

    main()

19. def main():
        ## Find states whose name and capital begin with the same letter.
        infile = open("StatesANC.txt", 'r')
        for line in infile:
            data = line.split(",")
            letter = data[0][0:1]
            if data[3].startswith(letter):
                print((data[3].rstrip()) + ",", data[0])
        infile.close()

    main()

21. def main():
        ## Display Oscar-winning films of requested genre.
        displayGenres()
        displayFilms()

    def displayGenres():
        print("The different film genres are as follows:")
        print("{0:12}{1:12}{2:10}{3:11}{4:11}".
              format("adventure","bioptic","comedy","crime","drama"))
        print("{0:12}{1:12}{2:10}{3:11}{4:11}".
              format("epic","fantasy","musical","romance","silent"))
        print("{0:12}{1:12}{2:10}{3:11}".
              format("sports","thriller","war","western"))
        print()

    def displayFilms():
        films = open("Oscars.txt",'r')
        genre = input("Enter a genre: ")
        print()
        print("The Academy Award winners are")
        for line in films:
            if line.endswith(genre + "\n"):
                temp = line.split(",")
                print("  " + temp[0])
        films.close()

    main()

23. def main():
        ## Create file of articles purchased by cowboys.
        articles = ["Colt Peacemaker,12.20\n", "Holster,2.00\n",
            "Levi Strauss jeans,1.35\n", "Saddle,40.00\n", "Stetson,10.00\n"]
        outfile = open("Cowboy.txt", 'w')
        outfile.writelines(articles)
        outfile.close()

    main()
```

25.
```python
def main():
    ## Create receipt
    createOrdersFile()
    total = 0
    infile1 = open("Cowboy.txt", 'r')
    infile2 = open("Orders.txt", 'r')
    for line in infile1:
        quantity = int(infile2.readline())
        cost = quantity * float(line.split(',')[1])
        print("{0} {1}: ${2:,.2f}".format(quantity, line.split(',')[0],
                                          cost))
        total += cost
    print("{0}: ${1:,.2f}".format("TOTAL", total))

def createOrdersFile():
    orders = ["3\n", "2\n", "10\n", "1\n", "4\n"]
    outfile = open("Orders.txt", 'w')
    outfile.writelines(orders)
    outfile.close()

main()
```

27.
```python
def main():
    ## Determine the day of the week for a date.
    infile = open("Calendar2015.txt", 'r')
    date = input("Enter a date in 2015: ")
    for line in infile:
        temp = line.split(',')
        if temp[0] == date:
            print(date, "falls on a", temp[1].rstrip())
            break

main()
```

EXERCISES 5.3

1. 3110.2

3. ['Three_Sisters_fall', "Olo'supena_falls", 'Tugela_falls', 'Angle_falls', 'Yumbilla_falls']

5. [('Three_Sisters_fall', 2998.5), ("Olo'supena_falls", 2953.3), ('Tugela_falls', 3110.2), ('Angle_falls', 3211.7), ('Yumbilla_falls', 2940)]

7. absent   9. Yumbilla_falls   11. 3111.0   13. 3110

15. Angle_falls Yumbilla_falls Three_Sisters_fall Tugela_falls Olo'supena_falls

17. 15213.7   19. 4   21. 4   23. False

25. std1   27. ['std1_age', 'std2_age', 'std1']   29. John

31. John   33. {'std1_age': 20, 'std2_age': 21, 'std1': 'John'}

35. 0   37. std1_age std2_age std1 std2

39. 20 25 John Smith   41. 20

43. {'std1': 'John', 'std2': 'Harry', 'std1_age': 30, 'std2_age': 45}

```
45. pres = input("Who was the youngest U.S. president? ")
    pres = pres.upper()
    trResponse = "Correct. He became president at age 42\n" + \
                 "when President McKinley was assassinated."
    jfkResponse = "Incorrect. He became president at age 43. However,\n" + \
                  "he was the youngest person elected president."
    responses = {}
    responses["THEODORE ROOSEVELT"] = trResponse
    responses["TEDDY ROOSEVELT"] = trResponse
    responses["JFK"] = jfkResponse
    responses["JOHN KENNEDY"] = jfkResponse
    responses["JOHN F. KENNEDY"] = jfkResponse
    print(responses.get(pres, "Nope."))

47. def main():
        ## Display batting averages of top hitters.
        topHitters = {"Gehrig":{"atBats":8061, "hits":2721},
                      "Ruth":{"atBats":8399, "hits":2873},
                      "Williams":{"atBats":7706, "hits":2654}}
        displayBattingAverage(topHitters)

    def displayBattingAverage(topHitters):
        for hitter in topHitters:
            print("{0:10} {1:.3f}".format(hitter,
                topHitters[hitter]["hits"] / topHitters[hitter]["atBats"]))

    main()

49. def main():
        ## Display average number of hits by the top three hitters.
        topHitters = {"Gehrig":{"atBats":8061, "hits":2721},
                      "Ruth":{"atBats":8399, "hits":2873},
                      "Williams":{"atBats":7706, "hits":2654}}
        displayAveNumberOfHits(topHitters)

    def displayAveNumberOfHits(topHitters):
        hitList = []
        for hitter in topHitters:
            hitList.append(topHitters[hitter]["hits"])
        value = "{0:.1f}".format(sum(hitList) / len(hitList))
        print("The average number of hits by")
        print("the baseball players was", value + '.')

    main()

51. import pickle

    def main():
        ## Display justices appointed by a specified president.
        justicesDict = createDictFromFile("JusticesDict.dat")
        displayPresidentialAppointees(justicesDict)

    def createDictFromFile(fileName):  # from binary file
        infile = open(fileName, 'rb')
        dictionaryName = pickle.load(infile)
```

```python
        infile.close()
        return dictionaryName

    def displayPresidentialAppointees(dictionaryName) :
        pres = input("Enter a president: ")
        for x in dictionaryName:
            if dictionaryName[x]["pres"] == pres:
                print("  {0:16} {1:d}".format(x, dictionaryName[x]["yrAppt"]))

    main()
```

53.
```python
import pickle

def main():
    ## display information about a specific justice.
    justicesDict = createDictFromFile("JusticesDict.dat")
    displayInfoAboutJustice(justicesDict)

def createDictFromFile(fileName):  # from binary file
    infile = open(fileName, 'rb')
    dictionaryName = pickle.load(infile)
    infile.close()
    return dictionaryName

def displayInfoAboutJustice(dictionaryName):
    justice = input("Enter name of a justice: ")
    print("Appointed by", dictionaryName[justice]["pres"])
    print("State:", dictionaryName[justice]["state"])
    print("Year of appointment:", dictionaryName[justice]["yrAppt"])
    if dictionaryName[justice]["yrLeft"] == 0:
        print("Currently serving on the Supreme Court.")
    else:
        print("Left court in", dictionaryName[justice]["yrLeft"])

main()
```

55.
```python
def main():
    ## Calculate letter frequencies for a sentence.
    sentence = input("Enter a sentence: ")
    sentence = sentence.upper()
    letterDict = dict([(chr(n),0) for n in range(65, 91)])
    for char in sentence:
        if 'A' <= char <= 'Z':
            letterDict[char] += 1
    displaySortedResults(letterDict)

def displaySortedResults(dictionaryName):
    letterList = list(dictionaryName.items())
    letterList.sort(key=f, reverse=True)
    for x in letterList:
        if x[1] != 0:
            print("   " + x[0] + ':', x[1])

def f(k):
    return k[1]

main()
```

57.
```python
import pickle

def main():
    ## Determine states that were home to three or more presidents.
    presidents = getDictionary("USpresStatesDict.dat")
    states = createStatesDict(presidents)
    sortedStates = [state for state in states if states[state] > 2]
    sortedStates.sort(key=lambda state: states[state], reverse=True)
    print("States that produced three or")
    print("more presidents as of 2016:")
    for state in sortedStates:
        print(" ", state + ":", states[state])

def getDictionary(fileName):
    infile = open(fileName, 'rb')
    dictName = pickle.load(infile)
    infile.close()
    return dictName

def createStatesDict(presidents):
    states = {}
    for state in presidents.values():
        if not states.get(state, False):
            states[state] = 1
        else:
            states[state] += 1
    return states

main()
```

59.
```python
def main():
    ## Determine the day of the week for a date.
    calender2015Dict = createDictionary("Calendar2015.txt")
    date = input("Enter a date in 2015: ")
    print(date, "falls on a", calender2015Dict[date])

def createDictionary(fileName):
    infile = open(fileName, 'r')
    textList = [line.rstrip() for line in infile]
    infile.close()
    return dict([x.split(',') for x in textList])

main()
```

61.
```python
import pickle

def main():
    ## Determine states having a specified number of large cities.
    largeCities = createDictionaryFromBinaryFile("LargeCitiesDict.dat")
    number = int(input("Enter an integer from 1 to 13: "))
    states = sorted(getStates(number, largeCities))
    displayResult(number, states)

def createDictionaryFromBinaryFile(fileName):
    infile = open(fileName, 'rb')
    dictionaryName = pickle.load(infile)
```

```
        infile.close()
        return dictionaryName

def getStates(number, dictionaryName):
    states = []
    for state in dictionaryName:
        if len(dictionaryName[state]) == number:
            states.append(state)
    return states

def displayResult(number, states):
    if len(states) == 0:
        print("No states have exactly", number, "large cities.")
    else:
        print("The following states have exactly", number, "large cities:")
        print("  ".join(states))

main()
```

CHAPTER 6

EXERCISES 6.1

1. f   **3.** l   **5.** d   **7.** i   **9.** s   **11.** o

13. j   **15.** n   **17.** d   **19.** h   **21.** r

23. You must enter a number.

25. string index out of range
Oops

27. File Salaries.txt contains an invalid salary.
Thank you for using our program.

29.
```
while True:
    try:
        n = int(input("Enter a nonzero integer: "))
        reciprocal = 1 / n
        print("The reciprocal of {0} is {1:,.3f}".format(n, reciprocal))
        break
    except ValueError:
        print("You did not enter a nonzero integer. Try again.")
    except ZeroDivisionError:
        print("You entered zero. Try again.")
```

31.
```
while True:
    try:
        num = int(input("Enter an integer from 1 to 100: "))
        if 1 <= num <= 100:
            print("Your number is", str(num) + '.')
            break
        else:
            print("Your number was not between 1 and 100.")
    except ValueError:
        print("You did not enter an integer.")
```

EXERCISES 6.2

1. A free hit by a cricketer who makes 50% of his or her free hits.

3. Breaking the target when hitting strength is greater than 50%.

5. The random selection of three colors for a flag.

7. Randomly selecting the order of presentations in a class.

9.
```python
import random
## Select three letters at random from the alphabet.
# Create a list of the 26 uppercase letters of the alphabet.
list1 = [chr(n) for n in range(ord('A'), ord('Z') + 1)]
# Select three letters at random.
list2 = random.sample(list1, 3)
# Display the three letters
print(", ".join(list2))
```

11.
```python
import random
## Randomly select two even numbers from 2 through 100.
# Create a list of the even numbers from 2 through 100.
list1 = [n for n in range(2, 101, 2)]
# Select two of the even numbers at random.
list2 = random.sample(list1, 2)
# Display the two numbers.
print(list2[0], list2[1])
```

13.
```python
import random
## Count the number of "Heads" in 100 coin tosses.
numberOfHeads = 0
for i in range(100):
    if (random.choice(["Head","Tail"]) == "Head"):
        numberOfHeads += 1
print("In 100 tosses, Heads occurred {0} times.".format(numberOfHeads))
```

15.
```python
import random
## Select three states at random from a file containing the 50 states.
allNumbers = [n for n in range(1, 51)]
# Randomly select three numbers from 1 through 50.
threeNumbers = random.sample(allNumbers, 3)
infile = open("StatesAlpha.txt", 'r')
line Number = 1
for line in infile:
    if lineNumber in threeNumbers:
        print(line.rstrip())
    lineNumber += 1
infile.close()
```

17.
```python
import random
import pickle
NUMBER_OF_TRIALS = 10000

def main():
    ## Carry out matching process NUMBER_OF_TRIALS times.
    totalNumberOfMatches = 0
```

```
        for i in range(NUMBER_OF_TRIALS):
            totalNumberOfMatches += matchTwoDecks()
        averageNumberOfMatches = totalNumberOfMatches / NUMBER_OF_TRIALS
        print("The average number of cards that")
        print("matched was {0:.3f}.".format(averageNumberOfMatches))

    def matchTwoDecks():
        ## Determine the number of matches when comparing
        ## two shuffled decks of cards.
        # Create two decks as lists using the binary file
        # DeckOfCardsList.dat from Example 2.
        infile = open("DeckOfCardsList.dat", 'rb')
        deck1 = pickle.load(infile)
        infile.close()
        infile = open("DeckOfCardsList.dat", 'rb')
        deck2 = pickle.load(infile)
        infile.close()
        # Shuffle both decks of cards.
        random.shuffle(deck1)
        random.shuffle(deck2)
        # Compare cards and determine the number of matches.
        numberOfMatches = 0
        for i in range(52):
            if (deck1[i] == deck2[i]):
                numberOfMatches += 1
        return numberOfMatches

    main()
```

19.
```
import random
## Simulate a Powerball Drawing.
whiteBalls = [num for num in range(1, 60)]
# Randomly sample and display five white balls.
whiteBallSelection = random.sample(whiteBalls, 5)
for i in range(5):
    whiteBallSelection[i] = str(whiteBallSelection[i])
print("White Balls:", " ".join(whiteBallSelection))
# Randomly select and display the Powerball.
powerBall = random.randint(1, 35)
print("Powerball:", powerBall)
```

21.
```
import random
## Simulate 32 coin tosses and check for runs of length five.
coin = ['T', 'H']
result = ""
for i in range(32):
        result += random.choice(coin)
print(result)
if ("TTTTT" in result) or ("HHHHH" in result):
    print("There was a run of five consecutive")
    print("same outcomes.")
else:
    print("There was not a run of five consecutive ")
    print("same outcomes.")
```

23.
```
import random
import pickle

def main():
    ## Calculate the High Point Count for a bridge hand.
    bridgeHand = getHand()
    print(", ".join(bridgeHand))  # Display the bridge hand.
    HCP = calculateHighCardPointCount(bridgeHand)
    print("HPC =", HCP)

def getHand():
    infile = open("DeckOfCardsList.dat", 'rb')
    deckOfCards = pickle.load(infile)
    infile.close()
    bridgeHand = random.sample(deckOfCards, 13)
    return bridgeHand

def calculateHighCardPointCount(bridgeHand):
    countDict = {'A':4, 'K':3, 'Q':2, 'J':1}
    HPC = 0
    for card in bridgeHand:
        rank = card[0]  # Each card is a string of
                        # two characters.
        if rank in "AKQJ":
            HPC += countDict[rank]
    return HPC

main()
```

EXERCISES 6.3

1.
```
import turtle
t = turtle.Turtle()
t.pencolor("blue")
t.hideturtle()
t.up()
t.goto(20, 30)
t.dot(5)
t.down()
t.goto(80, 90)
t.dot(5)
```

5.
```
import turtle
t = turtle.Turtle()
t.hideturtle()
t.color("red", "red")
t.up()
t.goto(-30, -40)
t.down()
t.begin_fill()
t.goto(-30, 60)
t.goto(50, 60)
t.goto(50, -40)
t.goto(-30, -40)
t.end_fill()
```

9.
```
import turtle
def main():
    ## Draw a yellow square inside a blue dot.
    t = turtle.Turtle()
    t.hideturtle()
    drawDot(t, 50, 50, 100, "blue")
    drawFilledRectangle(t, 20, 20, 60, 60, "red", "yellow")

def drawFilledRectangle(t, x, y, w, h, colorP="black", colorF="black"):
    ## Draw a filled rectangle with bottom-left corner (x, y),
```

```
                ## width w, height h, pen color colorP, and fill color colorF.
                t.pencolor(colorP)
                t.fillcolor(colorF)
                t.up()                      # Disable drawing of lines.
                t.goto(x, y)                # Move to bottom-left corner of rectangle.
                t.down()                    # Enable drawing of lines.
                t.begin_fill()
                t.goto(x + w, y)            # Draw line to bottom-right corner.
                t.goto(x + w, y + h)        # Draw line to top-right corner.
                t.goto(x, y + h)            # Draw line to top-left corner.
                t.goto(x, y)                # Draw line to bottom-left corner.
                t.end_fill()

        def drawDot(t, x, y, diameter, colorP):
                ## Draw dot with center (x, y) and color colorP.
                t.up()
                t.goto(x, y)
                t.dot(diameter, colorP)

        main()
```

13.
```
import turtle

def main():
        ## Draw a partial moon.
        t = turtle.Turtle()
        t.hideturtle()
        drawDot(t, 0, 0, 200, "orange")     # Draw moon.
        drawDot(t, -100,0, 200, "white")    # Take bite out of moon.

def drawDot(t, x, y, diameter, colorP):
        ## Draw a dot with center (x, y) having color colorP.
        t.up()
        t.goto(x, y)
        t.dot(diameter, colorP)

main()
```

17.
```
import turtle

def main():
        ## Draw a blue square containing the underlined word PYTHON.
        t = turtle.Turtle()
        t.hideturtle()
        drawFilledRectangle(t, 0, 0, 200, 200, "blue", "blue")      # Square
        drawFilledRectangle(t, 15, 75, 165, 5, "white", "white")   # Underline
        t.up()
        t.goto(100, 80)
        t.pencolor("white")
        t.write("PYTHON", align="center", font=("Arial", 25, "bold"))

def drawFilledRectangle(t, x, y, w, h, colorP="black", colorF="black"):
        ## Draw a solid rectangle with bottom-left corner (x, y),
        ## width w, height h, pen color colorP, and fill color colorF.
        t.pencolor(colorP)
        t.fillcolor(colorF)
        t.up()
```

```
            t.goto(x, y)                # Start at bottom-left corner of rectangle.
            t.down()
            t.begin_fill()
            t.goto(x + w, y)            # Draw line to bottom-right corner.
            t.goto(x + w, y + h)        # Draw line to top-right corner.
            t.goto(x, y + h)            # Draw line to top-left corner.
            t.goto(x, y)                # Draw line to bottom-left corner.
            t.end_fill()

        main()
```

21.
```
    import turtle

    def main():
        ## Draw the Italian flag.
        t = turtle.Turtle()
        t.hideturtle()
        drawFilledRectangle(t, 0, 0, 50, 100, "black", "green")
        drawFilledRectangle(t, 50, 0, 50, 100, "black", "white")
        drawFilledRectangle(t, 100, 0, 50, 100, "black", "red")

    def drawFilledRectangle(t, x, y, w, h, colorP="black", colorF="black"):
        ## Draw a filled rectangle with bottom-left corner (x, y),
        ## width w, height h, pen color colorP, and fill color colorF.
        t.pencolor(colorP)
        t.fillcolor(colorF)
        t.up()
        t.goto(x, y)                # Start at bottom-left corner of rectangle.
        t.down()
        t.begin_fill()
        t.goto(x + w, y)            # Draw line to bottom-right corner.
        t.goto(x + w, y + h)        # Draw line to top-right corner.
        t.goto(x, y + h)            # Draw line to top-left corner.
        t.goto(x, y)                # Draw line to bottom-left corner.
        t.end_fill()

    main()
```

25.
```
    import turtle

    def main():
        ## Draw the flag of Burkina Faso.
        t = turtle.Turtle()
        t.hideturtle()
        t.down()
        drawFilledRectangle(t, 0, 50, 150, 50, "red", "red")
        drawFilledRectangle(t, 0, 0, 150, 50, "forest green", "forest green")
        drawFivePointStar(t, 65, 33, 40, "yellow", "yellow")

    def drawFivePointStar(t, x, y, lenthOfSide, colorP="black",
                          colorF="white"):
        # Drawing begins at (x, y) and moves in a north-east direction.
        t.pencolor(colorP)
        t.fillcolor(colorF)
        t.up()
        t.goto(x, y)
```

```
            t.setheading(0)
            t.left(36)
            t.down()
            t.begin_fill()
            for i in range(6):
                t.forward(lenthOfSide)
                t.left(144)    # 144 = 180 - 36
            t.end_fill()

    def drawFilledRectangle(t, x, y, w, h, colorP="black",
                            colorF="black"):
        ## Draw a filled rectangle with bottom-left corner (x, y),
        ## width w, height h, pen color colorP, and fill color colorF.
        t.pencolor(colorP)
        t.fillcolor(colorF)
        t.up()
        t.goto(x, y)            # Start at bottom-left corner of rectangle.
        t.down()
        t.begin_fill()
        t.goto(x + w, y)        # Draw line to bottom-right corner.
        t.goto(x + w, y + h)    # Draw line to top-right corner.
        t.goto(x, y + h)        # Draw line to top-left corner.
        t.goto(x, y)            # Draw line to bottom-left corner.
        t.end_fill()

    main()
```

29.
```
    import turtle

    MALE_ENROLLMENTS = [1375, 2047, 2233, 2559, 3265]
    FEMALE_ENROLLMENTS = [945, 2479, 3007, 3390, 4415]

    def main():
        ## Draw line chart of two-year college enrollments.
        t = turtle.Turtle()
        t.hideturtle()
        drawLine(t, 0, 0, 200, 0)     # Draw x-axis.
        drawLine(t, 0, 0, 0, 200)     # Draw y-axis.
        ## Draw graphs.
        for i in range(4):
            drawLineWithDots(t, 20 + (40 * i), MALE_ENROLLMENTS[i]/ 25,
                            60 + 40 * i, MALE_ENROLLMENTS[i+1]/25, "black")
        for i in range(4):
            drawLineWithDots(t, 20 + (40 * i), FEMALE_ENROLLMENTS[i]/ 25,
                            60 + 40 * i, FEMALE_ENROLLMENTS[i+1]/25, "black")
        drawTickMarks(t)
        insertText(t)

    def drawLine(t, x1, y1, x2, y2, colorP="black"):
        ## Draw line segment from (x1, y1) to (x2, y2) having color colorP.
        t.up()
        t.goto(x1, y1)
        t.down()
        t.color(colorP)
        t.goto(x2, y2)
```

```
def drawLineWithDots(t, x1, y1, x2, y2, colorP="black"):
    ## Draw line segment from (x1, y1) to (x2, y2) having color
    ## colorP and insert dots at both ends of the line segment.
    t.pencolor(colorP)
    t.up()
    t.goto(x1, y1)
    t.dot(5)
    t.down()
    t.goto(x2, y2)
    t.dot(5)

def drawTickMarks(t):
    for i in range(5):
        drawLine(t, 20 + (40 * i), 0, 20 + 40 * i , 10)
    drawLine(t, 0, max(FEMALE_ENROLLMENTS)/25, 10,
            max(FEMALE_ENROLLMENTS)/25)
    drawLine(t, 0, min(FEMALE_ENROLLMENTS)/25, 10,
            min(FEMALE_ENROLLMENTS)/25)

def insertText(t):
    t.up()
    t.pencolor("black")
    t.goto(110, 150)
    t.write("Females")
    t.goto(120, 80)
    t.write("Males")
    # Display greatest enrollment value.
    t.color("blue")
    t.goto(-30, (max(FEMALE_ENROLLMENTS)/25)-10)
    t.write(max(FEMALE_ENROLLMENTS))
    # Display least enrollment value.
    t.goto(-22, (min(FEMALE_ENROLLMENTS)/25) - 10)
    t.write(min(FEMALE_ENROLLMENTS))
    # Display labels for tick marks on x-axis.
    t.goto(0, -20)
    x = 20
    for i in range(1970, 2011, 10):
        t.goto(x, -20)
        t.write(str(i), align="center")
        x += 40
    # Display title of line chart.
    t.goto(0, -40)
    t.write("Two-Year College Enrollments")
    t.goto(0, -55)
    t.write("(in thousands)")

main()
```

EXERCISES 6.4

1. 120   **3.** Six decreasing lines of stars.   **5.** hhhhhhhhhhhhhhhh

7.
```
def isAlpha(L):
    ## Determine whether items in a list are in alphabetical order.
```

```
        if len(L) == 1:
            return True
        elif L[0] > L[1]:
            return False
        else:
            return isAlpha(L[1:])
```

9.
```
def main():
    ## Determine the coefficients in a binomial expansion.
    n = int(input("Enter a positive integer: "))
    for r in range(0, n + 1):
        print(C(n, r), end=" ")

def C(n, r):
    if (n == 0) or (r == 0) or (n == r):
        return 1
    else:
        return C(n - 1, r - 1) + C(n - 1, r)

main()
```

11.
```
def main():
    ## Find the greatest common divisor of two non-negative integers.
    m = int(input("Enter the first integer: "))
    n = int(input("Enter the second integer: "))
    print("GCD =", GCD(m, n))

def GCD(m, n):
    if n == 0:
        return m
    else:
        return GCD(n, m % n)

main()
```

13.
```
def main():
    ## Reverse the order of items entered by the user.
    state = ""
    getState(state)

def getState(state):
    state = input("Enter a state: ")
    if state != "End":
        getState(state)
        print(state)

main()
```

CHAPTER 7

EXERCISES 7.1

1. The *self* parameter is missing from the second line.

3. The pair of parentheses in the first line should be replaced by a colon. Also, a colon should be placed at the end of the second line.

5. 1   7. 4   9. 12.56   11. 18.84

13.
```python
import point

def main():
    ## Determine the distance of a point from the origin.
    x = float(input("Enter x-coordinate of point: "))
    y = float(input("Enter y-coordinate of point: "))
    p = point.Point(x, y)
    print("Distance from origin: {0:,.2f}".
          format(p.distanceFromOrigin()))

main()
```

15.
```python
import pairOfDice

def main():
    ## Roll a pair of dice.
    dice = pairOfDice.PairOfDice()
    dice.roll()
    print("Red die:", dice.getRedDie())
    print("Blue die:", dice.getBlueDie())
    print("Sum of the dice:", dice.sum())

main()
```

17.
```python
import pairOfDice

def main():
    ## Determine the likelihood of obtaining 7
    ## when rolling a pair of dice.
    numberOfSevens = 0
    for i in range(100000):
        dice = pairOfDice.PairOfDice()
        dice.roll()
        if dice.sum() == 7:
            numberOfSevens += 1
    print("7 occurred {0:.2%} of the time.".
          format(numberOfSevens / 100000))

main()
```

19. queen of hearts   21. 10 of clubs   23. 7 of hearts

25.
```python
import pCard
import random

def main():
    ## Randomly select a face card.
    c = pCard.PlayingCard()
    c.selectAtRandom()
    picture = random.choice(["jack", "queen", "king"])
    c.setRank(picture)
    print(c)

main()
```

27.
```python
class Fraction:
    def __init__(self, numerator=0, denominator=1):
        self._numerator = numerator
        self._denominator = denominator

    def setNumerator(self, numerator):
        self._numerator = numerator

    def getNumerator(self):
        return self._numerator

    def setDenominator(self, denominator):
        self._denominator = denominator

    def getDenominator(self):
        return self._denominator

    def GCD(self, m, n):    # Greatest Common Divisor
        while n != 0:
            t = n
            n = m % n
            m = t
        return m

    def reduce(self):
        gcd = self.GCD(self._numerator, self._denominator)
        self._numerator = int(self._numerator / gcd)
        self._denominator = int(self._denominator / gcd)
```

29.
```python
import fraction

def main():
    ## Convert a decimal number to a fraction.
    decimal = input("Enter a positive decimal number less than 1: ")
    decimal = decimal[1:]     # Strip off decimal point.
    f = fraction.Fraction()
    f.setNumerator(int(decimal))
    f.setDenominator(10 ** len(decimal))
    f.reduce()
    msg = "Converted to fraction:"
    print(msg, str(f.getNumerator()) + '/' + str(f.getDenominator()))

main()
```

31.
```python
def main():
    ## Calculate a workers weekly pay.
    salary = Wages()
    name = input("Enter person's name: ")
    salary.setName(name)
    hours = float(input("Enter number of hours worked: "))
    salary.setHours(hours)
    wage = float(input("Enter hourly wage: "))
    salary.setWage(wage)
    print("Pay for", salary.getName() + ':', salary.payForWeek())
```

```
class Wages:
    def __init__(self, name="", hours=0.0, wage=0.0):
        self._name = name
        self._hours = hours      # Number of hours worked during week
        self._wage = wage        # Hourly wage

    def setName(self, name):
        self._name = name

    def getName(self):
        return self._name

    def setHours(self, hours):
        self._hours = hours

    def getHours(self):
        return self._hours

    def setWage(self, wage):
        self._wage = wage

    def getHours(self):
        return self._hours

    def payForWeek(self):
        amount = self._hours * self._wage
        if self._hours > 40:
            amount = 40 * self._wage + ((self._hours - 40) *
                        (1.5 * self._wage))
        return "${0:,.2f}".format(amount)

main()
```

33.
```
import random
import pCard

def main():
    ## Randomly select a poker hand.
    deckOfCards = []
    ranks = ['2', '3', '4', '5', '6', '7', '8', '9',
            "10", "jack", "queen", "king", "ace"]
    suits = ["spades", "hearts", "clubs", "diamonds"]
    for i in ranks:
        for j in suits:
            c = pCard.PlayingCard(i, j)
            deckOfCards.append(c)
    pokerHand = random.sample(deckOfCards, 5)
    pokerHand.sort(key = lambda x: x.getRank())
    for k in pokerHand:
        print(k)

main()
```

35.
```
def main():
    ## Check out at a shopping Web site.
    myPurchases = Cart()
    carryOn = 'Y'
```

```python
    while carryOn.upper() == 'Y':
        description = input("Enter description of article: ")
        price = float(input("Enter price of article: "))
        quantity = int(input("Enter quantity of article: "))
        article = Purchase(description, price, quantity)
        myPurchases.addItemToCart(article)
        carryOn = input("Do you want to enter more articles (Y/N)? ")
    printReceipt(myPurchases)

def printReceipt(myPurchases):
    print("\n{0:12}   {1:<s}   {2:<12}".format("ARTICLE",
            "PRICE", "QUANTITY"))
    for purchase in myPurchases.getItems():
        print("{0:12s} ${1:,.2f}   {2:5}".format(purchase.getDescription(),
                        purchase.getPrice(), purchase.getQuantity()))
    print("\nTOTAL COST: ${0:,.2f}".format(myPurchases.calculateTotal()))

class Purchase:
    def __init__(self, description="", price=0, quantity=0):
        self._description = description
        self._price = price
        self._quantity = quantity

    def setDescription(self, description):
        self._description = description

    def getDescription(self):
        return self._description

    def setPrice(self, price):
        self._price = price

    def getPrice(self):
        return self._price

    def setQuantity(self, quantity):
        self._quantity = quantity

    def getQuantity(self):
        return self._quantity

class Cart:
    def __init__(self, items=[]):
        self._items = items

    def addItemToCart(self, item):
        self._items.append(item)

    def getItems(self):
        return self._items

    def calculateTotal(self):
        amount = 0
        for item in self._items:
            amount += item.getPrice() * item.getQuantity()
        return amount

main()
```

EXERCISES 7.2

1. 4

3. 6.928

5. The rectangle has area 6.00.

7. Area of Rectangle is: 50
Area of Triangle is: 25

9. Change function *displayResults* to the following:

```
def displayResults(listOfStudents):
    listOfStudents.sort(key=lambda x: x.getName())
    for pupil in listOfStudents:
        if pupil.calcSemGrade() == 'A':
            print(pupil.getName())
```

11.
```
import random

def main():
    ## Play three games of rock, paper, scissors.
    # Get names of contestants and instantiate an object for each.
    nameOfHuman = input("Enter name of human: ")
    h = Human(nameOfHuman)
    nameOfComputer = input("Enter name of computer: ")
    c = Computer(nameOfComputer)
    print()
    # Play three games and keep score.
    for i in range(3):
        humanChoice = h.makeChoice()
        computerChoice = c.makeChoice()
        print("{0} chooses {1}".format(c.getName(), computerChoice))
        if humanChoice == "rock":
            if computerChoice == "scissors":
                h.incrementScore()
            elif computerChoice == "paper":
                c.incrementScore()
        elif humanChoice == "paper":
            if computerChoice == "rock":
                h.incrementScore()
            elif computerChoice == "scissors":
                c.incrementScore()
        else:  # humanChoice = scissors
            if computerChoice == "rock":
                c.incrementScore()
            elif computerChoice == "paper":
                h.incrementScore()
        print(h, end="  ")
        print(c)
        print()
    if h.getScore() > c.getScore():
        print(h.getName().upper(), "WINS")
    elif c.getScore() > h.getScore():
        print(c.getName().upper(), "WINS")
    else:
        print("TIE")
```

```python
class Contestant():
    def __init__(self, name="", score=0):
        self._name = name
        self._score = score

    def getName(self):
        return self._name

    def getScore(self):
        return self._score

    def incrementScore(self):
        self._score += 1

    def __str__(self):
        return "{0}: {1}".format(self._name, self._score)

class Human(Contestant):
    def makeChoice(self):
        choices = ["rock", "paper", "scissors"]
        while True:
            choice = input(self._name + ", enter your choice: ")
            if choice.lower() in choices:
                break
        return choice.lower()

class Computer(Contestant):
    def makeChoice(self):
        choices = ["rock", "paper", "scissors"]
        selection = random.choice(choices)
        return selection

main()
```

13.
```python
class Mortgage:
    def __init__(self, principal, interestRate, term):
        self._principal = principal
        self._interestRate = interestRate
        self._term = term

    def calculateMonthlyPayment(self):
        i = self._interestRate / 1200
        return ((i / (1 - ((1 + i) ** (-12 * self._term))))
                    * self._principal)
```

15.
```python
def main():
    ## Calculate the values for an interest-only mortgage.
    principal = float(input("Enter principal amount of mortgage: "))
    interestRate = float(input("Enter percent interest rate: "))
    term = float(input("Enter duration of mortgage in years: "))
    numberOfInterestOnlyYears = \
                    float(input("Enter number of interest-only years: "))
    mort = InterestOnlyMortgage(principal, interestRate,
                                term, numberOfInterestOnlyYears)
    print("Monthly payment for first {0:.0f} years: ${1:,.2f}"
        .format(numberOfInterestOnlyYears, mort.initialMonthlyPayment()))
```

```
            mort.setTerm(term - numberOfInterestOnlyYears)
            print("Monthly payment for last {0:.0f} years: ${1:,.2f}"
                    .format(mort.getTerm(), mort.calculateMonthlyPayment()))

class Mortgage:
    def __init__(self, principal, interestRate, term):
        self._principal = principal
        self._interestRate = interestRate
        self._term = term

    def calculateMonthlyPayment(self):
        i = self._interestRate / 1200
        return ((i / (1 - ((1 + i) ** (-12 * self._term))))
                    * self._principal)

class InterestOnlyMortgage(Mortgage):
    def __init__(self, principal, interestRate,
                    term, numberOfInterestOnlyYears):
        super().__init__(principal, interestRate, term)
        self._numberOfInterestOnlyYears = numberOfInterestOnlyYears

    def initialMonthlyPayment(self):
        return self._principal * (self._interestRate / 1200)

    def setTerm(self, numberOfInterestOnlyYears):
        self._term -= self._numberOfInterestOnlyYears

    def getTerm(self):
        return self._term

main()
```

INDEX

Some Available Pen Colors for use in Section 6.3 (Turtle Graphics).

red	dark red	saddle brown	tan
blue	dark blue	maroon	gold
green	navy blue	light green	goldenrod
yellow	midnight blue	forest green	aquamarine
orange	light blue	dark green	lavender
black	sky blue	gray	pink
brown	dark orange	dark gray	orchid
purple	dark turquoise	turquoise	salmon

In Exercises 9 through 20, write a program to create the output.

9.
10.
11.[1]
12.
13.

14.
15.
16.
17.

18. 19. 20. Python

---

[1]This figure illustrates the so-called "bullseye illusion." Although the tri-colored inner region has the same area as the outer black annulus, it appears to be larger.

In Exercises 21 through 26, write a program to create the flag of the designated country. *Note:* The Swiss flag is square. For the other five flags, the width is 1.5 times the height.

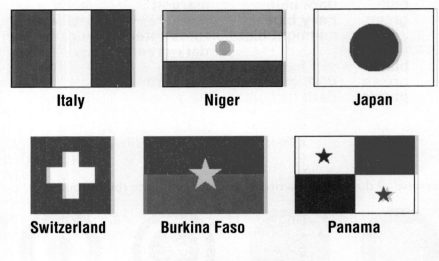

Italy   **Niger**   **Japan**

Switzerland   **Burkina Faso**   **Panama**

Flags of six countries.

21. Italy   **22.** Niger   **23.** Japan   **24.** Switzerland   **25.** Burkina Faso   **26.** Panama

Outcome of Programming Project 4 from Chapter 6.